Introducing Python

Bill Lubanovic

Beijing · Boston · Farnham · Sebastopol · Tokyo

Introducing Python

By Bill Lubanovic

Copyright © 2015 Bill Lubanovic. All rights reserved.

Printed in the United States of America.

Published by O'Reilly Media, Inc., 1005 Gravenstein Highway North, Sebastopol, CA 95472.

O'Reilly books may be purchased for educational, business, or sales promotional use. Online editions are also available for most titles (*http://safaribooksonline.com*). For more information, contact our corporate/institutional sales department: 800-998-9938 or corporate@oreilly.com.

Editors: Andy Oram and Allyson MacDonald	**Indexer:** Judy McConville
Production Editor: Nicole Shelby	**Interior Designer:** David Futato
Copyeditor: Octal Publishing	**Cover Designer:** Ellie Volckhausen
Proofreader: Sonia Saruba	**Illustrator:** Rebecca Demarest

November, 2014:   First Edition

Revision History for the First Edition

2014-11-07:	First release
2015-02-20:	Second release
2016-02-26:	Third release

See *http://oreilly.com/catalog/errata.csp?isbn=9781449359362* for release details.

978-1-449-35936-2

[LSI]

To Mary, Karin, Tom, and Roxie.

Table of Contents

Preface

This book will introduce you to the Python programming language. It's aimed at beginning programmers, but even if you've written programs before and just want to add Python to your list of languages, *Introducing Python* will get you started.

It's an unhurried introduction, taking small steps from the basics to more involved and varied topics. I mix cookbook and tutorial styles to explain new terms and ideas, but not too many at once. Real Python code is included early and often.

Even though this is an introduction, I include some topics that might seem advanced, such as NoSQL databases and message-passing libraries. I chose these because they can solve some problems better than standard solutions. You'll download and install external Python packages, which is good to know when the "batteries included" with Python don't fit your application. And it's fun to try something new.

I also include some examples of what *not* to do, especially if you've programmed in other languages and try to adapt those styles to Python. And I won't pretend that Python is perfect; I'll show you what to avoid.

 Sometimes, I'll include a note such as this when something might be confusing or there's a more appropriate *Pythonic* way to do it.

Audience

This book is for anybody interested in learning what seems to be emerging as the world's most popular computing language, whether or not you have learned any programming before.

Outline

The first seven chapters explain Python's basics, and you should read them in order. The later chapters show how Python is used in specific application areas such as the Web, databases, networks, and so on; read them in any order you like. The first three appendices showcase Python in the arts, business, and science. Then, you see how to install Python 3 if you don't have it. Next are answers to the end-of-chapter exercises, and then finally, a few cheat sheets of useful things.

Chapter 1

Programs are like directions for making socks or grilling potatoes. Some real Python programs give a little demonstration of the language's look, capabilities, and uses in the real world. Python fares well when compared with other languages, but it has some imperfections. An older version of Python (Python 2) is giving way to a newer one (Python 3). If you have Python 2, install Python 3 on your computer. Use the interactive interpreter to try examples from this book yourself.

Chapter 2

This chapter shows Python's simplest data types: booleans, integers, floating-point numbers, and text strings. You also learn the basic math and text operations.

Chapter 3

We step up to Python's higher-level built-in data structures: lists, tuples, dictionaries, and sets. You use these as you would Legos to build much more complicated structures. You learn how to step through them by using *iterators* and *comprehensions*.

Chapter 4

In Chapter 4, you weave the data structures of the previous chapters with code structures to compare, choose, or repeat. You see how to package code in *functions* and handle errors with *exceptions*.

Chapter 5

This chapter demonstrates how to scale out to larger code structures: modules, packages, and programs. You see where to put code and data, get data in and out, handle options, tour the Python Standard Library, and take a glance at what lies beyond.

Chapter 6

If you've done object-oriented programming in other languages, Python is a bit more relaxed. Chapter 6 explains when to use objects and classes, and when it's better to use modules or even lists and dictionaries.

Chapter 7

Learn to manage data like a pro. This chapter is all about text and binary data, the joy of Unicode characters, and I/O.

Chapter 8

Data needs to go somewhere. In this chapter, you begin with basic flat files, directories, and filesystems. Then, you see how to handle common file formats such as CSV, JSON, and XML. You also explore how to store and retrieve with relational databases, and even some recent NoSQL data stores.

Chapter 9

The Web gets its own chapter, which covers clients, servers, scraping, APIs, and frameworks. In Chapter 9, you work up a real website with request parameters and templates.

Chapter 10

This is the hard-core system chapter. In this one, you learn to manage programs, processes, and threads; deal with dates and times; and automate some system administration tasks.

Chapter 11

Networking is the subject here: services, protocols, and APIs. Examples range from low-level TCP sockets, to messaging libraries and queuing systems, to cloud deployment.

Chapter 12

This chapter contains tips for Python developers, including installing, using IDEs, testing, debugging, logging, source control, and documentation. Chapter 12 also helps you to find and install useful third-party packages, package your own code for reuse, and learn where to get more information. Good luck.

Appendix A

The first appendix delves into what people are doing with Python in the arts: graphics, music, animation, and games.

Appendix B

Python has specific applications for business: data visualization (plots, graphs, and maps), security, and regulation.

Appendix C

Python has a strong presence in science: math and statistics, physical science, bioscience, and medicine. Appendix C features NumPy, SciPy, and Pandas.

Appendix D

If you don't already have Python 3 on your computer, this appendix shows you how to install it, no matter if you're running Windows, Mac OS/X, Linux, or Unix.

Appendix E

This has the answers to the end-of-chapter exercises. Don't peek here until you've tried the exercises yourself.

Appendix F

This appendix contains cheat sheets to use as a quick reference.

Python Versions

Computer languages change over time as developers add features and fix mistakes. The examples in this book were written and tested while running Python version 3.3. Version 3.4 was released as this book was being edited, and I'll talk about a few of its additions. If you want to know what was added to Python and when, try the What's New in Python (*https://docs.python.org/3/whatsnew/*) page. It's a technical reference; a bit heavy when you're just starting with Python, but may be useful in the future if you ever have to get programs to work on computers with different Python versions.

Conventions Used in This Book

The following typographical conventions are used in this book:

Italic

> Indicates new terms, URLs, email addresses, filenames, and file extensions.

`Constant width`

> Used for program listings, as well as within paragraphs to refer to program elements such as variables, functions, and data types.

`Constant width bold`

> Shows commands or other text that should be typed literally by the user.

`Constant width italic`

> Shows text that should be replaced with user-supplied values or by values determined by context.

 This icon signifies a tip, suggestion, or general note.

This icon indicates a warning or caution.

Using Code Examples

The substantial code examples in this book—although not the exercises, which are challenges for the reader—are available online for you to download (*https://github.com/madscheme/introducing-python*). This book is here to help you get your job done. In general, you may use the code in this book in your programs and documentation. You do not need to contact us for permission unless you're reproducing a significant portion of the code. For example, writing a program that uses several chunks of code from this book does not require permission. Selling or distributing a CD-ROM of examples from O'Reilly books does require permission. Answering a question by citing this book and quoting example code does not require permission. Incorporating a significant amount of example code from this book into your product's documentation does require permission.

We appreciate, but do not require, attribution. An attribution usually includes the title, author, publisher, and ISBN. For example: "*Introducing Python* by Bill Lubanovic (O'Reilly). Copyright 2015 Bill Lubanovic, 978-1-449-35936-2."

If you feel your use of code examples falls outside fair use or the permission given here, feel free to contact us at *permissions@oreilly.com*.

Safari® Books Online

 Safari Books Online is an on-demand digital library that delivers expert content in both book and video form from the world's leading authors in technology and business.

Technology professionals, software developers, web designers, and business and creative professionals use Safari Books Online as their primary resource for research, problem solving, learning, and certification training.

Safari Books Online offers a range of plans and pricing for enterprise, government, education, and individuals.

Members have access to thousands of books, training videos, and prepublication manuscripts in one fully searchable database from publishers like O'Reilly Media, Prentice Hall Professional, Addison-Wesley Professional, Microsoft Press, Sams, Que, Peachpit Press, Focal Press, Cisco Press, John Wiley & Sons, Syngress, Morgan Kaufmann, IBM Redbooks, Packt, Adobe Press, FT Press, Apress, Manning, New Riders, McGraw-Hill, Jones & Bartlett, Course Technology, and hundreds more. For more information about Safari Books Online, please visit us online.

How to Contact Us

Please address comments and questions concerning this book to the publisher:

O'Reilly Media, Inc.
1005 Gravenstein Highway North
Sebastopol, CA 95472
800-998-9938 (in the United States or Canada)
707-829-0515 (international or local)
707-829-0104 (fax)

We have a web page for this book, where we list errata, examples, and any additional information. You can access this page at *http://bit.ly/introducing_python*.

To comment or ask technical questions about this book, send email to *bookquestions@oreilly.com*.

For more information about our books, courses, conferences, and news, see our website at *http://www.oreilly.com*.

Find us on Facebook: *http://facebook.com/oreilly*

Follow us on Twitter: *http://twitter.com/oreillymedia*

Watch us on YouTube: *http://www.youtube.com/oreillymedia*

Acknowledgments

Thanks go to the many people who read and commented on my draft. I'd like to particularly mention the careful reviews by Eli Bessert, Henry Canival, Jeremy Elliott, Monte Milanuk, Loïc Pefferkorn, and Steven Wayne.

CHAPTER 1

A Taste of Py

Let's begin with a mini-mystery and its solution. What do you think the following two lines mean?

```
(Row 1): (RS) K18,ssk,k1,turn work.
(Row 2): (WS) Sl 1 pwise,p5,p2tog,p1,turn.
```

It looks technical, like some kind of computer program. Actually, it's a *knitting pattern*; specifically, a fragment describing how to turn the heel of a sock. This makes as much sense to me as the *New York Times* crossword puzzle does to my cat, but my wife understands it perfectly. If you're a knitter, you do, too.

Let's try another example. You'll figure out its purpose right away, although you might not know its final product.

```
1/2 c. butter or margarine
1/2 c. cream
2 1/2 c. flour
1 t. salt
1 T. sugar
4 c. riced potatoes (cold)

Be sure all ingredients are cold before adding flour.
Mix all ingredients.
Knead thoroughly.
Form into 20 balls.  Store cold until the next step.
For each ball:
  Spread flour on cloth.
  Roll ball into a circle with a grooved rolling pin.
  Fry on griddle until brown spots appear.
  Turn over and fry other side.
```

Even if you don't cook, you probably recognized that it's a *recipe*: a list of food ingredients followed by directions for preparation. But what does it make? It's *lefse*, a Norwegian delicacy that resembles a tortilla. Slather on some butter and jam or whatever you like, roll it up, and enjoy.

The knitting pattern and the recipe share some features:

- A fixed vocabulary of words, abbreviations, and symbols. Some might be familiar, others mystifying.
- Rules about what can be said, and where—their *syntax*.
- A sequence of operations to be performed in order.
- Sometimes, a repetition of some operations (a *loop*), such as the method for frying each piece of lefse.
- Sometimes, a reference to another sequence of operations (in computer terms, a *function*). In the recipe, you might need to refer to another recipe for ricing potatoes.
- Assumed knowledge about the context. The recipe assumes you know what water is and how to boil it. The knitting pattern assumes that you can knit and purl without stabbing yourself too often.
- An expected result. In our examples, something for your feet and something for your stomach. Just don't mix them up.

You'll see all of these ideas in computer programs. I used these nonprograms to demonstrate that programming isn't that mysterious. It's just a matter of learning the right words and the rules.

Let's leave these stand-ins and see a real program. What does this do?

```
for countdown in 5, 4, 3, 2, 1, "hey!":
    print(countdown)
```

If you guessed that it's a Python program that prints the lines:

```
5
4
3
2
1
hey!
```

then you know that Python can be easier to learn than a recipe or knitting pattern. And, you can practice writing Python programs from the comfort and safety of your desk, far from the harrowing dangers of hot water and pointy sticks.

The Python program has some special words and symbols—for, in, print, commas, colons, parentheses, and so on—that are important parts of the language's syntax. The good news is that Python has a nicer syntax, and less of it to remember, than most computer languages. It seems more natural—almost like a recipe.

Here's another tiny Python program that selects a television news cliché from a Python *list* and prints it:

```python
cliches = [
    "At the end of the day",
    "Having said that",
    "The fact of the matter is",
    "Be that as it may",
    "The bottom line is",
    "If you will",
    ]
print(cliches[3])
```

The program prints the fourth cliché:

```
Be that as it may
```

A Python list such as `cliches` is a sequence of values, accessed by their *offset* from the beginning of the list. The first value is at offset 0, and the fourth value is at offset 3.

 People count from 1, so it might seem weird to count from 0. It helps to think in terms of offsets instead of positions.

Lists are very common in Python, and Chapter 3 shows how to use them.

Following is another program that also prints a quote, but this time referenced by the person who said it rather than its position in a list:

```python
quotes = {
    "Moe": "A wise guy, huh?",
    "Larry": "Ow!",
    "Curly": "Nyuk nyuk!",
    }
stooge = "Curly"
print(stooge, "says:", quotes[stooge])
```

If you were to run this little program, it would print the following:

```
Curly says: Nyuk nyuk!
```

`quotes` is a Python *dictionary*—a collection of unique *keys* (in this example, the name of the Stooge) and associated *values* (here, a notable quote of that Stooge). Using a dictionary, you can store and look up things by name, which is often a useful alternative to a list. You can read much more about dictionaries in Chapter 3.

The cliché example uses square brackets ([and]) to make a Python list, and the stooge example uses curly brackets ({ and }, which are no relation to Curly), to make a Python dictionary. These are examples of Python's syntax, and in the next few chapters, you'll see much more.

And now for something completely different: Example 1-1 presents a Python program performing a more complex series of tasks. Don't expect to understand how the program works yet; that's what this book is for! The intent is to introduce you to the look and feel of a typical nontrivial Python program. If you know other computer languages, evaluate how Python compares.

In earlier printings of this book, this sample program connected to a YouTube website and retrieved information on its most highly rated videos, like "Charlie Bit My Finger." It worked well until shortly after the ink was dry on the second printing. That's when Google dropped support for this service and the marquee sample program stopped working. Our new Example 1-1 goes to another site—the *Wayback Machine* at the Internet Archive (*http://archive.org*), which has saved billions of web pages (and movies, TV shows, music, games, and other digital artifacts) over twenty years.

The program will ask you to type a URL and a date. Then it asks the Wayback Machine if it has a copy of that website around that date. If it found one, it prints the URL and displays it in your web browser. The point is to show how Python handles a variety of tasks—get your typed input, talk across the Internet to a website, get back some content, extract a URL from it, and convince your web browser to display that URL.

If we got back a normal web page full of HTML-formatted text, it would be hard to dig out the information we want (I talk about *web scraping* in "Crawl and Scrape" on page 244). Instead, the program returns data in *JSON* format, which is meant for processing by computers. JSON, or JavaScript Object Notation, is a human-readable text format that describes the types, values, and order of the values within it. It's like a little programming language and has become a popular way to exchange data among different computer languages and systems. You read about JSON in "JSON" on page 189.

Python programs can translate JSON text into Python *data structures*—the kind you'll see in the next two chapters—as though you wrote a program to create them yourself. Our little program just selects one piece (the URL of the old page from the Archive). Again, this is a complete Python program that you can run yourself. We've included only a little error-checking, just to keep the example short.

Example 1-1. intro/archive.py

```
import webbrowser
import json
from urllib.request import urlopen

print("Let's find an old website.")
```

```
site = input("Type a website URL: ")
era = input("Type a year, month, and day, like 20150613: ")
url = "http://archive.org/wayback/available?url=%s&timestamp=%s" % (site, era)
response = urlopen(url)
contents = response.read()
text = contents.decode("utf-8")
data = json.loads(text)
try:
    old_site = data["archived_snapshots"]["closest"]["url"]
    print("Found this copy: ", old_site)
    print("It should appear in your browser now.")
    webbrowser.open(old_site)
except:
    print("Sorry, no luck finding", site)
```

When I ran this in a terminal window, I typed a site URL and a date, and got this text output:

```
$ python archive.py
Let's find an old website.
Type a website URL: lolcats.com
Type a year, month, and day, like 20150613: 20151022
Found this copy:  http://web.archive.org/web/20151102055938/http://www.lolcats.com/
It should appear in your browser now.
```

And this appeared in my browser:

This little Python program did a lot in a few fairly readable lines. You don't know all these terms, but don't worry; you will within the next few chapters:

- Line 1: import (make available to this program) all the code from the Python *standard library* called `webbrowser`
- Line 2: import all the code from the Python standard library called `json`
- Line 3: import only the `urlopen` function from the standard library `url lib.request`
- Line 4: a blank line, because we don't want to feel crowded
- Line 5: print some initial text to your display
- Line 6: print a question about a URL, read what you type, and save it in a program *variable* called `site`
- Line 7: print another question, this time reading a year, month and day, and saving it in a variable called `era`
- Line 8: construct another variable called `url` to make the Wayback Machine look up its copy of the site and date that you typed
- Line 9: connect to the web server at that URL and request a particular *web service*
- Line 10: get the response data and assign to the variable `contents`
- Line 11: *decode* `contents` to a text string in JSON format, and assign to the variable `text`
- Line 12: convert `text` to `data`—Python data structures
- Line 13: error-checking: `try` to run the next four lines, and if any fail, run the last line of the program (after the `except`)
- Line 14: if we got back a match for this site and date, extract its value from a three-level Python *dictionary*
- Line 15: print the URL that we found
- Line 16: print another messsage about what will happen in your browser now
- Line 17: display the URL we found in your web browser
- Line 18: if anything failed in the previous four lines, Python jumps down to here
- Line 19: if it failed, print a message and the site that we were looking for

In the previous example, we used some of Python's standard library modules (programs that are included with Python when it's installed), but there's nothing sacred about them. The code that follows shows a rewrite that uses an external Python software package called `requests`:

```python
import webbrowser
import requests

print("Let's find an old website.")
site = input("Type a website URL: ")
era = input("Type a year, month, and day, like 20150613: ")
url = "http://archive.org/wayback/available?url=%s&timestamp=%s" % (site, era)
response = requests.get(url)
data = response.json()
try:
    old_site = data["archived_snapshots"]["closest"]["url"]
    print("Found this copy: ", old_site)
    print("It should appear in your browser now.")
    webbrowser.open(old_site)
except:
    print("Sorry, no luck finding", site)
```

The new version is shorter, and I'd guess it's more readable for most people. I have a lot more to say about requests and other externally authored Python software in Chapter 5.

Python in the Real World

So, is learning Python worth the time and effort? Is it a fad or a toy? Actually, it's been around since 1991 (longer than Java), and is consistently in the top 10 most popular computing languages. People are paid to write Python programs—serious stuff that you use every day, such as Google, YouTube, Dropbox, Netflix, and Hulu. I've used it for production applications as varied as an email search appliance and an ecommerce website. Python has a reputation for productivity that appeals to fast-moving organizations.

You'll find Python in many computing environments, including the following:

- The command line in a monitor or terminal window
- Graphical user interfaces, including the Web
- The Web, on the client and server sides
- Backend servers supporting large popular sites
- The *cloud* (servers managed by third parties)
- Mobile devices
- Embedded devices

Python programs range from one-off *scripts*—such as those you've seen so far in this chapter—to million-line systems. We'll look at its uses in websites, system administration, and data manipulation. We'll also look at specific uses of Python in the arts, science, and business.

Python versus Language X

How does Python compare against other languages? Where and when would you choose one over the other? In this section, I'll show code samples from other languages, just so you can see what the competition looks like. You are *not* expected to understand these if you haven't worked with them. (By the time you get to the final Python sample, you might be relieved that you haven't had to work with some of the others.) If you're only interested in Python, you won't miss anything if you just skip to the next section.

Each program is supposed to print a number and say a little about the language.

If you use a terminal or terminal window, the program that reads what you type, runs it, and displays the results is called the *shell* program. The Windows shell is called cmd; it runs *batch* files with the suffix .bat. Linux and other Unix-like systems (including Mac OS X) have many shell programs, the most popular is called bash or sh. The shell has simple abilities, such as simple logic and expanding wildcard symbols such as * into filenames. You can save commands in files called *shell scripts* and run them later. These might be the first programs you encountered as a programmer. The problem is that shell scripts don't scale well beyond a few hundred lines, and they are much slower than the alternative languages. The next snippet shows a little shell program:

```
#!/bin/sh
language=0
echo "Language $language: I am the shell. So there."
```

If you saved this in a file as meh.sh and ran it with sh meh.sh, you would see the following on your display:

```
Language 0: I am the shell. So there.
```

Old stalwarts C and C++ are fairly low-level languages, used when speed is most important. They're harder to learn, and require you to keep track of many details, which can lead to crashes and problems that are hard to diagnose. Here's a look at a little C program:

```
#include <stdio.h>
int main(int argc, char *argv[]) {
    int language = 1;
    printf("Language %d: I am C! Behold me and tremble!\n", language);
    return 0;
}
```

C++ has the C family resemblance but with distinctive features:

```
#include <iostream>
using namespace std;
int main() {
```

```
    int language = 2;
    cout << "Language " << language << \
      ": I am C++!  Pay no attention to that C behind the curtain!" << \
      endl;
    return(0);
}
```

Java and C# are successors to C and C++ that avoid some of the latters' problems, but are somewhat verbose and restrictive. The example that follows shows some Java:

```
public class Overlord {
    public static void main (String[] args) {
        int language = 3;
        System.out.format("Language %d: I am Java! Scarier than C!\n", language);
    }
}
```

If you haven't written programs in any of these languages, you might wonder: *what* is all that *stuff*? Some languages carry substantial syntactic baggage. They're sometimes called *static languages* because they require you to specify some low-level details for the computer. Let me explain.

Languages have *variables*—names for values that you want to use in a program. Static languages make you declare the *type* of each variable: how much room it will use in memory, and what you can do with it. The computer uses this information to *compile* the program into very low-level *machine language* (specific to the computer's hardware and easier for it to understand, but harder for humans). Computer language designers often must decide between making things easier for people or for computers. Declaring variable types helps the computer to catch some mistakes and run faster, but it does require more up-front human thinking and typing. Much of the code that you saw in the C, C++, and Java examples was required to declare types. For example, in all of them the int declaration was needed to treat the variable language as an integer. (Other types include floating-point numbers such as 3.14159 and character or text data, which are stored differently.)

Then why are they called *static* languages? Because variables in those languages can't ever change their type; they're static. An integer is an integer, forever and ever.

In contrast, *dynamic languages* (also called *scripting languages*) do not force you to declare variable types before using them. If you type something such as x = 5, a dynamic language knows that 5 is an integer; thus, the variable x is, too. These languages let you accomplish more with fewer lines of code. Instead of being compiled, they are *interpreted* by a program called—surprise!—an *interpreter*. Dynamic languages are often slower than compiled static languages, but their speed is improving as their interpreters become more optimized. For a long time, dynamic languages were used mainly for short programs (*scripts*), often to prepare data for processing by longer programs written in static languages. Such programs have been called *glue code.* Although dynamic languages are well suited for this purpose, today they are able to tackle most big processing tasks as well.

The all-purpose dynamic language for many years was Perl (*http://www.perl.org/*). Perl is very powerful and has extensive libraries. Yet, its syntax can be awkward, and the language seems to have lost momentum in the last few years to Python and Ruby. This example regales you with a Perl bon mot:

```
my $language = 4;
print "Language $language: I am Perl, the camel of languages.\n";
```

Ruby (*http://www.ruby-lang.org/*) is a more recent language. It borrows a little from Perl, and is popular mostly because of *Ruby on Rails*, a web development framework. It's used in many of the same areas as Python, and the choice of one or the other might boil down to a matter of taste, or available libraries for your particular application. The code example here depicts a Ruby snippet:

```
language = 5
puts "Language #{language}: I am Ruby, ready and aglow."
```

PHP (*http://www.php.net/*), which you can see in the example that follows, is very popular for web development because it makes it easy to combine HTML and code. However, the PHP language itself has a number of gotchas, and PHP has not caught on as a general language outside of the Web.

```
<?PHP
$language = 6;
echo "Language $language: I am PHP. The web is <i>mine</i>, I say.\n";
?>
```

The example that follows presents Python's rebuttal:

```
language = 7
print("Language %s: I am Python. What's for supper?" % language)
```

So, Why Python?

Python is a good general-purpose, high-level language. Its design makes it very *readable*, which is more important than it sounds. Every computer program is written only once, but read and revised many times, often by many people. Being readable also makes it easier to learn and remember, hence more *writeable*. Compared with other popular languages, Python has a gentle learning curve that makes you productive sooner, yet it has depths that you can explore as you gain expertise.

Python's relative terseness makes it possible for you to write a program that's much smaller than its equivalent in a static language. Studies have shown that programmers tend to produce roughly the same number of lines of code per day—regardless of the language—so, writing half the lines of code doubles your productivity, just like that. Python is the not-so-secret weapon of many companies that think this is important.

Python is the most popular language for introductory computer science courses at the top American colleges (*http://bit.ly/popular-py*). It is also the most popular language for evaluating programming skill by over two thousand employers (*http://bit.ly/langs-2014*).

And of course, it's free, as in beer and speech. Write anything you want with Python, and use it anywhere, freely. No one can read your Python program and say, "That's a nice little program you have there. It would be too bad if something happened to it."

Python runs almost everywhere and has "batteries included"—a metric boatload of useful software in its standard library.

But, maybe the best reason to use Python is an unexpected one: people generally *like* it. They actually enjoy programming with it, rather than treating it as just another tool to get stuff done. Often they'll say that they miss some feature of Python when they need to work in another language. And that's what separates Python from most of its peers.

When Not to Use Python

Python isn't the best language for every situation.

It is not installed everywhere by default. Appendix D shows you how to install Python if you don't already have it on your computer.

It's fast enough for most applications, but it might not be fast enough for some of the more demanding ones. If your program spends most of its time calculating things (the technical term is *CPU-bound*), a program written in C, C++, or Java will generally run faster than its Python equivalent. But not always!

- Sometimes a better *algorithm* (a stepwise solution) in Python beats an inefficient one in C. The greater speed of development in Python gives you more time to experiment with alternatives.

- In many applications, a program twiddles its thumbs while awaiting a response from some server across a network. The CPU (central processing unit, the computer's *chip* that does all the calculating) is barely involved; consequently, end-to-end times between static and dynamic programs will be close.

- The standard Python interpreter is written in C and can be extended with C code. I discuss this a little in "Optimize Your Code" on page 335.

- Python interpreters are becoming faster. Java was terribly slow in its infancy, and a lot of research and money went into speeding it up. Python is not owned by a corporation, so its enhancements have been more gradual. In "PyPy" on page 338, I talk about the *PyPy* project and its implications.

- You might have an extremely demanding application, and no matter what you do, Python doesn't meet your needs. Then, as Ian Holm said in the movie *Alien*, you have my sympathies. The usual alternatives are C, C++, and Java, but a newer language called *Go* (*http://golang.org*) (which feels like Python but performs like C) could be an answer.

Python 2 versus Python 3

The biggest issue that you'll confront at the moment is that there are two versions of Python out there. Python 2 has been around forever and is preinstalled on Linux and Apple computers. It has been an excellent language, but nothing's perfect. In computer languages, as in many other areas, some mistakes are cosmetic and easy to fix, whereas others are hard. Hard fixes are *incompatible*: new programs written with them will not work on the old Python system, and old programs written before the fix will not work on the new system.

Python's creator (Guido van Rossum (*https://www.python.org/~guido*)) and others decided to bundle the hard fixes together and call it Python 3. Python 2 is the past, and Python 3 is the future. The last version of Python 2 is 2.7, and it will be supported for a long time, but it's the end of the line; there will be no Python 2.8. New development will be in Python 3.

This book features Python 3. If you've been using Python 2, it's almost identical. The most obvious change is how to call `print`. The most important change is the handling of *Unicode* characters, which is covered in Chapter 2 and Chapter 7. Conversion of popular Python software has been gradual, with the usual chicken-and-egg analogies. But now, it looks like we've finally reached a tipping point.

Installing Python

Rather than cluttering this chapter, the details on how to install Python 3 are in Appendix D. If you don't have Python 3, or aren't sure, go there and see what to do for your computer.

Running Python

After you have installed a working copy of Python 3, you can use it to run the Python programs in this book as well as your own Python code. How do you actually run a Python program? There are two main ways:

- Python's built-in *interactive interpreter* (also called its *shell*) is the easy way to experiment with small programs. You type commands line by line and see the results immediately. With the tight coupling between typing and seeing, you can

---

experiment faster. I'll use the interactive interpreter to demonstrate language features, and you can type the same commands in your own Python environment.

- For everything else, store your Python programs in text files, normally with the .py extension, and run them by typing python followed by those filenames.

Let's try both methods now.

Using the Interactive Interpreter

Most of the code examples in this book use the interactive interpreter. When you type the same commands as you see in the examples and get the same results, you'll know you're on the right track.

You start the interpreter by typing just the name of the main Python program on your computer: it should be python, python3, or something similar. For the rest of this book, we'll assume it's called python; if yours has a different name, type that wherever you see python in a code example.

The interactive interpreter works almost exactly the same as Python works on files, with one exception: when you type something that has a value, the interactive interpreter prints its value for you automatically. For example, if you start Python and type the number 61 in the interpreter, it will be echoed to your terminal.

 In the example that follows, $ is a sample system *prompt* for you to type a command like python in the terminal window. We'll use it for the code examples in this book, although your prompt might be different.

```
$ python
Python 3.5.1 (v3.5.1:37a07cee5969, Dec  5 2015, 21:12:44)
[GCC 4.2.1 (Apple Inc. build 5666) (dot 3)] on darwin
Type "help", "copyright", "credits" or "license" for more information.
>>> 61
61
>>>
```

This automatic printing of a value is a time-saving feature of the interactive interpreter, not a part of the Python language.

By the way, print() also works within the interpreter whenever you want to print something:

```
>>> print(61)
61
```

If you tried these examples with the interactive interpreter and saw the same results, you just ran some real (though tiny) Python code. In the next few chapters, you'll graduate from one-liners to longer Python programs.

Use Python Files

If you put `61` in a file by itself and run it through Python, it will run, but it won't print anything. In normal noninteractive Python programs, you need to call the `print` function to print things, as is demonstrated in the code that follows:

```
print(61)
```

Let's make a Python program file and run it:

1. Open your text editor.
2. Type the line `print(61)`, as it appears above.
3. Save this to a file called *61.py*. Make sure you save it as plain text, rather than a "rich" format such as RTF or Word. You don't need to use the .py suffix for your Python program files, but it does help you remember what they are.
4. If you're using a graphical user interface—that's almost everyone—open a terminal window.[1]
5. Run your program by typing the following:

```
$ python 61.py
```

You should see a single line of output:

```
61
```

Did that work? If it did, congratulations on running your first standalone Python program.

What's Next?

You'll be typing commands to an actual Python system, and they need to follow legal Python syntax. Rather than dumping the syntax rules on you all at once, we'll stroll through them over the next few chapters.

The basic way to develop Python programs is by using a plain-text editor and a terminal window. I use plain-text displays in this book, sometimes showing interactive terminal sessions and sometimes pieces of Python files. You should know that there are also many good *integrated development environments* (IDEs) for Python. These

---

1 If you're not sure what this means, see Appendix D for details for different operating systems.

may feature graphical user interfaces with advanced text editing and help displays. You can learn about details for some of these in Chapter 12.

Your Moment of Zen

Each computing language has its own style. In the preface, I mentioned that there is often a *Pythonic* way to express yourself. Embedded in Python is a bit of free verse that expresses the Python philosophy succinctly (as far as I know, Python is the only language to include such an Easter egg). Just type import this into your interactive interpreter and then press the Enter key whenever you need this moment of Zen:

```
>>> import this
The Zen of Python, by Tim Peters

Beautiful is better than ugly.
Explicit is better than implicit.
Simple is better than complex.
Complex is better than complicated.
Flat is better than nested.
Sparse is better than dense.
Readability counts.
Special cases aren't special enough to break the rules.
Although practicality beats purity.
Errors should never pass silently.
Unless explicitly silenced.
In the face of ambiguity, refuse the temptation to guess.
There should be one--and preferably only one--obvious way to do it.
Although that way may not be obvious at first unless you're Dutch.
Now is better than never.
Although never is often better than *right* now.
If the implementation is hard to explain, it's a bad idea.
If the implementation is easy to explain, it may be a good idea.
Namespaces are one honking great idea--let's do more of those!
```

I'll bring up examples of these sentiments throughout the book.

Things to Do

This chapter was an introduction to the Python language—what it does, how it looks, and where it fits in the computing world. At the end of each chapter, I'll suggest some mini-projects to help you remember what you just read and prepare you for what's to come.

1.1 If you don't already have Python 3 installed on your computer, do it now. Read Appendix D for the details for your computer system.

1.2 Start the Python 3 interactive interpreter. Again, details are in Appendix D. It should print a few lines about itself and then a single line starting with >>>. That's your prompt to type Python commands.

1.3 Play with the interpreter a little. Use it like a calculator and type this: 8 * 9. Press the Enter key to see the result. Python should print 72.

1.4 Type the number 47 and press the Enter key. Did it print 47 for you on the next line?

1.5 Now, type `print(47)` and press Enter. Did that also print 47 for you on the next line?

CHAPTER 2

Py Ingredients: Numbers, Strings, and Variables

In this chapter we'll begin by looking at Python's simplest built-in data types:

- *booleans* (which have the value `True` or `False`)
- *integers* (whole numbers such as `42` and `100000000`)
- *floats* (numbers with decimal points such as `3.14159`, or sometimes exponents like `1.0e8`, which means *one times ten to the eighth power*, or `100000000.0`)
- *strings* (sequences of text characters)

In a way, they're like atoms. We'll use them individually in this chapter. Chapter 3 shows how to combine them into larger "molecules."

Each type has specific rules for its usage and is handled differently by the computer. We'll also introduce *variables* (names that refer to actual data; more on these in a moment).

The code examples in this chapter are all valid Python, but they're snippets. We'll be using the Python interactive interpreter, typing these snippets and seeing the results immediately. Try running them yourself with the version of Python on your computer. You'll recognize these examples by the >>> prompt. In Chapter 4, we start writing Python programs that can run on their own.

Variables, Names, and Objects

In Python, *everything*—booleans, integers, floats, strings, even large data structures, functions, and programs—is implemented as an *object*. This gives the language a consistency (and useful features) that some other languages lack.

An object is like a clear plastic box that contains a piece of data (Figure 2-1). The object has a *type*, such as boolean or integer, that determines what can be done with the data. A real-life box marked "Pottery" would tell you certain things (it's probably heavy, and don't drop it on the floor). Similarly, in Python, if an object has the type `int`, you know that you could add it to another `int`.

Figure 2-1. An object is like a box

The type also determines if the data *value* contained by the box can be changed (*mutable*) or is constant (*immutable*). Think of an immutable object as a closed box with a clear window: you can see the value but you can't change it. By the same analogy, a mutable object is like an open box: not only can you see the value inside, you can also change it; however, you can't change its type.

Python is *strongly typed*, which means that the type of an object does not change, even if its value is mutable (Figure 2-2).

Figure 2-2. Strong typing does not mean push the keys harder

Programming languages allow you to define *variables*. These are names that refer to values in the computer's memory that you can define for use with your program. In Python, you use = to *assign* a value to a variable.

We all learned in grade school math that = means *equal to*. So why do many computer languages, including Python, use = for assignment? One reason is that standard keyboards lack logical alternatives such as a left arrow key, and = didn't seem too confusing. Also, in computer programs you use assignment much more than you test for equality.

The following is a two-line Python program that assigns the integer value 7 to the variable named a, and then prints the value currently associated with a:

```
>>> a = 7
>>> print(a)
7
```

Now, it's time to make a crucial point about Python variables: *variables are just names*. Assignment **does not copy** a value; it just **attaches a name** to the object that contains the data. The name is a *reference* to a thing rather than the thing itself. Think of a name as a sticky note (see Figure 2-3).

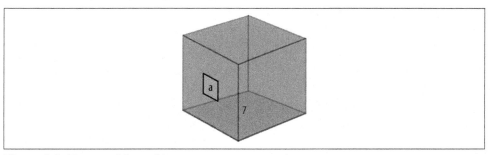

Figure 2-3. Names stick to objects

Try this with the interactive interpreter:

1. As before, assign the value 7 to the name a. This creates an object box containing the integer value 7.

2. Print the value of a.

3. Assign a to b, making b also stick to the object box containing 7.

4. Print the value of b.

```
>>> a = 7
>>> print(a)
7
>>> b = a
>>> print(b)
7
```

In Python, if you want to know the type of anything (a variable or a literal value), use type(*thing*). Let's try it with different literal values (58, 99.9, abc) and different variables (a, b):

```
>>> type(a)
<class 'int'>
>>> type(b)
<class 'int'>
>>> type(58)
<class 'int'>
>>> type(99.9)
<class 'float'>
>>> type('abc')
<class 'str'>
```

A *class* is the definition of an object; Chapter 6 covers classes in greater detail. In Python, "class" and "type" mean pretty much the same thing.

Variable names can only contain these characters:

- Lowercase letters (a through z)
- Uppercase letters (A through Z)
- Digits (0 through 9)
- Underscore (_)

Names cannot begin with a digit. Also, Python treats names that begin with an underscore in special ways (which you can read about in Chapter 4). These are valid names:

- a
- a1
- a_b_c___95
- _abc
- _1a

These names, however, are not valid:

- 1
- 1a
- 1_

Finally, don't use any of these for variable names, because they are Python's *reserved words*:

False	class	finally	is	return
None	continue	for	lambda	try
True	def	from	nonlocal	while
and	del	global	not	with
as	elif	if	or	yield
assert	else	import	pass	
break	except	in	raise	

These words, and some punctuation, are used to define Python's syntax. You'll see all of them as you progress through this book.

Numbers

Python has built-in support for *integers* (whole numbers such as 5 and 1,000,000,000) and *floating point* numbers (such as 3.1416, 14.99, and 1.87e4). You can calculate combinations of numbers with the simple math *operators* in this table:

Operator	Description	Example	Result
+	addition	5 + 8	13
-	subtraction	90 - 10	80
*	multiplication	4 * 7	28
/	floating point division	7 / 2	3.5
//	integer (truncating) division	7 // 2	3
%	modulus (remainder)	7 % 3	1
**	exponentiation	3 ** 4	81

For the next few pages, I'll show simple examples of Python acting as a glorified calculator.

Integers

Any sequence of digits in Python is assumed to be a literal *integer*:

```
>>> 5
5
```

You can use a plain zero (0):

```
>>> 0
0
```

But don't put it in front of other digits:

```
>>> 05
  File "<stdin>", line 1
    05
     ^
SyntaxError: invalid token
```

 This is the first time you've seen a Python *exception*—a program error. In this case, it's a warning that 05 is an "invalid token." I'll explain what this means in "Bases" on page 26. You'll see many more examples of exceptions in this book because they're Python's main error handling mechanism.

A sequence of digits specifies a positive integer. If you put a + sign before the digits, the number stays the same:

```
>>> 123
123
>>> +123
123
```

To specify a negative integer, insert a – before the digits:

```
>>> -123
-123
```

You can do normal arithmetic with Python, much as you would with a calculator, by using the operators listed in the table on the previous page. Addition and subtraction work as you'd expect:

```
>>> 5 + 9
14
>>> 100 - 7
93
>>> 4 - 10
-6
```

You can include as many numbers and operators as you'd like:

```
>>> 5 + 9 + 3
17
>>> 4 + 3 - 2 - 1 + 6
10
```

A style note: you're not required to have a space between each number and operator:

```
>>> 5+9   +      3
17
```

It just looks better and is easier to read.

Multiplication is also straightforward:

```
>>> 6 * 7
42
>>> 7 * 6
42
>>> 6 * 7 * 2 * 3
252
```

Division is a little more interesting, because it comes in two flavors:

- / carries out *floating-point* (decimal) division
- // performs *integer* (truncating) division

Even if you're dividing an integer by an integer, using a / will give you a floating-point result:

```
>>> 9 / 5
1.8
```

Truncating integer division gives you an integer answer, throwing away any remainder:

```
>>> 9 // 5
1
```

Dividing by zero with either kind of division causes a Python exception:

```
>>> 5 / 0
Traceback (most recent call last):
  File "<stdin>", line 1, in <module>
ZeroDivisionError: division by zero
>>> 7 // 0
Traceback (most recent call last):
  File "<stdin>", line 1, in <module>
ZeroDivisionError: integer division or modulo by z
```

All of the preceding examples used literal integers. You can mix literal integers and variables that have been assigned integer values:

```
>>> a = 95
>>> a
95
>>> a - 3
92
```

Earlier, when we said a - 3, we didn't assign the result to a, so the value of a did not change:

```
>>> a
95
```

If you wanted to change a, you would do this:

```
>>> a = a - 3
>>> a
92
```

This usually confuses beginning programmers, again because of our ingrained grade school math training, we see that = sign and think of equality. In Python, the expression on the right side of the = is calculated first, *then* assigned to the variable on the left side.

If it helps, think of it this way:

- Subtract 3 from a
- Assign the result of that subtraction to a temporary variable
- Assign the value of the temporary variable to a:

```
>>> a = 95
>>> temp = a - 3
>>> a = temp
```

So, when you say:

```
>>> a = a - 3
```

Python is calculating the subtraction on the righthand side, remembering the result, and then assigning it to a on the left side of the = sign. It's faster and neater than using a temporary variable.

You can combine the arithmetic operators with assignment by putting the operator before the =. Here, a -= 3 is like saying a = a - 3:

```
>>> a = 95
>>> a -= 3
>>> a
92
```

This is like a = a + 8:

```
>>> a += 8
>>> a
100
```

And this is like a = a * 2:

```
>>> a *= 2
>>> a
200
```

Here's a floating-point division example, such as a = a / 3:

```
>>> a /= 3
>>> a
66.66666666666667
```

Let's assign 13 to a, and then try the shorthand for a = a // 4 (truncating integer division):

```
>>> a = 13
>>> a //= 4
>>> a
3
```

The % character has multiple uses in Python. When it's between two numbers, it produces the remainder when the first number is divided by the second:

```
>>> 9 % 5
4
```

Here's how to get both the (truncated) quotient and remainder at once:

```
>>> divmod(9,5)
(1, 4)
```

Otherwise, you could have calculated them separately:

```
>>> 9 // 5
1
>>> 9 % 5
4
```

You just saw some new things here: a *function* named divmod is given the integers 9 and 5 and returns a two-item result called a *tuple*. Tuples will take a bow in Chapter 3; functions will make their debut in Chapter 4.

Precedence

What would you get if you typed the following?

```
>>> 2 + 3 * 4
```

If you do the addition first, 2 + 3 is 5, and 5 * 4 is 20. But if you do the multiplication first, 3 * 4 is 12, and 2 + 12 is 14. In Python, as in most languages, multiplication has higher *precedence* than addition, so the second version is what you'd see:

```
>>> 2 + 3 * 4
14
```

How do you know the precedence rules? There's a big table in Appendix F that lists them all, but I've found that in practice I never look up these rules. It's much easier to just add parentheses to group your code as you intend the calculation to be carried out:

```
>>> 2 + (3 * 4)
14
```

This way, anyone reading the code doesn't need to guess its intent or look up precedence rules.

Bases

Integers are assumed to be decimal (base 10) unless you use a prefix to specify another *base*. You might never need to use these other bases, but you'll probably see them in Python code somewhere, sometime.

We generally have 10 fingers or toes (one of my cats has a few more, but rarely uses them for counting). So, we count 0, 1, 2, 3, 4, 5, 6, 7, 8, 9. Next, we run out of digits and carry the one to the "ten's place" and put a 0 in the one's place: 10 means "1 ten and 0 ones". We don't have a single digit that represents "ten." Then, it's 11, 12, up to 19, carry the one to make 20 (2 tens and 0 ones), and so on.

A base is how many digits you can use until you need to "carry the one." In base 2 (binary), the only digits are 0 and 1. 0 is the same as a plain old decimal 0, and 1 is the same as a decimal 1. However, in base 2, if you add a 1 to a 1, you get 10 (1 decimal two plus 0 decimal ones).

In Python, you can express literal integers in three bases besides decimal:

- 0b or 0B for *binary* (base 2).
- 0o or 0O for *octal* (base 8).
- 0x or 0X for *hex* (base 16).

The interpreter prints these for you as decimal integers. Let's try each of these bases. First, a plain old decimal 10, which means *1 ten and 0 ones*:

```
>>> 10
10
```

Now, a binary (base two), which means *1 (decimal) two and 0 ones*:

```
>>> 0b10
2
```

Octal (base 8) for *1 (decimal) eight and 0 ones*:

```
>>> 0o10
8
```

Hexadecimal (base 16) for *1 (decimal) 16 and 0 ones*:

```
>>> 0x10
16
```

In case you're wondering what "digits" base 16 uses, they are: 0, 1, 2, 3, 4, 5, 6, 7, 8, 9, a, b, c, d, e, and f. 0xa is a decimal 10, and 0xf is a decimal 15. Add 1 to 0xf and you get 0x10 (decimal 16).

Why use a different base from 10? It's useful in *bit-level* operations, which are described in Chapter 7, along with more details about converting numbers from one base to another.

Type Conversions

To change other Python data types to an integer, use the `int()` function. This will keep the whole number and discard any fractional part.

Python's simplest data type is the *boolean*, which has only the values `True` and `False`. When converted to integers, they represent the values 1 and 0:

```
>>> int(True)
1
>>> int(False)
0
```

Converting a floating-point number to an integer just lops off everything after the decimal point:

```
>>> int(98.6)
98
>>> int(1.0e4)
10000
```

Finally, here's an example of converting a text string (you'll see more about strings in a few pages) that contains only digits, possibly with + or - signs:

```
>>> int('99')
99
>>> int('-23')
-23
>>> int('+12')
12
```

Converting an integer to an integer doesn't change anything but doesn't hurt either:

```
>>> int(12345)
12345
```

If you try to convert something that doesn't look like a number, you'll get an *exception*:

```
>>> int('99 bottles of beer on the wall')
Traceback (most recent call last):
  File "<stdin>", line 1, in <module>
ValueError: invalid literal for int() with base 10: '99 bottles of beer on the wall'
>>> int('')
Traceback (most recent call last):
  File "<stdin>", line 1, in <module>
ValueError: invalid literal for int() with base 10: ''
```

The preceding text string started with valid digit characters (99), but it kept on going with others that the int() function just wouldn't stand for.

 We'll get to exceptions in Chapter 4. For now, just know that it's how Python alerts you that an error occurred (rather than crashing the program, as some languages might do). Instead of assuming that things always go right, I'll show many examples of exceptions throughout this book, so you can see what Python does when they go wrong.

int() will make integers from floats or strings of digits, but won't handle strings containing decimal points or exponents:

```
>>> int('98.6')
Traceback (most recent call last):
  File "<stdin>", line 1, in <module>
ValueError: invalid literal for int() with base 10: '98.6'
>>> int('1.0e4')
Traceback (most recent call last):
  File "<stdin>", line 1, in <module>
ValueError: invalid literal for int() with base 10: '1.0e4'
```

If you mix numeric types, Python will sometimes try to automatically convert them for you:

```
>>> 4 + 7.0
11.0
```

The boolean value False is treated as 0 or 0.0 when mixed with integers or floats, and True is treated as 1 or 1.0:

```
>>> True + 2
3
>>> False + 5.0
5.0
```

How Big Is an int?

In Python 2, the size of an int was limited to 32 bits. This was enough room to store any integer from –2,147,483,648 to 2,147,483,647.

A long had even more room: 64 bits, allowing values from –9,223,372,036,854,775,808 to 9,223,372,036,854,775,807. In Python 3, long is long gone, and an int can be *any* size—even greater than 64 bits. Thus, you can say things like the following (10**100 is called a *googol*, and was the original name of Google before they decided on the easier spelling):

```
>>>
>>> googol = 10**100
>>> googol
10000000000000000000000000000000000000000000000000000000000000000000000000
00000000000000000000000
>>> googol * googol
10000000000000000000000000000000000000000000000000000000000000000000000000
00000000000000000000000000000000000000000000000000000000000000000000000000
0000000000000000000000000000000000000000000000000
```

In many languages, trying this would cause something called *integer overflow*, where the number would need more space than the computer allowed for it, causing various bad effects. Python handles humungous integers with no problem. Score one for Python.

Floats

Integers are whole numbers, but *floating-point* numbers (called *floats* in Python) have decimal points. Floats are handled similarly to integers: you can use the operators (+, -, *, /, //, **, and %) and `divmod()` function.

To convert other types to floats, you use the `float()` function. As before, booleans act like tiny integers:

```
>>> float(True)
1.0
>>> float(False)
0.0
```

Converting an integer to a float just makes it the proud possessor of a decimal point:

```
>>> float(98)
98.0
>>> float('99')
99.0
```

And, you can convert a string containing characters that would be a valid float (digits, signs, decimal point, or an e followed by an exponent) to a real float:

```
>>> float('98.6')
98.6
>>> float('-1.5')
-1.5
>>> float('1.0e4')
10000.0
```

Math Functions

Python has the usual math functions such as square roots, cosines, and so on. We'll save them for Appendix C, in which we also discuss Python uses in science.

Strings

Nonprogrammers often think that programmers must be good at math because they work with numbers. Actually, most programmers work with *strings* of text much more than numbers. Logical (and creative!) thinking is often more important than math skills.

Because of its support for the Unicode standard, Python 3 can contain characters from any written language in the world, plus a lot of symbols. Its handling of that standard was a big reason for its split from Python 2. It's also a good reason to use version 3. I'll get into Unicode in various places, because it can be daunting at times. In the string examples that follow, I'll mostly use ASCII examples.

Strings are our first example of a Python *sequence*. In this case, they're a sequence of characters.

Unlike other languages, strings in Python are *immutable*. You can't change a string in-place, but you can copy parts of strings to another string to get the same effect. You'll see how to do this shortly.

Create with Quotes

You make a Python string by enclosing characters in either single quotes or double quotes, as demonstrated in the following:

```
>>> 'Snap'
'Snap'
>>> "Crackle"
'Crackle'
```

The interactive interpreter echoes strings with a single quote, but all are treated exactly the same by Python.

Why have two kinds of quote characters? The main purpose is so that you can create strings containing quote characters. You can have single quotes inside double-quoted strings, or double quotes inside single-quoted strings:

```
>>> "'Nay,' said the naysayer."
"'Nay,' said the naysayer."
>>> 'The rare double quote in captivity: ".'
'The rare double quote in captivity: ".'
>>> 'A "two by four" is actually 1 1/2" × 3 1/2".'
'A "two by four is" actually 1 1/2" × 3 1/2".'
>>> "'There's the man that shot my paw!' cried the limping hound."
"'There's the man that shot my paw!' cried the limping hound."
```

You can also use three single quotes (''') or three double quotes ("""):

```
>>> '''Boom!'''
'Boom'
```

```
>>> """Eek!"""
'Eek!'
```

Triple quotes aren't very useful for short strings like these. Their most common use is to create *multiline strings*, like this classic poem from Edward Lear:

```
>>> poem =  '''There was a Young Lady of Norway,
... Who casually sat in a doorway;
... When the door squeezed her flat,
... She exclaimed, "What of that?"
... This courageous Young Lady of Norway.'''
>>>
```

(This was entered in the interactive interpreter, which prompted us with >>> for the first line and ... until we entered the final triple quotes and went to the next line.)

If you tried to create that poem with single quotes, Python would make a fuss when you went to the second line:

```
>>> poem = 'There was a young lady of Norway,
  File "<stdin>", line 1
    poem = 'There was a young lady of Norway,
                                             ^
SyntaxError: EOL while scanning string literal
>>>
```

If you have multiple lines within triple quotes, the line ending characters will be preserved in the string. If you have leading or trailing spaces, they'll also be kept:

```
>>> poem2 = '''I do not like thee, Doctor Fell.
...     The reason why, I cannot tell.
...     But this I know, and know full well:
...     I do not like thee, Doctor Fell.
... '''
>>> print(poem2)
I do not like thee, Doctor Fell.
    The reason why, I cannot tell.
    But this I know, and know full well:
    I do not like thee, Doctor Fell.

>>>
```

By the way, there's a difference between the output of print() and the automatic echoing done by the interactive interpreter:

```
>>> poem2
'I do not like thee, Doctor Fell.\n   The reason why, I cannot tell.\n    But
this I know, and know full well:\n   I do not like thee, Doctor Fell.\n'
```

print() strips quotes from strings and prints their contents. It's meant for human output. It helpfully adds a space between each of the things it prints, and a newline at the end:

```
>>> print(99, 'bottles', 'would be enough.')
99 bottles would be enough.
```

If you don't want the space or newline, you'll see how to avoid them shortly.

The interpreter prints the string with single quotes and *escape characters* such as \n, which are explained in "Escape with \" on page 32.

Finally, there is the *empty string*, which has no characters at all but is perfectly valid. You can create an empty string with any of the aforementioned quotes:

```
>>> ''
''
>>> ""
''
>>> ''''''
''
>>> """"""
''
>>>
```

Why would you need an empty string? Sometimes you might want to build a string from other strings, and you need to start with a blank slate.

```
>>> bottles = 99
>>> base = ''
>>> base += 'current inventory: '
>>> base += str(bottles)
>>> base
'current inventory: 99'
```

Convert Data Types by Using str()

You can convert other Python data types to strings by using the str() function:

```
>>> str(98.6)
'98.6'
>>> str(1.0e4)
'10000.0'
>>> str(True)
'True'
```

Python uses the str() function internally when you call print() with objects that are not strings and when doing *string interpolation*, which you'll see in Chapter 7.

Escape with \

Python lets you *escape* the meaning of some characters within strings to achieve effects that would otherwise be hard to express. By preceding a character with a backslash (\), you give it a special meaning. The most common escape sequence is \n,

---

which means to begin a new line. With this you can create multiline strings from a one-line string.

```
>>> palindrome = 'A man,\nA plan,\nA canal:\nPanama.'
>>> print(palindrome)
A man,
A plan,
A canal:
Panama.
```

You will see the escape sequence \t (tab) used to align text:

```
>>> print('\tabc')
    abc
>>> print('a\tbc')
a   bc
>>> print('ab\tc')
ab      c
>>> print('abc\t')
abc
```

(The final string has a terminating tab which, of course, you can't see.)

You might also need \' or \" to specify a literal single or double quote inside a string that's quoted by the same character:

```
>>> testimony = "\"I did nothing!\" he said. \"Not that either! Or the other
  thing.\""
>>> print(testimony)
"I did nothing!" he said. "Not that either! Or the other thing."
>>> fact = "The world's largest rubber duck was 54'2\" by 65'7\" by 105'"
>>> print(fact)
The world's largest rubber duck was 54'2" by 65'7" by 105'
```

And if you need a literal backslash, just type two of them:

```
>>> speech = 'Today we honor our friend, the backslash: \\.'
>>> print(speech)
Today we honor our friend, the backslash: \.
```

Combine with +

You can combine literal strings or string variables in Python by using the + operator, as demonstrated here:

```
>>> 'Release the kraken! ' + 'No, wait!'
'Release the kraken! No, wait!'
```

You can also combine *literal strings* (not string variables) just by having one after the other:

```
>>> "My word! " "A gentleman caller!"
'My word! A gentleman caller!'
```

Python does not add spaces for you when concatenating strings, so in the preceding example, we needed to include spaces explicitly. It does add a space between each argument to a `print()` statement, and a newline at the end:

```
>>> a = 'Duck.'
>>> b = a
>>> c = 'Grey Duck!'
>>> a + b + c
'Duck.Duck.Grey Duck!'
>>> print(a, b, c)
Duck. Duck. Grey Duck!
```

Duplicate with *

You use the * operator to duplicate a string. Try typing these lines into your interactive interpreter and see what they print:

```
>>> start = 'Na ' * 4 + '\n'
>>> middle = 'Hey ' * 3 + '\n'
>>> end = 'Goodbye.'
>>> print(start + start + middle + end)
```

Extract a Character with []

To get a single character from a string, specify its *offset* inside square brackets after the string's name. The first (leftmost) offset is 0, the next is 1, and so on. The last (rightmost) offset can be specified with −1 so you don't have to count; going to the left are −2, −3, and so on.

```
>>> letters = 'abcdefghijklmnopqrstuvwxyz'
>>> letters[0]
'a'
>>> letters[1]
'b'
>>> letters[-1]
'z'
>>> letters[-2]
'y'
>>> letters[25]
'z'
>>> letters[5]
'f'
```

If you specify an offset that is the length of the string or longer (remember, offsets go from 0 to length−1), you'll get an exception:

```
>>> letters[100]
Traceback (most recent call last):
  File "<stdin>", line 1, in <module>
IndexError: string index out of range
```

Indexing works the same with the other sequence types (lists and tuples), which we cover in Chapter 3.

Because strings are immutable, you can't insert a character directly into one or change the character at a specific index. Let's try to change `'Henny'` to `'Penny'` and see what happens:

```
>>> name = 'Henny'
>>> name[0] = 'P'
Traceback (most recent call last):
  File "<stdin>", line 1, in <module>
TypeError: 'str' object does not support item assignment
```

Instead you need to use some combination of string functions such as `replace()` or a *slice* (which you'll see in a moment):

```
>>> name = 'Henny'
>>> name.replace('H', 'P')
'Penny'
>>> 'P' + name[1:]
'Penny'
```

Slice with [*start*: *end*: *step*]

You can extract a *substring* (a part of a string) from a string by using a *slice*. You define a slice by using square brackets, a *start* offset, an *end* offset, and an optional *step* size. Some of these can be omitted. The slice will include characters from offset *start* to one before *end*.

- [:] extracts the entire sequence from start to end.
- [*start* :] specifies from the *start* offset to the end.
- [: *end*] specifies from the beginning to the *end* offset minus 1.
- [*start* : *end*] indicates from the *start* offset to the *end* offset minus 1.
- [*start* : *end* : *step*] extracts from the *start* offset to the *end* offset minus 1, skipping characters by *step*.

As before, offsets go 0, 1, and so on from the start to the right, and –1,–2, and so forth from the end to the left. If you don't specify *start*, the slice uses 0 (the beginning). If you don't specify *end*, it uses the end of the string.

Let's make a string of the lowercase English letters:

```
>>> letters = 'abcdefghijklmnopqrstuvwxyz'
```

Using a plain : is the same as 0: (the entire string):

```
>>> letters[:]
'abcdefghijklmnopqrstuvwxyz'
```

Here's an example from offset 20 to the end:

```
>>> letters[20:]
'uvwxyz'
```

Now, from offset 10 to the end:

```
>>> letters[10:]
'klmnopqrstuvwxyz'
```

And another, offset 12 to 14 (Python does not include the last offset):

```
>>> letters[12:15]
'mno'
```

The three last characters:

```
>>> letters[-3:]
'xyz'
```

In this next example, we go from offset 18 to the fourth before the end; notice the difference from the previous example, in which starting at –3 gets the x, but ending at –3 actually stops at –4, the w:

```
>>> letters[18:-3]
'stuvw'
```

In the following, we extract from 6 before the end to 3 before the end:

```
>>> letters[-6:-2]
'uvwx'
```

If you want a step size other than 1, specify it after a second colon, as shown in the next series of examples.

From the start to the end, in steps of 7 characters:

```
>>> letters[::7]
'ahov'
```

From offset 4 to 19, by 3:

```
>>> letters[4:20:3]
'ehknqt'
```

From offset 19 to the end, by 4:

```
>>> letters[19::4]
'tx'
```

From the start to offset 20 by 5:

```
>>> letters[:21:5]
'afkpu'
```

(Again, the *end* needs to be one more than the actual offset.)

And that's not all! Given a negative step size, this handy Python slicer can also step backward. This starts at the end and ends at the start, skipping nothing:

```
>>> letters[-1::-1]
'zyxwvutsrqponmlkjihgfedcba'
```

It turns out that you can get the same result by using this:

```
>>> letters[::-1]
'zyxwvutsrqponmlkjihgfedcba'
```

Slices are more forgiving of bad offsets than are single-index lookups. A slice offset earlier than the beginning of a string is treated as 0, and one after the end is treated as -1, as is demonstrated in this next series of examples.

From 50 before the end to the end:

```
>>> letters[-50:]
'abcdefghijklmnopqrstuvwxyz'
```

From 51 before the end to 50 before the end:

```
>>> letters[-51:-50]
''
```

From the start to 69 after the start:

```
>>> letters[:70]
'abcdefghijklmnopqrstuvwxyz'
```

From 70 after the start to 70 after the start:

```
>>> letters[70:71]
''
```

Get Length with len()

So far, we've used special punctuation characters such as + to manipulate strings. But there are only so many of these. Now, we start to use some of Python's built-in *functions*: named pieces of code that perform certain operations.

The len() function counts characters in a string:

```
>>> len(letters)
26
>>> empty = ""
>>> len(empty)
0
```

You can use len() with other sequence types, too, as is described in Chapter 3.

Split with split()

Unlike `len()`, some functions are specific to strings. To use a string function, type the name of the string, a dot, the name of the function, and any *arguments* that the function needs: *string . function (arguments)*. You'll see a longer discussion of functions in "Functions" on page 89.

You can use the built-in string `split()` function to break a string into a *list* of smaller strings based on some *separator*. You'll see lists in the next chapter. A list is a sequence of values, separated by commas and surrounded by square brackets.

```
>>> todos = 'get gloves,get mask,give cat vitamins,call ambulance'
>>> todos.split(',')
['get gloves', 'get mask', 'give cat vitamins', 'call ambulance']
```

In the preceding example, the string was called `todos` and the string function was called `split()`, with the single separator argument `','`. If you don't specify a separator, `split()` uses any sequence of white space characters—newlines, spaces, and tabs.

```
>>> todos.split()
['get', 'gloves,get', 'mask,give', 'cat', 'vitamins,call', 'ambulance']
```

You still need the parentheses when calling `split` with no arguments—that's how Python knows you're calling a function.

Combine with join()

In what may not be an earthshaking revelation, the `join()` function is the opposite of `split()`: it collapses a list of strings into a single string. It looks a bit backward because you specify the string that glues everything together first, and then the list of strings to glue: *string .join(list)*. So, to join the list `lines` with separating newlines, you would say `'\n'.join(lines)`. In the following example, let's join some names in a list with a comma and a space:

```
>>> crypto_list = ['Yeti', 'Bigfoot', 'Loch Ness Monster']
>>> crypto_string = ', '.join(crypto_list)
>>> print('Found and signing book deals:', crypto_string)
Found and signing book deals: Yeti, Bigfoot, Loch Ness Monster
```

Playing with Strings

Python has a large set of string functions. Let's explore how the most common of them work. Our test subject is the following string containing the text of the immortal poem "What Is Liquid?" by Margaret Cavendish, Duchess of Newcastle:

```
>>> poem = '''All that doth flow we cannot liquid name
Or else would fire and water be the same;
But that is liquid which is moist and wet
Fire that property can never get.
```

```
Then 'tis not cold that doth the fire put out
But 'tis the wet that makes it die, no doubt.'''
```

To begin, get the first 13 characters (offsets 0 to 12):

```
>>> poem[:13]
'All that doth'
```

How many characters are in this poem? (Spaces and newlines are included in the count.)

```
>>> len(poem)
250
```

Does it start with the letters All?

```
>>> poem.startswith('All')
True
```

Does it end with That's all, folks!?

```
>>> poem.endswith('That\'s all, folks!')
False
```

Now, let's find the offset of the first occurrence of the word the in the poem:

```
>>> word = 'the'
>>> poem.find(word)
73
```

And the offset of the last the:

```
>>> poem.rfind(word)
214
```

How many times does the three-letter sequence the occur?

```
>>> poem.count(word)
3
```

Are all of the characters in the poem either letters or numbers?

```
>>> poem.isalnum()
False
```

Nope, there were some punctuation characters.

Case and Alignment

In this section, we'll look at some more uses of the built-in string functions. Our test string is the following:

```
>>> setup = 'a duck goes into a bar...'
```

Remove . sequences from both ends:

```
>>> setup.strip('.')
'a duck goes into a bar'
```

 Because strings are immutable, none of these examples actually changes the `setup` string. Each example just takes the value of `setup`, does something to it, and returns the result as a new string.

Capitalize the first word:

```
>>> setup.capitalize()
'A duck goes into a bar...'
```

Capitalize all the words:

```
>>> setup.title()
'A Duck Goes Into A Bar...'
```

Convert all characters to uppercase:

```
>>> setup.upper()
'A DUCK GOES INTO A BAR...'
```

Convert all characters to lowercase:

```
>>> setup.lower()
'a duck goes into a bar...'
```

Swap upper- and lowercase:

```
>>> setup.swapcase()
'A DUCK GOES INTO A BAR...'
```

Now, we'll work with some layout alignment functions. The string is aligned within the specified total number of spaces (30 here).

Center the string within 30 spaces:

```
>>> setup.center(30)
'   a duck goes into a bar...   '
```

Left justify:

```
>>> setup.ljust(30)
'a duck goes into a bar...     '
```

Right justify:

```
>>> setup.rjust(30)
'     a duck goes into a bar...'
```

I have much more to say about string formatting and conversions in Chapter 7, including how to use % and `format()`.

Substitute with replace()

You use `replace()` for simple substring substitution. You give it the old substring, the new one, and how many instances of the old substring to replace. If you omit this final count argument, it replaces all instances. In this example, only one string is matched and replaced:

```
>>> setup.replace('duck', 'marmoset')
'a marmoset goes into a bar...'
```

Change up to 100 of them:

```
>>> setup.replace('a ', 'a famous ', 100)
'a famous duck goes into a famous bar...'
```

When you know the exact substring(s) you want to change, `replace()` is a good choice. But watch out. In the second example, if we had substituted for the single character string `'a'` rather than the two character string `'a '` (a followed by a space), we would have also changed a in the middle of other words:

```
>>> setup.replace('a', 'a famous', 100)
'a famous duck goes into a famous ba famousr...'
```

Sometimes, you want to ensure that the substring is a whole word, or the beginning of a word, and so on. In those cases, you need *regular expressions*, which are described in detail in Chapter 7.

More String Things

Python has many more string functions than I've shown here. Some will turn up in later chapters, but you can find all the details at the standard documentation link (*http://bit.ly/py-docs-strings*).

Things to Do

This chapter introduced the atoms of Python: numbers, strings, and variables. Let's try a few small exercises with them in the interactive interpreter.

2.1 How many seconds are in an hour? Use the interactive interpreter as a calculator and multiply the number of seconds in a minute (`60`) by the number of minutes in an hour (also `60`).

2.2 Assign the result from the previous task (seconds in an hour) to a variable called `seconds_per_hour`.

2.3 How many seconds are in a day? Use your `seconds_per_hour` variable.

2.4 Calculate seconds per day again, but this time save the result in a variable called `seconds_per_day`.

2.5 Divide seconds_per_day by seconds_per_hour. Use floating-point (/) division.

2.6 Divide seconds_per_day by seconds_per_hour, using integer (//) division. Did this number agree with the floating-point value from the previous question, aside from the final .0?

CHAPTER 3

Py Filling: Lists, Tuples, Dictionaries, and Sets

In Chapter 2 we started at the bottom with Python's basic data types: booleans, integers, floats, and strings. If you think of those as atoms, the data structures in this chapter are like molecules. That is, we combine those basic types in more complex ways. You will use these every day. Much of programming consists of chopping and glueing data into specific forms, and these are your hacksaws and glue guns.

Lists and Tuples

Most computer languages can represent a sequence of items indexed by their integer position: first, second, and so on down to the last. You've already seen Python *strings*, which are sequences of characters. You've also had a little preview of lists, which you'll now see are sequences of anything.

Python has two other sequence structures: *tuples* and *lists*. These contain zero or more elements. Unlike strings, the elements can be of different types. In fact, each element can be *any* Python object. This lets you create structures as deep and complex as you like.

Why does Python contain both lists and tuples? Tuples are *immutable*; when you assign elements to a tuple, they're baked in the cake and can't be changed. Lists are *mutable*, meaning you can insert and delete elements with great enthusiasm. I'll show many examples of each, with an emphasis on lists.

By the way, you might hear two different pronunciations for *tuple*. Which is right? If you guess wrong, do you risk being considered a Python poseur? No worries. Guido van Rossum, the creator of Python, tweeted (*http://bit.ly/tupletweet*) "I pronounce tuple too-pull on Mon/Wed/Fri and tub-pull on Tue/Thu/Sat. On Sunday I don't talk about them. :)"

Lists

Lists are good for keeping track of things by their order, especially when the order and contents might change. Unlike strings, lists are mutable. You can change a list in-place, add new elements, and delete or overwrite existing elements. The same value can occur more than once in a list.

Create with [] or list()

A list is made from zero or more elements, separated by commas, and surrounded by square brackets:

```
>>> empty_list = [ ]
>>> weekdays = ['Monday', 'Tuesday', 'Wednesday', 'Thursday', 'Friday']
>>> big_birds = ['emu', 'ostrich', 'cassowary']
>>> first_names = ['Graham', 'John', 'Terry', 'Terry', 'Michael']
```

You can also make an empty list with the list() function:

```
>>> another_empty_list = list()
>>> another_empty_list
[]
```

"Comprehensions" on page 84 shows one more way to create a list, called a *list comprehension*.

The weekdays list is the only one that actually takes advantage of list order. The first_names list shows that values do not need to be unique.

If you only want to keep track of unique values and don't care about order, a Python *set* might be a better choice than a list. In the previous example, big_birds could have been a set. You'll read about sets a little later in this chapter.

Convert Other Data Types to Lists with list()

Python's list() function converts other data types to lists. The following example converts a string to a list of one-character strings:

```
>>> list('cat')
['c', 'a', 't']
```

This example converts a *tuple* (coming up after lists in this chapter) to a list:

```
>>> a_tuple = ('ready', 'fire', 'aim')
>>> list(a_tuple)
['ready', 'fire', 'aim']
```

As I mentioned earlier in "Split with split()" on page 38, use split() to chop a string into a list by some separator string:

```
>>> birthday = '1/6/1952'
>>> birthday.split('/')
['1', '6', '1952']
```

What if you have more than one separator string in a row in your original string? Well, you get an empty string as a list item:

```
>>> splitme = 'a/b//c/d///e'
>>> splitme.split('/')
['a', 'b', '', 'c', 'd', '', '', 'e']
```

If you had used the two-character separator string // instead, you would get this:

```
>>> splitme = 'a/b//c/d///e'
>>> splitme.split('//')
>>>
['a/b', 'c/d', '/e']
```

Get an Item by Using [*offset*]

As with strings, you can extract a single value from a list by specifying its offset:

```
>>> marxes = ['Groucho', 'Chico', 'Harpo']
>>> marxes[0]
'Groucho'
>>> marxes[1]
'Chico'
>>> marxes[2]
'Harpo'
```

Again, as with strings, negative indexes count backward from the end:

```
>>> marxes[-1]
'Harpo'
>>> marxes[-2]
'Chico'
>>> marxes[-3]
'Groucho'
>>>
```

 The offset has to be a valid one for this list—a position you have assigned a value previously. If you specify an offset before the beginning or after the end, you'll get an exception (error). Here's what happens if we try to get the sixth Marx brother (offset 5 counting from 0), or the fifth before the end:

```
>>> marxes = ['Groucho', 'Chico', 'Harpo']
>>> marxes[5]
Traceback (most recent call last):
  File "<stdin>", line 1, in <module>
IndexError: list index out of range
>>> marxes[-5]
Traceback (most recent call last):
  File "<stdin>", line 1, in <module>
IndexError: list index out of range
```

Lists of Lists

Lists can contain elements of different types, including other lists, as illustrated here:

```
>>> small_birds = ['hummingbird', 'finch']
>>> extinct_birds = ['dodo', 'passenger pigeon', 'Norwegian Blue']
>>> carol_birds = [3, 'French hens', 2, 'turtledoves']
>>> all_birds = [small_birds, extinct_birds, 'macaw', carol_birds]
```

So what does all_birds, a list of lists, look like?

```
>>> all_birds
[['hummingbird', 'finch'], ['dodo', 'passenger pigeon', 'Norwegian Blue'], 'macaw',
[3, 'French hens', 2, 'turtledoves']]
```

Let's look at the first item in it:

```
>>> all_birds[0]
['hummingbird', 'finch']
```

The first item is a list: in fact, it's small_birds, the first item we specified when creating all_birds. You should be able to guess what the second item is:

```
>>> all_birds[1]
['dodo', 'passenger pigeon', 'Norwegian Blue']
```

It's the second item we specified, extinct_birds. If we want the first item of extinct_birds, we can extract it from all_birds by specifying two indexes:

```
>>> all_birds[1][0]
'dodo'
```

The [1] refers to the list that's the second item in all_birds, whereas the [0] refers to the first item in that inner list.

Change an Item by [*offset*]

Just as you can get the value of a list item by its offset, you can change it:

```
>>> marxes = ['Groucho', 'Chico', 'Harpo']
>>> marxes[2] = 'Wanda'
>>> marxes
['Groucho', 'Chico', 'Wanda']
```

Again, the list offset needs to be a valid one for this list.

You can't change a character in a string in this way, because strings are immutable. Lists are mutable. You can change how many items a list contains, and the items themselves.

Get a Slice to Extract Items by Offset Range

You can extract a subsequence of a list by using a *slice*:

```
>>> marxes = ['Groucho', 'Chico,' 'Harpo']
>>> marxes[0:2]
['Groucho', 'Chico']
```

A slice of a list is also a list.

As with strings, slices can step by values other than one. The next example starts at the beginning and goes right by 2:

```
>>> marxes[::2]
['Groucho', 'Harpo']
```

Here, we start at the end and go left by 2:

```
>>> marxes[::-2]
['Harpo', 'Groucho']
```

And finally, the trick to reverse a list:

```
>>> marxes[::-1]
['Harpo', 'Chico', 'Groucho']
```

Add an Item to the End with append()

The traditional way of adding items to a list is to append() them one by one to the end. In the previous examples, we forgot Zeppo, but that's all right because the list is mutable, so we can add him now:

```
>>> marxes.append('Zeppo')
>>> marxes
['Groucho', 'Chico', 'Harpo', 'Zeppo']
```

Combine Lists by Using extend() or +=

You can merge one list into another by using extend(). Suppose that a well-meaning person gave us a new list of Marxes called others, and we'd like to merge them into the main marxes list:

```
>>> marxes = ['Groucho', 'Chico', 'Harpo', 'Zeppo']
>>> others = ['Gummo', 'Karl']
>>> marxes.extend(others)
>>> marxes
['Groucho', 'Chico', 'Harpo', 'Zeppo', 'Gummo', 'Karl']
```

Alternatively, you can use +=:

```
>>> marxes = ['Groucho', 'Chico', 'Harpo', 'Zeppo']
>>> others = ['Gummo', 'Karl']
>>> marxes += others
>>> marxes
['Groucho', 'Chico', 'Harpo', 'Zeppo', 'Gummo', 'Karl']
```

If we had used append(), others would have been added as a *single* list item rather than merging its items:

```
>>> marxes = ['Groucho', 'Chico', 'Harpo', 'Zeppo']
>>> others = ['Gummo', 'Karl']
>>> marxes.append(others)
>>> marxes
['Groucho', 'Chico', 'Harpo', 'Zeppo', ['Gummo', 'Karl']]
```

This again demonstrates that a list can contain elements of different types. In this case, four strings, and a list of two strings.

Add an Item by Offset with insert()

The append() function adds items only to the end of the list. When you want to add an item before any offset in the list, use insert(). Offset 0 inserts at the beginning. An offset beyond the end of the list inserts at the end, like append(), so you don't need to worry about Python throwing an exception.

```
>>> marxes.insert(3, 'Gummo')
>>> marxes
```

```
['Groucho', 'Chico', 'Harpo', 'Gummo', 'Zeppo']
>>> marxes.insert(10, 'Karl')
>>> marxes
['Groucho', 'Chico', 'Harpo', 'Gummo', 'Zeppo', 'Karl']
```

Delete an Item by Offset with del

Our fact checkers have just informed us that Gummo was indeed one of the Marx Brothers, but Karl wasn't. Let's undo that last insertion:

```
>>> del marxes[-1]
>>> marxes
['Groucho', 'Chico', 'Harpo', 'Gummo', 'Zeppo']
```

When you delete an item by its position in the list, the items that follow it move back to take the deleted item's space, and the list's length decreases by one. If we delete 'Harpo' from the last version of the marxes list, we get this as a result:

```
>>> marxes = ['Groucho', 'Chico', 'Harpo', 'Gummo', 'Zeppo']
>>> marxes[2]
'Harpo'
>>> del marxes[2]
>>> marxes
['Groucho', 'Chico', 'Gummo', 'Zeppo']
>>> marxes[2]
'Gummo'
```

 del is a Python *statement*, not a list method—you don't say marxes[-2].del(). It's sort of the reverse of assignment (=): it detaches a name from a Python object and can free up the object's memory if that name was the last reference to it.

Delete an Item by Value with remove()

If you're not sure or don't care where the item is in the list, use remove() to delete it by value. Goodbye, Gummo:

```
>>> marxes = ['Groucho', 'Chico', 'Harpo', 'Gummo', 'Zeppo']
>>> marxes.remove('Gummo')
>>> marxes
['Groucho', 'Chico', 'Harpo', 'Zeppo']
```

Get an Item by Offset and Delete It by Using pop()

You can get an item from a list and delete it from the list at the same time by using pop(). If you call pop() with an offset, it will return the item at that offset; with no argument, it uses -1. So, pop(0) returns the head (start) of the list, and pop() or pop(-1) returns the tail (end), as shown here:

```
>>> marxes = ['Groucho', 'Chico', 'Harpo', 'Zeppo']
>>> marxes.pop()
'Zeppo'
>>> marxes
['Groucho', 'Chico', 'Harpo']
>>> marxes.pop(1)
'Chico'
>>> marxes
['Groucho', 'Harpo']
```

 It's computing jargon time! Don't worry, these won't be on the final exam. If you use `append()` to add new items to the end and `pop()` to remove them from the same end, you've implemented a data structure known as a *LIFO* (last in, first out) queue. This is more commonly known as a *stack*. `pop(0)` would create a *FIFO* (first in, first out) queue. These are useful when you want to collect data as they arrive and work with either the oldest first (FIFO) or the newest first (LIFO).

Find an Item's Offset by Value with index()

If you want to know the offset of an item in a list by its value, use `index()`:

```
>>> marxes = ['Groucho', 'Chico', 'Harpo', 'Zeppo']
>>> marxes.index('Chico')
1
```

Test for a Value with in

The Pythonic way to check for the existence of a value in a list is using `in`:

```
>>> marxes = ['Groucho', 'Chico', 'Harpo', 'Zeppo']
>>> 'Groucho' in marxes
True
>>> 'Bob' in marxes
False
```

The same value may be in more than one position in the list. As long as it's in there at least once, `in` will return `True`:

```
>>> words = ['a', 'deer', 'a' 'female', 'deer']
>>> 'deer' in words
True
```

 If you check for the existence of some value in a list often and don't care about the order of items, a Python *set* is a more appropriate way to store and look up unique values. We'll talk about sets a little later in this chapter.

Count Occurrences of a Value by Using count()

To count how many times a particular value occurs in a list, use count():

```
>>> marxes = ['Groucho', 'Chico', 'Harpo']
>>> marxes.count('Harpo')
1
>>> marxes.count('Bob')
0
>>> snl_skit = ['cheeseburger', 'cheeseburger', 'cheeseburger']
>>> snl_skit.count('cheeseburger')
3
```

Convert to a String with join()

"Combine with join()" on page 38 discusses join() in greater detail, but here's another example of what you can do with it:

```
>>> marxes = ['Groucho', 'Chico', 'Harpo']
>>> ', '.join(marxes)
'Groucho, Chico, Harpo'
```

But wait: you might be thinking that this seems a little backward. join() is a string method, not a list method. You can't say marxes.join(', '), even though it seems more intuitive. The argument to join() is a string or any iterable sequence of strings (including a list), and its output is a string. If join() were just a list method, you couldn't use it with other iterable objects such as tuples or strings. If you did want it to work with any iterable type, you'd need special code for each type to handle the actual joining. It might help to remember: *join()` is the opposite of `split(),* as demonstrated here:

```
>>> friends = ['Harry', 'Hermione', 'Ron']
>>> separator = ' * '
>>> joined = separator.join(friends)
>>> joined
'Harry * Hermione * Ron'
>>> separated = joined.split(separator)
>>> separated
['Harry', 'Hermione', 'Ron']
>>> separated == friends
True
```

Reorder Items with sort()

You'll often need to sort the items in a list by their values rather than their offsets. Python provides two functions:

- The list function sort() sorts the list itself, *in place.*

- The general function `sorted()` returns a sorted *copy* of the list.

If the items in the list are numeric, they're sorted by default in ascending numeric order. If they're strings, they're sorted in alphabetical order:

```
>>> marxes = ['Groucho', 'Chico', 'Harpo']
>>> sorted_marxes = sorted(marxes)
>>> sorted_marxes
['Chico', 'Groucho', 'Harpo']
```

`sorted_marxes` is a copy, and creating it did not change the original list:

```
>>> marxes
['Groucho', 'Chico', 'Harpo']
```

But, calling the list function `sort()` on the `marxes` list does change `marxes`:

```
>>> marxes.sort()
>>> marxes
['Chico', 'Groucho', 'Harpo']
```

If the elements of your list are all of the same type (such as strings in `marxes`), `sort()` will work correctly. You can sometimes even mix types—for example, integers and floats—because they are automatically converted to one another by Python in expressions:

```
>>> numbers = [2, 1, 4.0, 3]
>>> numbers.sort()
>>> numbers
[1, 2, 3, 4.0]
```

The default sort order is ascending, but you can add the argument `reverse=True` to set it to descending:

```
>>> numbers = [2, 1, 4.0, 3]
>>> numbers.sort(reverse=True)
>>> numbers
[4.0, 3, 2, 1]
```

Get Length by Using len()

`len()` returns the number of items in a list:

```
>>> marxes = ['Groucho', 'Chico', 'Harpo']
>>> len(marxes)
3
```

Assign with =, Copy with copy()

When you assign one list to more than one variable, changing the list in one place also changes it in the other, as illustrated here:

```
>>> a = [1, 2, 3]
>>> a
[1, 2, 3]
>>> b = a
>>> b
[1, 2, 3]
>>> a[0] = 'surprise'
>>> a
['surprise', 2, 3]
```

So what's in b now? Is it still [1, 2, 3], or ['surprise', 2, 3]? Let's see:

```
>>> b
['surprise', 2, 3]
```

Remember the sticky note analogy in Chapter 2? b just refers to the same list object as a; therefore, whether we change the list contents by using the name a or b, it's reflected in both:

```
>>> b
['surprise', 2, 3]
>>> b[0] = 'I hate surprises'
>>> b
['I hate surprises', 2, 3]
>>> a
['I hate surprises', 2, 3]
```

You can *copy* the values of a list to an independent, fresh list by using any of these methods:

- The list copy() function

- The list() conversion function

- The list slice [:]

Our original list will be a again. We'll make b with the list copy() function, c with the list() conversion function, and d with a list slice:

```
>>> a = [1, 2, 3]
>>> b = a.copy()
>>> c = list(a)
>>> d = a[:]
```

Again, b, c, and d are *copies* of a: they are new objects with their own values and no connection to the original list object [1, 2, 3] to which a refers. Changing a does *not* affect the copies b, c, and d:

```
>>> a[0] = 'integer lists are boring'
>>> a
['integer lists are boring', 2, 3]
>>> b
[1, 2, 3]
```

```
>>> c
[1, 2, 3]
>>> d
[1, 2, 3]
```

Tuples

Similar to lists, tuples are sequences of arbitrary items. Unlike lists, tuples are *immutable*, meaning you can't add, delete, or change items after the tuple is defined. So, a tuple is similar to a constant list.

Create a Tuple by Using ()

The syntax to make tuples is a little inconsistent, as we'll demonstrate in the examples that follow.

Let's begin by making an empty tuple using ():

```
>>> empty_tuple = ()
>>> empty_tuple
()
```

To make a tuple with one or more elements, follow each element with a comma. This works for one-element tuples:

```
>>> one_marx = 'Groucho',
>>> one_marx
('Groucho',)
```

If you have more than one element, follow all but the last one with a comma:

```
>>> marx_tuple = 'Groucho', 'Chico', 'Harpo'
>>> marx_tuple
('Groucho', 'Chico', 'Harpo')
```

Python includes parentheses when echoing a tuple. You don't need them—it's the trailing commas that really define a tuple—but using parentheses doesn't hurt. You can use them to enclose the values, which helps to make the tuple more visible:

```
>>> marx_tuple = ('Groucho', 'Chico', 'Harpo')
>>> marx_tuple
('Groucho', 'Chico', 'Harpo')
```

Tuples let you assign multiple variables at once:

```
>>> marx_tuple = ('Groucho', 'Chico', 'Harpo')
>>> a, b, c = marx_tuple
>>> a
'Groucho'
>>> b
'Chico'
```

```
>>> c
'Harpo'
```

This is sometimes called *tuple unpacking*.

You can use tuples to exchange values in one statement without using a temporary variable:

```
>>> password = 'swordfish'
>>> icecream = 'tuttifrutti'
>>> password, icecream = icecream, password
>>> password
'tuttifrutti'
>>> icecream
'swordfish'
>>>
```

The tuple() conversion function makes tuples from other things:

```
>>> marx_list = ['Groucho', 'Chico', 'Harpo']
>>> tuple(marx_list)
('Groucho', 'Chico', 'Harpo')
```

Tuples versus Lists

You can often use tuples in place of lists, but they have many fewer functions—there is no append(), insert(), and so on—because they can't be modified after creation. Why not just use lists instead of tuples everywhere?

- Tuples use less space.
- You can't clobber tuple items by mistake.
- You can use tuples as dictionary keys (see the next section).
- *Named tuples* (see "Named Tuples" on page 144) can be a simple alternative to objects.
- Function arguments are passed as tuples (see "Functions" on page 89).

I won't go into much more detail about tuples here. In everyday programming, you'll use lists and dictionaries more. Which is a perfect segue to...

Dictionaries

A *dictionary* is similar to a list, but the order of items doesn't matter, and they aren't selected by an offset such as 0 or 1. Instead, you specify a unique *key* to associate with each value. This key is often a string, but it can actually be any of Python's immutable types: boolean, integer, float, tuple, string, and others that you'll see in later chapters. Dictionaries are mutable, so you can add, delete, and change their key-value elements.

If you've worked with languages that support only arrays or lists, you'll love dictionaries.

In other languages, dictionaries might be called *associative arrays*, *hashes*, or *hashmaps*. In Python, a dictionary is also called a *dict* to save syllables.

Create with {}

To create a dictionary, you place curly brackets ({}) around comma-separated *key* : *value* pairs. The simplest dictionary is an empty one, containing no keys or values at all:

```
>>> empty_dict = {}
>>> empty_dict
{}
```

Let's make a small dictionary with quotes from Ambrose Bierce's *The Devil's Dictionary*:

```
>>> bierce = {
...     "day": "A period of twenty-four hours, mostly misspent",
...     "positive": "Mistaken at the top of one's voice",
...     "misfortune": "The kind of fortune that never misses",
...     }
>>>
```

Typing the dictionary's name in the interactive interpreter will print its keys and values:

```
>>> bierce
{'misfortune': 'The kind of fortune that never misses',
'positive': "Mistaken at the top of one's voice",
'day': 'A period of twenty-four hours, mostly misspent'}
```

In Python, it's okay to leave a comma after the last item of a list, tuple, or dictionary. Also, you don't need to indent, as I did in the preceding example, when you're typing keys and values within the curly braces. It just helps readability.

Convert by Using dict()

You can use the dict() function to convert two-value sequences into a dictionary. (You might run into such key-value sequences at times, such as "Strontium, 90, Carbon, 14", or "Vikings, 20, Packers, 7".) The first item in each sequence is used as the key and the second as the value.

First, here's a small example using `lol` (a list of two-item lists):

```
>>> lol = [ ['a', 'b'], ['c', 'd'], ['e', 'f'] ]
>>> dict(lol)
{'c': 'd', 'a': 'b', 'e': 'f'}
```

 Remember that the order of keys in a dictionary is arbitrary, and might differ depending on how you add items.

We could have used any sequence containing two-item sequences. Here are other examples.

A list of two-item tuples:

```
>>> lot = [ ('a', 'b'), ('c', 'd'), ('e', 'f') ]
>>> dict(lot)
{'c': 'd', 'a': 'b', 'e': 'f'}
```

A tuple of two-item lists:

```
>>> tol = ( ['a', 'b'], ['c', 'd'], ['e', 'f'] )
>>> dict(tol)
{'c': 'd', 'a': 'b', 'e': 'f'}
```

A list of two-character strings:

```
>>> los = [ 'ab', 'cd', 'ef' ]
>>> dict(los)
{'c': 'd', 'a': 'b', 'e': 'f'}
```

A tuple of two-character strings:

```
>>> tos = ( 'ab', 'cd', 'ef' )
>>> dict(tos)
{'c': 'd', 'a': 'b', 'e': 'f'}
```

The section "Iterate Multiple Sequences with zip()" on page 83 introduces you to a function called `zip()` that makes it easy to create these two-item sequences.

Add or Change an Item by [*key*]

Adding an item to a dictionary is easy. Just refer to the item by its key and assign a value. If the key was already present in the dictionary, the existing value is replaced by the new one. If the key is new, it's added to the dictionary with its value. Unlike lists, you don't need to worry about Python throwing an exception during assignment by specifying an index that's out of range.

Let's make a dictionary of most of the members of Monty Python, using their last names as keys, and first names as values:

```
>>> pythons = {
...     'Chapman': 'Graham',
...     'Cleese': 'John',
...     'Idle': 'Eric',
...     'Jones': 'Terry',
...     'Palin': 'Michael',
...     }
>>> pythons
{'Cleese': 'John', 'Jones': 'Terry', 'Palin': 'Michael',
'Chapman': 'Graham', 'Idle': 'Eric'}
```

We're missing one member: the one born in America, Terry Gilliam. Here's an attempt by an anonymous programmer to add him, but he's botched the first name:

```
>>> pythons['Gilliam'] = 'Gerry'
>>> pythons
{'Cleese': 'John', 'Gilliam': 'Gerry', 'Palin': 'Michael',
'Chapman': 'Graham', 'Idle': 'Eric', 'Jones': 'Terry'}
```

And here's some repair code by another programmer who is Pythonic in more than one way:

```
>>> pythons['Gilliam'] = 'Terry'
>>> pythons
{'Cleese': 'John', 'Gilliam': 'Terry', 'Palin': 'Michael',
'Chapman': 'Graham', 'Idle': 'Eric', 'Jones': 'Terry'}
```

By using the same key ('Gilliam'), we replaced the original value 'Gerry' with 'Terry'.

Remember that dictionary keys must be *unique*. That's why we used last names for keys instead of first names here—two members of Monty Python have the first name Terry! If you use a key more than once, the last value wins:

```
>>> some_pythons = {
...     'Graham': 'Chapman',
...     'John': 'Cleese',
...     'Eric': 'Idle',
...     'Terry': 'Gilliam',
...     'Michael': 'Palin',
...     'Terry': 'Jones',
...     }
>>> some_pythons
{'Terry': 'Jones', 'Eric': 'Idle', 'Graham': 'Chapman',
'John': 'Cleese', 'Michael': 'Palin'}
```

We first assigned the value 'Gilliam' to the key 'Terry' and then replaced it with the value 'Jones'.

Combine Dictionaries with update()

You can use the update() function to copy the keys and values of one dictionary into another.

Let's define the pythons dictionary, with all members:

```
>>> pythons = {
...     'Chapman': 'Graham',
...     'Cleese': 'John',
...     'Gilliam': 'Terry',
...     'Idle': 'Eric',
...     'Jones': 'Terry',
...     'Palin': 'Michael',
...     }
>>> pythons
{'Cleese': 'John', 'Gilliam': 'Terry', 'Palin': 'Michael',
'Chapman': 'Graham', 'Idle': 'Eric', 'Jones': 'Terry'}
```

We also have a dictionary of other humorous persons called others:

```
>>> others = { 'Marx': 'Groucho', 'Howard': 'Moe' }
```

Now, along comes another anonymous programmer who thinks the members of others should be members of Monty Python:

```
>>> pythons.update(others)
>>> pythons
{'Cleese': 'John', 'Howard': 'Moe', 'Gilliam': 'Terry',
'Palin': 'Michael', 'Marx': 'Groucho', 'Chapman': 'Graham',
'Idle': 'Eric', 'Jones': 'Terry'}
```

What happens if the second dictionary has the same key as the dictionary into which it's being merged? The value from the second dictionary wins:

```
>>> first = {'a': 1, 'b': 2}
>>> second = {'b': 'platypus'}
>>> first.update(second)
>>> first
{'b': 'platypus', 'a': 1}
```

Delete an Item by Key with del

Our anonymous programmer's code was correct—technically. But, he shouldn't have done it! The members of others, although funny and famous, were not in Monty Python. Let's undo those last two additions:

```
>>> del pythons['Marx']
>>> pythons
{'Cleese': 'John', 'Howard': 'Moe', 'Gilliam': 'Terry',
'Palin': 'Michael', 'Chapman': 'Graham', 'Idle': 'Eric',
'Jones': 'Terry'}
>>> del pythons['Howard']
```

```
>>> pythons
{'Cleese': 'John', 'Gilliam': 'Terry', 'Palin': 'Michael',
'Chapman': 'Graham', 'Idle': 'Eric', 'Jones': 'Terry'}
```

Delete All Items by Using clear()

To delete all keys and values from a dictionary, use clear() or just reassign an empty dictionary ({}) to the name:

```
>>> pythons.clear()
>>> pythons
{}
>>> pythons = {}
>>> pythons
{}
```

Test for a Key by Using in

If you want to know whether a key exists in a dictionary, use in. Let's redefine the pythons dictionary again, this time omitting a name or two:

```
>>> pythons = {'Chapman': 'Graham', 'Cleese': 'John',
'Jones': 'Terry', 'Palin': 'Michael'}
```

Now let's see who's in there:

```
>>> 'Chapman' in pythons
True
>>> 'Palin' in pythons
True
```

Did we remember to add Terry Gilliam this time?

```
>>> 'Gilliam' in pythons
False
```

Drat.

Get an Item by [*key*]

This is the most common use of a dictionary. You specify the dictionary and key to get the corresponding value:

```
>>> pythons['Cleese']
'John'
```

If the key is not present in the dictionary, you'll get an exception:

```
>>> pythons['Marx']
Traceback (most recent call last):
  File "<stdin>", line 1, in <module>
KeyError: 'Marx'
```

There are two good ways to avoid this. The first is to test for the key at the outset by using in, as you saw in the previous section:

```
>>> 'Marx' in pythons
False
```

The second is to use the special dictionary get() function. You provide the dictionary, key, and an optional value. If the key exists, you get its value:

```
>>> pythons.get('Cleese')
'John'
```

If not, you get the optional value, if you specified one:

```
>>> pythons.get('Marx', 'Not a Python')
'Not a Python'
```

Otherwise, you get None (which displays nothing in the interactive interpreter):

```
>>> pythons.get('Marx')
>>>
```

Get All Keys by Using keys()

You can use keys() to get all the keys in a dictionary. We'll use a different sample dictionary for the next few examples:

```
>>> signals = {'green': 'go', 'yellow': 'go faster', 'red': 'smile for the camera'}
>>> signals.keys()
dict_keys(['green', 'red', 'yellow'])
```

 In Python 2, keys() just returns a list. Python 3 returns dict_keys(), which is an iterable view of the keys. This is handy with large dictionaries because it doesn't use the time and memory to create and store a list that you might not use. But often you actually *do* want a list. In Python 3, you need to call list() to convert a dict_keys object to a list.

```
>>> list( signals.keys() )
['green', 'red', 'yellow']
```

In Python 3, you also need to use the list() function to turn the results of values() and items() into normal Python lists. I'm using that in these examples.

Get All Values by Using values()

To obtain all the values in a dictionary, use values():

```
>>> list( signals.values() )
['go', 'smile for the camera', 'go faster']
```

Get All Key-Value Pairs by Using items()

When you want to get all the key-value pairs from a dictionary, use the `items()` function:

```
>>> list( signals.items() )
[('green', 'go'), ('red', 'smile for the camera'), ('yellow', 'go faster')]
```

Each key and value is returned as a tuple, such as (`'green'`, `'go'`).

Assign with =, Copy with copy()

As with lists, if you make a change to a dictionary, it will be reflected in all the names that refer to it.

```
>>> signals = {'green': 'go', 'yellow': 'go faster', 'red': 'smile for the camera'}
>>> save_signals = signals
>>> signals['blue'] = 'confuse everyone'
>>> save_signals
{'blue': 'confuse everyone', 'green': 'go',
'red': 'smile for the camera', 'yellow': 'go faster'}
```

To actually copy keys and values from a dictionary to another dictionary and avoid this, you can use `copy()`:

```
>>> signals = {'green': 'go', 'yellow': 'go faster', 'red': 'smile for the camera'}
>>> original_signals = signals.copy()
>>> signals['blue'] = 'confuse everyone'
>>> signals
{'blue': 'confuse everyone', 'green': 'go',
'red': 'smile for the camera', 'yellow': 'go faster'}
>>> original_signals
{'green': 'go', 'red': 'smile for the camera', 'yellow': 'go faster'}
```

Sets

A *set* is like a dictionary with its values thrown away, leaving only the keys. As with a dictionary, each key must be unique. You use a set when you only want to know that something exists, and nothing else about it. Use a dictionary if you want to attach some information to the key as a value.

At some bygone time, in some places, set theory was taught in elementary school along with basic mathematics. If your school skipped it (or covered it and you were staring out the window as I often did), Figure 3-1 shows the ideas of union and intersection.

Suppose that you take the union of two sets that have some keys in common. Because a set must contain only one of each item, the union of two sets will contain only one of each key. The *null* or *empty* set is a set with zero elements. In Figure 3-1, an example of a null set would be female names beginning with X.

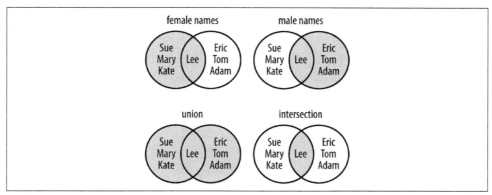

Figure 3-1. Common things to do with sets

Create with set()

To create a set, you use the set() function or enclose one or more comma-separated values in curly brackets, as shown here:

```
>>> empty_set = set()
>>> empty_set
set()
>>> even_numbers = {0, 2, 4, 6, 8}
>>> even_numbers
{0, 8, 2, 4, 6}
>>> odd_numbers = {1, 3, 5, 7, 9}
>>> odd_numbers
{9, 3, 1, 5, 7}
```

As with dictionary keys, sets are unordered.

Because [] creates an empty list, you might expect {} to create an empty set. Instead, {} creates an empty dictionary. That's also why the interpreter prints an empty set as set() instead of {}. Why? Dictionaries were in Python first and took possession of the curly brackets.

Convert from Other Data Types with set()

You can create a set from a list, string, tuple, or dictionary, discarding any duplicate values.

First, let's take a look at a string with more than one occurrence of some letters:

```
>>> set( 'letters' )
{'l', 'e', 't', 'r', 's'}
```

Notice that the set contains only one `'e'` or `'t'`, even though `'letters'` contained two of each.

Now, let's make a set from a list:

```
>>> set( ['Dasher', 'Dancer', 'Prancer', 'Mason-Dixon'] )
{'Dancer', 'Dasher', 'Prancer', 'Mason-Dixon'}
```

This time, a set from a tuple:

```
>>> set( ('Ummagumma', 'Echoes', 'Atom Heart Mother') )
{'Ummagumma', 'Atom Heart Mother', 'Echoes'}
```

When you give `set()` a dictionary, it uses only the keys:

```
>>> set( {'apple': 'red', 'orange': 'orange', 'cherry': 'red'} )
{'apple', 'cherry', 'orange'}
```

Test for Value by Using in

This is the most common use of a set. We'll make a dictionary called `drinks`. Each key is the name of a mixed drink, and the corresponding value is a set of its ingredients:

```
>>> drinks = {
...     'martini': {'vodka', 'vermouth'},
...     'black russian': {'vodka', 'kahlua'},
...     'white russian': {'cream', 'kahlua', 'vodka'},
...     'manhattan': {'rye', 'vermouth', 'bitters'},
...     'screwdriver': {'orange juice', 'vodka'}
...     }
```

Even though both are enclosed by curly braces ({ and }), a set is just a sequence of values, and a dictionary is one or more *key* : *value* pairs.

Which drinks contain vodka? (Note that I'm previewing the use of `for`, `if`, `and`, and `or` from the next chapter for these tests.)

```
>>> for name, contents in drinks.items():
...     if 'vodka' in contents:
...         print(name)
...
screwdriver
martini
black russian
white russian
```

We want something with vodka but are lactose intolerant, and think vermouth tastes like kerosene:

```
>>> for name, contents in drinks.items():
...     if 'vodka' in contents and not ('vermouth' in contents or
...         'cream' in contents):
```

```
...         print(name)
...
screwdriver
black russian
```

We'll rewrite this a bit more succinctly in the next section.

Combinations and Operators

What if you want to check for combinations of set values? Suppose that you want to find any drink that has orange juice or vermouth? We'll use the *set intersection operator*, which is an ampersand (&):

```
>>> for name, contents in drinks.items():
...     if contents & {'vermouth', 'orange juice'}:
...         print(name)
...
screwdriver
martini
manhattan
```

The result of the & operator is a set, which contains all the items that appear in both lists that you compare. If neither of those ingredients were in contents, the & returns an empty set, which is considered False.

Now, let's rewrite the example from the previous section, in which we wanted vodka but neither cream nor vermouth:

```
>>> for name, contents in drinks.items():
...     if 'vodka' in contents and not contents & {'vermouth', 'cream'}:
...         print(name)
...
screwdriver
black russian
```

Let's save the ingredient sets for these two drinks in variables, just to save typing in the coming examples:

```
>>> bruss = drinks['black russian']
>>> wruss = drinks['white russian']
```

The following are examples of all the set operators. Some have special punctuation, some have special functions, and some have both. We'll use test sets a (contains 1 and 2) and b (contains 2 and 3):

```
>>> a = {1, 2}
>>> b = {2, 3}
```

You get the *intersection* (members common to both sets) with the special punctuation symbol & or the set intersection() function, as demonstrated here:

```
>>> a & b
{2}
>>> a.intersection(b)
{2}
```

This snippet uses our saved drink variables:

```
>>> bruss & wruss
{'kahlua', 'vodka'}
```

In this example, you get the *union* (members of either set) by using | or the set union() function:

```
>>> a | b
{1, 2, 3}
>>> a.union(b)
{1, 2, 3}
```

And here's the alcoholic version:

```
>>> bruss | wruss
{'cream', 'kahlua', 'vodka'}
```

The *difference* (members of the first set but not the second) is obtained by using the character - or difference():

```
>>> a - b
{1}
>>> a.difference(b)
{1}

>>> bruss - wruss
set()
>>> wruss - bruss
{'cream'}
```

By far, the most common set operations are union, intersection, and difference. I've included the others for completeness in the examples that follow, but you might never use them.

The *exclusive or* (items in one set or the other, but not both) uses ^ or symmetric_difference():

```
>>> a ^ b
{1, 3}
>>> a.symmetric_difference(b)
{1, 3}
```

This finds the exclusive ingredient in our two russian drinks:

```
>>> bruss ^ wruss
{'cream'}
```

You can check whether one set is a *subset* of another (all members of the first set are also in the second set) by using <= or issubset():

```
>>> a <= b
False
>>> a.issubset(b)
False
```

Adding cream to a black russian makes a white russian, so wruss is a superset of bruss:

```
>>> bruss <= wruss
True
```

Is any set a subset of itself? Yup.

```
>>> a <= a
True
>>> a.issubset(a)
True
```

To be a *proper subset*, the second set needs to have all the members of the first and more. Calculate it by using <, as in this example:

```
>>> a < b
False
>>> a < a
False

>>> bruss < wruss
True
```

A *superset* is the opposite of a subset (all members of the second set are also members of the first). This uses >= or issuperset():

```
>>> a >= b
False
>>> a.issuperset(b)
False

>>> wruss >= bruss
True
```

Any set is a superset of itself:

```
>>> a >= a
True
>>> a.issuperset(a)
True
```

And finally, you can find a *proper superset* (the first set has all members of the second, and more) by using >, as shown here:

```
>>> a > b
False

>>> wruss > bruss
True
```

You can't be a proper superset of yourself:

```
>>> a > a
False
```

Compare Data Structures

To review: you make a list by using square brackets ([]), a tuple by using commas, and a dictionary by using curly brackets ({}). In each case, you access a single element with square brackets:

```
>>> marx_list = ['Groucho', 'Chico', 'Harpo']
>>> marx_tuple = 'Groucho', 'Chico', 'Harpo'
>>> marx_dict = {'Groucho': 'banjo', 'Chico': 'piano', 'Harpo': 'harp'}
>>> marx_list[2]
'Harpo'
>>> marx_tuple[2]
'Harpo'
>>> marx_dict['Harpo']
'harp'
```

For the list and tuple, the value between the square brackets is an integer offset. For the dictionary, it's a key. For all three, the result is a value.

Make Bigger Data Structures

We worked up from simple booleans, numbers, and strings to lists, tuples, sets, and dictionaries. You can combine these built-in data structures into bigger, more complex structures of your own. Let's start with three different lists:

```
>>> marxes = ['Groucho', 'Chico', 'Harpo']
>>> pythons = ['Chapman', 'Cleese', 'Gilliam', 'Jones', 'Palin']
>>> stooges = ['Moe', 'Curly', 'Larry']
```

We can make a tuple that contains each list as an element:

```
>>> tuple_of_lists = marxes, pythons, stooges
>>> tuple_of_lists
(['Groucho', 'Chico', 'Harpo'],
['Chapman', 'Cleese', 'Gilliam', 'Jones', 'Palin'],
['Moe', 'Curly', 'Larry'])
```

And, we can make a list that contains the three lists:

```
>>> list_of_lists = [marxes, pythons, stooges]
>>> list_of_lists
[['Groucho', 'Chico', 'Harpo'],
['Chapman', 'Cleese', 'Gilliam', 'Jones', 'Palin'],
['Moe', 'Curly', 'Larry']]
```

Finally, let's create a dictionary of lists. In this example, let's use the name of the comedy group as the key and the list of members as the value:

```
>>> dict_of_lists = {'Marxes': marxes, 'Pythons': pythons, 'Stooges': stooges}
>> dict_of_lists
{'Stooges': ['Moe', 'Curly', 'Larry'],
 'Marxes': ['Groucho', 'Chico', 'Harpo'],
 'Pythons': ['Chapman', 'Cleese', 'Gilliam', 'Jones', 'Palin']}
```

Your only limitations are those in the data types themselves. For example, dictionary keys need to be immutable, so a list, dictionary, or set can't be a key for another dictionary. But a tuple can be. For example, you could index sites of interest by GPS coordinates (latitude, longitude, and altitude; see "Maps" on page 366 for more mapping examples):

```
>>> houses = {
        (44.79, -93.14, 285): 'My House',
        (38.89, -77.03, 13): 'The White House'
        }
```

Things to Do

In this chapter, you saw more complex data structures: lists, tuples, dictionaries, and sets. Using these and those from Chapter 2 (numbers and strings), you can represent elements in the real world with great variety.

3.1. Create a list called years_list, starting with the year of your birth, and each year thereafter until the year of your fifth birthday. For example, if you were born in 1980. the list would be years_list = [1980, 1981, 1982, 1983, 1984, 1985].

If you're less than five years old and reading this book, I don't know what to tell you.

3.2. In which year in years_list was your third birthday? Remember, you were 0 years of age for your first year.

3.3. In which year in years_list were you the oldest?

3.4. Make a list called things with these three strings as elements: "mozzarella", "cinderella", "salmonella".

3.5. Capitalize the element in things that refers to a person and then print the list. Did it change the element in the list?

3.6. Make the cheesy element of things all uppercase and then print the list.

3.7. Delete the disease element from things, collect your Nobel Prize, and print the list.

3.8. Create a list called surprise with the elements "Groucho", "Chico", and "Harpo".

3.9. Lowercase the last element of the surprise list, reverse it, and then capitalize it.

3.10. Make an English-to-French dictionary called `e2f` and print it. Here are your starter words: dog is `chien`, cat is `chat`, and `walrus` is `morse`.

3.11. Using your three-word dictionary `e2f`, print the French word for `walrus`.

3.12. Make a French-to-English dictionary called `f2e` from `e2f`. Use the `items` method.

3.13. Using `f2e`, print the English equivalent of the French word `chien`.

3.14. Make and print a set of English words from the keys in `e2f`.

3.15. Make a multilevel dictionary called `life`. Use these strings for the topmost keys: `'animals'`, `'plants'`, and `'other'`. Make the `'animals'` key refer to another dictionary with the keys `'cats'`, `'octopi'`, and `'emus'`. Make the `'cats'` key refer to a list of strings with the values `'Henri'`, `'Grumpy'`, and `'Lucy'`. Make all the other keys refer to empty dictionaries.

3.16. Print the top-level keys of `life`.

3.17. Print the keys for `life['animals']`.

3.18. Print the values for `life['animals']['cats']`.

CHAPTER 4

Py Crust: Code Structures

In Chapters 1 through 3, you've seen many examples of data but have not done much with them. Most of the code examples used the interactive interpreter and were short. Now you'll see how to structure Python *code*, not just data.

Many computer languages use characters such as curly braces ({ and }) or keywords such as begin and end to mark off sections of code. In those languages, it's good practice to use consistent indentation to make your program more readable for yourself and others. There are even tools to make your code line up nicely.

When he was designing the language that became Python, Guido van Rossum decided that the indentation itself was enough to define a program's structure, and avoided typing all those parentheses and curly braces. Python is unusual in this use of *white space* to define program structure. It's one of the first aspects that newcomers notice, and it can seem odd to those who have experience with other languages. It turns out that after writing Python for a little while, it feels natural and you stop noticing it. You even get used to doing more while typing less.

Comment with

A *comment* is a piece of text in your program that is ignored by the Python interpreter. You might use comments to clarify nearby Python code, make notes to yourself to fix something someday, or for whatever purpose you like. You mark a comment by using the # character; everything from that point on to the end of the current line is part of the comment. You'll usually see a comment on a line by itself, as shown here:

```
>>> # 60 sec/min * 60 min/hr * 24 hr/day
>>> seconds_per_day = 86400
```

Or, on the same line as the code it's commenting:

```
>>> seconds_per_day = 86400 # 60 sec/min * 60 min/hr * 24 hr/day
```

The # character has many names: *hash*, *sharp*, *pound*, or the sinister-sounding *octo-thorpe*.[1] Whatever you call it,[2] its effect lasts only to the end of the line on which it appears.

Python does not have a multiline comment. You need to explicitly begin each comment line or section with a #.

```
>>> # I can say anything here, even if Python doesn't like it,
... # because I'm protected by the awesome
... # octothorpe.
...
>>>
```

However, if it's in a text string, the all-powerful octothorpe reverts back to its role as a plain old # character:

```
>>> print("No comment: quotes make the # harmless.")
No comment: quotes make the # harmless.
```

Continue Lines with \

Programs are more readable when lines are reasonably short. The recommended (not required) maximum line length is 80 characters. If you can't say everything you want to say in that length, you can use the *continuation character*: \ (backslash). Just put \ at the end of a line, and Python will suddenly act as though you're still on the same line.

For example, if I wanted to build a long string from smaller ones, I could do it in steps:

```
>>> alphabet = ''
>>> alphabet += 'abcdefg'
>>> alphabet += 'hijklmnop'
>>> alphabet += 'qrstuv'
>>> alphabet += 'wxyz'
```

Or, I could do it in one step, using the continuation character:

```
>>> alphabet = 'abcdefg' + \
...         'hijklmnop' + \
...         'qrstuv' + \
...         'wxyz'
```

---

1 Like that eight-legged green *thing* that's *right behind you.*

2 Please don't call it. It might come back.

Line continuation is also needed if a Python expression spans multiple lines:

```
>>> 1 + 2 +
  File "<stdin>", line 1
    1 + 2 +
          ^
SyntaxError: invalid syntax
>>> 1 + 2 + \
... 3
6
>>>
```

Compare with if, elif, and else

So far in this book, we've talked almost entirely about data structures. Now, we finally take our first step into the *code structures* that weave data into programs. (You got a little preview of these in the previous chapter's section on sets. I hope no lasting damage was done.) Our first example is this tiny Python program that checks the value of the boolean variable `disaster` and prints an appropriate comment:

```
>>> disaster = True
>>> if disaster:
...     print("Woe!")
... else:
...     print("Whee!")
...
Woe!
>>>
```

The `if` and `else` lines are Python *statements* that check whether a condition (here, the value of `disaster`) is `True`. Remember, `print()` is Python's built-in *function* to print things, normally to your screen.

 If you've programmed in other languages, note that you don't need parentheses for the `if` test. Don't say something such as `if (disaster == True)`. You do need the colon (`:`) at the end. If, like me, you forget to type the colon at times, Python will display an error message.

Each `print()` line is indented under its test. I used four spaces to indent each subsection. Although you can use any indentation you like, Python expects you to be consistent with code within a section—the lines need to be indented the same amount, lined up on the left. The recommended style, called *PEP-8* (*http://bit.ly/pep-8*), is to use four spaces. Don't use tabs, or mix tabs and spaces; it messes up the indent count.

We did a number of things here, which I'll explain more fully as the chapter progresses:

- Assigned the boolean value `True` to the variable named `disaster`
- Performed a *conditional comparison* by using `if` and `else`, executing different code depending on the value of `disaster`
- *Called* the `print()` *function* to print some text

You can have tests within tests, as many levels deep as needed:

```
>>> furry = True
>>> small = True
>>> if furry:
...     if small:
...         print("It's a cat.")
...     else:
...         print("It's a bear!")
... else:
...     if small:
...         print("It's a skink!")
...     else:
...         print("It's a human. Or a hairless bear.")
...
It's a cat.
```

In Python, indentation determines how the `if` and `else` sections are paired. Our first test was to check `furry`. Because `furry` is `True`, Python goes to the indented `if small` test. Because we had set `small` to `True`, `if small` is evaluated as `True`. This makes Python run the next line and print `It's a cat`.

If there are more than two possibilities to test, use `if`, `elif` (meaning *else if*), and `else`:

```
>>> color = "puce"
>>> if color == "red":
...     print("It's a tomato")
... elif color == "green":
...     print("It's a green pepper")
... elif color == "bee purple":
...     print("I don't know what it is, but only bees can see it")
... else:
...     print("I've never heard of the color", color)
...
I've never heard of the color puce
```

In the preceding example, we tested for equality with the == operator. Python's *comparison operators* are:

equality	==
inequality	!=
less than	<
less than or equal	<=
greater than	>
greater than or equal	>=
membership	in ...

These return the boolean values `True` or `False`. Let's see how these all work, but first, assign a value to x:

```
>>> x = 7
```

Now, let's try some tests:

```
>>> x == 5
False
>>> x == 7
True
>>> 5 < x
True
>>> x < 10
True
```

Note that two equals signs (==) are used to *test equality*; remember, a single equals sign (=) is what you use to assign a value to a variable.

If you need to make multiple comparisons at the same time, you use the *boolean operators* and, or, and not to determine the final boolean result.

Boolean operators have lower *precedence* than the chunks of code that they're comparing. This means that the chunks are calculated first, then compared. In this example, because we set x to 7, 5 < x is calculated to be `True` and x < 10 is also `True`, so we finally end up with `True and True`:

```
>>> 5 < x and x < 10
True
```

As "Precedence" on page 25 points out, the easiest way to avoid confusion about precedence is to add parentheses:

```
>>> (5 < x) and (x < 10)
True
```

Here are some other tests:

```
>>> 5 < x or x < 10
True
>>> 5 < x and x > 10
False
>>> 5 < x and not x > 10
True
```

If you're and-ing multiple comparisons with one variable, Python lets you do this:

```
>>> 5 < x < 10
True
```

It's the same as 5 < x and x < 10. You can also write longer comparisons:

```
>>> 5 < x < 10 < 999
True
```

What Is True?

What if the element we're checking isn't a boolean? What does Python consider True and False?

A false value doesn't necessarily need to explicitly be False. For example, these are all considered False:

boolean	False
null	None
zero integer	0
zero float	0.0
empty string	' '
empty list	[]
empty tuple	()
empty dict	{}
empty set	set()

Anything else is considered True. Python programs use this definition of "truthiness" (or in this case, "falsiness") to check for empty data structures as well as False conditions:

```
>>> some_list = []
>>> if some_list:
...     print("There's something in here")
... else:
...     print("Hey, it's empty!")
...
Hey, it's empty!
```

If what you're testing is an expression rather than a simple variable, Python evaluates the expression and returns a boolean result. So, if you type the following:

```
if color == "red":
```

Python evaluates `color == "red"`. In our example, we assigned the string `"puce"` to `color` earlier, so `color == "red"` is `False`, and Python moves on to the next test:

```
elif color == "green":
```

Do Multiple Comparisons with in

Say you have a letter and want to know if it's a vowel. One way would be to write a long `if` statement:

```
>>> letter = 'o'
>>> if letter == 'a' or letter == 'e' or letter == 'i' \
...     or letter == 'o' or letter == 'u':
...     print(letter, 'is a vowel')
... else:
...     print(letter, 'is not a vowel')
...
o is a vowel
>>>
```

Whenever you need to make a lot of comparisons like that, separated by `or`, use Python's `in` feature instead. Here's how to check vowel-ness more Pythonically, using `in` with a string made of vowel characters:

```
>>> vowels = 'aeiou'
>>> letter = 'o'
>>> letter in vowels
True
>>> if letter in vowels:
...     print(letter, 'is a vowel')
...
o is a vowel
```

In earlier chapters, we used `in` to see if a value exists in any of Python's iterable data types, notably lists, tuples, sets, strings. So, we could define `vowels` with any of those data types too:

```
>>> vowel_set = {'a', 'e', 'i', 'o', 'u'}
>>> letter in vowel_set
```

```
True
>>> vowel_list = ['a', 'e', 'i', 'o', 'u']
>>> letter in vowel_list
True
>>> vowel_tuple = ('a', 'e', 'i', 'o', 'u')
>>> letter in vowel_tuple
True
>>> vowel_dict = {'a': 'apple', 'e': 'elephant',
...               'i': 'impala', 'o': 'ocelot', 'u': 'unicorn'}
>>> letter in vowel_dict
True
```

For the dictionary, in looks at the keys instead of their values.

Repeat with while

Testing with if, elif, and else runs from top to bottom. Sometimes, we need to do something more than once. We need a *loop*, and the simplest looping mechanism in Python is while. Using the interactive interpreter, try this next example, which is a simple loop that prints the numbers from 1 to 5:

```
>>> count = 1
>>> while count <= 5:
...        print(count)
...        count += 1
...
1
2
3
4
5
>>>
```

We first assigned the value 1 to count. The while loop compared the value of count to 5 and continued if count was less than or equal to 5. Inside the loop, we printed the value of count and then *incremented* its value by one with the statement count += 1. Python goes back to the top of the loop, and again compares count with 5. The value of count is now 2, so the contents of the while loop are again executed, and count is incremented to 3.

This continues until count is incremented from 5 to 6 at the bottom of the loop. On the next trip to the top, count <= 5 is now False, and the while loop ends. Python moves on to the next lines.

Cancel with break

If you want to loop until something occurs, but you're not sure when that might happen, you can use an *infinite loop* with a break statement. This time we'll read a line of input from the keyboard via Python's input() function and then print it with the first letter capitalized. We break out of the loop when a line containing only the letter q is typed:

```
>>> while True:
...     stuff = input("String to capitalize [type q to quit]: ")
...     if stuff == "q":
...         break
...     print(stuff.capitalize())
...
String to capitalize [type q to quit]: test
Test
String to capitalize [type q to quit]: hey, it works
Hey, it works
String to capitalize [type q to quit]: q
>>>
```

Skip Ahead with continue

Sometimes you don't want to break out of a loop but just want to skip ahead to the next iteration for some reason. Here's a contrived example: let's read an integer, print its square if it's odd, and skip it if it's even. We even added a few comments. Again, we'll use q to stop the loop:

```
>>> while True:
...     value = input("Integer, please [q to quit]: ")
...     if value == 'q':      # quit
...         break
...     number = int(value)
...     if number % 2 == 0:   # an even number
...         continue
...     print(number, "squared is", number*number)
...
Integer, please [q to quit]: 1
1 squared is 1
Integer, please [q to quit]: 2
Integer, please [q to quit]: 3
3 squared is 9
Integer, please [q to quit]: 4
Integer, please [q to quit]: 5
5 squared is 25
Integer, please [q to quit]: q
>>>
```

Check break Use with else

If the while loop ended normally (no break call), control passes to an optional else. You use this when you've coded a while loop to check for something, and breaking as soon as it's found. The else would be run if the while loop completed but the object was not found:

```
>>> numbers = [1, 3, 5]
>>> position = 0
>>> while position < len(numbers):
...     number = numbers[position]
...     if number % 2 == 0:
...         print('Found even number', number)
...         break
...     position += 1
... else:  # break not called
...     print('No even number found')
...
No even number found
```

 This use of else might seem nonintuitive. Consider it a *break checker*.

Iterate with for

Python makes frequent use of *iterators*, for good reason. They make it possible for you to traverse data structures without knowing how large they are or how they are implemented. You can even iterate over data that is created on the fly, allowing processing of data *streams* that would otherwise not fit in the computer's memory all at once.

It's legal Python to step through a sequence like this:

```
>>> rabbits = ['Flopsy', 'Mopsy', 'Cottontail', 'Peter']
>>> current = 0
>>> while current < len(rabbits):
...     print(rabbits[current])
...     current += 1
...
Flopsy
Mopsy
Cottontail
Peter
```

But there's a better, more Pythonic way:

```
>>> for rabbit in rabbits:
...     print(rabbit)
...
Flopsy
Mopsy
Cottontail
Peter
```

Lists such as `rabbits` are one of Python's *iterable* objects, along with strings, tuples, dictionaries, sets, and some other elements. Tuple or list iteration produces an item at a time. String iteration produces a character at a time, as shown here:

```
>>> word = 'cat'
>>> for letter in word:
...     print(letter)
...
c
a
t
```

Iterating over a dictionary (or its `keys()` function) returns the keys. In this example, the keys are the types of cards in the board game Clue (Cluedo outside of North America):

```
>>> accusation = {'room': 'ballroom', 'weapon': 'lead pipe',
                  'person': 'Col. Mustard'}
>>> for card in accusation:    # or, for card in accusation.keys():
...     print(card)
...
room
weapon
person
```

To iterate over the values rather than the keys, you use the dictionary's `values()` function:

```
>>> for value in accusation.values():
...     print(value)
...
ballroom
lead pipe
Col. Mustard
```

To return both the key and value in a tuple, you can use the `items()` function:

```
>>> for item in accusation.items():
...     print(item)
...
('room', 'ballroom')
('weapon', 'lead pipe')
('person', 'Col. Mustard')
```

Remember that you can assign to a tuple in one step. For each tuple returned by `items()`, assign the first value (the key) to `card` and the second (the value) to `con tents`:

```
>>> for card, contents in accusation.items():
...     print('Card', card, 'has the contents', contents)
...
Card weapon has the contents lead pipe
```

```
Card person has the contents Col. Mustard
Card room has the contents ballroom
```

Cancel with break

A break in a for loop breaks out of the loop, as it does for a while loop.

Skip with continue

Inserting a continue in a for loop jumps to the next iteration of the loop, as it does for a while loop.

Check break Use with else

Similar to while, for has an optional else that checks if the for completed normally. If break was *not* called, the else statement is run.

This is useful when you want to verify that the previous for loop ran to completion, instead of being stopped early with a break. The for loop in the following example prints the name of the cheese and breaks if any cheese is found in the cheese shop:

```
>>> cheeses = []
>>> for cheese in cheeses:
...     print('This shop has some lovely', cheese)
...     break
... else:  # no break means no cheese
...     print('This is not much of a cheese shop, is it?')
...
This is not much of a cheese shop, is it?
```

 As with while, the use of else with for might seem nonintuitive. It makes more sense if you think of the for as looking for something, and else being called if you didn't find it. To get the same effect without else, use some variable to indicate whether you found what you wanted in the for loop, as demonstrated here:

```
>>> cheeses = []
>>> found_one = False
>>> for cheese in cheeses:
...     found_one = True
...     print('This shop has some lovely', cheese)
...     break
...
>>> if not found_one:
...     print('This is not much of a cheese shop, is it?')
...
This is not much of a cheese shop, is it?
```

Iterate Multiple Sequences with zip()

There's one more nice iteration trick: iterating over multiple sequences in parallel by using the zip() function:

```
>>> days = ['Monday', 'Tuesday', 'Wednesday']
>>> fruits = ['banana', 'orange', 'peach']
>>> drinks = ['coffee', 'tea', 'beer']
>>> desserts = ['tiramisu', 'ice cream', 'pie', 'pudding']
>>> for day, fruit, drink, dessert in zip(days, fruits, drinks, desserts):
...     print(day, ": drink", drink, "- eat", fruit, "- enjoy", dessert)
...
Monday : drink coffee - eat banana - enjoy tiramisu
Tuesday : drink tea - eat orange - enjoy ice cream
Wednesday : drink beer - eat peach - enjoy pie
```

zip() stops when the shortest sequence is done. One of the lists (desserts) was longer than the others, so no one gets any pudding unless we extend the other lists.

"Dictionaries" on page 55 shows you how the dict() function can create dictionaries from two-item sequences like tuples, lists, or strings. You can use zip() to walk through multiple sequences and make tuples from items at the same offsets. Let's make two tuples of corresponding English and French words:

```
>>> english = 'Monday', 'Tuesday', 'Wednesday'
>>> french = 'Lundi', 'Mardi', 'Mercredi'
```

Now, use zip() to pair these tuples. The value returned by zip() is itself not a tuple or list, but an iterable value that can be turned into one:

```
>>> list( zip(english, french) )
[('Monday', 'Lundi'), ('Tuesday', 'Mardi'), ('Wednesday', 'Mercredi')]
```

Feed the result of zip() directly to dict() and voilà: a tiny English-French dictionary!

```
>>> dict( zip(english, french) )
{'Monday': 'Lundi', 'Tuesday': 'Mardi', 'Wednesday': 'Mercredi'}
```

Generate Number Sequences with range()

The range() function returns a stream of numbers within a specified range. without first having to create and store a large data structure such as a list or tuple. This lets you create huge ranges without using all the memory in your computer and crashing your program.

You use range() similar to how to you use slices: range(*start*, *stop*, *step*). If you omit *start*, the range begins at 0. The only required value is *stop*; as with slices, the last value created will be just before *stop*. The default value of *step* is 1, but you can go backward with -1.

Like `zip()`, `range()` returns an *iterable* object, so you need to step through the values with `for ... in`, or convert the object to a sequence like a list. Let's make the range `0, 1, 2`:

```
>>> for x in range(0,3):
...     print(x)
...
0
1
2
>>> list( range(0, 3) )
[0, 1, 2]
```

Here's how to make a range from 2 down to 0:

```
>>> for x in range(2, -1, -1):
...     print(x)
...
2
1
0
>>> list( range(2, -1, -1) )
[2, 1, 0]
```

The following snippet uses a step size of 2 to get the even numbers from 0 to 10:

```
>>> list( range(0, 11, 2) )
[0, 2, 4, 6, 8, 10]
```

Other Iterators

Chapter 8 shows iteration over files. In Chapter 6, you can see how to enable iteration over objects that you've defined yourself.

Comprehensions

A *comprehension* is a compact way of creating a Python data structure from one or more iterators. Comprehensions make it possible for you to combine loops and conditional tests with a less verbose syntax. Using a comprehension is sometimes taken as a sign that you know Python at more than a beginner's level. In other words, it's more Pythonic.

List Comprehensions

You could build a list of integers from 1 to 5, one item at a time, like this:

```
>>> number_list = []
>>> number_list.append(1)
>>> number_list.append(2)
>>> number_list.append(3)
```

```
>>> number_list.append(4)
>>> number_list.append(5)
>>> number_list
[1, 2, 3, 4, 5]
```

Or, you could also use an iterator and the range() function:

```
>>> number_list = []
>>> for number in range(1, 6):
...         number_list.append(number)
...
>>> number_list
[1, 2, 3, 4, 5]
```

Or, you could just turn the output of range() into a list directly:

```
>>> number_list = list(range(1, 6))
>>> number_list
[1, 2, 3, 4, 5]
```

All of these approaches are valid Python code and will produce the same result. However, a more Pythonic way to build a list is by using a *list comprehension*. The simplest form of list comprehension is:

[*expression* for *item* in *iterable*]

Here's how a list comprehension would build the integer list:

```
>>> number_list = [number for number in range(1,6)]
>>> number_list
[1, 2, 3, 4, 5]
```

In the first line, you need the first number variable to produce values for the list: that is, to put a result of the loop into number_list. The second number is part of the for loop. To show that the first number is an expression, try this variant:

```
>>> number_list = [number-1 for number in range(1,6)]
>>> number_list
[0, 1, 2, 3, 4]
```

The list comprehension moves the loop inside the square brackets. This comprehension example really wasn't simpler than the previous example, but there's more. A list comprehension can include a conditional expression, looking something like this:

[*expression* for *item* in *iterable* if *condition*]

Let's make a new comprehension that builds a list of only the odd numbers between 1 and 5 (remember that number % 2 is True for odd numbers and False for even numbers):

```
>>> a_list = [number for number in range(1,6) if number % 2 == 1]
>>> a_list
[1, 3, 5]
```

Now, the comprehension is a little more compact than its traditional counterpart:

```
>>> a_list = []
>>> for number in range(1,6):
...     if number % 2 == 1:
...         a_list.append(number)
...
>>> a_list
[1, 3, 5]
```

Finally, just as there can be nested loops, there can be more than one set of for ...
clauses in the corresponding comprehension. To show this, let's first try a plain, old
nested loop and print the results:

```
>>> rows = range(1,4)
>>> cols = range(1,3)
>>> for row in rows:
...     for col in cols:
...         print(row, col)
...
1 1
1 2
2 1
2 2
3 1
3 2
```

Now, let's use a comprehension and assign it to the variable cells, making it a list of
(row, col) tuples:

```
>>> rows = range(1,4)
>>> cols = range(1,3)
>>> cells = [(row, col) for row in rows for col in cols]
>>> for cell in cells:
...     print(cell)
...
(1, 1)
(1, 2)
(2, 1)
(2, 2)
(3, 1)
(3, 2)
```

By the way, you can also use tuple unpacking to yank the row and col values from
each tuple as you iterate over the cells list:

```
>>> for row, col in cells:
...     print(row, col)
...
1 1
1 2
2 1
2 2
```

```
3 1
3 2
```

The `for row ...` and `for col ...` fragments in the list comprehension could also have had their own `if` tests.

Dictionary Comprehensions

Not to be outdone by mere lists, dictionaries also have comprehensions. The simplest form looks familiar:

{ *key_expression* : *value_expression* for *expression* in *iterable* }

Similar to list comprehensions, dictionary comprehensions can also have `if` tests and multiple for clauses:

```
>>> word = 'letters'
>>> letter_counts = {letter: word.count(letter) for letter in word}
>>> letter_counts
{'l': 1, 'e': 2, 't': 2, 'r': 1, 's': 1}
```

We are running a loop over each of the seven letters in the string `'letters'` and counting how many times that letter appears. Two of our uses of `word.count(letter)` are a waste of time because we have to count all the e's twice and all the t's twice. But, when we count the e's the second time, we do no harm because we just replace the entry in the dictionary that was already there; the same goes for counting the t's. So, the following would have been a teeny bit more Pythonic:

```
>>> word = 'letters'
>>> letter_counts = {letter: word.count(letter) for letter in set(word)}
>>> letter_counts
{'t': 2, 'l': 1, 'e': 2, 'r': 1, 's': 1}
```

The dictionary's keys are in a different order than the previous example, because iterating `set(word)` returns letters in a different order than iterating the string `word`.

Set Comprehensions

No one wants to be left out, so even sets have comprehensions. The simplest version looks like the list and dictionary comprehensions that you've just seen:

{ *expression* for *expression* in *iterable* }

The longer versions (`if` tests, multiple for clauses) are also valid for sets:

```
>>> a_set = {number for number in range(1,6) if number % 3 == 1}
>>> a_set
{1, 4}
```

Generator Comprehensions

Tuples do not have comprehensions! You might have thought that changing the square brackets of a list comprehension to parentheses would create a tuple comprehension. And it would appear to work because there's no exception if you type this:

```
>>> number_thing = (number for number in range(1, 6))
```

The thing between the parentheses is a *generator comprehension*, and it returns a *generator object*:

```
>>> type(number_thing)
<class 'generator'>
```

I'll get into generators in more detail in "Generators" on page 101. A generator is one way to provide data to an iterator.

You can iterate over this generator object directly, as illustrated here:

```
>>> for number in number_thing:
...     print(number)
...
1
2
3
4
5
```

Or, you can wrap a list() call around a generator comprehension to make it work like a list comprehension:

```
>>> number_list = list(number_thing)
>>> number_list
[1, 2, 3, 4, 5]
```

 A generator can be run only once. Lists, sets, strings, and dictionaries exist in memory, but a generator creates its values on the fly and hands them out one at a time through an iterator. It doesn't remember them, so you can't restart or back up a generator.

If you try to re-iterate this generator, you'll find that it's tapped out:

```
>>> try_again = list(number_thing)
>>> try_again
[]
```

You can create a generator from a generator comprehension, as we did here, or from a *generator function*. We'll talk about functions in general first, and then we'll get to the special case of generator functions.

Functions

So far, all our Python code examples have been little fragments. These are good for small tasks, but no one wants to retype fragments all the time. We need some way of organizing larger code into manageable pieces.

The first step to code reuse is the *function*: a named piece of code, separate from all others. A function can take any number and type of input *parameters* and return any number and type of output *results*.

You can do two things with a function:

- *Define* it
- *Call* it

To define a Python function, you type def, the function name, parentheses enclosing any input parameters to the function, and then finally, a colon (:). Function names have the same rules as variable names (they must start with a letter or _ and contain only letters, numbers, or _).

Let's take things one step at a time, and first define and call a function that has no parameters. Here's the simplest Python function:

```
>>> def do_nothing():
...     pass
```

Even for a function with no parameters like this one, you still need the parentheses and the colon in its definition. The next line needs to be indented, just as you would indent code under an if statement. Python requires the pass statement to show that this function does nothing. It's the equivalent of *This page intentionally left blank* (even though it isn't anymore).

You call this function just by typing its name and parentheses. It works as advertised, doing nothing very well:

```
>>> do_nothing()
>>>
```

Now, let's define and call another function that has no parameters but prints a single word:

```
>>> def make_a_sound():
...     print('quack')
...
>>> make_a_sound()
quack
```

When you called the make_a_sound() function, Python ran the code inside its definition. In this case, it printed a single word and returned to the main program.

Let's try a function that has no parameters but *returns* a value:

```
>>> def agree():
...     return True
...
```

You can call this function and test its returned value by using `if`:

```
>>> if agree():
...     print('Splendid!')
... else:
...     print('That was unexpected.')
...
Splendid!
```

You've just made a big step. The combination of functions with tests such as `if` and loops such as `while` make it possible for you to do things that you could not do before.

At this point, it's time to put something between those parentheses. Let's define the function `echo()` with one parameter called `anything`. It uses the `return` statement to send the value of `anything` back to its caller twice, with a space between:

```
>>> def echo(anything):
...     return anything + ' ' + anything
...
>>>
```

Now let's call `echo()` with the string `'Rumplestiltskin'`:

```
>>> echo('Rumplestiltskin')
'Rumplestiltskin Rumplestiltskin'
```

The values you pass into the function when you call it are known as *arguments*. When you call a function with arguments, the values of those arguments are copied to their corresponding *parameters* inside the function. In the previous example, the function `echo()` was called with the argument string `'Rumplestiltskin'`. This value was copied within `echo()` to the parameter `anything`, and then returned (in this case doubled, with a space) to the caller.

These function examples were pretty basic. Let's write a function that takes an input argument and actually does something with it. We'll adapt the earlier code fragment that comments on a color. Call it `commentary` and have it take an input string parameter called `color`. Make it return the string description to its caller, which can decide what to do with it:

```
>>> def commentary(color):
...     if color == 'red':
...         return "It's a tomato."
...     elif color == "green":
...         return "It's a green pepper."
...     elif color == 'bee purple':
```

```
...            return "I don't know what it is, but only bees can see it."
...        else:
...            return "I've never heard of the color "  + color +  "."
...
>>>
```

Call the function `commentary()` with the string argument `'blue'`.

```
>>> comment = commentary('blue')
```

The function does the following:

- Assigns the value `'blue'` to the function's internal `color` parameter
- Runs through the `if-elif-else` logic chain
- Returns a string
- Assigns the string to the variable `comment`

What do we get back?

```
>>> print(comment)
I've never heard of the color blue.
```

A function can take any number of input arguments (including zero) of any type. It can return any number of output results (also including zero) of any type. If a function doesn't call `return` explicitly, the caller gets the result `None`.

```
>>> print(do_nothing())
None
```

None Is Useful

None is a special Python value that holds a place when there is nothing to say. It is not the same as the boolean value `False`, although it looks false when evaluated as a boolean. Here's an example:

```
>>> thing = None
>>> if thing:
...     print("It's some thing")
... else:
...     print("It's no thing")
...
It's no thing
```

To distinguish None from a boolean False value, use Python's `is` operator:

```
>>> if thing is None:
...     print("It's nothing")
... else:
...     print("It's something")
...
```

```
    ...
    It's nothing
```

This seems like a subtle distinction, but it's important in Python. You'll need `None` to distinguish a missing value from an empty value. Remember that zero-valued integers or floats, empty strings (`''`), lists (`[]`), tuples (`(,)`), dictionaries (`{}`), and sets(`set()`) are all `False`, but are not equal to `None`.

Let's write a quick function that prints whether its argument is `None`:

```
>>> def is_none(thing):
...     if thing is None:
...         print("It's None")
...     elif thing:
...         print("It's True")
...     else:
...         print("It's False")
...
```

Now, let's run some tests:

```
>>> is_none(None)
It's None
>>> is_none(True)
It's True
>>> is_none(False)
It's False
>>> is_none(0)
It's False
>>> is_none(0.0)
It's False
>>> is_none(())
It's False
>>> is_none([])
It's False
>>> is_none({})
It's False
>>> is_none(set())
It's False
```

Positional Arguments

Python handles function arguments in a manner that's unusually flexible, when compared to many languages. The most familiar types of arguments are *positional arguments*, whose values are copied to their corresponding parameters in order.

This function builds a dictionary from its positional input arguments and returns it:

```
>>> def menu(wine, entree, dessert):
...     return {'wine': wine, 'entree': entree, 'dessert': dessert}
...
```

```
>>> menu('chardonnay', 'chicken', 'cake')
{'dessert': 'cake', 'wine': 'chardonnay', 'entree': 'chicken'}
```

Although very common, a downside of positional arguments is that you need to remember the meaning of each position. If we forgot and called menu() with wine as the last argument instead of the first, the meal would be very different:

```
>>> menu('beef', 'bagel', 'bordeaux')
{'dessert': 'bordeaux', 'wine': 'beef', 'entree': 'bagel'}
```

Keyword Arguments

To avoid positional argument confusion, you can specify arguments by the names of their corresponding parameters, even in a different order from their definition in the function:

```
>>> menu(entree='beef', dessert='bagel', wine='bordeaux')
{'dessert': 'bagel', 'wine': 'bordeaux', 'entree': 'beef'}
```

You can mix positional and keyword arguments. Let's specify the wine first, but use keyword arguments for the entree and dessert:

```
>>> menu('frontenac', dessert='flan', entree='fish')
{'entree': 'fish', 'dessert': 'flan', 'wine': 'frontenac'}
```

If you call a function with both positional and keyword arguments, the positional arguments need to come first.

Specify Default Parameter Values

You can specify default values for parameters. The default is used if the caller does not provide a corresponding argument. This bland-sounding feature can actually be quite useful. Using the previous example:

```
>>> def menu(wine, entree, dessert='pudding'):
...     return {'wine': wine, 'entree': entree, 'dessert': dessert}
```

This time, try calling menu() without the dessert argument:

```
>>> menu('chardonnay', 'chicken')
{'dessert': 'pudding', 'wine': 'chardonnay', 'entree': 'chicken'}
```

If you do provide an argument, it's used instead of the default:

```
>>> menu('dunkelfelder', 'duck', 'doughnut')
{'dessert': 'doughnut', 'wine': 'dunkelfelder', 'entree': 'duck'}
```

Default argument values are calculated when the function is *defined*, not when it is run. A common error with new (and sometimes not-so-new) Python programmers is to use a mutable data type such as a list or dictionary as a default argument.

In the following test, the buggy() function is expected to run each time with a fresh empty result list, add the arg argument to it, and then print a single-item list. However, there's a bug: it's empty only the first time it's called. The second time, result still has one item from the previous call:

```
>>> def buggy(arg, result=[]):
...     result.append(arg)
...     print(result)
...
>>> buggy('a')
['a']
>>> buggy('b')    # expect ['b']
['a', 'b']
```

It would have worked if it had been written like this:

```
>>> def works(arg):
...     result = []
...     result.append(arg)
...     return result
...
>>> works('a')
['a']
>>> works('b')
['b']
```

The fix is to pass in something else to indicate the first call:

```
>>> def nonbuggy(arg, result=None):
...     if result is None:
...         result = []
...     result.append(arg)
...     print(result)
...
>>> nonbuggy('a')
['a']
>>> nonbuggy('b')
['b']
```

Gather Positional Arguments with *

If you've programmed in C or C++, you might assume that an asterisk (*) in a Python program has something to do with a pointer. Nope, Python doesn't have pointers.

When used inside the function with a parameter, an asterisk groups a variable number of positional arguments into a tuple of parameter values. In the following example, args is the parameter tuple that resulted from the arguments that were passed to the function print_args():

```
>>> def print_args(*args):
...     print('Positional argument tuple:', args)
...
```

If you call it with no arguments, you get nothing in *args:

```
>>> print_args()
Positional argument tuple: ()
```

Whatever you give it will be printed as the args tuple:

```
>>> print_args(3, 2, 1, 'wait!', 'uh...')
Positional argument tuple: (3, 2, 1, 'wait!', 'uh...')
```

This is useful for writing functions such as print() that accept a variable number of arguments. If your function has required positional arguments as well, *args goes at the end and grabs all the rest:

```
>>> def print_more(required1, required2, *args):
...     print('Need this one:', required1)
...     print('Need this one too:', required2)
...     print('All the rest:', args)
...
>>> print_more('cap', 'gloves', 'scarf', 'monocle', 'mustache wax')
Need this one: cap
Need this one too: gloves
All the rest: ('scarf', 'monocle', 'mustache wax')
```

When using *, you don't need to call the tuple parameter args, but it's a common idiom in Python.

Gather Keyword Arguments with **

You can use two asterisks (**) to group keyword arguments into a dictionary, where the argument names are the keys, and their values are the corresponding dictionary values. The following example defines the function print_kwargs() to print its keyword arguments:

```
>>> def print_kwargs(**kwargs):
...     print('Keyword arguments:', kwargs)
...
```

Now, try calling it with some keyword arguments:

```
>>> print_kwargs(wine='merlot', entree='mutton', dessert='macaroon')
Keyword arguments: {'dessert': 'macaroon', 'wine': 'merlot', 'entree': 'mutton'}
```

Inside the function, kwargs is a dictionary.

If you mix positional parameters with *args and **kwargs, they need to occur in that order. As with args, you don't need to call this keyword parameter kwargs, but it's common usage.

Docstrings

Readability counts, says the Zen of Python. You can attach documentation to a function definition by including a string at the beginning of the function body. This is the function's *docstring*:

```
>>> def echo(anything):
...     'echo returns its input argument'
...     return anything
```

You can make a docstring quite long and even add rich formatting, if you want, as is demonstrated in the following:

```
def print_if_true(thing, check):
    '''
    Prints the first argument if a second argument is true.
    The operation is:
        1. Check whether the *second* argument is true.
        2. If it is, print the *first* argument.
    '''
    if check:
        print(thing)
```

To print a function's docstring, call the Python `help()` function. Pass the function's name to get a listing of arguments along with the nicely formatted docstring:

```
>>> help(echo)
Help on function echo in module __main__:

echo(anything)
    echo returns its input argument
```

If you want to see just the raw docstring, without the formatting:

```
>>> print(echo.__doc__)
echo returns its input argument
```

That odd-looking __doc__ is the internal name of the docstring as a variable within the function. "Uses of _ and __ in Names" on page 106 explains the reason behind all those underscores.

Functions Are First-Class Citizens

I've mentioned the Python mantra, *everything is an object*. This includes numbers, strings, tuples, lists, dictionaries—and functions, as well. Functions are first-class citizens in Python. You can assign them to variables, use them as arguments to other functions, and return them from functions. This gives you the capability to do some things in Python that are difficult-to-impossible to carry out in many other languages.

To test this, let's define a simple function called `answer()` that doesn't have any arguments; it just prints the number 42:

```
>>> def answer():
...     print(42)
```

If you run this function, you know what you'll get:

```
>>> answer()
42
```

Now, let's define another function named `run_something`. It has one argument called `func`, a function to run. Once inside, it just calls the function.

```
>>> def run_something(func):
...     func()
```

If we pass `answer` to `run_something()`, we're using a function as data, just as with anything else:

```
>>> run_something(answer)
42
```

Notice that you passed `answer`, not `answer()`. In Python, those parentheses mean *call this function*. With no parentheses, Python just treats the function like any other object. That's because, like everything else in Python, it *is* an object:

```
>>> type(run_something)
<class 'function'>
```

Let's try running a function with arguments. Define a function `add_args()` that prints the sum of its two numeric arguments, `arg1` and `arg2`:

```
>>> def add_args(arg1, arg2):
...     print(arg1 + arg2)
```

And what is `add_args()`?

```
>>> type(add_args)
<class 'function'>
```

At this point, let's define a function called `run_something_with_args()` that takes three arguments:

- `func`—The function to run
- `arg1`—The first argument for `func`
- `arg2`—The second argument for `func`

```
>>> def run_something_with_args(func, arg1, arg2):
...     func(arg1, arg2)
```

When you call `run_something_with_args()`, the function passed by the caller is assigned to the `func` parameter, whereas `arg1` and `arg2` get the values that follow in the argument list. Then, running `func(arg1, arg2)` executes that function with those arguments because the parentheses told Python to do so.

Let's test it by passing the function name `add_args` and the arguments 5 and 9 to `run_something_with_args()`:

```
>>> run_something_with_args(add_args, 5, 9)
14
```

Within the function `run_something_with_args()`, the function name argument `add_args` was assigned to the parameter `func`, 5 to `arg1`, and 9 to `arg2`. This ended up running:

```
add_args(5, 9)
```

You can combine this with the `*args` and `**kwargs` techniques.

Let's define a test function that takes any number of positional arguments, calculates their sum by using the `sum()` function, and then returns that sum:

```
>>> def sum_args(*args):
...     return sum(args)
```

I haven't mentioned `sum()` before. It's a built-in Python function that calculates the sum of the values in its iterable numeric (int or float) argument.

We'll define the new function `run_with_positional_args()`, which takes a function and any number of positional arguments to pass to it:

```
>>> def run_with_positional_args(func, *args):
...     return func(*args)
```

Now, go ahead and call it:

```
>>> run_with_positional_args(sum_args, 1, 2, 3, 4)
10
```

You can use functions as elements of lists, tuples, sets, and dictionaries. Functions are immutable, so you can also use them as dictionary keys.

Inner Functions

You can define a function within another function:

```
>>> def outer(a, b):
...     def inner(c, d):
...         return c + d
...     return inner(a, b)
...
>>>
```

```
>>> outer(4, 7)
11
```

An inner function can be useful when performing some complex task more than once within another function, to avoid loops or code duplication. For a string example, this inner function adds some text to its argument:

```
>>> def knights(saying):
...     def inner(quote):
...         return "We are the knights who say: '%s'" % quote
...     return inner(saying)
...
>>> knights('Ni!')
"We are the knights who say: 'Ni!'"
```

Closures

An inner function can act as a *closure*. This is a function that is dynamically generated by another function and can both change and remember the values of variables that were created outside the function.

The following example builds on the previous knights() example. Let's call the new one knights2(), because we have no imagination, and turn the inner() function into a closure called inner2(). Here are the differences:

- inner2() uses the outer saying parameter directly instead of getting it as an argument.
- knights2() returns the inner2 function name instead of calling it.

```
>>> def knights2(saying):
...     def inner2():
...         return "We are the knights who say: '%s'" % saying
...     return inner2
...
```

The inner2() function knows the value of saying that was passed in and remembers it. The line return inner2 returns this specialized copy of the inner2 function (but doesn't call it). That's a closure: a dynamically created function that remembers where it came from.

Let's call knights2() twice, with different arguments:

```
>>> a = knights2('Duck')
>>> b = knights2('Hasenpfeffer')
```

Okay, so what are a and b?

```
>>> type(a)
<class 'function'>
```

```
>>> type(b)
<class 'function'>
```

They're functions, but they're also closures:

```
>>> a
<function knights2.<locals>.inner2 at 0x10193e158>
>>> b
<function knights2.<locals>.inner2 at 0x10193e1e0>
```

If we call them, they remember the saying that was used when they were created by knights2:

```
>>> a()
"We are the knights who say: 'Duck'"
>>> b()
"We are the knights who say: 'Hasenpfeffer'"
```

Anonymous Functions: the lambda() Function

In Python, a *lambda function* is an anonymous function expressed as a single statement. You can use it instead of a normal tiny function.

To illustrate it, let's first make an example that uses normal functions. To begin, we'll define the function edit_story(). Its arguments are the following:

- words—a list of words
- func—a function to apply to each word in words

```
>>> def edit_story(words, func):
...     for word in words:
...         print(func(word))
```

Now, we need a list of words and a function to apply to each word. For the words, here's a list of (hypothetical) sounds made by my cat if he (hypothetically) missed one of the stairs:

```
>>> stairs = ['thud', 'meow', 'thud', 'hiss']
```

And for the function, this will capitalize each word and append an exclamation point, perfect for feline tabloid newspaper headlines:

```
>>> def enliven(word):   # give that prose more punch
...     return word.capitalize() + '!'
```

Mixing our ingredients:

```
>>> edit_story(stairs, enliven)
Thud!
Meow!
Thud!
Hiss!
```

Finally, we get to the lambda. The `enliven()` function was so brief that we could replace it with a lambda:

```
>>>
>>> edit_story(stairs, lambda word: word.capitalize() + '!')
Thud!
Meow!
Thud!
Hiss!
>>>
```

The lambda takes one argument, which we call `word` here. Everything between the colon and the terminating parenthesis is the definition of the function.

Often, using real functions such as `enliven()` is much clearer than using lambdas. Lambdas are mostly useful for cases in which you would otherwise need to define many tiny functions and remember what you called them all. In particular, you can use lambdas in graphical user interfaces to define *callback functions*; see Appendix A for examples.

Generators

A *generator* is a Python sequence creation object. With it, you can iterate through potentially huge sequences without creating and storing the entire sequence in memory at once. Generators are often the source of data for iterators. If you recall, we already used one of them, `range()`, in earlier code examples to generate a series of integers. In Python 2, `range()` returns a list, which limits it to fit in memory. Python 2 also has the generator `xrange()`, which became the normal `range()` in Python 3. This example adds all the integers from 1 to 100:

```
>>> sum(range(1, 101))
5050
```

Every time you iterate through a generator, it keeps track of where it was the last time it was called and returns the next value. This is different from a normal function, which has no memory of previous calls and always starts at its first line with the same state.

If you want to create a potentially large sequence, and the code is too large for a generator comprehension, write a *generator function*. It's a normal function, but it returns its value with a `yield` statement rather than `return`. Let's write our own version of `range()`:

```
>>> def my_range(first=0, last=10, step=1):
...     number = first
...     while number < last:
...         yield number
```

```
...          number += step
...
```

It's a normal function:

```
>>> my_range
<function my_range at 0x10193e268>
```

And it returns a generator object:

```
>>> ranger = my_range(1, 5)
>>> ranger
<generator object my_range at 0x101a0a168>
```

We can iterate over this generator object:

```
>>> for x in ranger:
...     print(x)
...
1
2
3
4
```

Decorators

Sometimes, you want to modify an existing function without changing its source code. A common example is adding a debugging statement to see what arguments were passed in.

A *decorator* is a function that takes one function as input and returns another function. We'll dig into our bag of Python tricks and use the following:

- *args and **kwargs
- Inner functions
- Functions as arguments

The function document_it() defines a decorator that will do the following:

- Print the function's name and the values of its arguments
- Run the function with the arguments
- Print the result
- Return the modified function for use

Here's what the code looks like:

```
>>> def document_it(func):
...     def new_function(*args, **kwargs):
...         print('Running function:', func.__name__)
```

```
...        print('Positional arguments:', args)
...        print('Keyword arguments:', kwargs)
...        result = func(*args, **kwargs)
...        print('Result:', result)
...        return result
...    return new_function
```

Whatever func you pass to document_it(), you get a new function that includes the extra statements that document_it() adds. A decorator doesn't actually have to run any code from func, but document_it() calls func part way through so that you get the results of func as well as all the extras.

So, how do you use this? You can apply the decorator manually:

```
>>> def add_ints(a, b):
...     return a + b
...
>>> add_ints(3, 5)
8
>>> cooler_add_ints = document_it(add_ints)   # manual decorator assignment
>>> cooler_add_ints(3, 5)
Running function: add_ints
Positional arguments: (3, 5)
Keyword arguments: {}
Result: 8
8
```

As an alternative to the manual decorator assignment above, just add @*decorator_name* before the function that you want to decorate:

```
>>> @document_it
... def add_ints(a, b):
...     return a + b
...
>>> add_ints(3, 5)
Start function add_ints
Positional arguments: (3, 5)
Keyword arguments: {}
Result: 8
8
```

You can have more than one decorator for a function. Let's write another decorator called square_it() that squares the result:

```
>>> def square_it(func):
...     def new_function(*args, **kwargs):
...         result = func(*args, **kwargs)
...         return result * result
...     return new_function
...
```

The decorator that's used closest to the function (just above the `def`) runs first and then the one above it. Either order gives the same end result, but you can see how the intermediate steps change:

```
>>> @document_it
... @square_it
... def add_ints(a, b):
...     return a + b
...
>>> add_ints(3, 5)
Running function: new_function
Positional arguments: (3, 5)
Keyword arguments: {}
Result: 64
64
```

Let's try reversing the decorator order:

```
>>> @square_it
... @document_it
... def add_ints(a, b):
...     return a + b
...
>>> add_ints(3, 5)
Running function: add_ints
Positional arguments: (3, 5)
Keyword arguments: {}
Result: 8
64
```

Namespaces and Scope

A name can refer to different things, depending on where it's used. Python programs have various *namespaces*—sections within which a particular name is unique and unrelated to the same name in other namespaces.

Each function defines its own namespace. If you define a variable called x in a main program and another variable called x in a function, they refer to different things. But the walls can be breached: if you need to, you can access names in other namespaces in various ways.

The main part of a program defines the *global* namespace; thus, the variables in that namespace are *global variables*.

You can get the value of a global variable from within a function:

```
>>> animal = 'fruitbat'
>>> def print_global():
...     print('inside print_global:', animal)
...
>>> print('at the top level:', animal)
```

```
at the top level: fruitbat
>>> print_global()
inside print_global: fruitbat
```

But, if you try to get the value of the global variable *and* change it within the function, you get an error:

```
>>> def change_and_print_global():
...     print('inside change_and_print_global:', animal)
...     animal = 'wombat'
...     print('after the change:', animal)
...
>>> change_and_print_global()
Traceback (most recent call last):
  File "<stdin>", line 1, in <module>
  File "<stdin>", line 2, in change_and_print_global
UnboundLocalError: local variable 'animal' referenced before assignment
```

If you just change it, it changes a different variable also named `animal`, but this variable is inside the function:

```
>>> def change_local():
...     animal = 'wombat'
...     print('inside change_local:', animal, id(animal))
...
>>> change_local()
inside change_local: wombat 4330406160
>>> animal
'fruitbat'
>>> id(animal)
4330390832
```

What happened here? The first line assigned the string `'fruitbat'` to a global variable named `animal`. The `change_local()` function also has a variable named `animal`, but that's in its local namespace.

We used the Python function `id()` here to print the unique value for each object and prove that the variable `animal` inside `change_local()` is not the same as `animal` at the main level of the program.

To access the global variable rather than the local one within a function, you need to be explicit and use the `global` keyword (you knew this was coming: *explicit is better than implicit*):

```
>>> animal = 'fruitbat'
>>> def change_and_print_global():
...     global animal
...     animal = 'wombat'
...     print('inside change_and_print_global:', animal)
...
>>> animal
'fruitbat'
```

```
>>> change_and_print_global()
inside change_and_print_global: wombat
>>> animal
'wombat'
```

If you don't say global within a function, Python uses the local namespace and the variable is local. It goes away after the function completes.

Python provides two functions to access the contents of your namespaces:

- locals() returns a dictionary of the contents of the local namespace.
- globals() returns a dictionary of the contents of the global namespace.

And, here they are in use:

```
>>> animal = 'fruitbat'
>>> def change_local():
...     animal = 'wombat'  # local variable
...     print('locals:', locals())
...
>>> animal
'fruitbat'
>>> change_local()
locals: {'animal': 'wombat'}
>>> print('globals:', globals()) # reformatted a little for presentation
globals: {'animal': 'fruitbat',
'__doc__': None,
'change_local': <function change_it at 0x1006c0170>,
'__package__': None,
'__name__': '__main__',
'__loader__': <class '_frozen_importlib.BuiltinImporter'>,
'__builtins__': <module 'builtins'>}
>>> animal
'fruitbat'
```

The local namespace within change_local() contained only the local variable animal. The global namespace contained the separate global variable animal and a number of other things.

Uses of _ and __ in Names

Names that begin and end with two underscores (__) are reserved for use within Python, so you should not use them with your own variables. This naming pattern was chosen because it seemed unlikely to be selected by application developers for their own variables.

For instance, the name of a function is in the system variable *function* .__name__, and its documentation string is *function* .__doc__:

```
>>> def amazing():
...     '''This is the amazing function.
...     Want to see it again?'''
...     print('This function is named:', amazing.__name__)
...     print('And its docstring is:', amazing.__doc__)
...
>>> amazing()
This function is named: amazing
And its docstring is: This is the amazing function.
    Want to see it again?
```

As you saw in the earlier globals printout, the main program is assigned the special name __main__.

Handle Errors with try and except

Do, or do not. There is no try.
—Yoda

In some languages, errors are indicated by special function return values. Python uses *exceptions*: code that is executed when an associated error occurs.

You've seen some of these already, such as accessing a list or tuple with an out-of-range position, or a dictionary with a nonexistent key. When you run code that might fail under some circumstances, you also need appropriate *exception handlers* to intercept any potential errors.

It's good practice to add exception handling anywhere an exception might occur to let the user know what is happening. You might not be able to fix the problem, but at least you can note the circumstances and shut your program down gracefully. If an exception occurs in some function and is not caught there, it *bubbles up* until it is caught by a matching handler in some calling function. If you don't provide your own exception handler, Python prints an error message and some information about where the error occurred and then terminates the program, as demonstrated in the following snippet.

```
>>> short_list = [1, 2, 3]
>>> position = 5
>>> short_list[position]
Traceback (most recent call last):
  File "<stdin>", line 1, in <module>
IndexError: list index out of range
```

Rather than leaving it to chance, use try to wrap your code, and except to provide the error handling:

```
>>> short_list = [1, 2, 3]
>>> position = 5
>>> try:
```

```
...         short_list[position]
... except:
...         print('Need a position between 0 and', len(short_list)-1, ' but got',
...             position)
...
Need a position between 0 and 2 but got 5
```

The code inside the `try` block is run. If there is an error, an exception is raised and the code inside the `except` block runs. If there are no errors, the `except` block is skipped.

Specifying a plain `except` with no arguments, as we did here, is a catchall for any exception type. If more than one type of exception could occur, it's best to provide a separate exception handler for each. No one forces you to do this; you can use a bare `except` to catch all exceptions, but your treatment of them would probably be generic (something akin to printing *Some error occurred*). You can use any number of specific exception handlers.

Sometimes, you want exception details beyond the type. You get the full exception object in the variable *name* if you use the form:

```
except exceptiontype as name
```

The example that follows looks for an `IndexError` first, because that's the exception type raised when you provide an illegal position to a sequence. It saves an `IndexError` exception in the variable `err`, and any other exception in the variable `other`. The example prints everything stored in `other` to show what you get in that object.

```
>>> short_list = [1, 2, 3]
>>> while True:
...         value = input('Position [q to quit]? ')
...         if value == 'q':
...             break
...         try:
...             position = int(value)
...             print(short_list[position])
...         except IndexError as err:
...             print('Bad index:', position)
...         except Exception as other:
...             print('Something else broke:', other)
...
Position [q to quit]? 1
2
Position [q to quit]? 0
1
Position [q to quit]? 2
3
Position [q to quit]? 3
Bad index: 3
Position [q to quit]? 2
3
```

```
Position [q to quit]? two
Something else broke: invalid literal for int() with base 10: 'two'
Position [q to quit]? q
```

Inputting position 3 raised an `IndexError` as expected. Entering `two` annoyed the `int()` function, which we handled in our second, catchall `except` code.

Make Your Own Exceptions

The previous section discussed handling exceptions, but all of the exceptions (such as `IndexError`) were predefined in Python or its standard library. You can use any of these for your own purposes. You can also define your own exception types to handle special situations that might arise in your own programs.

 This requires defining a new object type with a *class*—something we don't get into until Chapter 6. So, if you're unfamiliar with classes, you might want to return to this section later.

An exception is a class. It is a child of the class `Exception`. Let's make an exception called `UppercaseException` and raise it when we encounter an uppercase word in a string.

```
>>> class UppercaseException(Exception):
...     pass
...
>>> words = ['eeenie', 'meenie', 'miny', 'MO']
>>> for word in words:
...     if word.isupper():
...         raise UppercaseException(word)
...
Traceback (most recent call last):
  File "<stdin>", line 3, in <module>
__main__.UppercaseException: MO
```

We didn't even define any behavior for `UppercaseException` (notice we just used `pass`), letting its parent class `Exception` figure out what to print when the exception was raised.

You can access the exception object itself and print it:

```
>>> try:
...     raise OopsException('panic')
... except OopsException as exc:
...     print(exc)
...
panic
```

Things to Do

4.1 Assign the value 7 to the variable `guess_me`. Then, write the conditional tests (`if`, `else`, and `elif`) to print the string `'too low'` if `guess_me` is less than 7, `'too high'` if greater than 7, and `'just right'` if equal to 7.

4.2 Assign the value 7 to the variable `guess_me` and the value 1 to the variable `start`. Write a `while` loop that compares `start` with `guess_me`. Print `too low` if `start` is less than `guess me`. If `start` equals `guess_me`, print `'found it!'` and exit the loop. If `start` is greater than `guess_me`, print `'oops'` and exit the loop. Increment `start` at the end of the loop.

4.3 Use a `for` loop to print the values of the list `[3, 2, 1, 0]`.

4.4 Use a list comprehension to make a list of the even numbers in `range(10)`.

4.5 Use a dictionary comprehension to create the dictionary `squares`. Use `range(10)` to return the keys, and use the square of each key as its value.

4.6 Use a set comprehension to create the set `odd` from the odd numbers in `range(10)`.

4.7 Use a generator comprehension to return the string `'Got '` and a number for the numbers in `range(10)`. Iterate through this by using a `for` loop.

4.8 Define a function called `good` that returns the list `['Harry', 'Ron', 'Hermione']`.

4.9 Define a generator function called `get_odds` that returns the odd numbers from `range(10)`. Use a `for` loop to find and print the third value returned.

4.10 Define a decorator called `test` that prints `'start'` when a function is called and `'end'` when it finishes.

4.11 Define an exception called `OopsException`. Raise this exception to see what happens. Then write the code to catch this exception and print `'Caught an oops'`.

4.12 Use `zip()` to make a dictionary called `movies` that pairs these lists: `titles = ['Creature of Habit', 'Crewel Fate']` and `plots = ['A nun turns into a monster', 'A haunted yarn shop']`.

CHAPTER 5

Py Boxes: Modules, Packages, and Programs

During your bottom-up climb, you've progressed from built-in data types to constructing ever-larger data and code structures. In this chapter, you'll finally get down to brass tacks and learn how to write realistic, large programs in Python.

Standalone Programs

Thus far, you've been writing and running code fragments such as the following within Python's interactive interpreter:

```
>>> print("This interactive snippet works.")
This interactive snippet works.
```

Now let's make your first standalone program. On your computer, create a file called *test1.py* containing this single line of Python code:

```
print("This standalone program works!")
```

Notice that there's no >>> prompt, just a single line of Python code. Ensure that there is no indentation in the line before print.

If you're running Python in a text terminal or terminal window, type the name of your Python program followed by the program filename:

```
$ python test1.py
This standalone program works!
```

You can save all of the interactive snippets that you've seen in this book so far to files and run them directly. If you're cutting and pasting, ensure that you delete the initial >>> and ... (include the final space).

Command-Line Arguments

On your computer, create a file called *test2.py* that contains these two lines:

```
import sys
print('Program arguments:', sys.argv)
```

Now, use your version of Python to run this program. Here's how it might look in a Linux or Mac OS X terminal window using a standard shell program:

```
$ python test2.py
Program arguments: ['test2.py']
$ python test2.py tra la la
Program arguments: ['test2.py', 'tra', 'la', 'la']
```

Modules and the import Statement

We're going to step up another level, creating and using Python code in more than one file. A *module* is just a file of Python code.

The text of this book is organized in a hierarchy: words, sentences, paragraphs, and chapters. Otherwise, it would be unreadable after a page or two. Code has a roughly similar bottom-up organization: data types are like words, statements are like sentences, functions are like paragraphs, and modules are like chapters. To continue the analogy, in this book, when I say that something will be explained in Chapter 8, in programming, that's like referring to code in another module.

We refer to code of other modules by using the import statement. This makes the code and variables in the imported module available to your program.

Import a Module

The simplest use of the import statement is import *module*, where *module* is the name of another Python file, without the *.py* extension. Let's simulate a weather station and print a weather report. One main program prints the report, and a separate module with a single function returns the weather description used by the report.

Here's the main program (call it *weatherman.py*):

```
import report

description = report.get_description()
print("Today's weather:", description)
```

And here is the module (*report.py*):

```
def get_description():  # see the docstring below?
    """Return random weather, just like the pros"""
    from random import choice
    possibilities = ['rain', 'snow', 'sleet', 'fog', 'sun', 'who knows']
    return choice(possibilities)
```

If you have these two files in the same directory and instruct Python to run *weather-man.py* as the main program, it will access the report module and run its get_description() function. We wrote this version of get_description() to return a random result from a list of strings, so that's what the main program will get back and print:

```
$ python weatherman.py
Today's weather: who knows
$ python weatherman.py
Today's weather: sun
$ python weatherman.py
Today's weather: sleet
```

We used imports in two different places:

- The main program *weatherman.py* imported the module report.

- In the module file *report.py*, the get_description() function imported the choice function from Python's standard random module.

We also used imports in two different ways:

- The main program called import report and then ran report.get_descrip tion().

- The get_description() function in *report.py* called from random import choice and then ran choice(possibilities).

In the first case, we imported the entire report module but needed to use report. as a prefix to get_description(). After this import statement, everything in *report.py* is available to the main program, as long as we tack report. before its name. By *qualifying* the contents of a module with the module's name, we avoid any nasty naming conflicts. There could be a get_description() function in some other module, and we would not call it by mistake.

In the second case, we're within a function and know that nothing else named choice is here, so we imported the choice() function from the random module directly. We could have written the function like the following snippet, which returns random results:

```
def get_description():
    import random
    possibilities = ['rain', 'snow', 'sleet', 'fog', 'sun', 'who knows']
    return random.choice(possibilities)
```

Like many aspects of programming, pick the style that seems the most clear to you. The module-qualified name (random.choice) is safer but requires a little more typing.

These get_description() examples showed variations of *what* to import, but but not *where* to do the importing—they all called import from inside the function. We could have imported random from outside the function:

```
>>> import random
>>> def get_description():
...     possibilities = ['rain', 'snow', 'sleet', 'fog', 'sun', 'who knows']
...     return random.choice(possibilities)
...
>>> get_description()
'who knows'
>>> get_description()
'rain'
```

You should consider importing from outside the function if the imported code might be used in more than one place, and from inside if you know its use will be limited. Some people prefer to put all their imports at the top of the file, just to make all the dependencies of their code explicit. Either way works.

Import a Module with Another Name

In our main *weatherman.py* program, we called import report. But what if you have another module with the same name or want to use a name that is more mnemonic or shorter? In such a situation, you can import using an *alias*. Let's use the alias wr:

```
import report as wr
description = wr.get_description()
print("Today's weather:", description)
```

Import Only What You Want from a Module

With Python, you can import one or more parts of a module. Each part can keep its original name or you can give it an alias. First, let's import get_description() from the report module with its original name:

```
from report import get_description
description = get_description()
print("Today's weather:", description)
```

Now, import it as do_it:

```
from report import get_description as do_it
description = do_it()
print("Today's weather:", description)
```

Module Search Path

Where does Python look for files to import? It uses a list of directory names and ZIP archive files stored in the standard sys module as the variable path. You can access and modify this list. Here's the value of sys.path for Python 3.3 on my Mac:

```
>>> import sys
>>> for place in sys.path:
...     print(place)
...

/Library/Frameworks/Python.framework/Versions/3.3/lib/python33.zip
/Library/Frameworks/Python.framework/Versions/3.3/lib/python3.3
/Library/Frameworks/Python.framework/Versions/3.3/lib/python3.3/plat-darwin
/Library/Frameworks/Python.framework/Versions/3.3/lib/python3.3/lib-dynload
/Library/Frameworks/Python.framework/Versions/3.3/lib/python3.3/site-packages
```

That initial blank output line is the empty string '', which stands for the current directory. If '' is first in sys.path, Python looks in the current directory first when you try to import something: import report looks for report.py.

The first match will be used. This means that if you define a module named random and it's in the search path before the standard library, you won't be able to access the standard library's random now.

Packages

We went from single lines of code, to multiline functions, to standalone programs, to multiple modules in the same directory. To allow Python applications to scale even more, you can organize modules into file hierarchies called *packages*.

Maybe we want different types of text forecasts: one for the next day and one for the next week. One way to structure this is to make a directory named sources, and create two modules within it: *daily.py* and *weekly.py*. Each has a function called fore cast. The daily version returns a string, and the weekly version returns a list of seven strings.

Here's the main program and the two modules. (The enumerate() function takes apart a list and feeds each item of the list to the for loop, adding a number to each item as a little bonus.)

```
from sources import daily, weekly

print("Daily forecast:", daily.forecast())
print("Weekly forecast:")
```

```
for number, outlook in enumerate(weekly.forecast(), 1):
    print(number, outlook)
def forecast():
    'fake daily forecast'
    return 'like yesterday'
def forecast():
    """Fake weekly forecast"""
    return ['snow', 'more snow', 'sleet',
        'freezing rain', 'rain', 'fog', 'hail']
```

You'll need one more thing in the sources directory: a file named __init__.py. This can be empty, but Python needs it to treat the directory containing it as a package.

Run the main *weather.py* program to see what happens:

```
$ python weather.py
Daily forecast: like yesterday
Weekly forecast:
1 snow
2 more snow
3 sleet
4 freezing rain
5 rain
6 fog
7 hail
```

The Python Standard Library

One of Python's prominent claims is that it has "batteries included"—a large standard library of modules that perform many useful tasks, and are kept separate to avoid bloating the core language. When you're about to write some Python code, it's often worthwhile to first check whether there's a standard module that already does what you want. It's surprising how often you encounter little gems in the standard library. Python also provides authoritative documentation for the modules (*http://docs.python.org/3/library*), along with a tutorial (*http://bit.ly/library-tour*). Doug Hellmann's website *Python Module of the Week* (*http://bit.ly/py-motw*) and his book *The Python Standard Library by Example* (*http://bit.ly/py-libex*) (Addison-Wesley Professional) are also very useful guides.

Upcoming chapters in this book feature many of the standard modules that are specific to the Web, systems, databases, and so on. In this section, I'll talk about some standard modules that have generic uses.

Handle Missing Keys with setdefault() and defaultdict()

You've seen that trying to access a dictionary with a nonexistent key raises an exception. Using the dictionary get() function to return a default value avoids an excep-

---

tion. The `setdefault()` function is like `get()`, but also assigns an item to the dictionary if the key is missing:

```
>>> periodic_table = {'Hydrogen': 1, 'Helium': 2}
>>> print(periodic_table)
{'Helium': 2, 'Hydrogen': 1}
```

If the key was *not* already in the dictionary, the new value is used:

```
>>> carbon = periodic_table.setdefault('Carbon', 12)
>>> carbon
12
>>> periodic_table
{'Helium': 2, 'Carbon': 12, 'Hydrogen': 1}
```

If we try to assign a different default value to an *existing* key, the original value is returned and nothing is changed:

```
>>> helium = periodic_table.setdefault('Helium', 947)
>>> helium
2
>>> periodic_table
{'Helium': 2, 'Carbon': 12, 'Hydrogen': 1}
```

`defaultdict()` is similar, but specifies the default value for any new key up front, when the dictionary is created. Its argument is a function. In this example, we pass the function `int`, which will be called as `int()` and return the integer `0`:

```
>>> from collections import defaultdict
>>> periodic_table = defaultdict(int)
```

Now, any missing value will be an integer (`int`), with the value `0`:

```
>>> periodic_table['Hydrogen'] = 1
>>> periodic_table['Lead']
0
>>> periodic_table
defaultdict(<class 'int'>, {'Lead': 0, 'Hydrogen': 1})
```

The argument to `defaultdict()` is a function that returns the value to be assigned to a missing key. In the following example, `no_idea()` is executed to return a value when needed:

```
>>> from collections import defaultdict
>>>
>>> def no_idea():
...     return 'Huh?'
...
>>> bestiary = defaultdict(no_idea)
>>> bestiary['A'] = 'Abominable Snowman'
>>> bestiary['B'] = 'Basilisk'
>>> bestiary['A']
'Abominable Snowman'
>>> bestiary['B']
```

```
'Basilisk'
>>> bestiary['C']
'Huh?'
```

You can use the functions int(), list(), or dict() to return default empty values for those types: int() returns 0, list() returns an empty list ([]), and dict() returns an empty dictionary ({}). If you omit the argument, the initial value of a new key will be set to None.

By the way, you can use lambda to define your default-making function right inside the call:

```
>>> bestiary = defaultdict(lambda: 'Huh?')
>>> bestiary['E']
'Huh?'
```

Using int is one way to make your own counter:

```
>>> from collections import defaultdict
>>> food_counter = defaultdict(int)
>>> for food in ['spam', 'spam', 'eggs', 'spam']:
...     food_counter[food] += 1
...
>>> for food, count in food_counter.items():
...     print(food, count)
...
eggs 1
spam 3
```

In the preceding example, if food_counter had been a normal dictionary instead of a defaultdict, Python would have raised an exception every time we tried to increment the dictionary element food_counter[food] because it would not have been initialized. We would have needed to do some extra work, as shown here:

```
>>> dict_counter = {}
>>> for food in ['spam', 'spam', 'eggs', 'spam']:
...     if not food in dict_counter:
...         dict_counter[food] = 0
...     dict_counter[food] += 1
...
>>> for food, count in dict_counter.items():
...     print(food, count)
...
spam 3
eggs 1
```

Count Items with Counter()

Speaking of counters, the standard library has one that does the work of the previous example and more:

```
>>> from collections import Counter
>>> breakfast = ['spam', 'spam', 'eggs', 'spam']
>>> breakfast_counter = Counter(breakfast)
>>> breakfast_counter
Counter({'spam': 3, 'eggs': 1})
```

The `most_common()` function returns all elements in descending order, or just the top count elements if given a count:

```
>>> breakfast_counter.most_common()
[('spam', 3), ('eggs', 1)]
>>> breakfast_counter.most_common(1)
[('spam', 3)]
```

You can combine counters. First, let's see again what's in `breakfast_counter`:

```
>>> breakfast_counter
>>> Counter({'spam': 3, 'eggs': 1})
```

This time, we'll make a new list called `lunch`, and a counter called `lunch_counter`:

```
>>> lunch = ['eggs', 'eggs', 'bacon']
>>> lunch_counter = Counter(lunch)
>>> lunch_counter
Counter({'eggs': 2, 'bacon': 1})
```

The first way we combine the two counters is by addition, using +:

```
>>> breakfast_counter + lunch_counter
Counter({'spam': 3, 'eggs': 3, 'bacon': 1})
```

As you might expect, you subtract one counter from another by using -. What's for breakfast but not for lunch?

```
>>> breakfast_counter - lunch_counter
Counter({'spam': 3})
```

Okay, now what can we have for lunch that we can't have for breakfast?

```
>>> lunch_counter - breakfast_counter
Counter({'bacon': 1, 'eggs': 1})
```

Similar to sets in Chapter 4, you can get common items by using the intersection operator &:

```
>>> breakfast_counter & lunch_counter
Counter({'eggs': 1})
```

The intersection picked the common element ('eggs') with the lower count. This makes sense: breakfast only offered one egg, so that's the common count.

Finally, you can get all items by using the union operator |:

```
>>> breakfast_counter | lunch_counter
Counter({'spam': 3, 'eggs': 2, 'bacon': 1})
```

The item 'eggs' was again common to both. Unlike addition, union didn't add their counts, but picked the one with the larger count.

Order by Key with OrderedDict()

Many of the code examples in the early chapters of this book demonstrate that the order of keys in a dictionary is not predictable: you might add keys a, b, and c in that order, but keys() might return c, a, b. Here's a repurposed example from Chapter 1:

```
>>> quotes = {
...       'Moe': 'A wise guy, huh?',
...       'Larry': 'Ow!',
...       'Curly': 'Nyuk nyuk!',
...       }
>>> for stooge in quotes:
...    print(stooge)
...
Larry
Curly
Moe
```

An OrderedDict() remembers the order of key addition and returns them in the same order from an iterator. Try creating an OrderedDict from a sequence of (*key*, *value*) tuples:

```
>>> from collections import OrderedDict
>>> quotes = OrderedDict([
...       ('Moe', 'A wise guy, huh?'),
...       ('Larry', 'Ow!'),
...       ('Curly', 'Nyuk nyuk!'),
...       ])
>>>
>>> for stooge in quotes:
...       print(stooge)
...
Moe
Larry
Curly
```

Stack + Queue == deque

A deque (pronounced *deck*) is a double-ended queue, which has features of both a stack and a queue. It's useful when you want to add and delete items from either end of a sequence. Here, we'll work from both ends of a word to the middle to see if it's a palindrome. The function popleft() removes the leftmost item from the deque and returns it; pop() removes the rightmost item and returns it. Together, they work from the ends toward the middle. As long as the end characters match, it keeps popping until it reaches the middle:

```
>>> def palindrome(word):
...     from collections import deque
...     dq = deque(word)
...     while len(dq) > 1:
...         if dq.popleft() != dq.pop():
...             return False
...     return True
...
...
>>> palindrome('a')
True
>>> palindrome('racecar')
True
>>> palindrome('')
True
>>> palindrome('radar')
True
>>> palindrome('halibut')
False
```

I used this as a simple illustration of deques. If you really wanted a quick palindrome checker, it would be a lot simpler to just compare a string with its reverse. Python doesn't have a `reverse()` function for strings, but it does have a way to reverse a string with a slice, as illustrated here:

```
>>> def another_palindrome(word):
...     return word == word[::-1]
...
>>> another_palindrome('radar')
True
>>> another_palindrome('halibut')
False
```

Iterate over Code Structures with itertools

`itertools` (*http://bit.ly/py-itertools*) contains special-purpose iterator functions. Each returns one item at a time when called within a `for ... in` loop, and remembers its state between calls.

`chain()` runs through its arguments as though they were a single iterable:

```
>>> import itertools
>>> for item in itertools.chain([1, 2], ['a', 'b']):
...     print(item)
...
1
2
a
b
```

`cycle()` is an infinite iterator, cycling through its arguments:

```
>>> import itertools
>>> for item in itertools.cycle([1, 2]):
...     print(item)
...
1
2
1
2
.
.
.
```

…and so on.

accumulate() calculates accumulated values. By default, it calculates the sum:

```
>>> import itertools
>>> for item in itertools.accumulate([1, 2, 3, 4]):
...     print(item)
...
1
3
6
10
```

You can provide a function as the second argument to accumulate(), and it will be used instead of addition. The function should take two arguments and return a single result. This example calculates an accumulated product:

```
>>> import itertools
>>> def multiply(a, b):
...     return a * b
...
>>> for item in itertools.accumulate([1, 2, 3, 4], multiply):
...     print(item)
...
1
2
6
24
```

The itertools module has many more functions, notably some for combinations and permutations that can be time savers when the need arises.

Print Nicely with pprint()

All of our examples have used print() (or just the variable name, in the interactive interpreter) to print things. Sometimes, the results are hard to read. We need a *pretty printer* such as pprint():

```
>>> from pprint import pprint
>>> quotes = OrderedDict([
```

```
...        ('Moe', 'A wise guy, huh?'),
...        ('Larry', 'Ow!'),
...        ('Curly', 'Nyuk nyuk!'),
...        ])
>>>
```

Plain old `print()` just dumps things out there:

```
>>> print(quotes)
OrderedDict([('Moe', 'A wise guy, huh?'), ('Larry', 'Ow!'), ('Curly', 'Nyuk nyuk!')])
```

However, `pprint()` tries to align elements for better readability:

```
>>> pprint(quotes)
{'Moe': 'A wise guy, huh?',
 'Larry': 'Ow!',
 'Curly': 'Nyuk nyuk!'}
```

More Batteries: Get Other Python Code

Sometimes, the standard library doesn't have what you need, or doesn't do it in quite the right way. There's an entire world of open-source, third-party Python software. Good resources include:

- PyPi (*http://pypi.python.org*) (also known as the Cheese Shop, after an old Monty Python skit)
- github (*https://github.com/Python*)
- readthedocs (*https://readthedocs.org/*)

You can find many smaller code examples at activestate (*http://code.activestate.com/ recipes/langs/python/*).

Almost all of the Python code in this book uses the standard Python installation on your computer, which includes all the built-ins and the standard library. External packages are featured in some places: I mentioned `requests` in Chapter 1, and have more details in "Beyond the Standard Library: Requests" on page 229. Appendix D shows how to install third-party Python software, along with many other nuts-and-bolts development details.

Things to Do

5.1. Create a file called *zoo.py*. In it, define a function called `hours()` that prints the string `'Open 9-5 daily'`. Then, use the interactive interpreter to import the `zoo` module and call its `hours()` function.

5.2. In the interactive interpreter, import the `zoo` module as `menagerie` and call its `hours()` function.

5.3. Staying in the interpreter, import the `hours()` function from `zoo` directly and call it.

5.4. Import the `hours()` function as `info` and call it.

5.5. Make a dictionary called `plain` with the key-value pairs `'a': 1`, `'b': 2`, and `'c': 3`, and then print it.

5.6. Make an `OrderedDict` called `fancy` from the same pairs listed in 5.5 and print it. Did it print in the same order as `plain`?

5.7. Make a `defaultdict` called `dict_of_lists` and pass it the argument `list`. Make the list `dict_of_lists['a']` and append the value `'something for a'` to it in one assignment. Print `dict_of_lists['a']`.

CHAPTER 6

Oh Oh: Objects and Classes

No object is mysterious. The mystery is your eye.
—Elizabeth Bowen

Take an object. Do something to it. Do something else to it.
—Jasper Johns

Up to this point, you've seen data structures such as strings and dictionaries, and code structures such as functions and modules. In this chapter, you'll deal with custom data structures: *objects*.

What Are Objects?

As I mention in Chapter 2, everything in Python, from numbers to modules, is an object. However, Python hides most of the object machinery by means of special syntax. You can type `num = 7` to create a object of type integer with the value 7, and assign an object reference to the name `num`. The only time you need to look inside objects is when you want to make your own or modify the behavior of existing objects. You'll see how to do both in this chapter.

An object contains both data (variables, called *attributes*) and code (functions, called *methods*). It represents a unique instance of some concrete thing. For example, the integer object with the value 7 is an object that facilitates methods such as addition and multiplication, as is demonstrated in "Numbers" on page 21. 8 is a different object. This means there's an Integer class in Python, to which both 7 and 8 belong. The strings `'cat'` and `'duck'` are also objects in Python, and have string methods that you've seen, such as `capitalize()` and `replace()`.

When you create new objects no one has ever created before, you must create a class that indicates what they contain.

Think of objects as nouns and their methods as verbs. An object represents an individual thing, and its methods define how it interacts with other things.

Unlike modules, you can have multiple objects at the same time, each one with different values for its attributes. They're like super data structures, with code thrown in.

Define a Class with class

In Chapter 1, I compare an object to a plastic box. A *class* is like the mold that makes that box. For instance, a `String` is the built-in Python class that makes string objects such as `'cat'` and `'duck'`. Python has many other built-in classes to create the other standard data types, including lists, dictionaries, and so on. To create your own custom object in Python, you first need to define a class by using the `class` keyword. Let's walk through a simple example.

Suppose that you want to define objects to represent information about people. Each object will represent one person. You'll first want to define a class called `Person` as the mold. In the examples that follow, we'll try more than one version of this class as we build up from the simplest class to ones that actually do something useful.

Our first try is the simplest possible class, an empty one:

```
>>> class Person():
...     pass
```

Just as with functions, we needed to say `pass` to indicate that this class was empty. This definition is the bare minimum to create an object. You create an object from a class by calling the class name as though it were a function:

```
>>> someone = Person()
```

In this case, `Person()` creates an individual object from the `Person` class and assigns it the name `someone`. But, our `Person` class was empty, so the `someone` object that we create from it just sits there and can't do anything else. You would never actually define such a class, and I'm only showing it here to build up to the next example.

Let's try again, this time including the special Python object initialization method `__init__`:

```
>>> class Person():
...     def __init__(self):
...         pass
```

This is what you'll see in real Python class definitions. I admit that the `__init__()` and `self` look strange. `__init__()` is the special Python name for a method that initializes an individual object from its class definition. [1] The `self` argument specifies that it refers to the individual object itself.

When you define `__init__()` in a class definition, its first parameter should be `self`. Although `self` is not a reserved word in Python, it's common usage. No one reading your code later (including you!) will need to guess what you meant if you use `self`.

But even that second `Person` definition didn't create an object that really did anything. The third try is the charm that really shows how to create a simple object in Python. This time, we'll add the parameter `name` to the initialization method:

```
>>> class Person():
...     def __init__(self, name):
...         self.name = name
...
>>>
```

Now, we can create an object from the `Person` class by passing a string for the `name` parameter:

```
>>> hunter = Person('Elmer Fudd')
```

Here's what this line of code does:

- Looks up the definition of the `Person` class
- *Instantiates* (creates) a new object in memory
- Calls the object's `__init__` method, passing this newly-created object as `self` and the other argument (`'Elmer Fudd'`) as `name`
- Stores the value of `name` in the object
- Returns the new object
- Attaches the name `hunter` to the object

This new object is like any other object in Python. You can use it as an element of a list, tuple, dictionary, or set. You can pass it to a function as an argument, or return it as a result.

What about the `name` value that we passed in? It was saved with the object as an attribute. You can read and write it directly:

```
>>> print('The mighty hunter: ', hunter.name)
The mighty hunter: Elmer Fudd
```

---

1 You'll see many examples of double underscores in Python names; to save syllables, some people pronounce them as *dunder*.

Remember, *inside* the Person class definition, you access the name attribute as self.name. When you create an actual object such as hunter, you refer to it as hunter.name.

It is *not* necessary to have an __init__ method in every class definition; it's used to do anything that's needed to distinguish this object from others created from the same class.

Inheritance

When you're trying to solve some coding problem, often you'll find an existing class that creates objects that do almost what you need. What can you do? You could modify this old class, but you'll make it more complicated, and you might break something that used to work.

Of course, you could write a new class, cutting and pasting from the old one and merging your new code. But this means that you have more code to maintain, and the parts of the old and new classes that used to work the same might drift apart because they're now in separate places.

The solution is *inheritance*: creating a new class from an existing class but with some additions or changes. It's an excellent way to reuse code. When you use inheritance, the new class can automatically use all the code from the old class but without copying any of it.

You define only what you need to add or change in the new class, and this overrides the behavior of the old class. The original class is called a *parent*, *superclass*, or *base class*; the new class is called a *child*, *subclass*, or *derived class*. These terms are interchangeable in object-oriented programming.

So, let's inherit something. We'll define an empty class called Car. Next, define a subclass of Car called Yugo. You define a subclass by using the same class keyword but with the parent class name inside the parentheses (class Yugo(Car) below):

```
>>> class Car():
...     pass
...
>>> class Yugo(Car):
...     pass
...
```

Next, create an object from each class:

```
>>> give_me_a_car = Car()
>>> give_me_a_yugo = Yugo()
```

A child class is a specialization of a parent class; in object-oriented lingo, Yugo *is-a* Car. The object named give_me_a_yugo is an instance of class Yugo, but it also inherits whatever a Car can do. In this case, Car and Yugo are as useful as deckhands on a submarine, so let's try new class definitions that actually do something:

```
>>> class Car():
...     def exclaim(self):
...         print("I'm a Car!")
...
>>> class Yugo(Car):
...     pass
...
```

Finally, make one object from each class and call the exclaim method:

```
>>> give_me_a_car = Car()
>>> give_me_a_yugo = Yugo()
>>> give_me_a_car.exclaim()
I'm a Car!
>>> give_me_a_yugo.exclaim()
I'm a Car!
```

Without doing anything special, Yugo inherited the exclaim() method from Car. In fact, Yugo says that it *is* a Car, which might lead to an identity crisis. Let's see what we can do about that.

Override a Method

As you just saw, a new class initially inherits everything from its parent class. Moving forward, you'll see how to replace or *override* a parent method. Yugo should probably be different from Car in some way; otherwise, what's the point of defining a new class? Let's change how the exclaim() method works for a Yugo:

```
>>> class Car():
...     def exclaim(self):
...         print("I'm a Car!")
...
>>> class Yugo(Car):
...     def exclaim(self):
...         print("I'm a Yugo! Much like a Car, but more Yugo-ish.")
...
```

Now, make two objects from these classes:

```
>>> give_me_a_car = Car()
>>> give_me_a_yugo = Yugo()
```

What do they say?

```
>>> give_me_a_car.exclaim()
I'm a Car!
>>> give_me_a_yugo.exclaim()
I'm a Yugo! Much like a Car, but more Yugo-ish.
```

In these examples, we overrode the `exclaim()` method. We can override any methods, including `__init__()`. Here's another example that uses our earlier `Person` class. Let's make subclasses that represent doctors (`MDPerson`) and lawyers (`JDPerson`):

```
>>> class Person():
...     def __init__(self, name):
...         self.name = name
...
>>> class MDPerson(Person):
...     def __init__(self, name):
...         self.name = "Doctor " + name
...
>>> class JDPerson(Person):
...     def __init__(self, name):
...         self.name = name + ", Esquire"
...
```

In these cases, the initialization method `__init__()` takes the same arguments as the parent `Person` class but stores the value of `name` differently inside the object instance:

```
>>> person = Person('Fudd')
>>> doctor = MDPerson('Fudd')
>>> lawyer = JDPerson('Fudd')
>>> print(person.name)
Fudd
>>> print(doctor.name)
Doctor Fudd
>>> print(lawyer.name)
Fudd, Esquire
```

Add a Method

The child class can also *add* a method that was not present in its parent class. Going back to classes `Car` and `Yugo`, we'll define the new method `need_a_push()` for class `Yugo` only:

```
>>> class Car():
...     def exclaim(self):
...         print("I'm a Car!")
...
>>> class Yugo(Car):
...     def exclaim(self):
...         print("I'm a Yugo! Much like a Car, but more Yugo-ish.")
...     def need_a_push(self):
...         print("A little help here?")
...
```

Next, make a Car and a Yugo:

```
>>> give_me_a_car = Car()
>>> give_me_a_yugo = Yugo()
```

A Yugo object can react to a `need_a_push()` method call:

```
>>> give_me_a_yugo.need_a_push()
A little help here?
```

But a generic `Car` object cannot:

```
>>> give_me_a_car.need_a_push()
Traceback (most recent call last):
  File "<stdin>", line 1, in <module>
AttributeError: 'Car' object has no attribute 'need_a_push'
```

At this point, a Yugo can do something that a Car cannot, and the distinct personality of a Yugo can emerge.

Get Help from Your Parent with super

We saw how the child class could add or override a method from the parent. What if it wanted to call that parent method? "I'm glad you asked," says `super()`. We'll define a new class called `EmailPerson` that represents a `Person` with an email address. First, our familiar `Person` definition:

```
>>> class Person():
...     def __init__(self, name):
...         self.name = name
...
```

Notice that the `__init__()` call in the following subclass has an additional `email` parameter:

```
>>> class EmailPerson(Person):
...     def __init__(self, name, email):
...         super().__init__(name)
...         self.email = email
```

When you define an `__init__()` method for your class, you're replacing the `__init__()` method of its parent class, and the latter is not called automatically anymore. As a result, we need to call it explicitly. Here's what's happening:

- The `super()` gets the definition of the parent class, `Person`.

- The `__init__()` method calls the `Person.__init__()` method. It takes care of passing the `self` argument to the superclass, so you just need to give it any optional arguments. In our case, the only other argument `Person()` accepts is `name`.

- The `self.email = email` line is the new code that makes this `EmailPerson` different from a `Person`.

Moving on, let's make one of these creatures:

```
>>> bob = EmailPerson('Bob Frapples', 'bob@frapples.com')
```

We should be able to access both the `name` and `email` attributes:

```
>>> bob.name
'Bob Frapples'
>>> bob.email
'bob@frapples.com'
```

Why didn't we just define our new class as follows?

```
>>> class EmailPerson(Person):
...     def __init__(self, name, email):
...         self.name = name
...         self.email = email
```

We could have done that, but it would have defeated our use of inheritance. We used `super()` to make `Person` do its work, the same as a plain `Person` object would. There's another benefit: if the definition of `Person` changes in the future, using `super()` will ensure that the attributes and methods that `EmailPerson` inherits from `Person` will reflect the change.

Use `super()` when the child is doing something its own way but still needs something from the parent (as in real life).

In self Defense

One criticism of Python (besides the use of whitespace) is the need to include `self` as the first argument to instance methods (the kind of method you've seen in the previous examples). Python uses the `self` argument to find the right object's attributes and methods. For an example, I'll show how you would call an object's method, and what Python actually does behind the scenes.

Remember class `Car` from earlier examples? Let's call its `exclaim()` method again:

```
>>> car = Car()
>>> car.exclaim()
I'm a Car!
```

Here's what Python actually does, under the hood:

- Look up the class (`Car`) of the object `car`.
- Pass the object `car` to the `exclaim()` method of the `Car` class as the `self` parameter.

Just for fun, you can even run it this way yourself and it will work the same as the normal (`car.exclaim()`) syntax:

```
>>> Car.exclaim(car)
I'm a Car!
```

However, there's never a reason to use that lengthier style.

Get and Set Attribute Values with Properties

Some object-oriented languages support private object attributes that can't be accessed directly from the outside; programmers often need to write *getter* and *setter* methods to read and write the values of such private attributes.

Python doesn't need getters or setters, because all attributes and methods are public, and you're expected to behave yourself. If direct access to attributes makes you nervous, you can certainly write getters and setters. But be Pythonic—use *properties*.

In this example, we'll define a Duck class with a single attribute called hidden_name. (In the next section, I'll show you a better way to name attributes that you want to keep private.) We don't want people to access this directly, so we'll define two methods: a getter (get_name()) and a setter (set_name()). I've added a print() statement to each method to show when it's being called. Finally, we define these methods as properties of the name attribute:

```
>>> class Duck():
...     def __init__(self, input_name):
...         self.hidden_name = input_name
...     def get_name(self):
...         print('inside the getter')
...         return self.hidden_name
...     def set_name(self, input_name):
...         print('inside the setter')
...         self.hidden_name = input_name
...     name = property(get_name, set_name)
```

The new methods act as normal getters and setters until that last line; it defines the two methods as properties of the attribute called name. The first argument to prop erty() is the getter method, and the second is the setter. Now, when you refer to the name of any Duck object, it actually calls the get_name() method to return it:

```
>>> fowl = Duck('Howard')
>>> fowl.name
inside the getter
'Howard'
```

You can still call get_name() directly, too, like a normal getter method:

```
>>> fowl.get_name()
inside the getter
'Howard'
```

When you assign a value to the name attribute, the set_name() method will be called:

```
>>> fowl.name = 'Daffy'
inside the setter
```

```
>>> fowl.name
inside the getter
'Daffy'
```

You can still call the set_name() method directly:

```
>>> fowl.set_name('Daffy')
inside the setter
>>> fowl.name
inside the getter
'Daffy'
```

Another way to define properties is with *decorators*. In this next example, we'll define two different methods, each called name() but preceded by different decorators:

- @property, which goes before the getter method
- @name.setter, which goes before the setter method

Here's how they actually look in the code:

```
>>> class Duck():
...     def __init__(self, input_name):
...         self.hidden_name = input_name
...     @property
...     def name(self):
...         print('inside the getter')
...         return self.hidden_name
...     @name.setter
...     def name(self, input_name):
...         print('inside the setter')
...         self.hidden_name = input_name
```

You can still access name as though it were an attribute, but there are no visible get_name() or set_name() methods:

```
>>> fowl = Duck('Howard')
>>> fowl.name
inside the getter
'Howard'
>>> fowl.name = 'Donald'
inside the setter
>>> fowl.name
inside the getter
'Donald'
```

If anyone guessed that we called our attribute hidden_name, they could still read and write it directly as fowl.hidden_name. In the next section, you'll see how Python provides a special way to name private attributes.

In both of the previous examples, we used the name property to refer to a single attribute (ours was called hidden_name) stored within the object. A property can refer to a *computed value*, as well. Let's define a Circle class that has a radius attribute and a computed diameter property:

```
>>> class Circle():
...     def __init__(self, radius):
...         self.radius = radius
...     @property
...     def diameter(self):
...         return 2 * self.radius
...
```

We create a Circle object with an initial value for its radius:

```
>>> c = Circle(5)
>>> c.radius
5
```

We can refer to diameter as if it were an attribute such as radius:

```
>>> c.diameter
10
```

Here's the fun part: we can change the radius attribute at any time, and the diameter property will be computed from the current value of radius:

```
>>> c.radius = 7
>>> c.diameter
14
```

If you don't specify a setter property for an attribute, you can't set it from the outside. This is handy for read-only attributes:

```
>>> c.diameter = 20
Traceback (most recent call last):
  File "<stdin>", line 1, in <module>
AttributeError: can't set attribute
```

There's one more big advantage of using a property over direct attribute access: if you ever change the definition of the attribute, you only need to fix the code within the class definition, not in all the callers.

Name Mangling for Privacy

In the Duck class example in the previous section, we called our (not completely) hidden attribute hidden_name. Python has a naming convention for attributes that should not be visible outside of their class definition: begin by using with two underscores (__).

Let's rename hidden_name to __name, as demonstrated here:

```
>>> class Duck():
...     def __init__(self, input_name):
...         self.__name = input_name
...     @property
...     def name(self):
...         print('inside the getter')
...         return self.__name
...     @name.setter
...     def name(self, input_name):
...         print('inside the setter')
...         self.__name = input_name
...
```

Take a moment to see if everything still works:

```
>>> fowl = Duck('Howard')
>>> fowl.name
inside the getter
'Howard'
>>> fowl.name = 'Donald'
inside the setter
>>> fowl.name
inside the getter
'Donald'
```

Looks good. And, you can't access the __name attribute:

```
>>> fowl.__name
Traceback (most recent call last):
  File "<stdin>", line 1, in <module>
AttributeError: 'Duck' object has no attribute '__name'
```

This naming convention doesn't make it private, but Python does *mangle* the name to make it unlikely for external code to stumble upon it. If you're curious and promise not to tell everyone, here's what it becomes:

```
>>> fowl._Duck__name
'Donald'
```

Notice that it didn't print inside the getter. Although this isn't perfect protection, name mangling discourages accidental or intentional direct access to the attribute.

Method Types

Some data (*attributes*) and functions (*methods*) are part of the class itself, and some are part of the objects that are created from that class.

When you see an initial self argument in methods within a class definition, it's an *instance method*. These are the types of methods that you would normally write when creating your own classes. The first parameter of an instance method is self, and Python passes the object to the method when you call it.

In contrast, a *class method* affects the class as a whole. Any change you make to the class affects all of its objects. Within a class definition, a preceding @classmethod decorator indicates that that following function is a class method. Also, the first parameter to the method is the class itself. The Python tradition is to call the parameter cls, because class is a reserved word and can't be used here. Let's define a class method for A that counts how many object instances have been made from it:

```
>>> class A():
...     count = 0
...     def __init__(self):
...         A.count += 1
...     def exclaim(self):
...         print("I'm an A!")
...     @classmethod
...     def kids(cls):
...         print("A has", cls.count, "little objects.")
...
>>>
>>> easy_a = A()
>>> breezy_a = A()
>>> wheezy_a = A()
>>> A.kids()
A has 3 little objects.
```

Notice that we referred to A.count (the class attribute) rather than self.count (which would be an object instance attribute). In the kids() method, we used cls.count, but we could just as well have used A.count.

A third type of method in a class definition affects neither the class nor its objects; it's just in there for convenience instead of floating around on its own. It's a *static method*, preceded by a @staticmethod decorator, with no initial self or class parameter. Here's an example that serves as a commercial for the class CoyoteWeapon:

```
>>> class CoyoteWeapon():
...     @staticmethod
...     def commercial():
...         print('This CoyoteWeapon has been brought to you by Acme')
...
>>>
>>> CoyoteWeapon.commercial()
This CoyoteWeapon has been brought to you by Acme
```

Notice that we didn't need to create an object from class CoyoteWeapon to access this method. Very class-y.

Duck Typing

Python has a loose implementation of *polymorphism*; this means that it applies the same operation to different objects, regardless of their class.

Let's use the same __init__() initializer for all three Quote classes now, but add two new functions:

- who() just returns the value of the saved person string
- says() returns the saved words string with the specific punctuation

And here they are in action:

```
>>> class Quote():
...     def __init__(self, person, words):
...         self.person = person
...         self.words = words
...     def who(self):
...         return self.person
...     def says(self):
...         return self.words + '.'
...
>>> class QuestionQuote(Quote):
...     def says(self):
...         return self.words + '?'
...
>>> class ExclamationQuote(Quote):
...     def says(self):
...         return self.words + '!'
...
>>>
```

We didn't change how QuestionQuote or ExclamationQuote were initialized, so we didn't override their __init__() methods. Python then automatically calls the __init__() method of the parent class Quote to store the instance variables person and words. That's why we can access self.words in objects created from the subclasses QuestionQuote and ExclamationQuote.

Next up, let's make some objects:

```
>>> hunter = Quote('Elmer Fudd', "I'm hunting wabbits")
>>> print(hunter.who(), 'says:', hunter.says())
Elmer Fudd says: I'm hunting wabbits.

>>> hunted1 = QuestionQuote('Bugs Bunny', "What's up, doc")
>>> print(hunted1.who(), 'says:', hunted1.says())
Bugs Bunny says: What's up, doc?

>>> hunted2 = ExclamationQuote('Daffy Duck', "It's rabbit season")
>>> print(hunted2.who(), 'says:', hunted2.says())
Daffy Duck says: It's rabbit season!
```

Three different versions of the says() method provide different behavior for the three classes. This is traditional polymorphism in object-oriented languages. Python goes a little further and lets you run the who() and says() methods of *any* objects that have them. Let's define a class called `BabblingBrook` that has no relation to our previous woodsy hunter and huntees (descendants of the `Quote` class):

```
>>> class BabblingBrook():
...     def who(self):
...         return 'Brook'
...     def says(self):
...         return 'Babble'
...
>>> brook = BabblingBrook()
```

Now, run the `who()` and `says()` methods of various objects, one (`brook`) completely unrelated to the others:

```
>>> def who_says(obj):
...     print(obj.who(), 'says', obj.says())
...
>>> who_says(hunter)
Elmer Fudd says I'm hunting wabbits.
>>> who_says(hunted1)
Bugs Bunny says What's up, doc?
>>> who_says(hunted2)
Daffy Duck says It's rabbit season!
>>> who_says(brook)
Brook says Babble
```

This behavior is sometimes called *duck typing*, after the old saying:

> If it walks like a duck and quacks like a duck, it's a duck.
>
> —A Wise Person

Special Methods

You can now create and use basic objects, but now let's go a bit deeper and do more.

When you type something such as `a = 3 + 8`, how do the integer objects with values 3 and 8 know how to implement +? Also, how does `a` know how to use = to get the result? You can get at these operators by using Python's *special methods* (you might also see them called *magic methods*). You don't need Gandalf to perform any magic, and they're not even complicated.

The names of these methods begin and end with double underscores (__). You've already seen one: `__init__` initializes a newly created object from its class definition and any arguments that were passed in.

Suppose that you have a simple `Word` class, and you want an `equals()` method that compares two words but ignores case. That is, a `Word` containing the value `'ha'` would be considered equal to one containing `'HA'`.

The example that follows is a first attempt, with a normal method we're calling equals(). self.text is the text string that this Word object contains, and the equals() method compares it with the text string of word2 (another Word object):

```
>>> class Word():
...     def __init__(self, text):
...         self.text = text
...
...     def equals(self, word2):
...         return self.text.lower() == word2.text.lower()
...
```

Then, make three Word objects from three different text strings:

```
>>> first = Word('ha')
>>> second = Word('HA')
>>> third = Word('eh')
```

When strings 'ha' and 'HA' are compared to lowercase, they should be equal:

```
>>> first.equals(second)
True
```

But the string 'eh' will not match 'ha':

```
>>> first.equals(third)
False
```

We defined the method equals() to do this lowercase conversion and comparison. It would be nice to just say if first == second, just like Python's built-in types. So, let's do that. We change the equals() method to the special name __eq__() (you'll see why in a moment):

```
>>> class Word():
...     def __init__(self, text):
...         self.text = text
...     def __eq__(self, word2):
...         return self.text.lower() == word2.text.lower()
...
```

Let's see if it works:

```
>>> first = Word('ha')
>>> second = Word('HA')
>>> third = Word('eh')
>>> first == second
True
>>> first == third
False
```

Magic! All we needed was the Python's special method name for testing equality, __eq__(). Tables 6-1 and 6-2 list the names of the most useful magic methods.

Table 6-1. Magic methods for comparison

__eq__(*self, other*) *self == other*

__ne__(*self, other*) *self != other*

__lt__(*self, other*) *self < other*

__gt__(*self, other*) *self > other*

__le__(*self, other*) *self <= other*

__ge__(*self, other*) *self >= other*

Table 6-2. Magic methods for math

__add__(*self, other*) *self + other*

__sub__(*self, other*) *self - other*

__mul__(*self, other*) *self * other*

__floordiv__(*self, other*) *self // other*

__truediv__(*self, other*) *self / other*

__mod__(*self, other*) *self % other*

__pow__(*self, other*) *self ** other*

You aren't restricted to use the math operators such as + (magic method __add__())
and - (magic method __sub__()) with numbers. For instance, Python string objects
use + for concatenation and * for duplication. There are many more, documented
online at Special method names (*http://bit.ly/pydocs-smn*). The most common among
them are presented in Table 6-3.

Table 6-3. Other, miscellaneous magic methods

__str__(*self*) str(*self*)

__repr__(*self*) repr(*self*)

__len__(*self*) len(*self*)

Besides __init__(), you might find yourself using __str__() the most in your own methods. It's how you print your object. It's used by print(), str(), and the string formatters that you can read about in Chapter 7. The interactive interpreter uses the __repr__() function to echo variables to output. If you fail to define either __str__() or __repr__(), you get Python's default string version of your object:

```
>>> first = Word('ha')
>>> first
<__main__.Word object at 0x1006ba3d0>
>>> print(first)
<__main__.Word object at 0x1006ba3d0>
```

Let's add both __str__() and __repr__() methods to the Word class to make it prettier:

```
>>> class Word():
...     def __init__(self, text):
...         self.text = text
...     def __eq__(self, word2):
...         return self.text.lower() == word2.text.lower()
...     def __str__(self):
...         return self.text
...     def __repr__(self):
...         return 'Word("'  self.text  '")'
...
>>> first = Word('ha')
>>> first            # uses __repr__
Word("ha")
>>> print(first)    # uses __str__
ha
```

To explore even more special methods, check out the Python documentation (*http://bit.ly/pydocs-smn*).

Aggregation and Composition

Inheritance is a good technique to use when you want a child class to act like its parent class most of the time (when child *is-a* parent). It's tempting to build elaborate inheritance hierarchies, but sometimes *composition* or *aggregation* make more sense. What's the difference? In composition, one thing is part of another. A duck *is-a* bird (inheritance), but *has-a* tail (composition). A tail is not a kind of duck, but part of a duck. In this next example, let's make bill and tail objects and provide them to a new duck object:

```
>>> class Bill():
...     def __init__(self, description):
...         self.description = description
...
>>> class Tail():
...     def __init__(self, length):
```

```
...            self.length = length
...
>>> class Duck():
...     def __init__(self, bill, tail):
...         self.bill = bill
...         self.tail = tail
...     def about(self):
...         print('This duck has a', self.bill.description,
...             'bill and a', self.tail.length, 'tail')
...
>>> a_tail = Tail('long')
>>> a_bill = Bill('wide orange')
>>> duck = Duck(a_bill, a_tail)
>>> duck.about()
This duck has a wide orange bill and a long tail
```

Aggregation expresses relationships, but is a little looser: one thing *uses* another, but both exist independently. A duck *uses* a lake, but one is not a part of the other.

When to Use Classes and Objects versus Modules

Here are some guidelines for deciding whether to put your code in a class or a module:

- Objects are most useful when you need a number of individual instances that have similar behavior (methods), but differ in their internal states (attributes).

- Classes support inheritance, modules don't.

- If you want only one of something, a module might be best. No matter how many times a Python module is referenced in a program, only one copy is loaded. (Java and C++ programmers: if you're familiar with the book *Design Patterns: Elements of Reusable Object-Oriented Software* by Erich Gamma, you can use a Python module as a *singleton*.)

- If you have a number of variables that contain multiple values and can be passed as arguments to multiple functions, it might be better to define them as classes. For example, you might use a dictionary with keys such as `size` and `color` to represent a color image. You could create a different dictionary for each image in your program, and pass them as arguments to functions such as `scale()` or `transform()`. This can get messy as you add keys and functions. It's more coherent to define an `Image` class with attributes `size` or `color` and methods `scale()` and `transform()`. Then, all the data and methods for a color image are defined in one place.

- Use the simplest solution to the problem. A dictionary, list, or tuple is simpler, smaller, and faster than a module, which is usually simpler than a class.

Guido's advice:

> Avoid overengineering datastructures. Tuples are better than objects (try namedtuple too though). Prefer simple fields over getter/setter functions ... Built-in datatypes are your friends. Use more numbers, strings, tuples, lists, sets, dicts. Also check out the collections library, esp. deque.
>
> —Guido van Rossum (*http://bit.ly/ guido-vr*)

Named Tuples

Because Guido just mentioned them and I haven't yet, this is a good place to talk about *named tuples*. A named tuple is a subclass of tuples with which you can access values by name (with .*name*) as well as by position (with [*offset*]).

Let's take the example from the previous section and convert the Duck class to a named tuple, with bill and tail as simple string attributes. We'll call the namedtuple function with two arguments:

- The name
- A string of the field names, separated by spaces

Named tuples are not automatically supplied with Python, so you need to load a module before using them. We do that in the first line of the following example:

```
>>> from collections import namedtuple
>>> Duck = namedtuple('Duck', 'bill tail')
>>> duck = Duck('wide orange', 'long')
>>> duck
Duck(bill='wide orange', tail='long')
>>> duck.bill
'wide orange'
>>> duck.tail
'long'
```

You can also make a named tuple from a dictionary:

```
>>> parts = {'bill': 'wide orange', 'tail': 'long'}
>>> duck2 = Duck(**parts)
>>> duck2
Duck(bill='wide orange', tail='long')
```

In the preceding code, take a look at **parts. This is a *keyword argument*. It extracts the keys and values from the parts dictionary and supplies them as arguments to Duck(). It has the same effect as:

```
>>> duck2 = Duck(bill = 'wide orange', tail = 'long')
```

Named tuples are immutable, but you can replace one or more fields and return another named tuple:

```
>>> duck3 = duck2._replace(tail='magnificent', bill='crushing')
>>> duck3
Duck(bill='crushing', tail='magnificent')
```

We could have defined duck as a dictionary:

```
>>> duck_dict = {'bill': 'wide orange', 'tail': 'long'}
>>> duck_dict
{'tail': 'long', 'bill': 'wide orange'}
```

You can add fields to a dictionary:

```
>>> duck_dict['color'] = 'green'
>>> duck_dict
{'color': 'green', 'tail': 'long', 'bill': 'wide orange'}
```

But not to a named tuple:

```
>>> duck.color = 'green'
Traceback (most recent call last):
  File "<stdin>", line 1, in <module>
AttributeError: 'dict' object has no attribute 'color'
```

To recap, here are some of the pros of a named tuple:

- It looks and acts like an immutable object.
- It is more space- and time-efficient than objects.
- You can access attributes by using dot notation instead of dictionary-style square brackets.
- You can use it as a dictionary key.

Things to Do

6.1. Make a class called Thing with no contents and print it. Then, create an object called example from this class and also print it. Are the printed values the same or different?

6.2. Make a new class called Thing2 and assign the value 'abc' to a class attribute called letters. Print letters.

6.3. Make yet another class called, of course, Thing3. This time, assign the value 'xyz' to an instance (object) attribute called letters. Print letters. Do you need to make an object from the class to do this?

6.4. Make a class called Element, with instance attributes name, symbol, and number. Create an object of this class with the values 'Hydrogen', 'H', and 1.

6.5. Make a dictionary with these keys and values: `'name'`: `'Hydrogen'`, `'symbol'`: `'H'`, `'number'`: `1`. Then, create an object called hydrogen from class `Element` using this dictionary.

6.6. For the `Element` class, define a method called `dump()` that prints the values of the object's attributes (`name`, `symbol`, and `number`). Create the hydrogen object from this new definition and use `dump()` to print its attributes.

6.7. Call `print(hydrogen)`. In the definition of `Element`, change the name of method dump to `__str__`, create a new hydrogen object, and call `print(hydrogen)` again.

6.8. Modify `Element` to make the attributes `name`, `symbol`, and `number` private. Define a getter property for each to return its value.

6.9. Define three classes: `Bear`, `Rabbit`, and `Octothorpe`. For each, define only one method: `eats()`. This should return `'berries'` (`Bear`), `'clover'` (`Rabbit`), or `'campers'` (`Octothorpe`). Create one object from each and print what it eats.

6.10. Define these classes: `Laser`, `Claw`, and `SmartPhone`. Each has only one method: `does()`. This returns `'disintegrate'` (`Laser`), `'crush'` (`Claw`), or `'ring'` (Smart Phone). Then, define the class `Robot` that has one instance (object) of each of these. Define a `does()` method for the `Robot` that prints what its component objects do.

CHAPTER 7

Mangle Data Like a Pro

In this chapter, you'll learn many techniques for taming data. Most of them concern these built-in Python data types:

strings
  Sequences of *Unicode* characters, used for text data.

bytes and bytearrays
  Sequences of eight-bit integers, used for binary data.

Text Strings

Text is the most familiar type of data to most readers, so we'll begin with some of the powerful features of text strings in Python.

Unicode

All of the text examples in this book thus far have been plain old ASCII. ASCII was defined in the 1960s, when computers were the size of refrigerators and only slightly better at performing computations. The basic unit of computer storage is the *byte*, which can store 256 unique values in its eight *bits*. For various reasons, ASCII only used 7 bits (128 unique values): 26 uppercase letters, 26 lowercase letters, 10 digits, some punctuation symbols, some spacing characters, and some nonprinting control codes.

Unfortunately, the world has more letters than ASCII provides. You could have a hot dog at a diner, but never a Gewürztraminer[1] at a café. Many attempts have been made

---

1 This wine has an umlaut in Germany, but loses it in France.

to add more letters and symbols, and you'll see them at times. Just a couple of those include:

- *Latin-1*, or *ISO 8859-1*
- Windows code page *1252*

Each of these uses all eight bits, but even that's not enough, especially when you need non-European languages. *Unicode* is an ongoing international standard to define the characters of all the world's languages, plus symbols from mathematics and other fields.

> Unicode provides a unique number for every character, no matter what the platform, no matter what the program, no matter what the language.
>
> —The Unicode Consortium

The Unicode Code Charts page (*http://www.unicode.org/charts*) has links to all the currently defined character sets with images. The latest version (6.2) defines over 110,000 characters, each with a unique name and identification number. The characters are divided into eight-bit sets called *planes*. The first 256 planes are the *basic multilingual planes*. See the Wikipedia page about Unicode planes (*http://bit.ly/unicodeplane*) for details.

Python 3 Unicode strings

Python 3 strings are Unicode strings, not byte arrays. This is the single largest change from Python 2, which distinguished between normal byte strings and Unicode character strings.

If you know the Unicode ID or name for a character, you can use it in a Python string. Here are some examples:

- A \u followed by *four* hex numbers[1] specifies a character in one of Unicode's 256 basic multilingual planes. The first two are the plane number (00 to FF), and the next two are the index of the character within the plane. Plane 00 is good old ASCII, and the character positions within that plane are the same as ASCII.
- For characters in the higher planes, we need more bits. The Python escape sequence for these is \U followed by *eight* hex characters; the leftmost ones need to be 0.

---

1 Base 16, specified with characters 0-9 and A-F.

- For all characters, \N{ *name* } lets you specify it by its standard *name*. The Unicode Character Name Index page (*http://www.unicode.org/charts/charindex.html*) lists these.

The Python unicodedata module has functions that translate in both directions:

- lookup()—Takes a case-insensitive name and returns a Unicode character
- name()—Takes a Unicode character and returns an uppercase name

In the following example, we'll write a test function that takes a Python Unicode character, looks up its name, and looks up the character again from the name (it should match the original character):

```
>>> def unicode_test(value):
...     import unicodedata
...     name = unicodedata.name(value)
...     value2 = unicodedata.lookup(name)
...     print('value="%s", name="%s", value2="%s"' % (value, name, value2))
...
```

Let's try some characters, beginning with a plain ASCII letter:

```
>>> unicode_test('A')
value="A", name="LATIN CAPITAL LETTER A", value2="A"
```

ASCII punctuation:

```
>>> unicode_test('$')
value="$", name="DOLLAR SIGN", value2="$"
```

A Unicode currency character:

```
>>> unicode_test('\u00a2')
value="¢", name="CENT SIGN", value2="¢"
```

Another Unicode currency character:

```
>>> unicode_test('\u20ac')
value="€", name="EURO SIGN", value2="€"
```

The only problem you could potentially run into is limitations in the font you're using to display text. All fonts do not have images for all Unicode characters, and might display some placeholder character. For instance, here's the Unicode symbol for SNOWMAN, like symbols in dingbat fonts:

```
>>> unicode_test('\u2603')
value="☃", name="SNOWMAN", value2="☃"
```

Suppose that we want to save the word café in a Python string. One way is to copy and paste it from a file or website and hope that it works:

```
>>> place = 'café'
>>> place
'café'
```

This worked because I copied and pasted from a source that used UTF-8 encoding (which you'll see in a few pages) for its text.

How can we specify that final é character? If you look at character index for E (*http://bit.ly/e-index*), you see that the name E WITH ACUTE, LATIN SMALL LETTER has the value 00E9. Let's check with the name() and lookup() functions that we were just playing with. First give the code to get the name:

```
>>> unicodedata.name('\u00e9')
'LATIN SMALL LETTER E WITH ACUTE'
```

Next, give the name to look up the code:

```
>>> unicodedata.lookup('E WITH ACUTE, LATIN SMALL LETTER')
Traceback (most recent call last):
  File "<stdin>", line 1, in <module>
KeyError: "undefined character name 'E WITH ACUTE, LATIN SMALL LETTER'"
```

The names listed on the Unicode Character Name Index page were reformatted to make them sort nicely for display. To convert them to their real Unicode names (the ones that Python uses), remove the comma and move the part of the name that was after the comma to the beginning. Accordingly, change E WITH ACUTE, LATIN SMALL LETTER to LATIN SMALL LETTER E WITH ACUTE:

```
>>> unicodedata.lookup('LATIN SMALL LETTER E WITH ACUTE')
'é'
```

Now, we can specify the string café by code or by name:

```
>>> place = 'caf\u00e9'
>>> place
'café'
>>> place = 'caf\N{LATIN SMALL LETTER E WITH ACUTE}'
>>> place
'café'
```

In the preceding snippet, we inserted the é directly in the string, but we can also build a string by appending:

```
>>> u_umlaut = '\N{LATIN SMALL LETTER U WITH DIAERESIS}'
>>> u_umlaut
'ü'
>>> drink = 'Gew' + u_umlaut + 'rztraminer'
>>> print('Now I can finally have my', drink, 'in a', place)
Now I can finally have my Gewürztraminer in a café
```

The string len function counts Unicode *characters*, not bytes:

```
>>> len('$')
1
>>> len('\U0001f47b')
1
```

Encode and decode with UTF-8

You don't need to worry about how Python stores each Unicode character when you do normal string processing.

However, when you exchange data with the outside world, you need a couple of things:

- A way to *encode* character strings to bytes
- A way to *decode* bytes to character strings

If there were fewer than 64,000 characters in Unicode, we could store each Unicode character ID in two bytes. Unfortunately, there are more. We could encode each ID in three or four bytes, but that would increase the memory and disk storage space needs for common text strings by three or four times.

Ken Thompson and Rob Pike, whose names will be familiar to Unix developers, designed the *UTF-8* dynamic encoding scheme one night on a placemat in a New Jersey diner. It uses one to four bytes per Unicode character:

- One byte for ASCII
- Two bytes for most Latin-derived (but not Cyrillic) languages
- Three bytes for the rest of the basic multilingual plane
- Four bytes for the rest, including some Asian languages and symbols

UTF-8 is the standard text encoding in Python, Linux, and HTML. It's fast, complete, and works well. If you use UTF-8 encoding throughout your code, life will be much easier than trying to hop in and out of various encodings.

 If you create a Python string by copying and pasting from another source such as a web page, be sure the source is encoded in the UTF-8 format. It's *very* common to see text that was encoded as Latin-1 or Windows 1252 copied into a Python string, which causes an exception later with an invalid byte sequence.

Encoding

You *encode* a *string* to *bytes*. The string `encode()` function's first argument is the encoding name. The choices include those presented in Table 7-1.

Table 7-1. Encodings

`'ascii'`	Good old seven-bit ASCII
`'utf-8'`	Eight-bit variable-length encoding, and what you almost always want to use
`'latin-1'`	Also known as ISO 8859-1
`'cp-1252'`	A common Windows encoding
`'unicode-escape'`	Python Unicode literal format, `\u`*xxxx* or `\U`*xxxxxxxx*

You can encode anything as UTF-8. Let's assign the Unicode string `'\u2603'` to the name snowman:

```
>>> snowman = '\u2603'
```

snowman is a Python Unicode string with a single character, regardless of how many bytes might be needed to store it internally:

```
>>> len(snowman)
1
```

Next let's encode this Unicode character to a sequence of bytes:

```
>>> ds = snowman.encode('utf-8')
```

As I mentioned earlier, UTF-8 is a variable-length encoding. In this case, it used three bytes to encode the single snowman Unicode character:

```
>>> len(ds)
3
>>> ds
b'\xe2\x98\x83'
```

Now, len() returns the number of bytes (3) because ds is a bytes variable.

You can use encodings other than UTF-8, but you'll get errors if the Unicode string can't be handled by the encoding. For example, if you use the ascii encoding, it will fail unless your Unicode characters happen to be valid ASCII characters as well:

```
>>> ds = snowman.encode('ascii')
Traceback (most recent call last):
  File "<stdin>", line 1, in <module>
UnicodeEncodeError: 'ascii' codec can't encode character '\u2603'
in position 0: ordinal not in range(128)
```

The encode() function takes a second argument to help you avoid encoding exceptions. Its default value, which you can see in the previous example, is `'strict'`; it raises a UnicodeEncodeError if it sees a non-ASCII character. There are other encodings. Use 'ignore' to throw away anything that won't encode:

```
>>> snowman.encode('ascii', 'ignore')
b''
```

Use 'replace' to substitute ? for unknown characters:

```
>>> snowman.encode('ascii', 'replace')
b'?'
```

Use 'backslashreplace' to produce a Python Unicode character string, like unicode-escape:

```
>>> snowman.encode('ascii', 'backslashreplace')
b'\\u2603'
```

You would use this if you needed a printable version of the Unicode escape sequence.

The following produces character entity strings that you can use in web pages:

```
>>> snowman.encode('ascii', 'xmlcharrefreplace')
b'&#9731;'
```

Decoding

We *decode* byte strings to Unicode strings. Whenever we get text from some external source (files, databases, websites, network APIs, and so on), it's encoded as byte strings. The tricky part is knowing which encoding was actually used, so we can *run it backward* and get Unicode strings.

The problem is that nothing in the byte string itself says what encoding was used. I mentioned the perils of copying and pasting from websites earlier. You've probably visited websites with odd characters where plain old ASCII characters should be.

Let's create a Unicode string called place with the value 'café':

```
>>> place = 'caf\u00e9'
>>> place
'café'
>>> type(place)
<class 'str'>
```

Encode it in UTF-8 format in a bytes variable called place_bytes:

```
>>> place_bytes = place.encode('utf-8')
>>> place_bytes
b'caf\xc3\xa9'
>>> type(place_bytes)
<class 'bytes'>
```

Notice that `place_bytes` has five bytes. The first three are the same as ASCII (a strength of UTF-8), and the final two encode the `'é'`. Now, let's decode that byte string back to a Unicode string:

```
>>> place2 = place_bytes.decode('utf-8')
>>> place2
'café'
```

This worked because we encoded to UTF-8 and decoded from UTF-8. What if we told it to decode from some other encoding?

```
>>> place3 = place_bytes.decode('ascii')
Traceback (most recent call last):
  File "<stdin>", line 1, in <module>
UnicodeDecodeError: 'ascii' codec can't decode byte 0xc3 in position 3:
ordinal not in range(128)
```

The ASCII decoder threw an exception because the byte value `0xc3` is illegal in ASCII. There are some 8-bit character set encodings in which values between 128 (hex `80`) and 255 (hex `FF`) are legal but not the same as UTF-8:

```
>>> place4 = place_bytes.decode('latin-1')
>>> place4
'cafÃ©'
>>> place5 = place_bytes.decode('windows-1252')
>>> place5
'cafÃ©'
```

Urk.

The moral of this story: whenever possible, use UTF-8 encoding. It works, is supported everywhere, can express every Unicode character, and is quickly decoded and encoded.

For more information

If you would like to learn more, these links are particularly helpful:

- Unicode HOWTO (*http://bit.ly/unicode-howto*)
- Pragmatic Unicode (*http://bit.ly/pragmatic-uni*)
- The Absolute Minimum Every Software Developer Absolutely, Positively Must Know About Unicode and Character Sets (No Excuses!) (*http://bit.ly/jspolsky*)

Format

We've pretty much ignored text formatting—until now. Chapter 2 shows a few string alignment functions, and the code examples have used simple `print()` statements, or just let the interactive interpreter display values. But it's time we look at how to *inter-*

polate data values into strings—in other words, put the values inside the strings—using various formats. You can use this to produce reports and other outputs for which appearances need to be just so.

Python has two ways of formatting strings, loosely called *old style* and *new style*. Both styles are supported in Python 2 and 3 (new style in Python 2.6 and up). Old style is simpler, so we'll begin there.

Old style with %

The old style of string formatting has the form *string % data*. Inside the string are interpolation sequences. Table 7-2 illustrates that the very simplest sequence is a % followed by a letter indicating the data type to be formatted.

Table 7-2. Conversion types

%s	string
%d	decimal integer
%x	hex integer
%o	octal integer
%f	decimal float
%e	exponential float
%g	decimal or exponential float
%%	a literal %

Following are some simple examples. First, an integer:

```
>>> '%s' % 42
'42'
>>> '%d' % 42
'42'
>>> '%x' % 42
'2a'
>>> '%o' % 42
'52'
```

A float:

```
>>> '%s' % 7.03
'7.03'
>>> '%f' % 7.03
'7.030000'
```

```
>>> '%e' % 7.03
'7.030000e+00'
>>> '%g' % 7.03
'7.03'
```

An integer and a literal %:

```
>>> '%d%%' % 100
'100%'
```

Some string and integer interpolation:

```
>>> actor = 'Richard Gere'
>>> cat = 'Chester'
>>> weight = 28

>>> "My wife's favorite actor is %s" % actor
"My wife's favorite actor is Richard Gere"

>>> "Our cat %s weighs %s pounds" % (cat, weight)
'Our cat Chester weighs 28 pounds'
```

That %s inside the string means to interpolate a string. The number of % appearances in the string needs match the number of data items after the %. A single data item such as actor goes right after the %. Multiple data must be grouped into a tuple (bounded by parentheses, separated by commas) such as (cat, weight).

Even though weight is an integer, the %s inside the string converted it to a string.

You can add other values between the % and the type specifier to designate minimum and maximum widths, alignment, and character filling:

For variables, let's define an integer, n; a float, f; and a string, s:

```
>>> n = 42
>>> f = 7.03
>>> s = 'string cheese'
```

Format them using default widths:

```
>>> '%d %f %s' % (n, f, s)
'42 7.030000 string cheese'
```

Set a minimum field width of 10 characters for each variable, and align them to the right, filling unused spots on the left with spaces:

```
>>> '%10d %10f %10s' % (n, f, s)
'        42   7.030000 string cheese'
```

Use the same field width, but align to the left:

```
>>> '%-10d %-10f %-10s' % (n, f, s)
'42         7.030000   string cheese'
```

This time, the same field width, but a maximum character width of 4, and aligned to the right. This setting truncates the string, and limits the float to 4 digits after the decimal point:

```
>>> '%10.4d %10.4f %10.4s' % (n, f, s)
'      0042     7.0300       stri'
```

The same song as before, but right-aligned:

```
>>> '%.4d %.4f %.4s' % (n, f, s)
'0042 7.0300 stri'
```

Finally, get the field widths from arguments rather than hard-coding them:

```
>>> '%*.*d %*.*f %*.*s' % (10, 4, n, 10, 4, f, 10, 4, s)
'      0042     7.0300       stri'
```

New style formatting with {} and format

Old style formatting is still supported. In Python 2, which will freeze at version 2.7, it will be supported forever. However, new style formatting is recommended if you're using Python 3.

The simplest usage is demonstrated here:

```
>>> '{} {} {}'.format(n, f, s)
'42 7.03 string cheese'
```

Old-style arguments needed to be provided in the order in which their % placeholders appeared in the string. With new-style, you can specify the order:

```
>>> '{2} {0} {1}'.format(f, s, n)
'42 7.03 string cheese'
```

The value 0 referred to the first argument, f, whereas 1 referred to the string s, and 2 referred to the last argument, the integer n.

The arguments can be a dictionary or named arguments, and the specifiers can include their names:

```
>>> '{n} {f} {s}'.format(n=42, f=7.03, s='string cheese')
'42 7.03 string cheese'
```

In this next example, let's try combining our three values into a dictionary, which looks like this:

```
>>> d = {'n': 42, 'f': 7.03, 's': 'string cheese'}
```

In the following example, {0} is the entire dictionary, whereas {1} is the string 'other' that follows the dictionary:

```
>>> '{0[n]} {0[f]} {0[s]} {1}'.format(d, 'other')
'42 7.03 string cheese other'
```

These examples all printed their arguments with default formats. Old-style allows a type specifier after the % in the string, but new-style puts it after a :. First, with positional arguments:

```
>>> '{0:d} {1:f} {2:s}'.format(n, f, s)
'42 7.030000 string cheese'
```

In this example, we'll use the same values, but as named arguments:

```
>>> '{n:d} {f:f} {s:s}'.format(n=42, f=7.03, s='string cheese')
'42 7.030000 string cheese'
```

The other options (minimum field width, maximum character width, alignment, and so on) are also supported.

Minimum field width 10, right-aligned (default):

```
>>> '{0:10d} {1:10f} {2:10s}'.format(n, f, s)
'        42   7.030000 string cheese'
```

Same as the preceding example, but the > characters make the right-alignment more explicit:

```
>>> '{0:>10d} {1:>10f} {2:>10s}'.format(n, f, s)
'        42   7.030000 string cheese'
```

Minimum field width 10, left-aligned:

```
>>> '{0:<10d} {1:<10f} {2:<10s}'.format(n, f, s)
'42         7.030000   string cheese'
```

Minimum field width 10, centered:

```
>>> '{0:^10d} {1:^10f} {2:^10s}'.format(n, f, s)
'    42     7.030000   string cheese'
```

There is one change from old-style: the *precision* value (after the decimal point) still means the number of digits after the decimal for floats, and the maximum number of characters for strings, but you can't use it for integers:

```
>>> '{0:>10.4d} {1:>10.4f} {2:10.4s}'.format(n, f, s)
Traceback (most recent call last):
  File "<stdin>", line 1, in <module>
ValueError: Precision not allowed in integer format specifier
>>> '{0:>10d} {1:>10.4f} {2:>10.4s}'.format(n, f, s)
'        42     7.0300       stri'
```

The final option is the *fill character*. If you want something other than spaces to pad your output fields, put it right after the :, before any alignment (<, >, ^) or width specifiers:

```
>>> '{0:!^20s}'.format('BIG SALE')
'!!!!!!BIG SALE!!!!!!'
```

Match with Regular Expressions

Chapter 2 touched on simple string operations. Armed with that introductory information, you've probably used simple "wildcard" patterns on the command line, such as *ls *.py*, which means *list all filenames ending in .py*.

It's time to explore more complex pattern matching by using *regular expressions*. These are provided in the standard module re, which we'll import. You define a string *pattern* that you want to match, and the *source* string to match against. For simple matches, usage looks like this:

```
result = re.match('You', 'Young Frankenstein')
```

Here, 'You' is the *pattern* and 'Young Frankenstein' is the *source*—the string you want to check. match() checks whether the *source* begins with the *pattern*.

For more complex matches, you can *compile* your pattern first to speed up the match later:

```
youpattern = re.compile('You')
```

Then, you can perform your match against the compiled pattern:

```
result = youpattern.match('Young Frankenstein')
```

match() is not the only way to compare the pattern and source. Here are several other methods you can use:

- search() returns the first match, if any.
- findall() returns a list of all non-overlapping matches, if any.
- split() splits *source* at matches with *pattern* and returns a list of the string pieces.
- sub() takes another *replacement* argument, and changes all parts of *source* that are matched by *pattern* to *replacement*.

Exact match with match()

Does the string 'Young Frankenstein' begin with the word 'You'? Here's some code with comments:

```
>>> import re
>>> source = 'Young Frankenstein'
>>> m = re.match('You', source)  # match starts at the beginning of source
>>> if m:   # match returns an object; do this to see what matched
...     print(m.group())
...
You
>>> m = re.match('^You', source) # start anchor does the same
```

```
>>> if m:
...     print(m.group())
...
You
```

How about `'Frank'`?

```
>>> m = re.match('Frank', source)
>>> if m:
...     print(m.group())
...
```

This time `match()` returned nothing and the `if` did not run the `print` statement. As I said earlier, `match()` works only if the pattern is at the beginning of the source. But `search()` works if the pattern is anywhere:

```
>>> m = re.search('Frank', source)
>>> if m:
...     print(m.group())
...
Frank
```

Let's change the pattern:

```
>>> m = re.match('.*Frank', source)
>>> if m:   # match returns an object
...     print(m.group())
...
Young Frank
```

Following is a brief explanation of how our new pattern works:

- `.` means *any single character.*

- `*` means *any number of the preceding thing*. Together, `.*` mean *any number of characters* (even zero).

- `Frank` is the phrase that we wanted to match, somewhere.

`match()` returned the string that matched `.*Frank`: `'Young Frank'`.

First match with search()

You can use `search()` to find the pattern `'Frank'` anywhere in the source string `'Young Frankenstein'`, without the need for the `.*` wildcards:

```
>>> m = re.search('Frank', source)
>>> if m:   # search returns an object
...     print(m.group())
...
Frank
```

All matches with findall()

The preceding examples looked for one match only. But what if you want to know how many instances of the single-letter string 'n' are in the string?

```
>>> m = re.findall('n', source)
>>> m   # findall returns a list
['n', 'n', 'n', 'n']
>>> print('Found', len(m), 'matches')
Found 4 matches
```

How about 'n' followed by any character?

```
>>> m = re.findall('n.', source)
>>> m
['ng', 'nk', 'ns']
```

Notice that it did not match that final 'n'. We need to say that the character after 'n' is optional with ?:

```
>>> m = re.findall('n.?', source)
>>> m
['ng', 'nk', 'ns', 'n']
```

Split at matches with split()

The example that follows shows you how to split a string into a list by a pattern rather than a simple string (as the normal string `split()` method would do):

```
>>> m = re.split('n', source)
>>> m   # split returns a list
['You', 'g Fra', 'ke', 'stei', '']
```

Replace at matches with sub()

This is like the string `replace()` method, but for patterns rather than literal strings:

```
>>> m = re.sub('n', '?', source)
>>> m   # sub returns a string
'You?g Fra?ke?stei?'
```

Patterns: special characters

Many descriptions of regular expressions start with all the details of how to define them. I think that's a mistake. Regular expressions are a not-so-little language in their own right, with too many details to fit in your head at once. They use so much punctuation that they look like cartoon characters swearing.

With these expressions (`match()`, `search()`, `findall()`, and `sub()`) under your belt, let's get into the details of building them. The patterns you make apply to any of these functions.

You've seen the basics:

- Literal matches with any non-special characters
- Any single character except \n with .
- Any number (including zero) with *
- Optional (zero or one) with ?

First, special characters are shown in Table 7-3.

Table 7-3. Special characters

Pattern	Matches
\d	a single digit
\D	a single non-digit
\w	an alphanumeric character
\W	a non-alphanumeric character
\s	a whitespace character
\S	a non-whitespace character
\b	a word boundary (between a \w and a \W, in either order)
\B	a non-word boundary

The Python `string` module has predefined string constants that we can use for testing. We'll use `printable`, which contains 100 printable ASCII characters, including letters in both cases, digits, space characters, and punctuation:

```
>>> import string
>>> printable = string.printable
>>> len(printable)
100
>>> printable[0:50]
'0123456789abcdefghijklmnopqrstuvwxyzABCDEFGHIJKLMN'
>>> printable[50:]
'OPQRSTUVWXYZ!"#$%&\'()*+,-./:;<=>?@[\\]^_`{|}~ \t\n\r\x0b\x0c'
```

Which characters in `printable` are digits?

```
>>> re.findall('\d', printable)
['0', '1', '2', '3', '4', '5', '6', '7', '8', '9']
```

Which characters are digits, letters, or an underscore?

```
>>> re.findall('\w', printable)
['0', '1', '2', '3', '4', '5', '6', '7', '8', '9', 'a', 'b',
'c', 'd', 'e', 'f', 'g', 'h', 'i', 'j', 'k', 'l', 'm', 'n',
'o', 'p', 'q', 'r', 's', 't', 'u', 'v', 'w', 'x', 'y', 'z',
'A', 'B', 'C', 'D', 'E', 'F', 'G', 'H', 'I', 'J', 'K', 'L',
'M', 'N', 'O', 'P', 'Q', 'R', 'S', 'T', 'U', 'V', 'W', 'X',
'Y', 'Z', '_']
```

Which are spaces?

```
>>> re.findall('\s', printable)
[' ', '\t', '\n', '\r', '\x0b', '\x0c']
```

Regular expressions are not confined to ASCII. A \d will match whatever Unicode calls a digit, not just ASCII characters '0' through '9'. Let's add two non-ASCII lowercase letters from FileFormat.info (*http://bit.ly/unicode-letter*):

In this test, we'll throw in the following:

- Three ASCII letters
- Three punctuation symbols that should *not* match a \w
- A Unicode *LATIN SMALL LETTER E WITH CIRCUMFLEX* (\u00ea)
- A Unicode *LATIN SMALL LETTER E WITH BREVE* (\u0115)

```
>>> x = 'abc' + '-/*' + '\u00ea' + '\u0115'
```

As expected, this pattern found only the letters:

```
>>> re.findall('\w', x)
['a', 'b', 'c', 'ê', 'ĕ']
```

Patterns: using specifiers

Now, let's make "punctuation pizza," using the main pattern specifiers for regular expressions, which are presented in Table 7-4.

In the table, *expr* and the other italicized words mean any valid regular expression.

Table 7-4. Pattern specifiers

Pattern	Matches
abc	literal abc
(*expr*)	*expr*
expr1 | *expr2*	*expr1* or *expr2*
.	any character except \n

Pattern	Matches
^	start of source string
$	end of source string
prev ?	zero or one *prev*
prev *	zero or more *prev*, as many as possible
prev *?	zero or more *prev*, as few as possible
prev +	one or more *prev*, as many as possible
prev +?	one or more *prev*, as few as possible
prev { *m* }	*m* consecutive *prev*
prev { *m, n* }	*m* to *n* consecutive *prev*, as many as possible
prev { *m, n* }?	*m* to *n* consecutive *prev*, as few as possible
[*abc*]	a or b or c (same as a | b | c)
[^ *abc*]	*not* (a or b or c)
prev (?= *next*)	*prev* if followed by *next*
prev (?! *next*)	*prev* if *not* followed by *next*
(?<= *prev*) *next*	*next* if preceded by *prev*
(?<! *prev*) *next*	*next* if *not* preceded by *prev*

Your eyes might cross permanently when trying to read these examples. First, let's define our source string:

```
>>> source = '''I wish I may, I wish I might
... Have a dish of fish tonight.'''
```

First, find `wish` anywhere:

```
>>> re.findall('wish', source)
['wish', 'wish']
```

Next, find `wish` or `fish` anywhere:

```
>>> re.findall('wish|fish', source)
['wish', 'wish', 'fish']
```

Find `wish` at the beginning:

```
>>> re.findall('^wish', source)
[]
```

Find `I wish` at the beginning:

```
>>> re.findall('^I wish', source)
['I wish']
```

Find `fish` at the end:

```
>>> re.findall('fish$', source)
[]
```

Finally, find `fish tonight.` at the end:

```
>>> re.findall('fish tonight.$', source)
['fish tonight.']
```

The characters ^ and $ are called *anchors*: ^ anchors the search to the beginning of the search string, and $ anchors it to the end. `.$` matches any character at the end of the line, including a period, so that worked. To be more precise, we should escape the dot to match it literally:

```
>>> re.findall('fish tonight\.$', source)
['fish tonight.']
```

Begin by finding `w` or `f` followed by `ish`:

```
>>> re.findall('[wf]ish', source)
['wish', 'wish', 'fish']
```

Find one or more runs of `w`, `s`, or `h`:

```
>>> re.findall('[wsh]+', source)
['w', 'sh', 'w', 'sh', 'h', 'sh', 'sh', 'h']
```

Find `ght` followed by a non-alphanumeric:

```
>>> re.findall('ght\W', source)
['ght\n', 'ght.']
```

Find `I` followed by `wish`:

```
>>> re.findall('I (?=wish)', source)
['I ', 'I ']
```

And last, `wish` preceded by `I`:

```
>>> re.findall('(?<=I) wish', source)
[' wish', ' wish']
```

There are a few cases in which the regular expression pattern rules conflict with the Python string rules. The following pattern should match any word that begins with `fish`:

```
>>> re.findall('\bfish', source)
[]
```

Why doesn't it? As is discussed in Chapter 2, Python employs a few special *escape characters* for strings. For example, \b means backspace in strings, but in the mini-language of regular expressions it means the beginning of a word. Avoid the accidental use of escape characters by using Python's *raw strings* when you define your regular expression string. Always put an r character before your regular expression pattern string, and Python escape characters will be disabled, as demonstrated here:

```
>>> re.findall(r'\bfish', source)
['fish']
```

Patterns: specifying match output

When using match() or search(), all matches are returned from the result object m as m.group(). If you enclose a pattern in parentheses, the match will be saved to its own group, and a tuple of them will be available as m.groups(), as shown here:

```
>>> m = re.search(r'(. dish\b).*(\bfish)', source)
>>> m.group()
'a dish of fish'
>>> m.groups()
('a dish', 'fish')
```

If you use this pattern (?P< *name* > *expr*), it will match *expr*, saving the match in group *name*:

```
>>> m = re.search(r'(?P<DISH>. dish\b).*(?P<FISH>\bfish)', source)
>>> m.group()
'a dish of fish'
>>> m.groups()
('a dish', 'fish')
>>> m.group('DISH')
'a dish'
>>> m.group('FISH')
'fish'
```

Binary Data

Text data can be challenging, but binary data can be, well, interesting. You need to know about concepts such as *endianness* (how your computer's processor breaks data into bytes) and *sign bits* for integers. You might need to delve into binary file formats or network packets to extract or even change data. This section will show you the basics of binary data wrangling in Python.

bytes and bytearray

Python 3 introduced the following sequences of eight-bit integers, with possible values from 0 to 255, in two types:

- *bytes* is immutable, like a tuple of bytes
- *bytearray* is mutable, like a list of bytes

Beginning with a list called `blist`, this next example creates a `bytes` variable called `the_bytes` and a bytearray variable called `the_byte_array`:

```
>> blist = [1, 2, 3, 255]
>>> the_bytes = bytes(blist)
>>> the_bytes
b'\x01\x02\x03\xff'
>>> the_byte_array = bytearray(blist)
>>> the_byte_array
bytearray(b'\x01\x02\x03\xff')
```

 The representation of a bytes value begins with a b and a quote character, followed by hex sequences such as \x02 or ASCII characters, and ends with a matching quote character. Python converts the hex sequences or ASCII characters to little integers, but shows byte values that are also valid ASCII encodings as ASCII characters.

```
>>> b'\x61'
b'a'
>>> b'\x01abc\xff'
b'\x01abc\xff'
```

This next example demonstrates that you can't change a `bytes` variable:

```
>>> the_bytes[1] = 127
Traceback (most recent call last):
  File "<stdin>", line 1, in <module>
TypeError: 'bytes' object does not support item assignment
```

But a bytearray variable is mellow and mutable:

```
>>> the_byte_array = bytearray(blist)
>>> the_byte_array
bytearray(b'\x01\x02\x03\xff')
>>> the_byte_array[1] = 127
>>> the_byte_array
bytearray(b'\x01\x7f\x03\xff')
```

Each of these would create a 256-element result, with values from 0 to 255:

```
>>> the_bytes = bytes(range(0, 256))
>>> the_byte_array = bytearray(range(0, 256))
```

When printing bytes or bytearray data, Python uses \x *xx* for non-printable bytes and their ASCII equivalents for printable ones (plus some common escape characters, such as \n instead of \x0a). Here's the printed representation of the_bytes (manually reformatted to show 16 bytes per line):

```
>>> the_bytes
b'\x00\x01\x02\x03\x04\x05\x06\x07\x08\t\n\x0b\x0c\r\x0e\x0f
\x10\x11\x12\x13\x14\x15\x16\x17\x18\x19\x1a\x1b\x1c\x1d\x1e\x1f
!"#$%&\'()*+,-./
0123456789:;<=>?
@ABCDEFGHIJKLMNO
PQRSTUVWXYZ[\\]^_
`abcdefghijklmno
pqrstuvwxyz{|}~\x7f
\x80\x81\x82\x83\x84\x85\x86\x87\x88\x89\x8a\x8b\x8c\x8d\x8e\x8f
\x90\x91\x92\x93\x94\x95\x96\x97\x98\x99\x9a\x9b\x9c\x9d\x9e\x9f
\xa0\xa1\xa2\xa3\xa4\xa5\xa6\xa7\xa8\xa9\xaa\xab\xac\xad\xae\xaf
\xb0\xb1\xb2\xb3\xb4\xb5\xb6\xb7\xb8\xb9\xba\xbb\xbc\xbd\xbe\xbf
\xc0\xc1\xc2\xc3\xc4\xc5\xc6\xc7\xc8\xc9\xca\xcb\xcc\xcd\xce\xcf
\xd0\xd1\xd2\xd3\xd4\xd5\xd6\xd7\xd8\xd9\xda\xdb\xdc\xdd\xde\xdf
\xe0\xe1\xe2\xe3\xe4\xe5\xe6\xe7\xe8\xe9\xea\xeb\xec\xed\xee\xef
\xf0\xf1\xf2\xf3\xf4\xf5\xf6\xf7\xf8\xf9\xfa\xfb\xfc\xfd\xfe\xff'
```

This can be confusing, because they're bytes (teeny integers), not characters.

Convert Binary Data with struct

As you've seen, Python has many tools for manipulating text. Tools for binary data are much less prevalent. The standard library contains the struct module, which handles data similar to *structs* in C and C++. Using struct, you can convert binary data to and from Python data structures.

Let's see how this works with data from a PNG file—a common image format that you'll see along with GIF and JPEG files. We'll write a small program that extracts the width and height of an image from some PNG data.

We'll use the O'Reilly logo—the little bug-eyed tarsier shown in Figure 7-1.

Figure 7-1. The O'Reilly tarsier

The PNG file for this image is available on Wikipedia (*http://bit.ly/orm-logo*). We don't show how to read files until Chapter 8, so I downloaded this file, wrote a little program to print its values as bytes, and just typed the values of the first 30 bytes into a Python `bytes` variable called `data` for the example that follows. (The PNG format specification stipulates that the width and height are stored within the first 24 bytes, so we don't need more than that for now.)

```
>>> import struct
>>> valid_png_header = b'\x89PNG\r\n\x1a\n'
>>> data = b'\x89PNG\r\n\x1a\n\x00\x00\x00\rIHDR' + \
...        b'\x00\x00\x00\x9a\x00\x00\x00\x8d\x08\x02\x00\x00\x00\xc0'
>>> if data[:8] == valid_png_header:
...        width, height = struct.unpack('>LL', data[16:24])
...        print('Valid PNG, width', width, 'height', height)
... else:
...        print('Not a valid PNG')
...
Valid PNG, width 154 height 141
```

Here's what this code does:

- `data` contains the first 30 bytes from the PNG file. To fit on the page, I joined two byte strings with + and the continuation character (\).

- `valid_png_header` contains the 8-byte sequence that marks the start of a valid PNG file.

- `width` is extracted from bytes 16-20, and `height` from bytes 21-24.

The `>LL` is the format string that instructs `unpack()` how to interpret its input byte sequences and assemble them into Python data types. Here's the breakdown:

- The > means that integers are stored in *big-endian* format.

- Each L specifies a 4-byte unsigned long integer.

You can examine each 4-byte value directly:

```
>>> data[16:20]
b'\x00\x00\x00\x9a'
>>> data[20:24]0x9a
b'\x00\x00\x00\x8d'
```

Big-endian integers have the most significant bytes to the left. Because the width and height are each less than 255, they fit into the last byte of each sequence. You can verify that these hex values match the expected decimal values:

```
>>> 0x9a
154
>>> 0x8d
141
```

When you want to go in the other direction and convert Python data to bytes, use the struct pack() function:

```
>>> import struct
>>> struct.pack('>L', 154)
b'\x00\x00\x00\x9a'
>>> struct.pack('>L', 141)
b'\x00\x00\x00\x8d'
```

Table 7-5 and Table 7-6 show the format specifiers for pack() and unpack().

The endian specifiers go first in the format string.

Table 7-5. Endian specifiers

Specifier	Byte order
<	little endian
>	big endian

Table 7-6. Format specifiers

Specifier	Description	Bytes
x	skip a byte	1
b	signed byte	1
B	unsigned byte	1
h	signed short integer	2
H	unsigned short integer	2
i	signed integer	4
I	unsigned integer	4
l	signed long integer	4
L	unsigned long integer	4
Q	unsigned long long integer	8
f	single precision float	4
d	double precision float	8

Specifier	Description	Bytes
p	*count* and characters	1 + *count*
s	characters	*count*

The type specifiers follow the endian character. Any specifier may be preceded by a number that indicates the *count*; 5B is the same as BBBBB.

You can use a *count* prefix instead of >LL:

```
>>> struct.unpack('>2L', data[16:24])
(154, 141)
```

We used the slice data[16:24] to grab the interesting bytes directly. We could also use the x specifier to skip the uninteresting parts:

```
>>> struct.unpack('>16x2L6x', data)
(154, 141)
```

This means:

- Use big-endian integer format (>)
- Skip 16 bytes (16x)
- Read 8 bytes—two unsigned long integers (2L)
- Skip the final 6 bytes (6x)

Other Binary Data Tools

Some third-party open source packages offer the following, more declarative ways of defining and extracting binary data:

- bitstring (*http://bit.ly/py-bitstring*)
- construct (*http://bit.ly/py-construct*)
- hachoir (*http://bit.ly/hachoir-pkg*)
- binio (*http://spika.net/py/binio/*)

Appendix D has details on how to download and install external packages such as these. For the next example, you need to install construct. Here's all you need to do:

```
$ pip install construct
```

Here's how to extract the PNG dimensions from our data bytestring by using construct:

```
>>> from construct import Struct, Magic, UBInt32, Const, String
>>> # adapted from code at https://github.com/construct
>>> fmt = Struct('png',
...     Magic(b'\x89PNG\r\n\x1a\n'),
...     UBInt32('length'),
...     Const(String('type', 4), b'IHDR'),
...     UBInt32('width'),
...     UBInt32('height')
...     )
>>> data = b'\x89PNG\r\n\x1a\n\x00\x00\x00\rIHDR' + \
...     b'\x00\x00\x00\x9a\x00\x00\x00\x8d\x08\x02\x00\x00\x00\xc0'
>>> result = fmt.parse(data)
>>> print(result)
Container:
    length = 13
    type = b'IHDR'
    width = 154
    height = 141
>>> print(result.width, result.height)
154, 141
```

Convert Bytes/Strings with binascii()

The standard `binascii` module has functions with which you can convert between
binary data and various string representations: hex (base 16), base 64, uuencoded,
and others. For example, in the next snippet, let's print that 8-byte PNG header as a
sequence of hex values, instead of the mixture of ASCII and \x *xx* escapes that
Python uses to display *bytes* variables:

```
>>> import binascii
>>> valid_png_header = b'\x89PNG\r\n\x1a\n'
>>> print(binascii.hexlify(valid_png_header))
b'89504e470d0a1a0a'
```

Hey, this thing works backwards, too:

```
>>> print(binascii.unhexlify(b'89504e470d0a1a0a'))
b'\x89PNG\r\n\x1a\n'
```

Bit Operators

Python provides bit-level integer operators, similar to those in the C language.
Table 7-7 summarizes them and includes examples with the integers a (decimal 5,
binary 0b0101) and b (decimal 1, binary 0b0001).

Table 7-7. Bit-level integer operators

Operator	Description	Example	Decimal result	Binary result
&	and	a & b	1	0b0001
|	or	a | b	5	0b0101
^	exclusive or	a ^ b	4	0b0100
~	flip bits	~a	-6	*binary representation depends on int size*
<<	left shift	a << 1	10	0b1010
>>	right shift	a >> 1	2	0b0010

These operators work something like the set operators in Chapter 3. The & operator returns bits that are the same in both arguments, and | returns bits that are set in either of them. The ^ operator returns bits that are in one or the other, but not both. The ~ operator reverses all the bits in its single argument; this also reverses the sign because an integer's highest bit indicates its sign (1 = negative) in *two's complement* arithmetic, used in all modern computers. The << and >> operators just move bits to the left or right. A left shift of one bit is the same as multiplying by two, and a right shift is the same as dividing by two.

Things to Do

7.1. Create a Unicode string called mystery and assign it the value '\U0001f4a9'. Print mystery. Look up the Unicode name for mystery.

7.2. Encode mystery, this time using UTF-8, into the bytes variable pop_bytes. Print pop_bytes.

7.3. Using UTF-8, decode pop_bytes into the string variable pop_string. Print pop_string. Is pop_string equal to mystery?

7.4. Write the following poem by using old-style formatting. Substitute the strings 'roast beef', 'ham', 'head', and 'clam' into this string:

```
My kitty cat likes %s,
My kitty cat likes %s,
My kitty cat fell on his %s
And now thinks he's a %s.
```

7.5. Write a form letter by using new-style formatting. Save the following string as letter (you'll use it in the next exercise):

```
Dear {salutation} {name},

Thank you for your letter. We are sorry that our {product} {verbed} in your
{room}. Please note that it should never be used in a {room}, especially
near any {animals}.

Send us your receipt and {amount} for shipping and handling. We will send
you another {product} that, in our tests, is {percent}% less likely to
have {verbed}.

Thank you for your support.

Sincerely,
{spokesman}
{job_title}
```

7.6. Make a dictionary called response with values for the string keys 'salutation', 'name', 'product', 'verbed' (past tense verb), 'room', 'animals', 'amount', 'per cent', 'spokesman', and 'job_title'. Print letter with the values from response.

7.7. When you're working with text, regular expressions come in very handy. We'll apply them in a number of ways to our featured text sample. It's a poem titled "Ode on the Mammoth Cheese," written by James McIntyre in 1866 in homage to a seven-thousand-pound cheese that was crafted in Ontario and sent on an international tour. If you'd rather not type all of it, use your favorite search engine and cut and paste the words into your Python program. Or, just grab it from Project Gutenberg (*http:// bit.ly/mcintyre-poetry*). Call the text string mammoth.

```
We have seen thee, queen of cheese,
Lying quietly at your ease,
Gently fanned by evening breeze,
Thy fair form no flies dare seize.

All gaily dressed soon you'll go
To the great Provincial show,
To be admired by many a beau
In the city of Toronto.

Cows numerous as a swarm of bees,
Or as the leaves upon the trees,
It did require to make thee please,
And stand unrivalled, queen of cheese.

May you not receive a scar as
We have heard that Mr. Harris
Intends to send you off as far as
The great world's show at Paris.

Of the youth beware of these,
For some of them might rudely squeeze
```

```
And bite your cheek, then songs or glees
We could not sing, oh! queen of cheese.

We'rt thou suspended from balloon,
You'd cast a shade even at noon,
Folks would think it was the moon
About to fall and crush them soon.
```

7.8. Import the `re` module to use Python's regular expression functions. Use `re.findall()` to print all the words that begin with c.

7.9. Find all four-letter words that begin with c.

7.10. Find all the words that end with r.

7.11. Find all words that contain exactly three vowels in a row.

7.12. Use `unhexlify` to convert this hex string (combined from two strings to fit on a page) to a `bytes` variable called `gif`:

```
'47494638396101000100800000000000ffffff21f9' +
'0401000000002c00000000010001000020144003b'
```

7.13. The bytes in `gif` define a one-pixel transparent GIF file, one of the most common graphics file formats. A legal GIF starts with the string *GIF89a*. Does `gif` match this?

7.14. The pixel width of a GIF is a 16-bit little-endian integer beginning at byte offset 6, and the height is the same size, starting at offset 8. Extract and print these values for `gif`. Are they both 1?

Data Has to Go Somewhere

It is a capital mistake to theorize before one has data.
—Arthur Conan Doyle

An active program accesses data that is stored in Random Access Memory, or RAM. RAM is very fast, but it is expensive and requires a constant supply of power; if the power goes out, all the data in memory is lost. Disk drives are slower than RAM but have more capacity, cost less, and retain data even after someone trips over the power cord. Thus, a huge amount of effort in computer systems has been devoted to making the best tradeoffs between storing data on disk and RAM. As programmers, we need *persistence*: storing and retrieving data using nonvolatile media such as disks.

This chapter is all about the different flavors of data storage, each optimized for different purposes: flat files, structured files, and databases. File operations other than input and output are covered in "Files" on page 247.

 This is also the first chapter to show examples of nonstandard Python modules; that is, Python code apart from the standard library. You'll install them by using the `pip` command, which is painless. There are more details on its usage in Appendix D.

File Input/Output

The simplest kind of persistence is a plain old file, sometimes called a *flat file*. This is just a sequence of bytes stored under a *filename*. You *read* from a file into memory and *write* from memory to a file. Python makes these jobs easy. Its file operations were modeled on the familiar and popular Unix equivalents.

Before reading or writing a file, you need to *open* it:

```
fileobj = open( filename, mode )
```

Here's a brief explanation of the pieces of this call:

- *fileobj* is the file object returned by open()
- *filename* is the string name of the file
- *mode* is a string indicating the file's type and what you want to do with it

The first letter of *mode* indicates the *operation*:

- r means read.
- w means write. If the file doesn't exist, it's created. If the file does exist, it's over-written.
- x means write, but only if the file does *not* already exist.
- a means append (write after the end) if the file exists.

The second letter of *mode* is the file's *type*:

- t (or nothing) means text.
- b means binary.

After opening the file, you call functions to read or write data; these will be shown in the examples that follow.

Last, you need to *close* the file.

Let's create a file from a Python string in one program and then read it back in the next.

Write a Text File with write()

For some reason, there aren't many limericks about special relativity. This one will just have to do for our data source:

```
>>> poem = '''There was a young lady named Bright,
... Whose speed was far faster than light;
... She started one day
... In a relative way,
... And returned on the previous night.'''
>>> len(poem)
150
```

The following code writes the entire poem to the file 'relativity' in one call:

```
>>> fout = open('relativity', 'wt')
>>> fout.write(poem)
```

```
150
>>> fout.close()
```

The write() function returns the number of bytes written. It does not add any spaces or newlines, as print() does. You can also print() to a text file:

```
>>> fout = open('relativity', 'wt')
>>> print(poem, file=fout)
>>> fout.close()
```

This brings up the question: should I use write() or print()? By default, print() adds a space after each argument and a newline at the end. In the previous example, it appended a newline to the relativity file. To make print() work like write(), pass the following two arguments:

- sep (separator, which defaults to a space, ' ')
- end (end string, which defaults to a newline, '\n')

print() uses the defaults unless you pass something else. We'll pass empty strings to suppress all of the fussiness normally added by print():

```
>>> fout = open('relativity', 'wt')
>>> print(poem, file=fout, sep='', end='')
>>> fout.close()
```

If you have a large source string, you can also write chunks until the source is done:

```
>>> fout = open('relativity', 'wt')
>>> size = len(poem)
>>> offset = 0
>>> chunk = 100
>>> while True:
...     if offset > size:
...         break
...     fout.write(poem[offset:offset+chunk])
...     offset += chunk
...
100
50
>>> fout.close()
```

This wrote 100 characters on the first try and the last 50 characters on the next.

If the relativity file is precious to us, let's see if using mode x really protects us from overwriting it:

```
>>> fout = open('relativity', 'xt')
Traceback (most recent call last):
  File "<stdin>", line 1, in <module>
FileExistsError: [Errno 17] File exists: 'relativity'
```

You can use this with an exception handler:

```
>>> try:
...     fout = open('relativity', 'xt')]
...     fout.write('stomp stomp stomp')
... except FileExistsError:
...     print('relativity already exists!. That was a close one.')
...
relativity already exists!. That was a close one.
```

Read a Text File with read(), readline(), or readlines()

You can call read() with no arguments to slurp up the entire file at once, as shown in the example that follows. Be careful when doing this with large files; a gigabyte file will consume a gigabyte of memory.

```
>>> fin = open('relativity', 'rt' )
>>> poem = fin.read()
>>> fin.close()
>>> len(poem)
150
```

You can provide a maximum character count to limit how much read() returns at one time. Let's read 100 characters at a time and append each chunk to a poem string to rebuild the original:

```
>>> poem = ''
>>> fin = open('relativity', 'rt' )
>>> chunk = 100
>>> while True:
...     fragment = fin.read(chunk)
...     if not fragment:
...         break
...     poem += fragment
...
>>> fin.close()
>>> len(poem)
150
```

After you've read all the way to the end, further calls to read() will return an empty string (''), which is treated as False in if not fragment. This breaks out of the while True loop.

You can also read the file a line at a time by using readline(). In this next example, we'll append each line to the poem string to rebuild the original:

```
>>> poem = ''
>>> fin = open('relativity', 'rt' )
>>> while True:
...     line = fin.readline()
...     if not line:
...         break
...     poem += line
...
```

```
>>> fin.close()
>>> len(poem)
150
```

For a text file, even a blank line has a length of one (the newline character), and is evaluated as True. When the file has been read, readline() (like read()) also returns an empty string, which is also evaluated as False.

The easiest way to read a text file is by using an *iterator*. This returns one line at a time. It's similar to the previous example, but with less code:

```
>>> poem = ''
>>> fin = open('relativity', 'rt' )
>>> for line in fin:
...     poem += line
...
>>> fin.close()
>>> len(poem)
150
```

All of the preceding examples eventually built the single string poem. The read lines() call reads a line at a time, and returns a list of one-line strings:

```
>>> fin = open('relativity', 'rt' )
>>> lines = fin.readlines()
>>> fin.close()
>>> print(len(lines), 'lines read')
5 lines read
>>> for line in lines:
...     print(line, end='')
...
There was a young lady named Bright,
Whose speed was far faster than light;
She started one day
In a relative way,
And returned on the previous night.>>>
```

We told print() to suppress the automatic newlines because the first four lines already had them. The last line did not, causing the interactive prompt >>> to occur right after the last line.

Write a Binary File with write()

If you include a 'b' in the *mode* string, the file is opened in binary mode. In this case, you read and write bytes instead of a string.

We don't have a binary poem lying around, so we'll just generate the 256 byte values from 0 to 255:

```
>>> bdata = bytes(range(0, 256))
>>> len(bdata)
256
```

Open the file for writing in binary mode and write all the data at once:

```
>>> fout = open('bfile', 'wb')
>>> fout.write(bdata)
256
>>> fout.close()
```

Again, `write()` returns the number of bytes written.

As with text, you can write binary data in chunks:

```
>>> fout = open('bfile', 'wb')
>>> size = len(bdata)
>>> offset = 0
>>> chunk = 100
>>> while True:
...     if offset > size:
...         break
...     fout.write(bdata[offset:offset+chunk])
...     offset += chunk
...
100
100
56
>>> fout.close()
```

Read a Binary File with read()

This one is simple; all you need to do is just open with `'rb'`:

```
>>> fin = open('bfile', 'rb')
>>> bdata = fin.read()
>>> len(bdata)
256
>>> fin.close()
```

Close Files Automatically by Using with

If you forget to close a file that you've opened, it will be closed by Python after it's no longer referenced. This means that if you open a file within a function and don't close it explicitly, it will be closed automatically when the function ends. But you might have opened the file in a long-running function or the main section of the program. The file should be closed to force any remaining writes to be completed.

Python has *context managers* to clean up things such as open files. You use the form `with` *expression* as *variable*:

```
>>> with open('relativity', 'wt') as fout:
...     fout.write(poem)
...
```

That's it. After the block of code under the context manager (in this case, one line) completes (normally *or* by a raised exception), the file is closed automatically.

Change Position with seek()

As you read and write, Python keeps track of where you are in the file. The `tell()` function returns your current offset from the beginning of the file, in bytes. The `seek()` function lets you jump to another byte offset in the file. This means that you don't have to read every byte in a file to read the last one; you can `seek()` to the last one and just read one byte.

For this example, use the 256-byte binary file `'bfile'` that you wrote earlier:

```
>>> fin = open('bfile', 'rb')
>>> fin.tell()
0
```

Use `seek()` to one byte before the end of the file:

```
>>> fin.seek(255)
255
```

Read until the end of the file:

```
>>> bdata = fin.read()
>>> len(bdata)
1
>>> bdata[0]
255
```

`seek()` also returns the current offset.

You can call `seek()` with a second argument: `seek( offset, origin )`:

- If `origin` is `0` (the default), go *offset* bytes from the start
- If `origin` is `1`, go *offset* bytes from the current position
- If `origin` is `2`, go *offset* bytes relative to the end

These values are also defined in the standard `os` module:

```
>>> import os
>>> os.SEEK_SET
0
>>> os.SEEK_CUR
1
>>> os.SEEK_END
2
```

So, we could have read the last byte in different ways:

```
>>> fin = open('bfile', 'rb')
```

One byte before the end of the file:

```
>>> fin.seek(-1, 2)
255
>>> fin.tell()
255
```

Read until the end of the file:

```
>>> bdata = fin.read()
>>> len(bdata)
1
>>> bdata[0]
255
```

 You don't need to call tell() for seek() to work. I just wanted to show that they both report the same offset.

Here's an example of seeking from the current position in the file:

```
>>> fin = open('bfile', 'rb')
```

This next example ends up two bytes before the end of the file:

```
>>> fin.seek(254, 0)
254
>>> fin.tell()
254
```

Now, go forward one byte:

```
>>> fin.seek(1, 1)
255
>>> fin.tell()
255
```

Finally, read until the end of the file:

```
>>> bdata = fin.read()
>>> len(bdata)
1
>>> bdata[0]
255
```

These functions are most useful for binary files. You can use them with text files, but unless the file is ASCII (one byte per character), you would have a hard time calculating offsets. These would depend on the text encoding, and the most popular encoding (UTF-8) uses varying numbers of bytes per character.

Structured Text Files

With simple text files, the only level of organization is the line. Sometimes, you want more structure than that. You might want to save data for your program to use later, or send data to another program.

There are many formats, and here's how you can distinguish them:

- A *separator*, or *delimiter*, character like tab ('\t'), comma (','), or vertical bar ('|'). This is an example of the comma-separated values (CSV) format.
- '<' and '>' around *tags*. Examples include XML and HTML.
- Punctuation. An example is JavaScript Object Notation (JSON).
- Indentation. An example is YAML (which depending on the source you use means "YAML Ain't Markup Language;" you'll need to research that one yourself).
- Miscellaneous, such as configuration files for programs.

Each of these structured file formats can be read and written by at least one Python module.

CSV

Delimited files are often used as an exchange format for spreadsheets and databases. You could read CSV files manually, a line at a time, splitting each line into fields at comma separators, and adding the results to data structures such as lists and dictionaries. But it's better to use the standard csv module, because parsing these files can get more complicated than you think.

- Some have alternate delimiters besides a comma: '|' and '\t' (tab) are common.
- Some have *escape sequences*. If the delimiter character can occur within a field, the entire field might be surrounded by quote characters or preceded by some escape character.
- Files have different line-ending characters. Unix uses '\n', Microsoft uses '\r\n', and Apple used to use '\r' but now uses '\n'.
- There can be column names in the first line.

First, we'll see how to read and write a list of rows, each containing a list of columns:

```
>>> import csv
>>> villains = [
...     ['Doctor', 'No'],
...     ['Rosa', 'Klebb'],
```

```
...         ['Mister', 'Big'],
...         ['Auric', 'Goldfinger'],
...         ['Ernst', 'Blofeld'],
...         ]
>>> with open('villains', 'wt') as fout:  # a context manager
...     csvout = csv.writer(fout)
...     csvout.writerows(villains)
```

This creates the file villains with these lines:

```
Doctor,No
Rosa,Klebb
Mister,Big
Auric,Goldfinger
Ernst,Blofeld
```

Now, we'll try to read it back in:

```
>>> import csv
>>> with open('villains', 'rt') as fin:  # context manager
...     cin = csv.reader(fin)
...     villains = [row for row in cin]  # This uses a list comprehension
...
>>> print(villains)
[['Doctor', 'No'], ['Rosa', 'Klebb'], ['Mister', 'Big'],
['Auric', 'Goldfinger'], ['Ernst', 'Blofeld']]
```

Take a moment to think about list comprehensions (feel free to go to "Comprehensions" on page 84 and brush up on that syntax). We took advantage of the structure created by the reader() function. It obligingly created rows in the cin object that we can extract in a for loop.

Using reader() and writer() with their default options, the columns are separated by commas and the rows by line feeds.

The data can be a list of dictionaries rather than a list of lists. Let's read the villains file again, this time using the new DictReader() function and specifying the column names:

```
>>> import csv
>>> with open('villains', 'rt') as fin:
...     cin = csv.DictReader(fin, fieldnames=['first', 'last'])
...     villains = [row for row in cin]
...
>>> print(villains)
[{'last': 'No', 'first': 'Doctor'},
{'last': 'Klebb', 'first': 'Rosa'},
{'last': 'Big', 'first': 'Mister'},
{'last': 'Goldfinger', 'first': 'Auric'},
{'last': 'Blofeld', 'first': 'Ernst'}]
```

Let's rewrite the CSV file by using the new DictWriter() function. We'll also call writeheader() to write an initial line of column names to the CSV file:

```
import csv
villains = [
    {'first': 'Doctor', 'last': 'No'},
    {'first': 'Rosa', 'last': 'Klebb'},
    {'first': 'Mister', 'last': 'Big'},
    {'first': 'Auric', 'last': 'Goldfinger'},
    {'first': 'Ernst', 'last': 'Blofeld'},
    ]
with open('villains', 'wt') as fout:
    cout = csv.DictWriter(fout, ['first', 'last'])
    cout.writeheader()
    cout.writerows(villains)
```

That creates a `villains` file with a header line:

```
first,last
Doctor,No
Rosa,Klebb
Mister,Big
Auric,Goldfinger
Ernst,Blofeld
```

Now we'll read it back. By omitting the `fieldnames` argument in the `DictReader()` call, we instruct it to use the values in the first line of the file (`first,last`) as column labels and matching dictionary keys:

```
>>> import csv
>>> with open('villains', 'rt') as fin:
...     cin = csv.DictReader(fin)
...     villains = [row for row in cin]
...
>>> print(villains)
[{'last': 'No', 'first': 'Doctor'},
 {'last': 'Klebb', 'first': 'Rosa'},
 {'last': 'Big', 'first': 'Mister'},
 {'last': 'Goldfinger', 'first': 'Auric'},
 {'last': 'Blofeld', 'first': 'Ernst'}]
```

XML

Delimited files convey only two dimensions: rows (lines) and columns (fields within a line). If you want to exchange data structures among programs, you need a way to encode hierarchies, sequences, sets, and other structures as text.

XML is the most prominent *markup* format that suits the bill. It uses *tags* to delimit data, as in this sample *menu.xml* file:

```
<?xml version="1.0"?>
<menu>
  <breakfast hours="7-11">
    <item price="$6.00">breakfast burritos</item>
    <item price="$4.00">pancakes</item>
```

```
      </breakfast>
      <lunch hours="11-3">
        <item price="$5.00">hamburger</item>
      </lunch>
      <dinner hours="3-10">
        <item price="8.00">spaghetti</item>
      </dinner>
    </menu>
```

Following are a few important characteristics of XML:

- Tags begin with a < character. The tags in this sample were `menu`, `breakfast`, `lunch`, `dinner`, and `item`.

- Whitespace is ignored.

- Usually a *start tag* such as `<menu>` is followed by other content and then a final matching *end tag* such as `</menu>`.

- Tags can *nest* within other tags to any level. In this example, `item` tags are children of the `breakfast`, `lunch`, and `dinner` tags; they, in turn, are children of `menu`.

- Optional *attributes* can occur within the start tag. In this example, `price` is an attribute of `item`.

- Tags can contain *values*. In this example, each `item` has a value, such as `pancakes` for the second breakfast item.

- If a tag named `thing` has no values or children, it can be expressed as the single tag by including a forward slash just before the closing angle bracket, such as `<thing/>`, rather than a start and end tag, like `<thing></thing>`.

- The choice of where to put data—attributes, values, child tags—is somewhat arbitrary. For instance, we could have written the last `item` tag as `<item price="$8.00" food="spaghetti"/>`.

XML is often used for data *feeds* and *messages*, and has subformats like RSS and Atom. Some industries have many specialized XML formats, such as the finance field (*http://bit.ly/xml-finance*).

XML's über-flexibility has inspired multiple Python libraries that differ in approach and capabilities.

The simplest way to parse XML in Python is by using `ElementTree`. Here's a little program to parse the *menu.xml* file and print some tags and attributes:

```
>>> import xml.etree.ElementTree as et
>>> tree = et.ElementTree(file='menu.xml')
>>> root = tree.getroot()
>>> root.tag
```

```
'menu'
>>> for child in root:
...     print('tag:', child.tag, 'attributes:', child.attrib)
...     for grandchild in child:
...         print('\ttag:', grandchild.tag, 'attributes:', grandchild.attrib)
...
tag: breakfast attributes: {'hours': '7-11'}
    tag: item attributes: {'price': '$6.00'}
    tag: item attributes: {'price': '$4.00'}
tag: lunch attributes: {'hours': '11-3'}
    tag: item attributes: {'price': '$5.00'}
tag: dinner attributes: {'hours': '3-10'}
    tag: item attributes: {'price': '8.00'}
>>> len(root)      # number of menu sections
3
>>> len(root[0])  # number of breakfast items
2
```

For each element in the nested lists, `tag` is the tag string and `attrib` is a dictionary of its attributes. `ElementTree` has many other ways of searching XML-derived data, modifying it, and even writing XML files. The `ElementTree` documentation (*http://bit.ly/elementtree*) has the details.

Other standard Python XML libraries include:

`xml.dom`

The Document Object Model (DOM), familiar to JavaScript developers, represents Web documents as hierarchical structures. This module loads the entire XML file into memory and lets you access all the pieces equally.

`xml.sax`

Simple API for XML, or SAX, parses XML on the fly, so it does not have to load everything into memory at once. Therefore, it can be a good choice if you need to process very large streams of XML.

HTML

Enormous amounts of data are saved as Hypertext Markup Language (HTML), the basic document format of the Web. The problem is so much of it doesn't follow the HTML rules, which can make it difficult to parse. Also, much of HTML is intended more to format output than interchange data. Because this chapter is intended to describe fairly well-defined data formats, I have separated out the discussion about HTML to Chapter 9.

JSON

JavaScript Object Notation (JSON) (*http://www.json.org*) has become a very popular data interchange format, beyond its JavaScript origins. The JSON format is a subset of

JavaScript, and often legal Python syntax as well. Its close fit to Python makes it a good choice for data interchange among programs. You'll see many examples of JSON for web development in Chapter 9.

Unlike the variety of XML modules, there's one main JSON module, with the unforgettable name json. This program encodes (dumps) data to a JSON string and decodes (loads) a JSON string back to data. In this next example, let's build a Python data structure containing the data from the earlier XML example:

```
>>> menu = \
... {
... "breakfast": {
...         "hours": "7-11",
...         "items": {
...                 "breakfast burritos": "$6.00",
...                 "pancakes": "$4.00"
...                 }
...         },
... "lunch" : {
...         "hours": "11-3",
...         "items": {
...                 "hamburger": "$5.00"
...                 }
...         },
... "dinner": {
...         "hours": "3-10",
...         "items": {
...                 "spaghetti": "$8.00"
...                 }
...         }
... }
.
```

Next, encode the data structure (menu) to a JSON string (menu_json) by using dumps():

```
>>> import json
>>> menu_json = json.dumps(menu)
>>> menu_json
'{"dinner": {"items": {"spaghetti": "$8.00"}, "hours": "3-10"},
"lunch": {"items": {"hamburger": "$5.00"}, "hours": "11-3"},
"breakfast": {"items": {"breakfast burritos": "$6.00", "pancakes":
"$4.00"}, "hours": "7-11"}}'
```

And now, let's turn the JSON string menu_json back into a Python data structure (menu2) by using loads():

```
>>> menu2 = json.loads(menu_json)
>>> menu2
{'breakfast': {'items': {'breakfast burritos': '$6.00', 'pancakes':
'$4.00'}, 'hours': '7-11'}, 'lunch': {'items': {'hamburger': '$5.00'},
'hours': '11-3'}, 'dinner': {'items': {'spaghetti': '$8.00'}, 'hours': '3-10'}}
```

menu and menu2 are both dictionaries with the same keys and values. As always with standard dictionaries, the order in which you get the keys varies.

You might get an exception while trying to encode or decode some objects, including objects such as datetime (covered in detail in "Calendars and Clocks" on page 256), as demonstrated here.

```
>>> import datetime
>>> now = datetime.datetime.utcnow()
>>> now
datetime.datetime(2013, 2, 22, 3, 49, 27, 483336)
>>> json.dumps(now)
Traceback (most recent call last):
# ... (deleted stack trace to save trees)
TypeError: datetime.datetime(2013, 2, 22, 3, 49, 27, 483336) is not JSON serializable
>>>
```

This can happen because the JSON standard does not define date or time types; it expects you to define how to handle them. You could convert the datetime to something JSON understands, such as a string or an *epoch* value (coming in Chapter 10):

```
>>> now_str = str(now)
>>> json.dumps(now_str)
'"2013-02-22 03:49:27.483336"'
>>> from time import mktime
>>> now_epoch = int(mktime(now.timetuple()))
>>> json.dumps(now_epoch)
'1361526567'
```

If the datetime value could occur in the middle of normally converted data types, it might be annoying to make these special conversions. You can modify how JSON is encoded by using inheritance, which is described in "Inheritance" on page 128. Python's JSON documentation (*http://bit.ly/json-docs*) gives an example of this for complex numbers, which also makes JSON play dead. Let's modify it for datetime:

```
>>> class DTEncoder(json.JSONEncoder):
...     def default(self, obj):
...         # isinstance() checks the type of obj
...         if isinstance(obj, datetime.datetime):
...             return int(mktime(obj.timetuple()))
...         # else it's something the normal decoder knows:
...         return json.JSONEncoder.default(self, obj)
...
>>> json.dumps(now, cls=DTEncoder)
'1361526567'
```

The new class DTEncoder is a subclass, or child class, of JSONEncoder. We only need to override its default() method to add datetime handling. Inheritance ensures that everything else will be handled by the parent class.

The `isinstance()` function checks whether the object `obj` is of the class `date time.datetime`. Because everything in Python is an object, `isinstance()` works everywhere:

```
>>> type(now)
<class 'datetime.datetime'>
>>> isinstance(now, datetime.datetime)
True
>>> type(234)
<class 'int'>
>>> isinstance(234, int)
True
>>> type('hey')
<class 'str'>
>>> isinstance('hey', str)
True
```

 For JSON and other structured text formats, you can load from a file into data structures without knowing anything about the structures ahead of time. Then, you can walk through the structures by using `isinstance()` and type-appropriate methods to examine their values. For example, if one of the items is a dictionary, you can extract contents through `keys()`, `values()`, and `items()`.

YAML

Similar to JSON, YAML (*http://www.yaml.org*) has keys and values, but handles more data types such as dates and times. The standard Python library does not yet include YAML handling, so you need to install a third-party library named `yaml` (*http://pyyaml.org/wiki/PyYAML*) to manipulate it. `load()` converts a YAML string to Python data, whereas `dump()` does the opposite.

The following YAML file, *mcintyre.yaml*, contains information on the Canadian poet James McIntyre, including two of his poems:

```
name:
  first: James
  last: McIntyre
dates:
  birth: 1828-05-25
  death: 1906-03-31
details:
  bearded: true
  themes: [cheese, Canada]
books:
  url: http://www.gutenberg.org/files/36068/36068-h/36068-h.htm
poems:
  - title: 'Motto'
    text: |
```

```
        Politeness, perseverance and pluck,
        To their possessor will bring good luck.
  - title: 'Canadian Charms'
    text: |
        Here industry is not in vain,
        For we have bounteous crops of grain,
        And you behold on every field
        Of grass and roots abundant yield,
        But after all the greatest charm
        Is the snug home upon the farm,
        And stone walls now keep cattle warm.
```

Values such as `true`, `false`, `on`, and `off` are converted to Python Booleans. Integers and strings are converted to their Python equivalents. Other syntax creates lists and dictionaries:

```
>>> import yaml
>>> with open('mcintyre.yaml', 'rt') as fin:
>>>     text = fin.read()
>>> data = yaml.load(text)
>>> data['details']
{'themes': ['cheese', 'Canada'], 'bearded': True}
>>> len(data['poems'])
2
```

The data structures that are created match those in the YAML file, which in this case are more than one level deep in places. You can get the title of the second poem with this dict/list/dict reference:

```
>>> data['poems'][1]['title']
'Canadian Charms'
```

 PyYAML can load Python objects from strings, and this is dangerous. Use `safe_load()` instead of `load()` if you're importing YAML that you don't trust. Better yet, *always* use `safe_load()`. Read war is peace (*http://bit.ly/war-is-peace*) for a description of how unprotected YAML loading compromised the Ruby on Rails platform.

A Security Note

You can use all the formats described in this chapter to save objects to files and read them back again. It's possible to exploit this process and cause security problems.

For example, the following XML snippet from the billion laughs Wikipedia page defines ten nested entities, each expanding the lower level ten times for a total expansion of one billion:

```
<?xml version="1.0"?>
<!DOCTYPE lolz [
 <!ENTITY lol "lol">
```

```
<!ENTITY lol1 "&lol;&lol;&lol;&lol;&lol;&lol;&lol;&lol;&lol;&lol;">
<!ENTITY lol2 "&lol1;&lol1;&lol1;&lol1;&lol1;&lol1;&lol1;&lol1;&lol1;&lol1;">
<!ENTITY lol3 "&lol2;&lol2;&lol2;&lol2;&lol2;&lol2;&lol2;&lol2;&lol2;">
<!ENTITY lol4 "&lol3;&lol3;&lol3;&lol3;&lol3;&lol3;&lol3;&lol3;&lol3;">
<!ENTITY lol5 "&lol4;&lol4;&lol4;&lol4;&lol4;&lol4;&lol4;&lol4;&lol4;">
<!ENTITY lol6 "&lol5;&lol5;&lol5;&lol5;&lol5;&lol5;&lol5;&lol5;&lol5;">
<!ENTITY lol7 "&lol6;&lol6;&lol6;&lol6;&lol6;&lol6;&lol6;&lol6;&lol6;">
<!ENTITY lol8 "&lol7;&lol7;&lol7;&lol7;&lol7;&lol7;&lol7;&lol7;&lol7;">
<!ENTITY lol9 "&lol8;&lol8;&lol8;&lol8;&lol8;&lol8;&lol8;&lol8;&lol8;">
]>
<lolz>&lol9;</lolz>
```

The bad news: billion laughs would blow up all of the XML libraries mentioned in the previous sections. Defused XML (*https://bitbucket.org/tiran/defusedxml*) lists this attack and others, along with the vulnerability of Python libraries. The link shows how to change the settings for many of the libraries to avoid these problems. Also, you can use the defusedxml library as a security frontend for the other libraries:

```
>>> # insecure:
>>> from xml.etree.ElementTree import parse
>>> et = parse(xmlfile)
>>> # protected:
>>> from defusedxml.ElementTree import parse
>>> et = parse(xmlfile)
```

Configuration Files

Most programs offer various *options* or *settings*. Dynamic ones can be provided as program arguments, but long-lasting ones need to be kept somewhere. The temptation to define your own quick and dirty *config file* format is strong—but resist it. It often turns out to be dirty, but not so quick. You need to maintain both the writer program and the reader program (sometimes called a *parser*). There are good alternatives that you can just drop into your program, including those in the previous sections.

Here, we'll use the standard configparser module, which handles Windows-style *.ini* files. Such files have sections of *key = value* definitions. Here's a minimal *settings.cfg* file:

```
[english]
greeting = Hello

[french]
greeting = Bonjour

[files]
home = /usr/local
# simple interpolation:
bin = %(home)s/bin
```

Here's the code to read it into Python data structures:

```
>>> import configparser
>>> cfg = configparser.ConfigParser()
>>> cfg.read('settings.cfg')
['settings.cfg']
>>> cfg
<configparser.ConfigParser object at 0x1006be4d0>
>>> cfg['french']
<Section: french>
>>> cfg['french']['greeting']
'Bonjour'
>>> cfg['files']['bin']
'/usr/local/bin'
```

Other options are available, including fancier interpolation. See the configparser documentation (*http://bit.ly/configparser*). If you need deeper nesting than two levels, try YAML or JSON.

Other Interchange Formats

These binary data interchange formats are usually more compact and faster than XML or JSON:

- MsgPack (*http://msgpack.org*)
- Protocol Buffers (*https://code.google.com/p/protobuf/*)
- Avro (*http://avro.apache.org/docs/current/*)
- Thrift (*http://thrift.apache.org/*)

Because they are binary, none can be easily edited by a human with a text editor.

Serialize by Using pickle

Saving data structures to a file is called *serializing*. Formats such as JSON might require some custom converters to serialize all the data types from a Python program. Python provides the pickle module to save and restore any object in a special binary format.

Remember how JSON lost its mind when encountering a datetime object? Not a problem for pickle:

```
>>> import pickle
>>> import datetime
>>> now1 = datetime.datetime.utcnow()
>>> pickled = pickle.dumps(now1)
>>> now2 = pickle.loads(pickled)
>>> now1
datetime.datetime(2014, 6, 22, 23, 24, 19, 195722)
```

```
>>> now2
datetime.datetime(2014, 6, 22, 23, 24, 19, 195722)
```

pickle works with your own classes and objects, too. We'll define a little class called Tiny that returns the string 'tiny' when treated as a string:

```
>>> import pickle
>>> class Tiny():
...     def __str__(self):
...         return 'tiny'
...
>>> obj1 = Tiny()
>>> obj1
<__main__.Tiny object at 0x10076ed10>
>>> str(obj1)
'tiny'
>>> pickled = pickle.dumps(obj1)
>>> pickled
b'\x80\x03c__main__\nTiny\nq\x00)\x81q\x01.'
>>> obj2 = pickle.loads(pickled)
>>> obj2
<__main__.Tiny object at 0x10076e550>
>>> str(obj2)
'tiny'
```

pickled is the pickled binary string made from the object obj1. We converted that back to the object obj2 to make a copy of obj1. Use dump() to pickle to a file, and load() to unpickle from one.

 Because pickle can create Python objects, the same security warnings that were discussed in earlier sections apply. Don't unpickle something that you don't trust.

Structured Binary Files

Some file formats were designed to store particular data structures but are neither relational nor NoSQL databases. The sections that follow present some of them.

Spreadsheets

Spreadsheets, notably Microsoft Excel, are widespread binary data formats. If you can save your spreadsheet to a CSV file, you can read it by using the standard csv module that was described earlier. If you have a binary xls file, xlrd (*http://pypi.python.org/pypi/xlrd*) is a third-party package for reading and writing.

HDF5

HDF5 (*http://www.hdfgroup.org/why_hdf*) is a binary data format for multidimensional or hierarchical numeric data. It's used mainly in science, where fast random access to large datasets (gigabytes to terabytes) is a common requirement. Even though HDF5 could be a good alternative to databases in some cases, for some reason HDF5 is almost unknown in the business world. It's best suited to *WORM* (write once/read many) applications for which database protection against conflicting writes is not needed. Here are a couple of modules that you might find useful:

- h5py is a full-featured low-level interface. Read the documentation (*http://www.h5py.org/*) and code (*https://github.com/h5py/h5py*).
- PyTables is a bit higher-level, with database-like features. Read the documentation (*http://www.pytables.org/*) and code (*http://pytables.github.com/*).

Both of these are discussed in terms of scientific applications of Python in Appendix C. I'm mentioning HDF5 here in case you have a need to store and retrieve large amounts of data and are willing to consider something outside the box, as well as the usual database solutions. A good example is the Million Song dataset (*http://bit.ly/millionsong*), which has downloadable song data in HDF5 format.

Relational Databases

Relational databases are only about 40 years old but are ubiquitous in the computing world. You'll almost certainly have to deal with them at one time or another. When you do, you'll appreciate what they provide:

- Access to data by multiple simultaneous users
- Protection from corruption by those users
- Efficient methods to store and retrieve the data
- Data defined by *schemas* and limited by *constraints*
- *Joins* to find relationships across diverse types of data
- A declarative (rather than imperative) query language: *SQL* (Structured Query Language)

These are called *relational* because they show relationships among different kinds of data in the form of *tables* (as they are usually called nowadays). For instance, in our menu example earlier, there is a relationship between each item and its price.

A table is a grid of rows and columns, similar to a spreadsheet. To create a table, name it and specify the order, names, and types of its columns. Each row has the same columns, although a column may be defined to allow missing data (called *nulls*). In the menu example, you could create a table with one row for each item being sold. Each item has the same columns, including one for the price.

A column or group of columns is usually the table's *primary key*; its values must be unique in the table. This prevents adding the same data to the table more than once. This key is *indexed* for fast lookups during queries. An index works a little like a book index, making it fast to find a particular row.

Each table lives within a parent *database*, like a file within a directory. Two levels of hierarchy help keep things organized a little better.

 Yes, the word *database* is used in multiple ways: as the server, the table container, and the data stored therein. If you'll be referring to all of them at the same time, it might help to call them *database server*, *database*, and *data*.

If you want to find rows by some non-key column value, define a *secondary index* on that column. Otherwise, the database server must perform a *table scan*—a brute-force search of every row for matching column values.

Tables can be related to each other with *foreign keys*, and column values can be constrained to these keys.

SQL

SQL is not an API or a protocol, but a declarative *language*: you say *what* you want rather than *how* to do it. It's the universal language of relational databases. SQL queries are text strings, that a client sends to the database server, which figures out what to do with them.

There have been various SQL standard definitions, but all database vendors have added their own tweaks and extensions, resulting in many SQL *dialects*. If you store your data in a relational database, SQL gives you some portability. Still, dialect and operational differences can make it difficult to move your data to another type of database.

There are two main categories of SQL statements:

DDL (data definition language)
    Handles creation, deletion, constraints, and permissions for tables, databases, and uses

DML (data manipulation language)
    Handles data insertions, selects, updates, and deletions

Table 8-1 lists the basic SQL DDL commands.

Table 8-1. Basic SQL DDL commands

Operation	SQL pattern	SQL example
Create a database	CREATE DATABASE *dbname*	CREATE DATABASE d
Select current database	USE *dbname*	USE d
Delete a database and its tables	DROP DATABASE *dbname*	DROP DATABASE d
Create a table	CREATE TABLE *tbname* (*coldefs*)	CREATE TABLE t (id INT, count INT)
Delete a table	DROP TABLE *tbname*	DROP TABLE t
Remove all rows from a table	TRUNCATE TABLE *tbname*	TRUNCATE TABLE t

 Why all the CAPITAL LETTERS? SQL is case-insensitive, but it's tradition (don't ask me why) to SHOUT its keywords in code examples to distinguish them from column names.

The main DML operations of a relational database are often known by the acronym CRUD:

- Create by using the SQL INSERT statement
- Read by using SELECT
- Update by using UPDATE
- Delete by using DELETE

Table 8-2 looks at the commands available for SQL DML.

Table 8-2. Basic SQL DML commands

Operation	SQL pattern	SQL example
Add a row	INSERT INTO *tbname* VALUES(...)	INSERT INTO t VALUES(7, 40)
Select all rows and columns	SELECT * FROM *tbname*	SELECT * FROM t
Select all rows, some columns	SELECT *cols* FROM *tbname*	SELECT id, count FROM t

Operation	SQL pattern	SQL example
Select some rows, some columns	SELECT *cols* FROM *tbname* WHERE *condition*	SELECT id, count from t WHERE count > 5 AND id = 9
Change some rows in a column	UPDATE *tbname* SET *col* = *value* WHERE *condition*	UPDATE t SET count=3 WHERE id=5
Delete some rows	DELETE FROM *tbname* WHERE *condition*	DELETE FROM t WHERE count <= 10 OR id = 16

DB-API

An application programming interface (API) is a set of functions that you can call to get access to some service. DB-API (*http://bit.ly/db-api*) is Python's standard API for accessing relational databases. Using it, you can write a single program that works with multiple kinds of relational databases instead of writing a separate program for each one. It's similar to Java's JDBC or Perl's dbi.

Its main functions are the following:

connect()
> Make a connection to the database; this can include arguments such as username, password, server address, and others.

cursor()
> Create a *cursor* object to manage queries.

execute() *and* executemany()
> Run one or more SQL commands against the database.

fetchone(), fetchmany(), *and* fetchall()
> Get the results from execute.

The Python database modules in the coming sections conform to DB-API, often with extensions and some differences in details.

SQLite

SQLite (*http://www.sqlite.org*) is a good, light, open source relational database. It's implemented as a standard Python library, and stores databases in normal files. These files are portable across machines and operating systems, making SQLite a very portable solution for simple relational database applications. It isn't as full-featured as MySQL or PostgreSQL, but it does support SQL, and it manages multiple simultaneous users. Web browsers, smart phones, and other applications use SQLite as an embedded database.

You begin with a `connect()` to the local SQLite database file that you want to use or create. This file is the equivalent of the directory-like *database* that parents tables in other servers. The special string `':memory:'` creates the database in memory only; this is fast and useful for testing but will lose data when your program terminates or if your computer goes down.

For the next example, let's make a database called `enterprise.db` and the table `zoo` to manage our thriving roadside petting zoo business. The table columns are as follows:

`critter`
> A variable length string, and our primary key

`count`
> An integer count of our current inventory for this animal

`damages`
> The dollar amount of our current losses from animal-human interactions

```
>>> import sqlite3
>>> conn = sqlite3.connect('enterprise.db')
>>> curs = conn.cursor()
>>> curs.execute('''CREATE TABLE zoo
    (critter VARCHAR(20) PRIMARY KEY,
     count INT,
     damages FLOAT)''')
<sqlite3.Cursor object at 0x1006a22d0>
```

Python's triple quotes are handy when creating long strings such as SQL queries.

Now, add some animals to the zoo:

```
>>> curs.execute('INSERT INTO zoo VALUES("duck", 5, 0.0)')
<sqlite3.Cursor object at 0x1006a22d0>
>>> curs.execute('INSERT INTO zoo VALUES("bear", 2, 1000.0)')
<sqlite3.Cursor object at 0x1006a22d0>
```

There's a safer way to insert data, using a *placeholder*:

```
>>> ins = 'INSERT INTO zoo (critter, count, damages) VALUES(?, ?, ?)'
>>> curs.execute(ins, ('weasel', 1, 2000.0))
<sqlite3.Cursor object at 0x1006a22d0>
```

This time, we used three question marks in the SQL to indicate that we plan to insert three values, and then pass those three values as a tuple to the `execute()` function. Placeholders handle tedious details such as quoting. They protect you against *SQL injection*—a kind of external attack that is common on the Web that inserts malicious SQL commands into the system.

Now, let's see if we can get all our animals out again:

```
>>> curs.execute('SELECT * FROM zoo')
<sqlite3.Cursor object at 0x1006a22d0>
>>> rows = curs.fetchall()
>>> print(rows)
[('duck', 5, 0.0), ('bear', 2, 1000.0), ('weasel', 1, 2000.0)]
```

Let's get them again, but ordered by their counts:

```
>>> curs.execute('SELECT * from zoo ORDER BY count')
<sqlite3.Cursor object at 0x1006a22d0>
>>> curs.fetchall()
[('weasel', 1, 2000.0), ('bear', 2, 1000.0), ('duck', 5, 0.0)]
```

Hey, we wanted them in descending order:

```
>>> curs.execute('SELECT * from zoo ORDER BY count DESC')
<sqlite3.Cursor object at 0x1006a22d0>
>>> curs.fetchall()
[('duck', 5, 0.0), ('bear', 2, 1000.0), ('weasel', 1, 2000.0)]
```

Which type of animal is costing us the most?

```
>>> curs.execute('''SELECT * FROM zoo WHERE
...     damages = (SELECT MAX(damages) FROM zoo)''')
<sqlite3.Cursor object at 0x1006a22d0>
>>> curs.fetchall()
[('weasel', 1, 2000.0)]
```

You would have thought it was the bears. It's always best to check the actual data.

Before we leave SQLite, we need to clean up. If we opened a connection and a cursor, we need to close them when we're done:

```
>>> curs.close()
>>> conn.close()
```

MySQL

MySQL (*http://www.mysql.com*) is a very popular open source relational database. Unlike SQLite, it's an actual server, so clients can access it from different devices across the network.

MysqlDB (*http://sourceforge.net/projects/mysql-python*) has been the most popular MySQL driver, but it has not yet been ported to Python 3. Table 8-3 lists the drivers you can use to access MySQL from Python.

Table 8-3. MySQL drivers

Name	Link	Pypi package	Import as	Notes
MySQL Connector	http://bit.ly/mysql-cpdg	mysql-connector-python	`mysql.connector`	

Name	Link	Pypi package	Import as	Notes
PYMySQL	https://github.com/petehunt/ PyMySQL/	pymysql	`pymysql`	
oursql	http://pythonhosted.org/oursql/	oursql	`oursql`	Requires the MySQL C client libraries.

PostgreSQL

PostgreSQL (*http://www.postgresql.org*) is a full-featured open source relational database, in many ways more advanced than MySQL. Table 8-4 presents the Python drivers you can use to access it.

Table 8-4. PostgreSQL drivers

Name	Link	Pypi package	Import as	Notes
psycopg2	http://initd.org/psycopg/	psycopg2	psycopg2	Needs `pg_config` from PostgreSQL client tools
py-postgresql	http://python.projects.pgfoundry.org/	py-postgresql	postgresql	

The most popular driver is `psycopg2`, but its installation requires the PostgreSQL client libraries.

SQLAlchemy

SQL is not quite the same for all relational databases, and DB-API takes you only so far. Each database implements a particular *dialect* reflecting its features and philosophy. Many libraries try to bridge these differences in one way or another. The most popular cross-database Python library is SQLAlchemy (*http://www.sqlalchemy.org*).

It isn't in the standard library, but it's well known and used by many people. You can install it on your system by using this command:

```
$ pip install sqlalchemy
```

You can use SQLAlchemy on several levels:

- The lowest level handles database connection *pools*, executing SQL commands, and returning results. This is closest to the DB-API.
- Next up is the *SQL expression language*, a Pythonic SQL builder.
- Highest is the ORM (Object Relational Model) layer, which uses the SQL Expression Language and binds application code with relational data structures.

As we go along, you'll understand what the terms mean in those levels. SQLAlchemy works with the database drivers documented in the previous sections. You don't need to import the driver; the initial connection string you provide to SQLAlchemy will determine it. That string looks like this:

dialect + *driver* : // *user* : *password* @ *host* : *port* / *dbname*

The values you put in this string are as follows:

dialect
> The database type

driver
> The particular driver you want to use for that database

user *and* password
> Your database authentication strings

host *and* port
> The database server's location (: port is only needed if it's not the standard one for this server)

dbname
> The database to initially connect to on the server

Table 8-5 lists the dialects and drivers.

Table 8-5. SQLAlchemy connection

dialect	driver
sqlite	pysqlite (or omit)
mysql	mysqlconnector
mysql	pymysql
mysql	oursql
postgresql	psycopg2
postgresql	pypostgresql

The engine layer

First, we'll try the lowest level of SQLAlchemy, which does little more than the base DB-API functions.

Let's try it with SQLite, which is already built into Python. The connection string for SQLite skips the *host*, *port*, *user*, and *password*. The *dbname* informs SQLite as to what file to use to store your database. If you omit the *dbname*, SQLite builds a database in memory. If the *dbname* starts with a slash (/), it's an absolute filename on your computer (as in Linux and OS X; for example, C:\\ on Windows). Otherwise, it's relative to your current directory.

The following segments are all part of one program, separated here for explanation.

To begin, you need to import what we need. The following is an example of an *import alias*, which lets us use the string `sa` to refer to SQLAlchemy methods. I do this mainly because `sa` is a lot easier to type than `sqlalchemy`:

```
>>> import sqlalchemy as sa
```

Connect to the database and create the storage for it in memory (the argument string `'sqlite:///:memory:'` also works):

```
>>> conn = sa.create_engine('sqlite://')
```

Create a database table called `zoo` that comprises three columns:

```
>>> conn.execute('''CREATE TABLE zoo
...     (critter VARCHAR(20) PRIMARY KEY,
...      count INT,
...      damages FLOAT)''')
<sqlalchemy.engine.result.ResultProxy object at 0x1017efb10>
```

Running `conn.execute()` returns a SQLAlchemy object called a `ResultProxy`. You'll soon see what to do with it.

By the way, if you've never made a database table before, congratulations. Check that one off your bucket list.

Now, insert three sets of data into your new empty table:

```
>>> ins = 'INSERT INTO zoo (critter, count, damages) VALUES (?, ?, ?)'
>>> conn.execute(ins, 'duck', 10, 0.0)
<sqlalchemy.engine.result.ResultProxy object at 0x1017efb50>
>>> conn.execute(ins, 'bear', 2, 1000.0)
<sqlalchemy.engine.result.ResultProxy object at 0x1017ef090>
>>> conn.execute(ins, 'weasel', 1, 2000.0)
<sqlalchemy.engine.result.ResultProxy object at 0x1017ef450>
```

Next, ask the database for everything that we just put in:

```
>>> rows = conn.execute('SELECT * FROM zoo')
```

In SQLAlchemy, `rows` is not a list; it's that special `ResultProxy` thing that we can't print directly:

```
>>> print(rows)
<sqlalchemy.engine.result.ResultProxy object at 0x1017ef9d0>
```

However, you can iterate over it like a list, so we can get a row at a time:

```
>>> for row in rows:
...     print(row)
...
('duck', 10, 0.0)
('bear', 2, 1000.0)
('weasel', 1, 2000.0)
```

That was almost the same as the SQLite DB-API example that you saw earlier. The one advantage is that we didn't need to import the database driver at the top; SQLAlchemy figured that out from the connection string. Just changing the connection string would make this code portable to another type of database. Another plus is SQLAlchemy's *connection pooling*, which you can read about at its documentation site (*http://bit.ly/conn-pooling*).

The SQL Expression Language

The next level up is SQLAlchemy's SQL Expression Language. It introduces functions to create the SQL for various operations. The Expression Language handles more of the SQL dialect differences than the lower-level engine layer does. It can be a handy middle-ground approach for relational database applications.

Here's how to create and populate the zoo table. Again, these are successive fragments of a single program.

The import and connection are the same as before:

```
>>> import sqlalchemy as sa
>>> conn = sa.create_engine('sqlite://')
```

To define the zoo table, we'll begin using some of the Expression Language instead of SQL:

```
>>> meta = sa.MetaData()
>>> zoo = sa.Table('zoo', meta,
...     sa.Column('critter', sa.String, primary_key=True),
...     sa.Column('count', sa.Integer),
...     sa.Column('damages', sa.Float)
...     )
>>> meta.create_all(conn)
```

Check out the parentheses in that multiline call in the preceding example. The structure of the `Table()` method matches the structure of the table. Just as our table contains three columns, there are three calls to `Column()` inside the parentheses of the `Table()` method call.

Meanwhile, zoo is some magic object that bridges the SQL database world and the Python data structure world.

Insert the data with more Expression Language functions:

```
... conn.execute(zoo.insert(('bear', 2, 1000.0)))
<sqlalchemy.engine.result.ResultProxy object at 0x1017ea910>
>>> conn.execute(zoo.insert(('weasel', 1, 2000.0)))
<sqlalchemy.engine.result.ResultProxy object at 0x1017eab10>
>>> conn.execute(zoo.insert(('duck', 10, 0)))
<sqlalchemy.engine.result.ResultProxy object at 0x1017eac50>
```

Next, create the SELECT statement (`zoo.select()` selects everything from the table represented by the zoo object, such as `SELECT * FROM zoo` would do in plain SQL):

```
>>> result = conn.execute(zoo.select())
```

Finally, get the results:

```
>>> rows = result.fetchall()
>>> print(rows)
[('bear', 2, 1000.0), ('weasel', 1, 2000.0), ('duck', 10, 0.0)]
```

The Object-Relational Mapper

In the last section, the zoo object was a mid-level connection between SQL and Python. At the top layer of SQLAlchemy, the Object-Relational Mapper (ORM) uses the SQL Expression Language but tries to make the actual database mechanisms invisible. You define classes, and the ORM handles how to get their data in and out of the database. The basic idea behind that complicated phrase, "object-relational mapper," is that you can refer to objects in your code, and thus stay close to the way Python likes to operate, while still using a relational database.

We'll define a Zoo class and hook it into the ORM. This time, we'll make SQLite use the file *zoo.db* so that we can confirm that the ORM worked.

As in the previous two sections, the snippets that follow are actually one program separated by explanations. Don't worry if you don't understand some if it. The SQLAlchemy documentation has all the details, and this stuff can get complex. I just want you to get an idea of how much work it is to do this, so that you can decide which of the approaches discussed in this chapter suits you.

The initial import is the same, but this time we need another something also:

```
>>> import sqlalchemy as sa
>>> from sqlalchemy.ext.declarative import declarative_base
```

Here, we make the connection:

```
>>> conn = sa.create_engine('sqlite:///zoo.db')
```

Now, we get into SQLAlchemy's ORM. We define the Zoo class and associate its attributes with table columns:

```
>>> Base = declarative_base()
>>> class Zoo(Base):
...     __tablename__ = 'zoo'
```

```
...     critter = sa.Column('critter', sa.String, primary_key=True)
...     count = sa.Column('count', sa.Integer)
...     damages = sa.Column('damages', sa.Float)
...     def __init__(self, critter, count, damages):
...         self.critter = critter
...         self.count = count
...         self.damages = damages
...     def __repr__(self):
...         return "<Zoo({}, {}, {})>".format(self.critter, self.count, self.damages)
```

The following line magically creates the database and table:

```
>>> Base.metadata.create_all(conn)
```

You can then insert data by creating Python objects. The ORM manages these internally:

```
>>> first = Zoo('duck', 10, 0.0)
>>> second = Zoo('bear', 2, 1000.0)
>>> third = Zoo('weasel', 1, 2000.0)
>>> first
<Zoo(duck, 10, 0.0)>
```

Next, we get the ORM to take us to SQL land. We create a session to talk to the database:

```
>>> from sqlalchemy.orm import sessionmaker
>>> Session = sessionmaker(bind=conn)
>>> session = Session()
```

Within the session, we write the three objects that we created to the database. The add() function adds one object, and add_all() adds a list:

```
>>> session.add(first)
>>> session.add_all([second, third])
```

Finally, we need to force everything to complete:

```
>>> session.commit()
```

Did it work? Well, it created a *zoo.db* file in the current directory. You can use the command-line sqlite3 program to check it:

```
$ sqlite3 zoo.db
SQLite version 3.6.12
Enter ".help" for instructions
Enter SQL statements terminated with a ";"
sqlite> .tables
zoo
sqlite> select * from zoo;
duck|10|0.0
bear|2|1000.0
weasel|1|2000.0
```

The purpose of this section was to show what an ORM is and how it works at a high level. The author of SQLAlchemy has written a full tutorial (*http://bit.ly/obj-rel-tutorial*). After reading this, decide which of the following levels would best fit your needs:

- Plain DB-API, as in the earlier SQLite section
- The SQLAlchemy engine room
- The SQLAlchemy Expression Language
- The SQLAlchemy ORM

It seems like a natural choice to use an ORM to avoid the complexities of SQL. Should you use one? Some people think ORMs should be avoided (*http://bit.ly/obj-rel-map*), but others think the criticism is overdone (*http://bit.ly/fowler-orm*). Whoever's right, an ORM is an abstraction, and all abstractions break down at some point; they're leaky (*http://bit.ly/leaky-law*). When your ORM doesn't do what you want, you must figure out both how it works and how to fix it in SQL. To borrow an Internet meme: *Some people, when confronted with a problem, think, "I know, I'll use an ORM." Now they have two problems.* Use ORMs sparingly, and mostly for simple applications. If the application is that simple, maybe you can just use straight SQL (or the SQL Expression Language), anyhow.

Or, you can try something simpler such as `dataset` (*https://dataset.readthedocs.org/*). It's built on SQLAlchemy and provides a simple ORM for SQL, JSON, and CSV storage.

NoSQL Data Stores

Some databases are not relational and don't support SQL. These were written to handle very large data sets, allow more flexible data definitions, or support custom data operations. They've been collectively labeled *NoSQL* (formerly meaning *no SQL*; now the less confrontational *not only SQL*).

The dbm Family

The `dbm` formats were around long before *NoSQL* was coined. They're *key-value stores*, often embedded in applications such as web browsers to maintain various settings. A dbm database is like a Python dictionary in the following ways:

- You can assign a value to a key, and it's automatically saved to the database on disk.
- You can get a value from a key.

The following is a quick example. The second argument to the following `open()` method is `'r'` to read, `'w'` to write, and `'c'` for both, creating the file if it doesn't exist:

```
>>> import dbm
>>> db = dbm.open('definitions', 'c')
```

To create key-value pairs, just assign a value to a key just as you would a dictionary:

```
>>> db['mustard'] = 'yellow'
>>> db['ketchup'] = 'red'
>>> db['pesto'] = 'green'
```

Let's pause and check what we have so far:

```
>>> len(db)
3
>>> db['pesto']
b'green'
```

Now close, then reopen to see if it actually saved what we gave it:

```
>>> db.close()
>>> db = dbm.open('definitions', 'r')
>>> db['mustard']
b'yellow'
```

Keys and values are stored as `bytes`. You cannot iterate over the database object `db`, but you can get the number of keys by using `len()`. Note that `get()` and `setdefault()` work as they do for dictionaries.

Memcached

`memcached` (*http://memcached.org/*) is a fast in-memory key-value *cache* server. It's often put in front of a database, or used to store web server session data. You can download versions for Linux and OS X (*http://bit.ly/install-osx*), and for Windows (*http://bit.ly/memcache-win*). If you want to try out this section, you'll need a memcached server and Python driver.

There are many Python drivers; one that works with Python 3 is `python3-memcached` (*https://github.com/eguven/python3-memcached*), which you can install by using this command:

```
$ pip install python-memcached
```

To use it, connect to a memcached server, after which you can do the following:

- Set and get values for keys
- Increment or decrement a value
- Delete a key

Data is *not* persistent, and data that you wrote earlier might disappear. This is inherent in memcached, being that it's a cache server. It avoids running out of memory by discarding old data.

You can connect to multiple memcached servers at the same time. In this next example, we're just talking to one on the same computer:

```
>>> import memcache
>>> db = memcache.Client(['127.0.0.1:11211'])
>>> db.set('marco', 'polo')
True
>>> db.get('marco')
'polo'
>>> db.set('ducks', 0)
True
>>> db.get('ducks')
0
>>> db.incr('ducks', 2)
2
>>> db.get('ducks')
2
```

Redis

Redis (*http://redis.io*) is a *data structure server*. Like memcached, all of the data in a Redis server should fit in memory (although there is now an option to save the data to disk). Unlike memcached, Redis can do the following:

- Save data to disk for reliability and restarts
- Keep old data
- Provide more data structures than simple strings

The Redis data types are a close match to Python's, and a Redis server can be a useful intermediary for one or more Python applications to share data. I've found it so useful that it's worth a little extra coverage here.

The Python driver `redis-py` has its source code and tests on GitHub (*https://github.com/andymccurdy/redis-py*), as well as online documentation (*http://bit.ly/redis-py-docs*). You can install it by using this command:

```
$ pip install redis
```

The Redis server (*http://redis.io*) itself has good documentation. If you install and start the Redis server on your local computer (with the network nickname `local host`), you can try the programs in the following sections.

Strings

A key with a single value is a Redis *string*. Simple Python data types are automatically converted. Connect to a Redis server at some host (default is `localhost`) and port (default is 6379):

```
>>> import redis
>>> conn = redis.Redis()
```

`redis.Redis('localhost')` or `redis.Redis('localhost', 6379)` would have given the same result.

List all keys (none so far):

```
>>> conn.keys('*')
[]
```

Set a simple string (key `'secret'`), integer (key `'carats'`), and float (key `'fever'`):

```
>>> conn.set('secret', 'ni!')
True
>>> conn.set('carats', 24)
True
>>> conn.set('fever', '101.5')
True
```

Get the values back by key:

```
>>> conn.get('secret')
b'ni!'
>>> conn.get('carats')
b'24'
>>> conn.get('fever')
b'101.5'
```

Here, the `setnx()` method sets a value only if the key does not exist:

```
>>> conn.setnx('secret', 'icky-icky-icky-ptang-zoop-boing!')
False
```

It failed because we had already defined `'secret'`:

```
>>> conn.get('secret')
b'ni!'
```

The `getset()` method returns the old value and sets it to a new one at the same time:

```
>>> conn.getset('secret', 'icky-icky-icky-ptang-zoop-boing!')
b'ni!'
```

Let's not get too far ahead of ourselves. Did it work?

```
>>> conn.get('secret')
b'icky-icky-icky-ptang-zoop-boing!'
```

Now, get a substring by using `getrange()` (as in Python, offset 0=start, -1=end):

```
>>> conn.getrange('secret', -6, -1)
b'boing!'
```

Replace a substring by using setrange() (using a zero-based offset):

```
>>> conn.setrange('secret', 0, 'ICKY')
32
>>> conn.get('secret')
b'ICKY-icky-icky-ptang-zoop-boing!'
```

Next, set multiple keys at once by using mset():

```
>>> conn.mset({'pie': 'cherry', 'cordial': 'sherry'})
True
```

Get more than one value at once by using mget():

```
>>> conn.mget(['fever', 'carats'])
[b'101.5', b'24']
```

Delete a key by using delete():

```
>>> conn.delete('fever')
True
```

Increment by using the incr() or incrbyfloat() commands, and decrement with decr():

```
>>> conn.incr('carats')
25
>>> conn.incr('carats', 10)
35
>>> conn.decr('carats')
34
>>> conn.decr('carats', 15)
19
>>> conn.set('fever', '101.5')
True
>>> conn.incrbyfloat('fever')
102.5
>>> conn.incrbyfloat('fever', 0.5)
103.0
```

There's no decrbyfloat(). Use a negative increment to reduce the fever:

```
>>> conn.incrbyfloat('fever', -2.0)
101.0
```

Lists

Redis lists can contain only strings. The list is created when you do your first insertion. Insert at the beginning by using lpush():

```
>>> conn.lpush('zoo', 'bear')
1
```

Insert more than one item at the beginning:

```
>>> conn.lpush('zoo', 'alligator', 'duck')
3
```

Insert before or after a value by using linsert():

```
>>> conn.linsert('zoo', 'before', 'bear', 'beaver')
4
>>> conn.linsert('zoo', 'after', 'bear', 'cassowary')
5
```

Insert at an offset by using lset() (the list must exist already):

```
>>> conn.lset('zoo', 2, 'marmoset')
True
```

Insert at the end by using rpush():

```
>>> conn.rpush('zoo', 'yak')
6
```

Get the value at an offset by using lindex():

```
>>> conn.lindex('zoo', 3)
b'bear'
```

Get the values in an offset range by using lrange() (0 to -1 for all):

```
>>> conn.lrange('zoo', 0, 2)
[b'duck', b'alligator', b'marmoset']
```

Trim the list with ltrim(), keeping only those in a range of offsets:

```
>>> conn.ltrim('zoo', 1, 4)
True
```

Get a range of values (use 0 to -1 for all) by using lrange():

```
>>> conn.lrange('zoo', 0, -1)
[b'alligator', b'marmoset', b'bear', b'cassowary']
```

Chapter 10 shows you how you can use Redis lists and *publish-subscribe* to implement job queues.

Hashes

Redis *hashes* are similar to Python dictionaries but can contain only strings. Thus, you can go only one level deep, not make deep-nested structures. Here are examples that create and play with a Redis hash called song:

Set the fields do and re in hash song at once by using hmset():

```
>>> conn.hmset('song', {'do': 'a deer', 're': 'about a deer'})
True
```

Set a single field value in a hash by using hset():

```
>>> conn.hset('song', 'mi', 'a note to follow re')
1
```

Get one field's value by using hget():

```
>>> conn.hget('song', 'mi')
b'a note to follow re'
```

Get multiple field values by using hmget():

```
>>> conn.hmget('song', 're', 'do')
[b'about a deer', b'a deer']
```

Get all field keys for the hash by using hkeys():

```
>>> conn.hkeys('song')
[b'do', b're', b'mi']
```

Get all field values for the hash by using hvals():

```
>>> conn.hvals('song')
[b'a deer', b'about a deer', b'a note to follow re']
```

Get the number of fields in the hash by using hlen():

```
>>> conn.hlen('song')
3
```

Get all field keys and values in the hash by using hgetall():

```
>>> conn.hgetall('song')
{b'do': b'a deer', b're': b'about a deer', b'mi': b'a note to follow re'}
```

Set a field if its key doesn't exist by using hsetnx():

```
>>> conn.hsetnx('song', 'fa', 'a note that rhymes with la')
1
```

Sets

Redis sets are similar to Python sets, as you can see in the series of examples that follow.

Add one or more values to a set:

```
>>> conn.sadd('zoo', 'duck', 'goat', 'turkey')
3
```

Get the number of values from the set:

```
>>> conn.scard('zoo')
3
```

Get all the set's values:

```
>>> conn.smembers('zoo')
{b'duck', b'goat', b'turkey'}
```

Remove a value from the set:

```
>>> conn.srem('zoo', 'turkey')
True
```

Let's make a second set to show some set operations:

```
>>> conn.sadd('better_zoo', 'tiger', 'wolf', 'duck')
0
```

Intersect (get the common members of) the zoo and better_zoo sets:

```
>>> conn.sinter('zoo', 'better_zoo')
{b'duck'}
```

Get the intersection of zoo and better_zoo, and store the result in the set fowl_zoo:

```
>>> conn.sinterstore('fowl_zoo', 'zoo', 'better_zoo')
1
```

Who's in there?

```
>>> conn.smembers('fowl_zoo')
{b'duck'}
```

Get the union (all members) of zoo and better_zoo:

```
>>> conn.sunion('zoo', 'better_zoo')
{b'duck', b'goat', b'wolf', b'tiger'}
```

Store that union result in the set fabulous_zoo:

```
>>> conn.sunionstore('fabulous_zoo', 'zoo', 'better_zoo')
4
>>> conn.smembers('fabulous_zoo')
{b'duck', b'goat', b'wolf', b'tiger'}
```

What does zoo have that better_zoo doesn't? Use sdiff() to get the set difference, and sdiffstore() to save it in the zoo_sale set:

```
>>> conn.sdiff('zoo', 'better_zoo')
{b'goat'}
>>> conn.sdiffstore('zoo_sale', 'zoo', 'better_zoo')
1
>>> conn.smembers('zoo_sale')
{b'goat'}
```

Sorted sets

One of the most versatile Redis data types is the *sorted set*, or *zset*. It's a set of unique values, but each value has an associated floating point *score*. You can access each item by its value or score. Sorted sets have many uses:

- Leader boards
- Secondary indexes
- Timeseries, using timestamps as scores

We'll show the last use case, tracking user logins via timestamps. We're using the Unix *epoch* value (more on this in Chapter 10) that's returned by the Python `time()` function:

```
>>> import time
>>> now = time.time()
>>> now
1361857057.576483
```

Let's add our first guest, looking nervous:

```
>>> conn.zadd('logins', 'smeagol', now)
1
```

Five minutes later, another guest:

```
>>> conn.zadd('logins', 'sauron', now+(5*60))
1
```

Two hours later:

```
>>> conn.zadd('logins', 'bilbo', now+(2*60*60))
1
```

One day later, not hasty:

```
>>> conn.zadd('logins', 'treebeard', now+(24*60*60))
1
```

In what order did `bilbo` arrive?

```
>>> conn.zrank('logins', 'bilbo')
2
```

When was that?

```
>>> conn.zscore('logins', 'bilbo')
1361864257.576483
```

Let's see everyone in login order:

```
>>> conn.zrange('logins', 0, -1)
[b'smeagol', b'sauron', b'bilbo', b'treebeard']
```

With their times, please:

```
>>> conn.zrange('logins', 0, -1, withscores=True)
[(b'smeagol', 1361857057.576483), (b'sauron', 1361857357.576483),
(b'bilbo', 1361864257.576483), (b'treebeard', 1361943457.576483)]
```

Bits

This is a very space-efficient and fast way to deal with large sets of numbers. Suppose that you have a website with registered users. You'd like to track how often people log in, how many users visit on a particular day, how often the same user visits on following days, and so on. You could use Redis sets, but if you've assigned increasing numeric user IDs, bits are more compact and faster.

Let's begin by creating a bitset for each day. For this test, we'll just use three days and a few user IDs:

```
>>> days = ['2013-02-25', '2013-02-26', '2013-02-27']
>>> big_spender = 1089
>>> tire_kicker = 40459
>>> late_joiner = 550212
```

Each date is a separate key. Set the bit for a particular user ID for that date. For example, on the first date (2013-02-25), we had visits from big_spender (ID 1089) and tire_kicker (ID 40459):

```
>>> conn.setbit(days[0], big_spender, 1)
0
>>> conn.setbit(days[0], tire_kicker, 1)
0
```

The next day, big_spender came back:

```
>>> conn.setbit(days[1], big_spender, 1)
0
```

The next day had yet another visit from our friend, big_spender, and a new person whom we're calling late_joiner:

```
>>> conn.setbit(days[2], big_spender, 1)
0
>>> conn.setbit(days[2], late_joiner, 1)
0
```

Let's get the daily visitor count for these three days:

```
>>> for day in days:
...     conn.bitcount(day)
...
2
1
2
```

Did a particular user visit on a particular day?

```
>>> conn.getbit(days[1], tire_kicker)
0
```

So, tire_kicker did not visit on the second day.

How many users visited every day?

```
>>> conn.bitop('and', 'everyday', *days)
68777
>>> conn.bitcount('everyday')
1
```

I'll give you three guesses who it was:

```
>>> conn.getbit('everyday', big_spender)
1
```

Finally, what was the number of total unique users in these three days?

```
>>> conn.bitop('or', 'alldays', *days)
68777
>>> conn.bitcount('alldays')
3
```

Caches and expiration

All Redis keys have a time-to-live, or *expiration date*. By default, this is forever. We can use the expire() function to instruct Redis how long to keep the key. As is demonstrated here, the value is a number of seconds:

```
>>> import time
>>> key = 'now you see it'
>>> conn.set(key, 'but not for long')
True
>>> conn.expire(key, 5)
True
>>> conn.ttl(key)
5
>>> conn.get(key)
b'but not for long'
>>> time.sleep(6)
>>> conn.get(key)
>>>
```

The expireat() command expires a key at a given epoch time. Key expiration is useful to keep caches fresh and to limit login sessions.

Other NoSQL

The NoSQL servers listed here handle data larger than memory, and many of them use multiple computers. Table 8-6 presents notable servers and their Python libraries.

Table 8-6. NoSQL databases

Site	Python API
Cassandra (*http://cassandra.apache.org/*)	pycassa (*https://github.com/pycassa/pycassa*)

Site	Python API
CouchDB (*http://couchdb.apache.org/*)	couchdb-python (*https://github.com/djc/couchdb-python*)
HBase (*http://hbase.apache.org/*)	happybase (*https://github.com/wbolster/happybase*)
Kyoto Cabinet (*http://fallabs.com/kyotocabinet/*)	kyotocabinet (*http://bit.ly/kyotocabinet*)
MongoDB (*http://www.mongodb.org/*)	mongodb (*http://api.mongodb.org/python/current/*)
Riak (*http://basho.com/riak/*)	riak-python-client (*https://github.com/basho/riak-python-client*)

Full-Text Databases

Finally, there's a special category of databases for *full-text* search. They index everything, so you can find that poem that talks about windmills and giant wheels of cheese. You can see some popular open source examples, and their Python APIs, in Table 8-7.

Table 8-7. Full-text databases

Site	Python API
Lucene (*http://lucene.apache.org/*)	pylucene (*http://lucene.apache.org/pylucene/*)
Solr (*http://lucene.apache.org/solr/*)	SolPython (*http://wiki.apache.org/solr/SolPython*)
ElasticSearch (*http://www.elasticsearch.org/*)	pyes (*https://github.com/aparo/pyes/*)
Sphinx (*http://sphinxsearch.com/*)	sphinxapi (*http://bit.ly/sphinxapi*)
Xapian (*http://xapian.org/*)	xappy (*https://code.google.com/p/xappy/*)
Whoosh (*http://bit.ly/mchaput-whoosh*)	(written in Python, includes an API)

Things to Do

8.1. Assign the string `'This is a test of the emergency text system'` to the variable `test1`, and write `test1` to a file called *test.txt*.

8.2. Open the file *test.txt* and read its contents into the string `test2`. Are `test1` and `test2` the same?

8.3. Save these text lines to a file called *books.csv*. Notice that if the fields are separated by commas, you need to surround a field with quotes if it contains a comma.

```
author,book
J R R Tolkien,The Hobbit
Lynne Truss,"Eats, Shoots & Leaves"
```

8.4. Use the csv module and its DictReader method to read *books.csv* to the variable books. Print the values in books. Did DictReader handle the quotes and commas in the second book's title?

8.5. Create a CSV file called *books.csv* by using these lines:

```
title,author,year
The Weirdstone of Brisingamen,Alan Garner,1960
Perdido Street Station,China Miéville,2000
Thud!,Terry Pratchett,2005
The Spellman Files,Lisa Lutz,2007
Small Gods,Terry Pratchett,1992
```

8.6. Use the sqlite3 module to create a SQLite database called *books.db*, and a table called books with these fields: title (text), author (text), and year (integer).

8.7. Read *books.csv* and insert its data into the book table.

8.8. Select and print the title column from the book table in alphabetical order.

8.9. Select and print all columns from the book table in order of publication.

8.10. Use the sqlalchemy module to connect to the sqlite3 database *books.db* that you just made in exercise 8.6. As in 8.8, select and print the title column from the book table in alphabetical order.

8.11. Install the Redis server and the Python redis library (pip install redis) on your computer. Create a Redis hash called test with the fields count (1) and name ('Fester Bestertester'). Print all the fields for test.

8.12. Increment the count field of test and print it.

CHAPTER 9

The Web, Untangled

Straddling the French-Swiss border is CERN—a particle physics research institute that would seem a good lair for a Bond villain. Luckily, its quest is not world domination but to understand how the universe works. This has always led CERN to generate prodigious amounts of data, challenging physicists and computer scientists just to keep up.

In 1989, the English scientist Tim Berners-Lee first circulated a proposal to help disseminate information within CERN and the research community. He called it the *World Wide Web*, and soon distilled its design into three simple ideas:

HTTP (Hypertext Transfer Protocol)
    A specification for web clients and servers to interchange requests and responses

HTML (Hypertext Markup Language)
    A presentation format for results

URL (Uniform Resource Locator)
    A way to uniquely represent a server and a *resource* on that server

In its simplest usage, a web client (I think Berners-Lee was the first to use the term *browser*) connected to a web server with HTTP, requested a URL, and received HTML.

He wrote the first web browser and server on a NeXT computer, invented by a short-lived company Steve Jobs founded during his hiatus from Apple Computer. Web awareness really expanded in 1993, when a group of students at the University of Illinois released the Mosaic web browser (for Windows, the Macintosh, and Unix) and NCSA *httpd* server. When I downloaded these and started building sites, I had no idea that the Web and the Internet would soon become part of everyday life. At the time, the Internet was still officially noncommercial; there were about 500 known web servers in the world (*http://home.web.cern.ch/about/birth-web*). By the end of 1994, the number of web servers had grown to 10,000. The Internet was opened to commercial use, and the authors of Mosaic founded Netscape to write commercial web software. Netscape went public as part of the Internet frenzy that was occurring at the time, and the Web's explosive growth has never stopped.

Almost every computer language has been used to write web clients and web servers. The dynamic languages Perl, PHP, and Ruby have been especially popular. In this chapter, I'll show why Python is a particularly good language for web work at every level:

- Clients, to access remote sites
- Servers, to provide data for websites and web APIs
- Web APIs and services, to interchange data in other ways than viewable web pages

And while we're at it, we'll build an actual interactive website in the exercises at the end of this chapter.

Web Clients

The low-level network plumbing of the Internet is called Transmission Control Protocol/Internet Protocol, or more commonly, simply TCP/IP ("TCP/IP" on page 286 goes into more detail about this). It moves bytes among computers, but doesn't care about what those bytes mean. That's the job of higher-level *protocols*—syntax definitions for specific purposes. HTTP is the standard protocol for web data interchange.

The Web is a client-server system. The client makes a *request* to a server: it opens a TCP/IP connection, sends the URL and other information via HTTP, and receives a *response*.

The format of the response is also defined by HTTP. It includes the status of the request, and (if the request succeeded) the response's data and format.

The most well-known web client is a web *browser*. It can make HTTP requests in a number of ways. You might initiate a request manually by typing a URL into the location bar or clicking on a link in a web page. Very often, the data returned is used to display a website—HTML documents, JavaScript files, CSS files, and images—but it can be any type of data, not just that intended for display.

An important aspect of HTTP is that it's *stateless*. Each HTTP connection that you make is independent of all the others. This simplifies basic web operations but complicates others. Here are just a few samples of the challenges:

Caching
> Remote content that doesn't change should be saved by the web client and used to avoid downloading from the server again.

Sessions
> A shopping website should remember the contents of your shopping cart.

Authentication
> Sites that require your username and password should remember them while you're logged in.

Solutions to statelessness include *cookies*, in which the server sends the client enough specific information to be able to identify it uniquely when the client sends the cookie back.

Test with telnet

HTTP is a text-based protocol, so you can actually type it yourself for web testing. The ancient `telnet` program lets you connect to any server and port and type commands.

Let's ask everyone's favorite test site, Google, some basic information about its home page. Type this:

```
$ telnet www.google.com 80
```

If there is a web server on port 80 at *google.com* (I think that's a safe bet), `telnet` will print some reassuring information and then display a final blank line that's your cue to type something else:

```
Trying 74.125.225.177...
Connected to www.google.com.
Escape character is '^]'.
```

Now, type an actual HTTP command for `telnet` to send to the Google web server. The most common HTTP command (the one your browser uses when you type a URL in its location bar) is `GET`. This retrieves the contents of the specified resource, such as an HTML file, and returns it to the client. For our first test, we'll use the HTTP command `HEAD`, which just retrieves some basic information *about* the resource:

```
HEAD / HTTP/1.1
```

That `HEAD /` sends the HTTP `HEAD` *verb* (command) to get information about the home page (`/`). Add an extra carriage return to send a blank line so the remote server knows you're all done and want a response. You'll receive a response such as this (we trimmed some of the long lines using ... so they wouldn't stick out of the book):

```
HTTP/1.1 200 OK
Date: Sat, 26 Oct 2013 17:05:17 GMT
Expires: -1
Cache-Control: private, max-age=0
Content-Type: text/html; charset=ISO-8859-1
Set-Cookie: PREF=ID=962a70e9eb3db9d9:FF=0:TM=1382807117:LM=1382807117:S=y...
  expires=Mon, 26-Oct-2015 17:05:17 GMT;
  path=/;
  domain=.google.com
Set-Cookie: NID=67=hTvtVC7dZJmZzGktimbwVbNZxPQnaDijCz716B1L56GM9qvsqqeIGb...
  expires=Sun, 27-Apr-2014 17:05:17 GMT
  path=/;
  domain=.google.com;
  HttpOnly
P3P: CP="This is not a P3P policy! See http://www.google.com/support/accounts...
Server: gws
X-XSS-Protection: 1; mode=block
X-Frame-Options: SAMEORIGIN
Alternate-Protocol: 80:quic
Transfer-Encoding: chunked
```

These are HTTP response headers and their values. Some, like `Date` and `Content-Type`, are required. Others, such as `Set-Cookie`, are used to track your activity across multiple visits (we'll talk about *state management* a little later in this chapter). When you make an HTTP `HEAD` request, you get back only headers. If you had used the HTTP `GET` or `POST` commands, you would also receive data from the home page (a mixture of HTML, CSS, JavaScript, and whatever else Google decided to throw into its home page).

I don't want to leave you stranded in telnet. To close telnet, type the following:

```
q
```

Python's Standard Web Libraries

In Python 2, web client and server modules were a bit scattered. One of the Python 3 goals was to bundle these modules into two *packages* (remember from Chapter 5 that a package is just a directory containing module files):

- `http` manages all the client-server HTTP details:
  - `client` does the client-side stuff
  - `server` helps you write Python web servers
  - `cookies` and `cookiejar` manage cookies, which save data between site visits
- `urllib` runs on top of `http`:
  - `request` handles the client request
  - `response` handles the server response

— `parse` cracks the parts of a URL

Let's use the standard library to get something from a website. The URL in the following example returns information about movies from the IMDB movie database:

```
>>> import urllib.request as ur
>>> from urllib.parse import quote
>>> import json
>>>
>>> title = input('Type a movie title: ')
Type a movie title: eegah
>>> url = 'http://www.omdbapi.com/?t=%s' % quote(title)
>>> conn = ur.urlopen(url)
```

For our example, we typed the movie title eegah; as you'll soon see, there was a movie with that name. But first, some web computing details.

This little chunk of Python opened a TCP/IP connection to the remote quote server, made an HTTP request, and received an HTTP response. The response contained more than just the page data (the movie info). In the official documentation (*http://bit.ly/httpresponse-docs*), we find that `conn` is an `HTTPResponse` object with a number of methods and attributes. One of the most important parts of the response is the HTTP *status code*:

```
>>> print(conn.status)
200
```

A `200` means that everything was peachy. There are dozens of HTTP status codes, grouped into five ranges by their first (hundreds) digit:

1xx (information)
The server received the request but has some extra information for the client.

2xx (success)
It worked; every success code other than 200 conveys extra details.

3xx (redirection)
The resource moved, so the response returns the new URL to the client.

4xx (client error)
Some problem from the client side, such as the famous 404 (not found). 418 (*I'm a teapot*) was an April Fool's joke.

5xx (server error)
500 is the generic whoops; you might see a 502 (bad gateway) if there's some disconnect between a web server and a backend application server.

To get the actual data contents from the web page, use the `read()` method of the `conn` variable:

```
>>> data = conn.read()
>>> print(data)
```

```
b'{"Title":"Eegah","Year":"1962","Rated":"UNRATED","Released":"01 Apr
1965","Runtime":"90 min","Genre":"Comedy","Director":"Arch Hall
Sr.","Writer":"Bob Wehling (screenplay), Arch Hall Sr. (original
story)","Actors":"Arch Hall Jr., Marilyn Manning, Richard Kiel, Arch
Hall Sr.","Plot":"Teenagers stumble across a prehistoric caveman, who
goes on a rampage.","Language":"English","Country":"USA","Awards":"N/A",
"Poster":"http://ia.media-imdb.com/images/M/MV5BMTY4MDE3NDQ1MF5BM15BanB
nXkFtZTcwODI3MDQyMQ@@._V1_SX300.jpg","Metascore":"N/A","imdbRating":"2.2",
"imdbVotes":"4,387","imdbID":"tt0055946","Type":"movie","Response":"True"}'
```

That didn't look like plain text or HTML. Web servers can send data back to you in any format they like. The data format is specified by the HTTP response *header* value with the name Content-Type, which we also saw in our *google.com* example:

```
>>> print(conn.getheader('Content-Type'))
application/json; charset=utf-8
```

That application/json string is a *MIME type*, and it means JSON format, not plain text or HTML. The MIME type for HTML, which the *google.com* example sent, is text/html. I'll show you more MIME types in this chapter.

Now that we know it's JSON, we can convert it into Python data structures and print the ones we want:

```
>>> try:
...     str_data = data.decode('utf8')
...     js_data = json.loads(str_data)
...     print('title:', js_data['Title'])
...     print('plot:', js_data['Plot'])
... except:
...     print('Sorry, no match for', title)
...
title: Eegah
plot: Teenagers stumble across a prehistoric caveman, who goes on a rampage.
```

In this example, the returned JSON string was converted to a Python dictionary, and we printed the two elements with the string keys Title and Plot.

Out of sheer curiosity, what other HTTP headers were sent back to us?

```
>>> for key, value in conn.getheaders():
...     print(key, value)
...
Date Tue, 09 Feb 2016 02:57:47 GMT
Content-Type application/json; charset=utf-8
Content-Length 627
Connection close
Set-Cookie __cfduid=dc4315212f945a15f879910e5f92c79651454986667;
expires=Wed, 08-Feb-17 02:57:47 GMT; path=/; domain=.omdbapi.com;
HttpOnly
```

```
Cache-Control public, max-age=14400
Expires Tue, 09 Feb 2016 06:57:47 GMT
Last-Modified Tue, 09 Feb 2016 01:43:08 GMT
Vary Accept-Encoding
X-AspNet-Version 4.0.30319
X-Powered-By ASP.NET
Access-Control-Allow-Origin *
CF-Cache-Status HIT
Server cloudflare-nginx
CF-RAY 271c4f0fe6da109f-ORD
```

Remember that `telnet` example a little earlier? Now, our Python library is parsing all those HTTP response headers and providing them in a dictionary. `Date` and `Server` seem straightforward; some of the others, less so. It's helpful to know that HTTP has a set of standard headers such as `Content-Type`, and many optional ones.

Beyond the Standard Library: Requests

At the beginning of Chapter 1, there's a program that accessed a Wayback Machine API by using the standard libraries `urllib.request` and `json`. Following that example is a version that uses the third-party module `requests`. The `requests` version is shorter and easier to understand.

For most purposes, I think web client development with `requests` is easier. You can browse the documentation (*http://docs.python-requests.org/*) (which is pretty good) for full details. I'll show the basics of `requests` in this section and use it throughout this book for web client tasks.

First, install the `requests` library into your Python environment. From a terminal window (Windows users, type `cmd` to make one), type the following command to make the Python package installer `pip` download the latest version of the `requests` package and install it:

```
$ pip install requests
```

If you have trouble, read Appendix D for details on how to install and use `pip`.

Let's redo our previous call to the movie service with `requests`. This time, just for cinematic variety, we'll input the name of a different wretched movie from days gone by:

```
>>> import requests
>>> import json
>>>
>>> url = 'http://www.omdbapi.com'
>>> title = input('Type a movie title: ')
Type a movie title: from hell it came
>>> args = {'t': title}
>>> resp = requests.get(url, params=args)
>>> resp
```

```
<Response [200]>
>>> js_data = resp.json()
>>> try:
...     print('title:', js_data['Title'])
...     print('plot:', js_data['Plot'])
... except:
...     print('Sorry, no match for', title)
...
title: From Hell It Came
plot: A wrongfully accused South Seas prince is executed, and returns
as a walking tree stump.
```

It isn't that different from using `urllib.request.urlopen`, but I think it's a little more convenient and less wordy.

Web Servers

Web developers have found Python to be an excellent language for writing web servers and server-side programs. This has led to such a variety of Python-based web *frameworks* that it can be hard to navigate among them and make choices—not to mention deciding what deserves to go into a book.

A web framework provides features with which you can build websites, so it does more than a simple web (HTTP) server. You'll see features such as routing (URL to server function), templates (HTM with dynamic inclusions), debugging, and more.

I'm not going to cover all of the frameworks here—just those that I've found to be relatively simple to use and suitable for real websites. I'll also show how to run the dynamic parts of a website with Python and other parts with a traditional web server.

The Simplest Python Web Server

You can run a simple web server by typing just one line of Python:

```
$ python -m http.server
```

This implements a bare-bones Python HTTP server. If there are no problems, this will print an initial status message:

```
Serving HTTP on 0.0.0.0 port 8000 ...
```

That `0.0.0.0` means *any TCP address*, so web clients can access it no matter what address the server has. There's more low-level details on TCP and other network plumbing for you to read about in Chapter 11.

You can now request files, with paths relative to your current directory, and they will be returned. If you type `http://localhost:8000` in your web browser, you should see a directory listing there, and the server will print access log lines such as this:

```
127.0.0.1 - - [20/Feb/2013 22:02:37] "GET / HTTP/1.1" 200 -
```

`localhost` and `127.0.0.1` are TCP synonyms for *your local computer*, so this works regardless of whether you're connected to the Internet. You can interpret this line as follows:

- `127.0.0.1` is the client's IP address
- The first `"-"` is the remote username, if found
- The second `"-"` is the login username, if required
- `[20/Feb/2013 22:02:37]` is the access date and time
- `"GET / HTTP/1.1"` is the command sent to the web server:
  — The HTTP method (`GET`)
  — The resource requested (`/`, the top)
  — The HTTP version (`HTTP/1.1`)
- The final `200` is the HTTP status code returned by the web server

Click any file. If your browser can recognize the format (HTML, PNG, GIF, JPEG, and so on) it should display it, and the server will log the request. For instance, if you have the file *oreilly.png* in your current directory, a request for *http://localhost:8000/oreilly.png* should return the image of the unsettling fellow in Figure 7-1, and the log should show something such as this:

```
127.0.0.1 - - [20/Feb/2013 22:03:48] "GET /oreilly.png HTTP/1.1" 200 -
```

If you have other files in the same directory on your computer, they should show up in a listing on your display, and you can click any one to download it. If your browser is configured to display that file's format, you'll see the results on your screen; otherwise, your browser will ask you if you want to download and save the file.

The default port number used is 8000, but you can specify another:

```
$ python -m http.server 9999
```

You should see this:

```
Serving HTTP on 0.0.0.0 port 9999 ...
```

This Python-only server is best suited for quick tests. You can stop it by killing its process; in most terminals, press Ctrl+C.

You should not use this basic server for a busy production website. Traditional web servers such as Apache and Nginx are much faster for serving static files. In addition, this simple server has no way to handle dynamic content, which more extensive servers can do by accepting parameters.

Web Server Gateway Interface

All too soon, the allure of serving simple files wears off, and we want a web server that can also run programs dynamically. In the early days of the Web, the *Common Gateway Interface* (CGI) was designed for clients to make web servers run external programs and return the results. CGI also handled getting input arguments from the client through the server to the external programs. However, the programs were started anew for *each* client access. This could not scale well, because even small programs have appreciable startup time.

To avoid this startup delay, people began merging the language interpreter into the web server. Apache ran PHP within its mod_php module, Perl in mod_perl, and Python in mod_python. Then, code in these dynamic languages could be executed within the long-running Apache process itself rather than in external programs.

An alternative method was to run the dynamic language within a separate long-running program and have it communicate with the web server. FastCGI and SCGI are examples.

Python web development made a leap with the definition of *Web Server Gateway Interface* (WSGI), a universal API between Python web applications and web servers. All of the Python web frameworks and web servers in the rest of this chapter use WSGI. You don't normally need to know how WSGI works (there really isn't much to it), but it helps to know what some of the parts under the hood are called.

Frameworks

Web servers handle the HTTP and WSGI details, but you use web *frameworks* to actually write the Python code that powers the site. So, we'll talk about frameworks for a while and then get back to alternative ways of actually serving sites that use them.

If you want to write a website in Python, there are many Python web frameworks (some might say too many). A web framework handles, at a minimum, client requests and server responses. It might provide some or all of these features:

Routes
> Interpret URLs and find the corresponding server files or Python server code

Templates
> Merge server-side data into pages of HTML

Authentication and authorization
> Handle usernames, passwords, permissions

Sessions
> Maintain transient data storage during a user's visit to the website

In the coming sections, we'll write example code for two frameworks (`bottle` and `flask`). Then, we'll talk about alternatives, especially for database-backed websites. You can find a Python framework to power any site that you can think of.

Bottle

Bottle consists of a single Python file, so it's very easy to try out, and it's easy to deploy later. Bottle isn't part of standard Python, so to install it, type the following command:

```
$ pip install bottle
```

Here's code that will run a test web server and return a line of text when your browser accesses the URL *http://localhost:9999/*. Save it as *bottle1.py*:

```
from bottle import route, run

@route('/')
def home():
    return "It isn't fancy, but it's my home page"

run(host='localhost', port=9999)
```

Bottle uses the `route` decorator to associate a URL with the following function; in this case, / (the home page) is handled by the `home()` function. Make Python run this server script by typing this:

```
$ python bottle1.py
```

You should see this on your browser when you access *http://localhost:9999*:

```
It isn't fancy, but it's my home page
```

The `run()` function executes `bottle`'s built-in Python test web server. You don't need to use this for `bottle` programs, but it's useful for initial development and testing.

Now, instead of creating text for the home page in code, let's make a separate HTML file called *index.html* that contains this line of text:

```
My <b>new</b> and <i>improved</i> home page!!!
```

Make `bottle` return the contents of this file when the home page is requested. Save this script as *bottle2.py*:

```
from bottle import route, run, static_file

@route('/')
def main():
    return static_file('index.html', root='.')

run(host='localhost', port=9999)
```

In the call to static_file(), we want the file index.html in the directory indicated by root (in this case, '.', the current directory). If your previous server example code was still running, stop it. Now, run the new server:

```
$ python bottle2.py
```

When you ask your browser to get *http:/localhost:9999/*, you should see:

My **new** and *improved* home page!!!

Let's add one last example that shows how to pass arguments to a URL and use them. Of course, this will be *bottle3.py*:

```
from bottle import route, run, static_file

@route('/')
def home():
    return static_file('index.html', root='.')

@route('/echo/<thing>')
def echo(thing):
    return "Say hello to my little friend: %s!" % thing

run(host='localhost', port=9999)
```

We have a new function called echo() and want to pass it a string argument in a URL. That's what the line @route('/echo/<thing>') in the preceding example does. That <thing> in the route means that whatever was in the URL after /echo/ is assigned to the string argument thing, which is then passed to the echo function. To see what happens, stop the old server if it's still running, and start it with the new code:

```
$ python bottle3.py
```

Then, access *http://localhost:9999/echo/Mothra* in your web browser. You should see the following:

```
Say hello to my little friend: Mothra!
```

Now, leave *bottle3.py* running for a minute so that we can try something else. You've been verifying that these examples work by typing URLs into your browser and looking at the displayed pages. You can also use client libraries such as requests to do your work for you. Save this as *bottle_test.py*:

```
import requests

resp = requests.get('http://localhost:9999/echo/Mothra')
if resp.status_code == 200 and \
   resp.text == 'Say hello to my little friend: Mothra!':
    print('It worked! That almost never happens!')
else:
    print('Argh, got this:', resp.text)
```

Great! Now, run it:

```
$ python bottle_test.py
```

You should see this in your terminal:

```
It worked! That almost never happens!
```

This is a little example of a *unit test*. Chapter 8 provides more details on why tests are good and how to write them in Python.

There's more to `bottle` than I've shown here. In particular, you can try adding these arguments when you call `run()`:

- `debug=True` creates a debugging page if you get an HTTP error;
- `reloader=True` reloads the page in the browser if you change any of the Python code.

It's well documented at the developer site (*http://bottlepy.org/docs/dev/*).

Flask

Bottle is a good initial web framework. If you need a few more cowbells and whistles, try Flask. It started in 2010 as an April Fools' joke, but enthusiastic response encouraged the author, Armin Ronacher, to make it a real framework. He named the result `Flask` as a wordplay on `bottle`.

Flask is about as simple to use as Bottle, but it supports many extensions that are useful in professional web development, such as Facebook authentication and database integration. It's my personal favorite among Python web frameworks because it balances ease of use with a rich feature set.

The Flask package includes the `werkzeug` WSGI library and the `jinja2` template library. You can install it from a terminal:

```
$ pip install flask
```

Let's replicate the final `bottle` example code in `flask`. First, though, we need to make a few changes:

- Flask's default directory home for static files is `static`, and URLs for files there also begin with `/static`. We change the folder to `'.'` (current directory) and the URL prefix to `''` (empty) to allow the URL `/` to map to the file *index.html*.
- In the `run()` function, setting `debug=True` also activates the automatic reloader; `bottle` used separate arguments for debugging and reloading.

Save this file to *flask1.py*:

```
from flask import Flask

app = Flask(__name__, static_folder='.', static_url_path='')

@app.route('/')
def home():
    return app.send_static_file('index.html')

@app.route('/echo/<thing>')
def echo(thing):
    return "Say hello to my little friend: %s" % thing

app.run(port=9999, debug=True)
```

Then, run the server from a terminal or window:

```
$ python flask1.py
```

Test the home page by typing this URL into your browser:

```
http://localhost:9999/
```

You should see the following (as you did for `bottle`):

My **new** and *improved* home page!!!

Try the /echo endpoint:

```
http://localhost:9999/echo/Godzilla
```

You should see this:

```
Say hello to my little friend: Godzilla
```

There's another benefit to setting `debug` to `True` when calling `run`. If an exception occurs in the server code, Flask returns a specially formatted page with useful details about what went wrong, and where. Even better, you can type some commands to see the values of variables in the server program.

 Do not set debug = `True` in production web servers. It exposes too much information about your server to potential intruders.

So far, the Flask example just replicates what we did with `bottle`. What can Flask do that `bottle` can't? Flask includes `jinja2`, a more extensive templating system. Here's a tiny example of how to use `jinja2` and `flask` together.

Create a directory called `templates`, and a file within it called *flask2.html*:

```
<html>
<head>
```

```
<title>Flask2 Example</title>
</head>
<body>
Say hello to my little friend: {{ thing }}
</body>
</html>
```

Next, we'll write the server code to grab this template, fill in the value of *thing* that we passed it, and render it as HTML (I'm dropping the home() function here to save space). Save this as *flask2.py*:

```
from flask import Flask, render_template

app = Flask(__name__)

@app.route('/echo/<thing>')
def echo(thing):
    return render_template('flask2.html', thing=thing)

app.run(port=9999, debug=True)
```

That thing = thing argument means to pass a variable named thing to the template, with the value of the string thing.

Ensure that *flask1.py* isn't still running, and start *flask2.py*:

```
$ python flask2.py
```

Now, type this URL:

```
http://localhost:9999/echo/Gamera
```

You should see the following:

```
Say hello to my little friend: Gamera
```

Let's modify our template and save it in the *templates* directory as *flask3.html*:

```
<html>
<head>
<title>Flask3 Example</title>
</head>
<body>
Say hello to my little friend: {{ thing }}.
Alas, it just destroyed {{ place }}!
</body>
</html>
```

You can pass this second argument to the echo URL in many ways.

Pass an argument as part of the URL path

Using this method, you simply extend the URL itself (save this as *flask3a.py*):

```
from flask import Flask, render_template

app = Flask(__name__)

@app.route('/echo/<thing>/<place>')
def echo(thing, place):
    return render_template('flask3.html', thing=thing, place=place)

app.run(port=9999, debug=True)
```

As usual, stop the previous test server script if it's still running and then try this new one:

```
$ python flask3a.py
```

The URL would look like this:

```
http://localhost:9999/echo/Rodan/McKeesport
```

And you should see the following:

```
Say hello to my little friend: Rodan. Alas, it just destroyed McKeesport!
```

Or, you can provide the arguments as GET parameters (save this as *flask3b.py*):

```
from flask import Flask, render_template, request

app = Flask(__name__)

@app.route('/echo/')
def echo():
    thing = request.args.get('thing')
    place = request.args.get('place')
    return render_template('flask3.html', thing=thing, place=place)

app.run(port=9999, debug=True)
```

Run the new server script:

```
$ python flask3b.py
```

This time, use this URL:

```
http://localhost:9999/echo?thing=Gorgo&place=Wilmerding
```

You should get back what you see here:

```
Say hello to my little friend: Gorgo. Alas, it just destroyed Wilmerding!
```

When a GET command is used for a URL, any arguments are passed in the form *&key1=val1&key2=val2&...*

You can also use the dictionary ** operator to pass multiple arguments to a template from a single dictionary (call this *flask3c.py*):

```
from flask import Flask, render_template, request

app = Flask(__name__)

@app.route('/echo/')
def echo():
    kwargs = {}
    kwargs['thing'] = request.args.get('thing')
    kwargs['place'] = request.args.get('place')
    return render_template('flask3.html', **kwargs)

app.run(port=9999, debug=True)
```

That **kwargs acts like thing=thing, place=place. It saves some typing if there are a lot of input arguments.

The jinja2 templating language does a lot more than this. If you've programmed in PHP, you'll see many similarities.

Non-Python Web Servers

So far, the web servers we've used have been simple: the standard library's http.server or the debugging servers in Bottle and Flask. In production, you'll want to run Python with a faster web server. The usual choices are the following:

- apache with the mod_wsgi module
- nginx with the uWSGI app server

Both work well; apache is probably the most popular, and nginx has a reputation for stability and lower memory use.

Apache

The apache (*http://httpd.apache.org/*) web server's best WSGI module is mod_wsgi (*https://code.google.com/p/modwsgi/*). This can run Python code within the Apache process or in separate processes that communicate with Apache.

You should already have apache if your system is Linux or OS X. For Windows, you'll need to install apache (*http://bit.ly/apache-http*).

Finally, install your preferred WSGI-based Python web framework. Let's try bottle here. Almost all of the work involves configuring Apache, which can be a dark art.

Create this test file and save it as */var/www/test/home.wsgi*:

```
import bottle

application = bottle.default_app()
```

```
@bottle.route('/')
def home():
    return "apache and wsgi, sitting in a tree"
```

Do not call `run()` this time, because that starts the built-in Python web server. We need to assign to the variable `application` because that's what `mod_wsgi` looks for to marry the web server and the Python code.

If `apache` and its `mod_wsgi` module are working correctly, we just need to connect them to our Python script. We want to add one line to the file that defines the default website for this `apache` server, but finding that file is a task in and of itself. It could be */etc/apache2/httpd.conf,* or */etc/apache2/sites-available/default,* or the Latin name of someone's pet salamander.

Let's assume for now that you understand `apache` and found that file. Add this line inside the `<VirtualHost>` section that governs the default website:

```
WSGIScriptAlias / /var/www/test/home.wsgi
```

That section might then look like this:

```
<VirtualHost *:80>
    DocumentRoot /var/www

    WSGIScriptAlias / /var/www/test/home.wsgi

    <Directory /var/www/test>
    Order allow,deny
    Allow from all
    </Directory>
</VirtualHost>
```

Start `apache`, or restart it if it was running to make it use this new configuration. If you then browse to *http://localhost/,* you should see:

```
apache and wsgi, sitting in a tree
```

This runs `mod_wsgi` in *embedded mode,* as part of `apache` itself.

You can also run it in *daemon mode*: as one or more processes, separate from `apache`. To do this, add two new directive lines to your `apache` config file:

```
$ WSGIDaemonProcess domain-name user=user-name group=group-name threads=25
WSGIProcessGroup domain-name
```

In the preceding example, *user-name* and *group-name* are the operating system user and group names, and the *domain-name* is the name of your Internet domain. A minimal `apache` config might look like this:

```
<VirtualHost *:80>
    DocumentRoot /var/www
```

```
    WSGIScriptAlias / /var/www/test/home.wsgi

    WSGIDaemonProcess mydomain.com user=myuser group=mygroup threads=25
    WSGIProcessGroup mydomain.com

    <Directory /var/www/test>
    Order allow,deny
    Allow from all
    </Directory>
  </VirtualHost>
```

The nginx Web Server

The nginx (*http://nginx.org/*) web server does not have an embedded Python module. Instead, it communicates by using a separate WSGI server such as uWSGI. Together they make a very fast and configurable platform for Python web development.

You can install nginx from its website (*http://wiki.nginx.org/Install*). You also need to install uWSGI (*http://bit.ly/uWSGI*). uWSGI is a large system, with many levers and knobs to adjust. A short documentation page (*http://bit.ly/flask-uwsgi*) gives you instructions on how to combine Flask, nginx, and uWSGI.

Other Frameworks

Websites and databases are like peanut butter and jelly—you see them together a lot. The smaller frameworks such as bottle and flask do not include direct support for databases, although some of their contributed add-ons do.

If you need to crank out database-backed websites, and the database design doesn't change very often, it might be worth the effort to try one of the larger Python web frameworks. The current main contenders include:

django *(https://www.djangoproject.com/)*
>   This is the most popular, especially for large sites. It's worth learning for many reasons, among them the frequent requests for django experience in Python job ads. It includes ORM code (we talked about ORMs in "The Object-Relational Mapper" on page 207) to create automatic web pages for the typical database *CRUD* functions (create, replace, update, delete) that I discussed in "SQL" on page 198. You don't have to use django's ORM if you prefer another, such as SQLAlchemy, or direct SQL queries.

web2py *(http://www.web2py.com/)*
>   This covers much the same ground as django, with a different style.

pyramid *(http://www.pylonsproject.org/)*
>   This grew from the earlier pylons project, and is similar to django in scope.

`turbogears` *(http://turbogears.org/)*
> This framework supports an ORM, many databases, and multiple template languages.

`wheezy.web` *(http://pythonhosted.org/wheezy.web/)*
> This is a newer framework optimized for performance. It was faster *(http://bit.ly/wheezyweb)* than the others in a recent test.

You can compare the frameworks by viewing this online table *(http://bit.ly/webframes)*.

If you want to build a website backed by a relational database, you don't necessarily need one of these larger frameworks. You can use `bottle`, `flask`, and others directly with relational database modules, or use SQLAlchemy to help gloss over the differences. Then, you're writing generic SQL instead of specific ORM code, and more developers know SQL than any particular ORM's syntax.

Also, there's nothing written in stone demanding that your database must be a relational one. If your data schema varies significantly—columns that differ markedly across rows—it might be worthwhile to consider a *schemaless* database, such as one of the *NoSQL* databases discussed in "NoSQL Data Stores" on page 209. I once worked on a website that initially stored its data in a NoSQL database, switched to a relational one, on to another relational one, to a different NoSQL one, and then finally back to one of the relational ones.

Other Python Web Servers

Following are some of the independent Python-based WSGI servers that work like `apache` or `nginx`, using multiple processes and/or threads (see "Concurrency" on page 268) to handle simultaneous requests:

- `uwsgi` *(http://projects.unbit.it/uwsgi/)*
- `cherrypy` *(http://www.cherrypy.org/)*
- `pylons` *(http://www.pylonsproject.org/)*

Here are some *event-based* servers, which use a single process but avoid blocking on any single request:

- `tornado` *(http://www.tornadoweb.org)*
- `gevent` *(http://gevent.org/)*
- `gunicorn` *(http://gunicorn.org/)*

I have more to say about events in the discussion about *concurrency* in Chapter 11.

Web Services and Automation

We've just looked at traditional web client and server applications, consuming and generating HTML pages. Yet the Web has turned out to be a powerful way to glue applications and data in many more formats than HTML.

The webbrowser Module

Let's start begin a little surprise. Start a Python session in a terminal window and type the following:

```
>>> import antigravity
```

This secretly calls the standard library's `webbrowser` module and directs your browser to an enlightening Python link.[1]

You can use this module directly. This program loads the main Python site's page in your browser:

```
>>> import webbrowser
>>> url = 'http://www.python.org/'
>>> webbrowser.open(url)
True
```

This opens it in a new window:

```
>>> webbrowser.open_new(url)
True
```

And this opens it in a new tab, if your browser supports tabs:

```
>>> webbrowser.open_new_tab('http://www.python.org/')
True
```

The `webbrowser` makes your browser do all the work.

Web APIs and Representational State Transfer

Often, data is only available within web pages. If you want to access it, you need to access the pages through a web browser and read it. If the authors of the website made any changes since the last time you visited, the location and style of the data might have changed.

Instead of publishing web pages, you can provide data through a web *application programming interface* (API). Clients access your service by making requests to URLs and getting back responses containing status and data. Instead of HTML pages, the

---

1 If you don't see it for some reason, visit xkcd (*http://xkcd.com/353/*).

data is in formats that are easier for programs to consume, such as JSON or XML (refer to Chapter 8 for more about these formats).

Representational State Transfer (REST) was defined by Roy Fielding in his doctoral thesis. Many products claim to have a *REST interface* or a *RESTful interface*. In practice, this often only means that they have a *web* interface—definitions of URLs to access a web service.

A *RESTful* service uses the HTTP *verbs* in specific ways, as is described here:

HEAD
> Gets information about the resource, but not its data.

GET
> As its name implies, GET retrieves the resource's data from the server. This is the standard method used by your browser. Any time you see a URL with a question mark (?) followed by a bunch of arguments, that's a GET request. GET should not be used to create, change, or delete data.

POST
> This verb updates data on the server. It's often used by HTML forms and web APIs.

PUT
> This verb creates a new resource.

DELETE
> This one speaks for itself: DELETE deletes. Truth in advertising!

A RESTful client can also request one or more content types from the server by using HTTP request headers. For example, a complex service with a REST interface might prefer its input and output to be JSON strings.

JSON

Chapter 1 shows two Python code samples to get information on popular YouTube videos, and Chapter 8 introduces JSON. JSON is especially well suited to web client-server data interchange. It's especially popular in web-based APIs, such as OpenStack.

Crawl and Scrape

Sometimes, you might want a little bit of information—a movie rating, stock price, or product availability—but the information is available only in HTML pages, surrounded by ads and extraneous content.

You could extract what you're looking for manually by doing the following:

1. Type the URL into your browser.
2. Wait for the remote page to load.
3. Look through the displayed page for the information you want.
4. Write it down somewhere.
5. Possibly repeat the process for related URLs.

However, it's much more satisfying to automate some or all of these steps. An automated web fetcher is called a *crawler* or *spider* (unappealing terms to arachnophobes). After the contents have been retrieved from the remote web servers, a *scraper* parses it to find the needle in the haystack.

If you need an industrial-strength combined crawler *and* scraper, Scrapy (*http://scrapy.org/*) is worth downloading:

```
$ pip install scrapy
```

Scrapy is a framework, not a module such as BeautifulSoup. It does more, but it's more complex to set up. To learn more about Scrapy, read the documentation (*http://scrapy.org*) or the online introduction (*http://bit.ly/using-scrapy*).

Scrape HTML with BeautifulSoup

If you already have the HTML data from a website and just want to extract data from it, BeautifulSoup (*http://www.crummy.com/software/BeautifulSoup/*) is a good choice. HTML parsing is harder than it sounds. This is because much of the HTML on public web pages is technically invalid: unclosed tags, incorrect nesting, and other complications. If you try to write your own HTML parser by using regular expressions (discussed in Chapter 7) you'll soon encounter these messes.

To install BeautifulSoup, type the following command (don't forget the final 4, or pip will try to install an older version and probably fail):

```
$ pip install beautifulsoup4
```

Now, let's use it to get all the links from a web page. The HTML a element represents a link, and href is its attribute representing the link destination. In the following example, we'll define the function get_links() to do the grunt work, and a main program to get one or more URLs as command-line arguments:

```
def get_links(url):
    import requests
    from bs4 import BeautifulSoup as soup
    result = requests.get(url)
    page = result.text
    doc = soup(page)
    links = [element.get('href') for element in doc.find_all('a')]
    return links
```

```
if __name__ == '__main__':
    import sys
    for url in sys.argv[1:]:
        print('Links in', url)
        for num, link in enumerate(get_links(url), start=1):
            print(num, link)
        print()
```

I saved this program as *links.py* and then ran this command:

```
$ python links.py http://boingboing.net
```

Here are the first few lines that it printed:

```
Links in http://boingboing.net/
1 http://boingboing.net/suggest.html
2 http://boingboing.net/category/feature/
3 http://boingboing.net/category/review/
4 http://boingboing.net/category/podcasts
5 http://boingboing.net/category/video/
6 http://bbs.boingboing.net/
7 javascript:void(0)
8 http://shop.boingboing.net/
9 http://boingboing.net/about
10 http://boingboing.net/contact
```

Things to Do

9.1. If you haven't installed flask yet, do so now. This will also install werkzeug, jinja2, and possibly other packages.

9.2. Build a skeleton website, using Flask's debug/reload development web server. Ensure that the server starts up for hostname localhost on default port 5000. If your computer is already using port 5000 for something else, use another port number.

9.3. Add a home() function to handle requests for the home page. Set it up to return the string It's alive!.

9.4. Create a Jinja2 template file called home.html with the following contents:

```
<html>
<head>
<title>It's alive!</title>
<body>
I'm of course referring to {{thing}}, which is {{height}} feet tall and {{color}}.
</body>
</html>
```

9.5. Modify your server's home() function to use the *home.html* template. Provide it with three GET parameters: thing, height, and color.

CHAPTER 10

Systems

One thing a computer can do that most humans can't is be sealed up in a cardboard box and
sit in a warehouse.
—Jack Handey

In your everyday use of a computer, you do such things as list the contents of a folder or directory, create and remove files, and other housekeeping that's necessary if not particularly exciting. You can also carry out these tasks, and more, within your own Python programs. Will this power drive you mad or cure your insomnia? We'll see.

Python provides many system functions through a module named os (for "operating system"), which we'll import for all the programs in this chapter.

Files

Python, like many other languages, patterned its file operations after Unix. Some functions, such as chown() and chmod(), have the same names, but there are a few new ones.

Create with open()

"File Input/Output" on page 177 introduced you to the open() function and explains how you can use it to open a file or create one if it doesn't already exist. Let's create a text file called *oops.txt*:

```
>>> fout = open('oops.txt', 'wt')
>>> print('Oops, I created a file.', file=fout)
>>> fout.close()
```

With that done, let's perform some tests with it.

Check Existence with exists()

To verify whether the file or directory is really there or you just imagined it, you can provide exists(), with a relative or absolute pathname, as demonstrated here:

```
>>> import os
>>> os.path.exists('oops.txt')
True
>>> os.path.exists('./oops.txt')
True
>>> os.path.exists('waffles')
False
>>> os.path.exists('.')
True
>>> os.path.exists('..')
True
```

Check Type with isfile()

The functions in this section check whether a name refers to a file, directory, or symbolic link (see the examples that follow for a discussion of links).

The first function we'll look at, isfile, asks a simple question: is it a plain old law-abiding file?

```
>>> name = 'oops.txt'
>>> os.path.isfile(name)
True
```

Here's how you determine a directory:

```
>>> os.path.isdir(name)
False
```

A single dot (.) is shorthand for the current directory, and two dots (..) stands for the parent directory. These always exist, so a statement such as the following will always report True:

```
>>> os.path.isdir('.')
True
```

The os module contains many functions dealing with *pathnames* (fully qualified file-names, starting with / and including all parents). One such function, isabs(), determines whether its argument is an absolute pathname. The argument doesn't need to be the name of a real file:

```
>>> os.path.isabs(name)
False
>>> os.path.isabs('/big/fake/name')
True
>>> os.path.isabs('big/fake/name/without/a/leading/slash')
False
```

Copy with copy()

The copy() function comes from another module, shutil. This example copies the file *oops.txt* to the file *ohno.txt*:

```
>>> import shutil
>>> shutil.copy('oops.txt', 'ohno.txt')
```

The shutil.move() function copies a file and then removes the original.

Change Name with rename()

This function does exactly what it says. In the example here, it renames *ohno.txt* to *ohwell.txt*:

```
>>> import os
>>> os.rename('ohno.txt', 'ohwell.txt')
```

Link with link() or symlink()

In Unix, a file exists in one place, but it can have multiple names, called *links*. In low-level *hard links*, it's not easy to find all the names for a given file. A *symbolic link* is an alternative method that stores the new name as its own file, making it possible for you to get both the original and new names at once. The link() call creates a hard link, and symlink() makes a symbolic link. The islink() function checks whether the file is a symbolic link.

Here's how to make a hard link to the existing file *oops.txt* from the new file *yikes.txt*:

```
>>> os.link('oops.txt', 'yikes.txt')
>>> os.path.isfile('yikes.txt')
True
```

To create a symbolic link to the existing file *oops.txt* from the new file *jeepers.txt*, use the following:

```
>>> os.path.islink('yikes.txt')
False
>>> os.symlink('oops.txt', 'jeepers.txt')
>>> os.path.islink('jeepers.txt')
True
```

Change Permissions with chmod()

On a Unix system, chmod() changes file permissions. There are read, write, and execute permissions for the user (that's usually you, if you created the file), the main group that the user is in, and the rest of the world. The command takes an intensely compressed octal (base 8) value that combines user, group, and other permissions. For instance, to make *oops.txt* only readable by its owner, type the following:

```
>>> os.chmod('oops.txt', 0o400)
```

If you don't want to deal with cryptic octal values and would rather deal with (slightly) obscure cryptic symbols, you can import some constants from the `stat` module and use a statement such as the following:

```
>>> import stat
>>> os.chmod('oops.txt', stat.S_IRUSR)
```

Change Ownership with chown()

This function is also Unix/Linux/Mac–specific. You can change the owner and/or group ownership of a file by specifying the numeric user ID (*uid*) and group ID (*gid*):

```
>>> uid = 5
>>> gid = 22
>>> os.chown('oops', uid, gid)
```

Get a Pathname with abspath()

This function expands a relative name to an absolute one. If your current directory is */usr/gaberlunzie* and the file *oops.txt* is there, also, you can type the following:

```
>>> os.path.abspath('oops.txt')
'/usr/gaberlunzie/oops.txt'
```

Get a symlink Pathname with realpath()

In one of the earlier sections, we made a symbolic link to *oops.txt* from the new file *jeepers.txt*. In circumstances such as this, you can get the name of *oops.txt* from *jeepers.txt* by using the `realpath()` function, as shown here:

```
>>> os.path.realpath('jeepers.txt')
'/usr/gaberlunzie/oops.txt'
```

Delete a File with remove()

In this snippet, we use the `remove()` function and say farewell to *oops.txt*:

```
>>> os.remove('oops.txt')
>>> os.path.exists('oops.txt')
False
```

Directories

In most operating systems, files exist in a hierarchy of *directories* (more often called *folders* these days). The container of all of these files and directories is a *file system* (sometimes called a *volume*). The standard `os` module deals with operating specifics such as these and provides the following functions with which you can manipulate them.

Create with mkdir()

This example shows how to create a directory called `poems` to store that precious verse:

```
>>> os.mkdir('poems')
>>> os.path.exists('poems')
True
```

Delete with rmdir()

Upon second thought, you decide you don't need that directory after all. Here's how to delete it:

```
>>> os.rmdir('poems')
>>> os.path.exists('poems')
False
```

List Contents with listdir()

Okay, take two; let's make `poems` again, with some contents:

```
>>> os.mkdir('poems')
```

Now, get a list of its contents (none so far):

```
>>> os.listdir('poems')
[]
```

Next, make a subdirectory:

```
>>> os.mkdir('poems/mcintyre')
>>> os.listdir('poems')
['mcintyre']
```

Create a file in this subdirectory (don't type all these lines unless you really feel poetic; just make sure you begin and end with matching quotes, either single or tripled):

```
>>> fout = open('poems/mcintyre/the_good_man', 'wt')
>>> fout.write('''Cheerful and happy was his mood,
... He to the poor was kind and good,
... And he oft' times did find them food,
... Also supplies of coal and wood,
... He never spake a word was rude,
... And cheer'd those did o'er sorrows brood,
... He passed away not understood,
... Because no poet in his lays
... Had penned a sonnet in his praise,
... 'Tis sad, but such is world's ways.
... ''')
```

```
>>> fout.close()
```

Finally, let's see what we have. It had better be there:

```
>>> os.listdir('poems/mcintyre')
['the_good_man']
```

Change Current Directory with chdir()

With this function, you can go from one directory to another. Let's leave the current directory and spend a little time in poems:

```
>>> import os
>>> os.chdir('poems')
>>> os.listdir('.')
['mcintyre']
```

List Matching Files with glob()

The glob() function matches file or directory names by using Unix shell rules rather than the more complete regular expression syntax. Here are those rules:

- * matches everything (re would expect .*)
- ? matches a single character
- [abc] matches character a, b, or c
- [!abc] matches any character *except* a, b, or c

Try getting all files or directories that begin with m:

```
>>> import glob
>>> glob.glob('m*')
['mcintyre']
```

How about any two-letter files or directories?

```
>>> glob.glob('??')
[]
```

I'm thinking of an eight-letter word that begins with m and ends with e:

```
>>> glob.glob('m??????e')
['mcintyre']
```

What about anything that begins with a k, l, or m, and ends with e?

```
>>> glob.glob('[klm]*e')
['mcintyre']
```

Programs and Processes

When you run an individual program, your operating system creates a single *process*. It uses system resources (CPU, memory, disk space) and data structures in the operating system's *kernel* (file and network connections, usage statistics, and so on). A process is isolated from other processes—it can't see what other processes are doing or interfere with them.

The operating system keeps track of all the running processes, giving each a little time to run and then switching to another, with the twin goals of spreading the work around fairly and being responsive to the user. You can see the state of your processes with graphical interfaces such as the Mac's Activity Monitor (OS X), or Task Manager on Windows-based computers.

You can also access process data from your own programs. The standard library's os module provides a common way of accessing some system information. For instance, the following functions get the *process ID* and the *current working directory* of the running Python interpreter:

```
>>> import os
>>> os.getpid()
76051
>>> os.getcwd()
'/Users/williamlubanovic'
```

And these get my *user ID* and *group ID*:

```
>>> os.getuid()
501
>>> os.getgid()
20
```

Create a Process with subprocess

All of the programs that you've seen here so far have been individual processes. You can start and stop other existing programs from Python by using the standard library's subprocess module. If you just want to run another program in a shell and grab whatever output it created (both standard output and standard error output), use the getoutput() function. Here, we'll get the output of the Unix date program:

```
>>> import subprocess
>>> ret = subprocess.getoutput('date')
>>> ret
'Sun Mar 30 22:54:37 CDT 2014'
```

You won't get anything back until the process ends. If you need to call something that might take a lot of time, see the discussion on *concurrency* in "Concurrency" on page 268. Because the argument to getoutput() is a string representing a complete shell command, you can include arguments, pipes, < and > I/O redirection, and so on:

```
>>> ret = subprocess.getoutput('date -u')
>>> ret
'Mon Mar 31 03:55:01 UTC 2014'
```

Piping that output string to the wc command counts one line, six "words," and 29 characters:

```
>>> ret = subprocess.getoutput('date -u | wc')
>>> ret
'       1       6      29'
```

A variant method called check_output() takes a list of the command and arguments. By default it only returns standard output as type bytes rather than a string and does not use the shell:

```
>>> ret = subprocess.check_output(['date', '-u'])
>>> ret
b'Mon Mar 31 04:01:50 UTC 2014\n'
```

To show the exit status of the other program, getstatusoutput() returns a tuple with the status code and output:

```
>>> ret = subprocess.getstatusoutput('date')
>>> ret
(0, 'Sat Jan 18 21:36:23 CST 2014')
```

If you don't want to capture the output but might want to know its exit status, use call():

```
>>> ret = subprocess.call('date')
Sat Jan 18 21:33:11 CST 2014
>>> ret
0
```

(In Unix-like systems, 0 is usually the exit status for success.)

That date and time was printed to output but not captured within our program. So, we saved the return code as ret.

You can run programs with arguments in two ways. The first is to specify them in a single string. Our sample command is date -u, which prints the current date and time in UTC (you'll read more about UTC in a few pages):

```
>>> ret = subprocess.call('date -u', shell=True)
Tue Jan 21 04:40:04 UTC 2014
```

You need that shell=True to recognize the command line date -u, splitting it into separate strings and possibly expanding any wildcard characters such as * (we didn't use any in this example).

The second method makes a list of the arguments, so it doesn't need to call the shell:

```
>>> ret = subprocess.call(['date', '-u'])
Tue Jan 21 04:41:59 UTC 2014
```

Create a Process with multiprocessing

You can run a Python function as a separate process or even run multiple independent processes in a single program with the `multiprocessing` module. Here's a short example that does nothing useful; save it as *mp.py* and then run it by typing `python mp.py`:

```
import multiprocessing
import os

def do_this(what):
    whoami(what)

def whoami(what):
    print("Process %s says: %s" % (os.getpid(), what))

if __name__ == "__main__":
    whoami("I'm the main program")
    for n in range(4):
        p = multiprocessing.Process(target=do_this,
          args=("I'm function %s" % n,))
        p.start()
```

When I run this, my output looks like this:

```
Process 6224 says: I'm the main program
Process 6225 says: I'm function 0
Process 6226 says: I'm function 1
Process 6227 says: I'm function 2
Process 6228 says: I'm function 3
```

The `Process()` function spawned a new process and ran the `do_this()` function in it. Because we did this in a loop that had four passes, we generated four new processes that executed `do_this()` and then exited.

The `multiprocessing` module has more bells and whistles than a clown on a calliope. It's really intended for those times when you need to farm out some task to multiple processes to save overall time; for example, downloading web pages for scraping, resizing images, and so on. It includes ways to queue tasks, enable intercommunication among processes, and wait for all the processes to finish. "Concurrency" on page 268 delves into some of these details.

Kill a Process with terminate()

If you created one or more processes and want to terminate one for some reason (perhaps it's stuck in a loop, or maybe you're bored, or you want to be an evil overlord), use `terminate()`. In the example that follows, our process would count to a million, sleeping at each step for a second, and printing an irritating message. However, our main program runs out of patience in five seconds and nukes it from orbit:

```
import multiprocessing
import time
import os

def whoami(name):
    print("I'm %s, in process %s" % (name, os.getpid()))

def loopy(name):
    whoami(name)
    start = 1
    stop = 1000000
    for num in range(start, stop):
        print("\tNumber %s of %s. Honk!" % (num, stop))
        time.sleep(1)

if __name__ == "__main__":
    whoami("main")
    p = multiprocessing.Process(target=loopy, args=("loopy",))
    p.start()
    time.sleep(5)
    p.terminate()
```

When I run this program, I get the following:

```
I'm main, in process 97080
I'm loopy, in process 97081
    Number 1 of 1000000. Honk!
    Number 2 of 1000000. Honk!
    Number 3 of 1000000. Honk!
    Number 4 of 1000000. Honk!
    Number 5 of 1000000. Honk!
```

Calendars and Clocks

Programmers devote a surprising amount of effort to dates and times. Let's talk about some of the problems they encounter, and then get to some best practices and tricks to make the situation a little less messy.

Dates can be represented in many ways—too many ways, actually. Even in English with the Roman calendar, you'll see many variants of a simple date:

- July 29 1984
- 29 Jul 1984
- 29/7/1984
- 7/29/1984

Among other problems, date representations can be ambiguous. In the previous examples, it's easy to determine that 7 stands for the month and 29 is the day of the month, largely because months don't go to 29. But how about 1/6/2012? Is that referring to January 6 or June 1?

The month name varies by language within the Roman calendar. Even the year and month can have a different definition in other cultures.

Leap years are another wrinkle. You probably know that every four years is a leap year (and the summer Olympics and the American presidential election). Did you also know that every 100 years is not a leap year, but that every 400 years is? Here's code to test various years for leapiness:

```
>>> import calendar
>>> calendar.isleap(1900)
False
>>> calendar.isleap(1996)
True
>>> calendar.isleap(1999)
False
>>> calendar.isleap(2000)
True
>>> calendar.isleap(2002)
False
>>> calendar.isleap(2004)
True
```

Times have their own sources of grief, especially because of time zones and daylight savings time. If you look at a time zone map, the zones follow political and historic boundaries rather than every 15 degrees (360 degrees / 24) of longitude. And countries start and end daylight saving times on different days of the year. In fact, countries in the southern hemisphere advance their clocks when the northern hemisphere is winding them back, and vice versa. (If you think about it a bit, you will see why.)

Python's standard library has many date and time modules: `datetime`, `time`, `calendar`, `dateutil`, and others. There's some overlap, and it's a bit confusing.

The datetime Module

Let's begin by investigating the standard `datetime` module. It defines four main objects, each with many methods:

- `date` for years, months, and days
- `time` for hours, minutes, seconds, and fractions
- `datetime` for dates and times together
- `timedelta` for date and/or time intervals

You can make a `date` object by specifying a year, month, and day. Those values are then available as attributes:

```
>>> from datetime import date
>>> halloween = date(2014, 10, 31)
>>> halloween
datetime.date(2014, 10, 31)
>>> halloween.day
31
>>> halloween.month
10
>>> halloween.year
2014
```

You can print a `date` with its `isoformat()` method:

```
>>> halloween.isoformat()
'2014-10-31'
```

The `iso` refers to ISO 8601, an international standard for representing dates and times. It goes from most general (year) to most specific (day). It also sorts correctly: by year, then month, then day. I usually pick this format for date representation in programs, and for filenames that save data by date. The next section describes the more complex `strptime()` and `strftime()` methods for parsing and formatting dates.

This example uses the `today()` method to generate today's date:

```
>>> from datetime import date
>>> now = date.today()
>>> now
datetime.date(2014, 2, 2)
```

This one makes use of a `timedelta` object to add some time interval to a `date`:

```
>>> from datetime import timedelta
>>> one_day = timedelta(days=1)
>>> tomorrow = now + one_day
>>> tomorrow
datetime.date(2014, 2, 3)
>>> now + 17*one_day
datetime.date(2014, 2, 19)
>>> yesterday = now - one_day
>>> yesterday
datetime.date(2014, 2, 1)
```

The range of `date` is from `date.min` (year=1, month=1, day=1) to `date.max` (year=9999, month=12, day=31). As a result, you can't use it for historic or astronomical calculations.

The `datetime` module's `time` object is used to represent a time of day:

```
>>> from datetime import time
>>> noon = time(12, 0, 0)
>>> noon
datetime.time(12, 0)
```

```
>>> noon.hour
12
>>> noon.minute
0
>>> noon.second
0
>>> noon.microsecond
0
```

The arguments go from the largest time unit (hours) to the smallest (microseconds). If you don't provide all the arguments, `time` assumes all the rest are zero. By the way, just because you can store and retrieve microseconds doesn't mean you can retrieve time from your computer to the exact microsecond. The accuracy of subsecond measurements depends on many factors in the hardware and operating system.

The `datetime` object includes both the date and time of day. You can create one directly, such as the one that follows, which is for January 2, 2014, at 3:04 A.M., plus 5 seconds and 6 microseconds:

```
>>> from datetime import datetime
>>> some_day = datetime(2014, 1, 2, 3, 4, 5, 6)
>>> some_day
datetime.datetime(2014, 1, 2, 3, 4, 5, 6)
```

The `datetime` object also has an `isoformat()` method:

```
>>> some_day.isoformat()
'2014-01-02T03:04:05.000006'
```

That middle T separates the date and time parts.

`datetime` has a `now()` method with which you can get the current date and time:

```
>>> from datetime import datetime
>>> now = datetime.now()
>>> now
datetime.datetime(2014, 2, 2, 23, 15, 34, 694988)
14
>>> now.month
2
>>> now.day
2
>>> now.hour
23
>>> now.minute
15
>>> now.second
34
>>> now.microsecond
694988
```

You can merge a `date` object and a `time` object into a `datetime` object by using `combine()`:

```
>>> from datetime import datetime, time, date
>>> noon = time(12)
>>> this_day = date.today()
>>> noon_today = datetime.combine(this_day, noon)
>>> noon_today
datetime.datetime(2014, 2, 2, 12, 0)
```

You can yank the date and time from a datetime by using the date() and time() methods:

```
>>> noon_today.date()
datetime.date(2014, 2, 2)
>>> noon_today.time()
datetime.time(12, 0)
```

Using the time Module

It is confusing that Python has a datetime module with a time object, and a separate time module. Furthermore, the time module has a function called—wait for it—time().

One way to represent an absolute time is to count the number of seconds since some starting point. *Unix time* uses the number of seconds since midnight on January 1, 1970.[1] This value is often called the *epoch*, and it is often the simplest way to exchange dates and times among systems.

The time module's time() function returns the current time as an epoch value:

```
>>> import time
>>> now = time.time()
>>> now
1391488263.664645
```

If you do the math, you'll see that it has been over one billion seconds since New Year's, 1970. Where did the time go?

You can convert an epoch value to a string by using ctime():

```
>>> time.ctime(now)
'Mon Feb  3 22:31:03 2014'
```

In the next section, you'll see how to produce more attractive formats for dates and times.

Epoch values are a useful least-common denominator for date and time exchange with different systems, such as JavaScript. Sometimes, though, you need actual days, hours, and so forth, which time provides as struct_time objects. localtime() provides the time in your system's time zone, and gmtime() provides it in UTC:

---

1 This starting point is roughly when Unix was born.

```
>>> time.localtime(now)
time.struct_time(tm_year=2014, tm_mon=2, tm_mday=3, tm_hour=22, tm_min=31,
tm_sec=3, tm_wday=0, tm_yday=34, tm_isdst=0)
>>> time.gmtime(now)
time.struct_time(tm_year=2014, tm_mon=2, tm_mday=4, tm_hour=4, tm_min=31,
tm_sec=3, tm_wday=1, tm_yday=35, tm_isdst=0)
```

In my (Central) time zone, 22:31 was 04:31 of the next day in UTC (formerly called *Greenwich time* or *Zulu time*). If you omit the argument to localtime() or gmtime(), they assume the current time.

The opposite of these is mktime(), which converts a struct_time object to epoch seconds:

```
>>> tm = time.localtime(now)
>>> time.mktime(tm)
1391488263.0
```

This doesn't exactly match our earlier epoch value of now() because the struct_time object preserves time only to the second.

Some advice: wherever possible, *use UTC* instead of time zones. UTC is an absolute time, independent of time zones. If you have a server, set its time to UTC; do not use local time.

Here's some more advice (free of charge, no less): *never use daylight savings time* if you can avoid it. If you use daylight savings time, an hour disappears at one time of year ("spring ahead") and occurs twice at another time ("fall back"). For some reason, many organizations use daylight savings in their computer systems, but are mystified every year by data duplicates and dropouts. It all ends in tears.

Remember, your friends are UTC for times, and UTF-8 for strings (for more about UTF-8, see Chapter 7).

Read and Write Dates and Times

isoformat() is not the only way to write dates and times. You already saw the ctime() function in the time module, which you can use to convert epochs to strings:

```
>>> import time
>>> now = time.time()
>>> time.ctime(now)
'Mon Feb  3 21:14:36 2014'
```

You can also convert dates and times to strings by using strftime(). This is provided as a method in the datetime, date, and time objects, and as a function in the time module. `strftime()` uses format strings to specify the output, which you can see in Table 10-1.

Table 10-1. Outut specifiers for `strftime()`

Format string	Date/time unit	Range
%Y	year	1900-...
%m	month	01-12
%B	month name	January, ...
%b	month abbrev	Jan, ...
%d	day of month	01-31
%A	weekday name	Sunday, ...
a	weekday abbrev	Sun, ...
%H	hour (24 hr)	00-23
%I	hour (12 hr)	01-12
%p	AM/PM	AM, PM
%M	minute	00-59
%S	second	00-59

Numbers are zero-padded on the left.

Here's the `strftime()` function provided by the `time` module. It converts a `struct_time` object to a string. We'll first define the format string `fmt` and use it again later:

```
>>> import time
>>> fmt = "It's %A, %B %d, %Y, local time %I:%M:%S%p"
>>> t = time.localtime()
>>> t
time.struct_time(tm_year=2014, tm_mon=2, tm_mday=4, tm_hour=19,
tm_min=28, tm_sec=38, tm_wday=1, tm_yday=35, tm_isdst=0)
>>> time.strftime(fmt, t)
"It's Tuesday, February 04, 2014, local time 07:28:38PM"
```

If we try this with a `date` object, only the date parts will work, and the time defaults to midnight:

```
>>> from datetime import date
>>> some_day = date(2014, 7, 4)
>>> fmt = "It's %B %d, %Y, local time %I:%M:%S%p"
>>> some_day.strftime(fmt)
"It's Friday, July 04, 2014, local time 12:00:00AM"
```

For a time object, only the time parts are converted:

```
>>> from datetime import time
>>> some_time = time(10, 35)
>>> some_time.strftime(fmt)
"It's Monday, January 01, 1900, local time 10:35:00AM"
```

Clearly, you won't want to use the day parts from a time object, because they're meaningless.

To go the other way and convert a string to a date or time, use strptime() with the same format string. There's no regular expression pattern matching; the nonformat parts of the string (without %) need to match exactly. Let's specify a format that matches *year-month-day*, such as 2012-01-29. What happens if the date string you want to parse has spaces instead of dashes?

```
>>> import time
>>> fmt = "%Y-%m-%d"
>>> time.strptime("2012 01 29", fmt)
Traceback (most recent call last):
  File "<stdin>", line 1, in <module>
  File "/Library/Frameworks/Python.framework/Versions/3.3/lib/
  python3.3/_strptime.py", line 494, in _strptime_time
    tt = _strptime(data_string, format)[0]
  File "/Library/Frameworks/Python.framework/Versions/3.3/lib/
  python3.3/_strptime.py", line 337, in _strptime
    (data_string, format))
ValueError: time data '2012 01 29' does not match format '%Y-%m-%d'
```

If we feed strptime() some dashes, is it happy now?

```
>>> time.strptime("2012-01-29", fmt)
time.struct_time(tm_year=2012, tm_mon=1, tm_mday=29, tm_hour=0, tm_min=0,
tm_sec=0, tm_wday=6, tm_yday=29, tm_isdst=-1)
```

Yes.

Even if the string seems to match its format, an exception is raised if a value is out of range:

```
>>> time.strptime("2012-13-29", fmt)
Traceback (most recent call last):
  File "<stdin>", line 1, in <module>
  File "/Library/Frameworks/Python.framework/Versions/3.3/lib/
  python3.3/_strptime.py", line 494, in _strptime_time
    tt = _strptime(data_string, format)[0]
  File "/Library/Frameworks/Python.framework/Versions/3.3/lib/
```

```
python3.3/_strptime.py", line 337, in _strptime
    (data_string, format))
ValueError: time data '2012-13-29' does not match format '%Y-%m-%d'
```

Names are specific to your *locale*—internationalization settings for your operating system. To print different month and day names, change your locale by using setlocale(); its first argument is locale.LC_TIME for dates and times, and the second is a string combining the language and country abbreviation. Let's invite some international friends to a Halloween party. We'll print the month, day, and day of week in US English, French, German, Spanish, and Icelandic. (What? You think Icelanders don't enjoy a good party as much as anyone else? They even have real elves.)

```
>>> import locale
>>> from datetime import date
>>> halloween = date(2014, 10, 31)
>>> for lang_country in ['en_us', 'fr_fr', 'de_de', 'es_es', 'is_is',]:
...     locale.setlocale(locale.LC_TIME, lang_country)
...     halloween.strftime('%A, %B %d')
...
'en_us'
'Friday, October 31'
'fr_fr'
'Vendredi, octobre 31'
'de_de'
'Freitag, Oktober 31'
'es_es'
'viernes, octubre 31'
'is_is'
'föstudagur, október 31'
>>>
```

Where do you find these magic values for lang_country? This is a bit wonky, but you can try this to get all of them (there are a few hundred):

```
>>> import locale
>>> names = locale.locale_alias.keys()
```

From names, let's get just locale names that seem to work with setlocale(), such as the ones we used in the preceding example—a two-character language code (*http:// bit.ly/iso-639-1*) followed by an underscore and a two-character country code (*http:// bit.ly/iso-3166-1*):

```
>>> good_names = [name for name in names if \
len(name) == 5 and name[2] == '_']
```

What do the first five look like?

```
>>> good_names[:5]
['sr_cs', 'de_at', 'nl_nl', 'es_ni', 'sp_yu']
```

So, if you wanted all the German language locales, try this:

```
>>> de = [name for name in good_names if name.startswith('de')]
>>> de
['de_at', 'de_de', 'de_ch', 'de_lu', 'de_be']
```

Alternative Modules

If you find the standard library modules confusing, or lacking a particular conversion that you want, there are many third-party alternatives. Here are just a few of them:

arrow *(http://crsmithdev.com/arrow/)*
   This combines many date and time functions with a simple API.

dateutil *(http://labix.org/python-dateutil)*
   This module parses almost any date format and handles relative dates and times well.

iso8601 *(https://pypi.python.org/pypi/iso8601)*
   This fills in gaps in the standard library for the ISO8601 format.

fleming *(https://github.com/ambitioninc/fleming)*
   This module offers many time zone functions.

Things to Do

10.1 Write the current date as a string to the text file *today.txt*.

10.2 Read the text file *today.txt* into the string today_string.

10.3 Parse the date from today_string.

10.4 List the files in your current directory.

10.5 List the files in your parent directory.

10.6 Use multiprocessing to create three separate processes. Make each one wait a random number of seconds between one and five, print the current time, and then exit.

10.7 Create a date object of your day of birth.

10.8 What day of the week was your day of birth?

10.9 When will you be (or when were you) 10,000 days old?

CHAPTER 11

Concurrency and Networks

Time is nature's way of keeping everything from happening at once. Space is what prevents everything from happening to me.
—Quotes about Time (*http://bit.ly/wiki-time*)

So far, most of the programs that you've written run in one place (a single machine) and one line at a time (*sequential*). But, we can do more than one thing at a time (*concurrency*) and in more than one place (*distributed computing* or *networking*). There are many good reasons to challenge time and space:

Performance
Your goal is to keep fast components busy, not waiting for slow ones.

Robustness
There's safety in numbers, so you want to duplicate tasks to work around hardware and software failures.

Simplicity
It's best practice to break complex tasks into many little ones that are easier to create, understand, and fix.

Communication
It's just plain fun to send your footloose bytes to distant places, and bring friends back with them.

We'll start with concurrency, first building on the non-networking techniques that are described in Chapter 10—processes and threads. Then we'll look at other approaches, such as callbacks, green threads, and coroutines. Finally, we'll arrive at networking, initially as a concurrency technique, and then spreading outward.

Some Python packages discussed in this chapter were not yet ported to Python 3 when this was written. In many cases, I'll show example code that would need to be run with a Python 2 interpreter, which we're calling python2.

Concurrency

The official Python site discusses concurrency in general and in the standard library (*http://bit.ly/concur-lib*). Those pages have many links to various packages and techniques; we'll show the most useful ones in this chapter.

In computers, if you're waiting for something, it's usually for one of two reasons:

I/O bound
> This is by far more common. Computer CPUs are ridiculously fast—hundreds of times faster than computer memory and many thousands of times faster than disks or networks.

CPU bound
> This happens with *number crunching* tasks such as scientific or graphic calculations.

Two more terms are related to concurrency:

synchronous
> One thing follows the other, like a funeral procession.

asynchronous
> Tasks are independent, like party-goers dropping in and tearing off in separate cars.

As you progress from simple systems and tasks to real-life problems, you'll need at some point to deal with concurrency. Consider a website, for example. You can usually provide static and dynamic pages to web clients fairly quickly. A fraction of a second is considered interactive, but if the display or interaction takes longer, people become impatient. Tests by companies such as Google and Amazon showed that traffic drops off quickly if the page loads even a little slower.

But what if you can't help it when something takes a long time, such as uploading a file, resizing an image, or querying a database? You can't do it within your synchronous web server code anymore, because someone's waiting.

On a single machine, if you want to perform multiple tasks as fast as possible, you want to make them independent. Slow tasks shouldn't block all the others.

"Programs and Processes" on page 253 demonstrates how multiprocessing can be used to overlap work on a single machine. If you needed to resize an image, your web server code could call a separate, dedicated image resizing process to run asynchronously and concurrently. It could scale your application horizontally by invoking multiple resizing processes.

The trick is getting them all to work with one another. Any shared control or state means that there will be bottlenecks. An even bigger trick is dealing with failures, because concurrent computing is harder than regular computing. Many more things can go wrong, and your odds of end-to-end success are lower.

All right. What methods can help you to deal with these complexities? Let's begin with a good way to manage multiple tasks: *queues*.

Queues

A queue is like a list: things are added at one end and taken away from the other. The most common is referred to as *FIFO* (first in, first out).

Suppose that you're washing dishes. If you're stuck with the entire job, you need to wash each dish, dry it, and put it away. You can do this in a number of ways. You might wash the first dish, dry it, and then put it away. You then repeat with the second dish, and so on. Or, you might *batch* operations and wash all the dishes, dry them all, and then put them away; this assumes you have space in your sink and drainer for all the dishes that accumulate at each step. These are all synchronous approaches—one worker, one thing at a time.

As an alternative, you could get a helper or two. If you're the washer, you can hand each cleaned dish to the dryer, who hands each dried dish to the put-away-er (look it up; it's absolutely a real word!). As long as each of you works at the same pace, you should finish much faster than by yourself.

However, what if you wash faster than the dryer dries? Wet dishes either fall on the floor, or you pile them up between you and the dryer, or you just whistle off-key until the dryer is ready. And if the last person is slower than the dryer, dry dishes can end up falling on the floor, or piling up, or the dryer does the whistling. You have multiple workers, but the overall task is still synchronous and can proceed only as fast as the slowest worker.

Many hands make light work, goes the old saying (I always thought it was Amish, because it makes me think of barn building). Adding workers can build a barn, or do the dishes, faster. This involves *queues*.

In general, queues transport *messages*, which can be any kind of information. In this case, we're interested in queues for distributed task management, also known as *work queues*, *job queues*, or *task queues*. Each dish in the sink is given to an available washer, who washes and hands it off to the first available dryer, who dries and hands it to a put-away-er. This can be synchronous (workers wait for a dish to handle and another worker to whom to give it), or asynchronous (dishes are stacked between workers with different paces). As long as you have enough workers, and they keep up with the dishes, things move a lot faster.

Processes

You can implement queues in many ways. For a single machine, the standard library's `multiprocessing` module (which you can see in "Programs and Processes" on page 253) contains a `Queue` function. Let's simulate just a single washer and multiple dryer processes (someone can put the dishes away later) and an intermediate `dish_queue`. Call this program *dishes.py*:

```
import multiprocessing as mp

def washer(dishes, output):
    for dish in dishes:
        print('Washing', dish, 'dish')
        output.put(dish)

def dryer(input):
    while True:
        dish = input.get()
        print('Drying', dish, 'dish')
        input.task_done()

dish_queue = mp.JoinableQueue()
dryer_proc = mp.Process(target=dryer, args=(dish_queue,))
dryer_proc.daemon = True
dryer_proc.start()

dishes = ['salad', 'bread', 'entree', 'dessert']
washer(dishes, dish_queue)
dish_queue.join()
```

Run your new program thusly:

```
$ python dishes.py
Washing salad dish
Washing bread dish
Washing entree dish
Washing dessert dish
Drying salad dish
Drying bread dish
Drying entree dish
Drying dessert dish
```

This queue looked a lot like a simple Python iterator, producing a series of dishes. It actually started up separate processes along with the communication between the washer and dryer. I used a `JoinableQueue` and the final `join()` method to let the washer know that all the dishes have been dried. There are other queue types in the multiprocessing module, and you can read the documentation (*http://bit.ly/multi-docs*) for more examples.

Threads

A *thread* runs within a process with access to everything in the process, similar to a multiple personality. The multiprocessing module has a cousin called threading that uses threads instead of processes (actually, multiprocessing was designed later as its process-based counterpart). Let's redo our process example with threads:

```
import threading

def do_this(what):
    whoami(what)

def whoami(what):
    print("Thread %s says: %s" % (threading.current_thread(), what))

if __name__ == "__main__":
    whoami("I'm the main program")
    for n in range(4):
        p = threading.Thread(target=do_this,
          args=("I'm function %s" % n,))
        p.start()
```

Here's what prints for me:

```
Thread <_MainThread(MainThread, started 140735207346960)> says: I'm the main
program
Thread <Thread(Thread-1, started 4326629376)> says: I'm function 0
Thread <Thread(Thread-2, started 4342157312)> says: I'm function 1
Thread <Thread(Thread-3, started 4347412480)> says: I'm function 2
Thread <Thread(Thread-4, started 4342157312)> says: I'm function 3
```

We can reproduce our process-based dish example by using threads:

```
import threading, queue
import time

def washer(dishes, dish_queue):
    for dish in dishes:
        print ("Washing", dish)
        time.sleep(5)
        dish_queue.put(dish)

def dryer(dish_queue):
    while True:
        dish = dish_queue.get()
        print ("Drying", dish)
        time.sleep(10)
        dish_queue.task_done()
```

```
dish_queue = queue.Queue()
for n in range(2):
    dryer_thread = threading.Thread(target=dryer, args=(dish_queue,))
    dryer_thread.start()

dishes = ['salad', 'bread', 'entree', 'dessert']
washer(dishes, dish_queue)
dish_queue.join()
```

One difference between multiprocessing and threading is that threading does not have a terminate() function. There's no easy way to terminate a running thread, because it can cause all sorts of problems in your code, and possibly in the space-time continuum itself.

Threads can be dangerous. Like manual memory management in languages such as C and C++, they can cause bugs that are extremely hard to find, let alone fix. To use threads, all the code in the program—and in external libraries that it uses—must be *thread-safe*. In the preceding example code, the threads didn't share any global variables, so they could run independently without breaking anything.

Imagine that you're a paranormal investigator in a haunted house. Ghosts roam the halls, but none are aware of the others, and at any time, any of them can view, add, remove, or move any of the house's contents.

You're walking apprehensively through the house, taking readings with your impressive instruments. Suddenly you notice that the candlestick you passed seconds ago is now missing.

The contents of the house are like the variables in a program. The ghosts are threads in a process (the house). If the ghosts only looked at the house's contents, there would be no problem. It's like a thread reading the value of a constant or variable without trying to change it.

Yet, some unseen entity could grab your flashlight, blow cold air down your neck, put marbles on the stairs, or make the fireplace come ablaze. The *really* subtle ghosts would change things in other rooms that you might never notice.

Despite your fancy instruments, you'd have a very hard time figuring out who did it, and how, and when.

If you used multiple processes instead of threads, it would be like having a number of houses but with only one (living) person in each. If you put your brandy in front of the fireplace, it would still be there an hour later. Some lost to evaporation, perhaps, but in the same place.

Threads can be useful and safe when global data is not involved. In particular, threads are useful for saving time while waiting for some I/O operation to complete. In these cases, they don't have to fight over data, because each has completely separate variables.

But threads do sometimes have good reasons to change global data. In fact, one common reason to launch multiple threads is to let them divide up the work on some data, so a certain degree of change to the data is expected.

The usual way to share data safely is to apply a software *lock* before modifying a variable in a thread. This keeps the other threads out while the change is made. It's like having a Ghostbuster guard the room you want to remain unhaunted. The trick, though, is that you need to remember to unlock it. Plus, locks can be nested—what if another Ghostbuster is also watching the same room, or the house itself? The use of locks is traditional but notoriously hard to get right.

 In Python, threads do not speed up CPU-bound tasks because of an implementation detail in the standard Python system called the *Global Interpreter Lock* (GIL). This exists to avoid threading problems in the Python interpreter, and can actually make a multithreaded program slower than its single-threaded counterpart, or even a multi-process version.

So for Python, the recommendations are as follows:

- Use threads for I/O bound problems
- Use processes, networking, or events (discussed in the next section) for CPU-bound problems

Green Threads and gevent

As you've seen, developers traditionally avoid slow spots in programs by running them in separate threads or processes. The Apache web server is an example of this design.

One alternative is *event-based* programming. An event-based program runs a central *event loop*, doles out any tasks, and repeats the loop. The nginx web server follows this design, and is generally faster than Apache.

The gevent library is event-based and accomplishes a cool trick: you write normal imperative code, and it magically converts pieces to *coroutines*. These are like generators that can communicate with one another and keep track of where they are. gevent modifies many of Python's standard objects such as socket to use its mechanism instead of blocking. This does not work with Python add-in code that was written in C, as some database drivers are.

As of this writing, gevent was not completely ported to Python 3, so these code examples use the Python 2 tools pip2 and python2.

You install gevent by using the Python 2 version of pip:

```
$ pip2 install gevent
```

Here's a variation of sample code at the gevent website (*http://www.gevent.org*). You'll see the socket module's gethostbyname() function in the upcoming DNS section. This function is synchronous, so you wait (possibly many seconds) while it chases name servers around the world to look up that address. But you could use the gevent version to look up multiple sites independently. Save this as *gevent_test.py*:

```python
import gevent
from gevent import socket
hosts = ['www.crappytaxidermy.com', 'www.walterpottertaxidermy.com',
    'www.antique-taxidermy.com']
jobs = [gevent.spawn(gevent.socket.gethostbyname, host) for host in hosts]
gevent.joinall(jobs, timeout=5)
for job in jobs:
    print(job.value)
```

There's a one-line for-loop in the preceding example. Each hostname is submitted in turn to a gethostbyname() call, but they can run asynchronously because it's the gevent version of gethostbyname().

Run *gevent_test.py* with Python 2 by typing the following (in bold):

```
$ python2 gevent_test.py
66.6.44.4
74.125.142.121
78.136.12.50
```

gevent.spawn() creates a *greenlet* (also known sometimes as a *green thread* or a *microthread*) to execute each gevent.socket.gethostbyname(url).

The difference from a normal thread is that it doesn't block. If something occurred that would have blocked a normal thread, gevent switches control to one of the other greenlets.

The gevent.joinall() method waits for all the spawned jobs to finish. Finally, we dump the IP addresses that we got for these hostnames.

Instead of the gevent version of socket, you can use its evocatively named *monkey-patching* functions. These modify standard modules such as socket to use greenlets rather than calling the gevent version of the module. This is useful when you want gevent to be applied all the way down, even into code that you might not be able to access.

At the top of your program, add the following call:

```
from gevent import monkey
monkey.patch_socket()
```

This inserts the **gevent** socket everywhere the normal socket is called, anywhere in your program, even in the standard library. Again, this works only for Python code, not libraries written in C.

Another function monkey-patches even more standard library modules:

```
from gevent import monkey
monkey.patch_all()
```

Use this at the top of your program to get as many **gevent** speedups as possible.

Save this program as *gevent_monkey.py*:

```
import gevent
from gevent import monkey; monkey.patch_all()
import socket
hosts = ['www.crappytaxidermy.com', 'www.walterpottertaxidermy.com',
    'www.antique-taxidermy.com']
jobs = [gevent.spawn(socket.gethostbyname, host) for host in hosts]
gevent.joinall(jobs, timeout=5)
for job in jobs:
    print(job.value)
```

Again, using Python 2, run the program:

```
$ python2 gevent_monkey.py
66.6.44.4
74.125.192.121
78.136.12.50
```

There are potential dangers when using **gevent**. As with any event-based system, each chunk of code that you execute should be relatively quick. Although it's non-blocking, code that does a lot of work is still slow.

The very idea of monkey-patching makes some people nervous. Yet, many large sites such as Pinterest use **gevent** to speed up their sites significantly. Like the fine print on a bottle of pills, use **gevent** as directed.

 Two other popular event-driven frameworks are **tornado** (*http://www.tornadoweb.org*) and **gunicorn** (*http://gunicorn.org/*). They provide both the low-level event handling and a fast web server. They're worth a look if you'd like to build a fast website without messing with a traditional web server such as Apache.

twisted

`twisted` (*http://twistedmatrix.com/trac/*) is an asynchronous, event-driven networking framework. You connect functions to events such as data received or connection closed, and those functions are called when those events occur. This is a *callback* design, and if you've written anything in JavaScript, it might seem familiar. If it's new to you, it can seem backwards. For some developers, callback-based code becomes harder to manage as the application grows.

Like `gevent`, `twisted` has not yet been ported to Python 3. We'll use the Python 2 installer and interpreter for this section. Type the following to install it:

```
$ pip2 install twisted
```

`twisted` is a large package, with support for many Internet protocols on top of TCP and UDP. To be short and simple, we'll show a little knock-knock server and client, adapted from twisted examples (*http://bit.ly/twisted-ex*). First, let's look at the server, *knock_server.py* (notice the Python 2 syntax for `print()`):

```python
from twisted.internet import protocol, reactor

class Knock(protocol.Protocol):
    def dataReceived(self, data):
        print 'Client:', data
        if data.startswith("Knock knock"):
            response = "Who's there?"
        else:
            response = data + " who?"
        print 'Server:', response
        self.transport.write(response)

class KnockFactory(protocol.Factory):
    def buildProtocol(self, addr):
        return Knock()

reactor.listenTCP(8000, KnockFactory())
reactor.run()
```

Now, let's take a glance at its trusty companion, *knock_client.py*:

```python
from twisted.internet import reactor, protocol

class KnockClient(protocol.Protocol):
    def connectionMade(self):
        self.transport.write("Knock knock")

    def dataReceived(self, data):
        if data.startswith("Who's there?"):
            response = "Disappearing client"
            self.transport.write(response)
        else:
```

```
            self.transport.loseConnection()
            reactor.stop()

    class KnockFactory(protocol.ClientFactory):
        protocol = KnockClient

    def main():
        f = KnockFactory()
        reactor.connectTCP("localhost", 8000, f)
        reactor.run()

    if __name__ == '__main__':
        main()
```

Start the server first:

```
$ python2 knock_server.py
```

Then start the client:

```
$ python2 knock_client.py
```

The server and client exchange messages, and the server prints the conversation:

```
Client: Knock knock
Server: Who's there?
Client: Disappearing client
Server: Disappearing client who?
```

Our trickster client then ends, keeping the server waiting for the punch line.

If you'd like to enter the twisted passages, try some of the other examples from its documentation.

asyncio

Recently, Guido van Rossum (remember him?) became involved with the Python concurrency issue. Many packages had their own event loop, and each event loop kind of likes to be the only one. How could he reconcile mechanisms such as callbacks, greenlets, and others? After many discussions and visits, he proposed Asynchronous IO Support Rebooted: the "asyncio" Module (*http://bit.ly/pep-3156*), codenamed Tulip. This first appeared in Python 3.4 as the asyncio module. For now, it offers a common event loop that could be compatible with twisted, gevent, and other asynchronous methods. The goal is to provide a standard, clean, well-performing asynchronous API. Watch it expand in future releases of Python.

Redis

Our earlier dishwashing code examples, using processes or threads, were run on a single machine. Let's take another approach to queues that can run on a single machine or across a network. Even with multiple singing processes and dancing threads, sometimes one machine isn't enough, You can treat this section as a bridge between single-box (one machine) and multiple-box concurrency.

To try the examples in this section, you'll need a Redis server and its Python module. You can see where to get them in "Redis" on page 211. In that chapter, Redis's role is that of a database. Here, we're featuring its concurrency personality.

A quick way to make a queue is with a Redis list. A Redis server runs on one machine; this can be the same one as its clients, or another that the clients can access through a network. In either case, clients talk to the server via TCP, so they're networking. One or more provider clients pushes messages onto one end of the list. One or more client workers watches this list with a *blocking pop* operation. If the list is empty, they all just sit around playing cards. As soon as a message arrives, the first eager worker gets it.

Like our earlier process- and thread-based examples, *redis_washer.py* generates a sequence of dishes:

```
import redis
conn = redis.Redis()
print('Washer is starting')
dishes = ['salad', 'bread', 'entree', 'dessert']
for dish in dishes:
    msg = dish.encode('utf-8')
    conn.rpush('dishes', msg)
    print('Washed', dish)
conn.rpush('dishes', 'quit')
print('Washer is done')
```

The loop generates four messages containing a dish name, followed by a final message that says "quit." It appends each message to a list called dishes in the Redis server, similar to appending to a Python list.

And as soon as the first dish is ready, *redis_dryer.py* does its work:

```
import redis
conn = redis.Redis()
print('Dryer is starting')
while True:
    msg = conn.blpop('dishes')
    if not msg:
        break
    val = msg[1].decode('utf-8')
    if val == 'quit':
        break
    print('Dried', val)
print('Dishes are dried')
```

This code waits for messages whose first token is "dishes" and prints that each one is dried. It obeys the *quit* message by ending the loop.

Start the dryer, and then the washer. Using the & at the end puts the first program in the *background*; it keeps running, but doesn't listen to the keyboard anymore. This works on Linux, OS X, and Windows, although you might see different output on the next line. In this case (OS X), it's some information about the background dryer process. Then, we start the washer process normally (in the *foreground*). You'll see the mingled output of the two processes:

```
$ python redis_dryer.py &
[2] 81691
Dryer is starting
$ python redis_washer.py
Washer is starting
Washed salad
Dried salad
Washed bread
Dried bread
Washed entree
Dried entree
Washed dessert
Washer is done
Dried dessert
Dishes are dried
[2]+  Done                    python redis_dryer.py
```

As soon as dish IDs started arriving at Redis from the washer process, our hard-working dryer process started pulling them back out. Each dish ID was a number, except the final *sentinel* value, the string 'quit'. When the dryer process read that quit dish ID, it quit, and some more background process information printed to the terminal (also system-dependent). You can use a sentinel (an otherwise invalid value) to indicate something special from the data stream itself—in this case, that we're done. Otherwise, we'd need to add a lot more program logic, such as the following:

- Agreeing ahead of time on some maximum dish number, which would kind of be a sentinel anyway.
- Doing some special *out-of-band* (not in the data stream) interprocess communication.
- Timing out after some interval with no new data.

Let's make a few last changes:

- Create multiple dryer processes.
- Add a timeout to each dryer rather than looking for a sentinel.

The new *redis_dryer2.py*:

```
def dryer():
    import redis
    import os
    import time
    conn = redis.Redis()
    pid = os.getpid()
    timeout = 20
    print('Dryer process %s is starting' % pid)
    while True:
        msg = conn.blpop('dishes', timeout)
        if not msg:
            break
        val = msg[1].decode('utf-8')
        if val == 'quit':
            break
        print('%s: dried %s' % (pid, val))
        time.sleep(0.1)
    print('Dryer process %s is done' % pid)

import multiprocessing
DRYERS=3
for num in range(DRYERS):
    p = multiprocessing.Process(target=dryer)
    p.start()
```

Start the dryer processes in the background, and then the washer process in the foreground:

```
$ python redis_dryer2.py &
Dryer process 44447 is starting
Dryer process 44448 is starting
Dryer process 44446 is starting
$ python redis_washer.py
Washer is starting
Washed salad
44447: dried salad
Washed bread
44448: dried bread
Washed entree
44446: dried entree
Washed dessert
Washer is done
44447: dried dessert
```

One dryer process reads the quit ID and quits:

```
Dryer process 44448 is done
```

After 20 seconds, the other dryer processes get a return value of None from their blpop calls, indicating that they've timed out. They say their last words and exit:

```
Dryer process 44447 is done
Dryer process 44446 is done
```

After the last dryer subprocess quits, the main dryer program ends:

```
[1]+  Done                    python redis_dryer2.py
```

Beyond Queues

With more moving parts, there are more possibilities for our lovely assembly lines to be disrupted. If we need to wash the dishes from a banquet, do we have enough workers? What if the dryers get drunk? What if the sink clogs? Worries, worries!

How will you cope with it all? Fortunately, there are some techniques available that you can apply. They include the following:

Fire and forget
> Just pass things on and don't worry about the consequences, even if no one is there. That's the dishes-on-the-floor approach.

Request-reply
> The washer receives an acknowledgement from the dryer, and the dryer from the put-away-er, for each dish in the pipeline.

Back pressure or throttling
> This technique directs a fast worker to take it easy if someone downstream can't keep up.

In real systems, you need to be careful that workers are keeping up with the demand; otherwise, you hear the dishes hitting the floor. You might add new tasks to a *pending* list, while some worker process pops the latest message and adds it to a *working* list. When the message is done, it's removed from the working list and added to a *completed* list. This lets you know what tasks have failed or are taking too long. You can do this with Redis yourself, or use a system that someone else has already written and tested. Some Python-based queue packages that add this extra level of management—some of which use Redis—include:

celery *(http://www.celeryproject.org)*
> This particular package is well worth a look. It can execute distributed tasks synchronously or asynchronously, using the methods we've discussed: multiprocessing, gevent, and others.

thoonk *(https://github.com/andyet/thoonk.py)*
> This package builds on Redis to provide job queues and *pub-sub* (coming in the next section).

rq *(http://python-rq.org/)*
> This is a Python library for job queues, also based on Redis.

Queues (http://queues.io/)
This site offers a discussion of queuing software, Python-based and otherwise.

Networks

In our discussion of concurrency, we talked mostly about time: single-machine solutions (processes, threads, green threads). We also briefly touched upon some solutions that can span networks (Redis, ZeroMQ). Now, we'll look at networking in its own right, distributing computing across space.

Patterns

You can build networking applications from some basic patterns.

The most common pattern is *request-reply*, also known as *client-server*. This pattern is synchronous: the client waits until the server responds. You've seen many examples of request-reply in this book. Your web browser is also a client, making an HTTP request to a web server, which returns a reply.

Another common pattern is *push*, or *fanout*: you send data to any available worker in a pool of processes. An example is a web server behind a load balancer.

The opposite of push is *pull*, or *fanin*: you accept data from one or more sources. An example would be a logger that takes text messages from multiple processes and writes them to a single log file.

One pattern is similar to radio or television broadcasting: *publish-subscribe*, or *pub-sub*. With this pattern, a publisher sends out data. In a simple pub-sub system, all subscribers would receive a copy. More often, subscribers can indicate that they're interested only in certain types of data (often called a *topic*), and the publisher will send just those. So, unlike the push pattern, more than one subscriber might receive a given piece of data. If there's no subscriber for a topic, the data is ignored.

Let's show a few examples of pub-sub code now, before getting into low-level networking details later in the chapter.

The Publish-Subscribe Model

Publish-subscribe is not a queue but a broadcast. One or more processes publish messages. Each subscriber process indicates what type of messages it would like to receive. A copy of each message is sent to each subscriber that matched its type. Thus, a given message might be processed once, more than once, or not at all. Each publisher is just broadcasting and doesn't know who—if anyone—is listening.

Redis

You can build a quick pub-sub system by using Redis. The publisher emits messages with a topic and a value, and subscribers say which topics they want to receive.

Here's the publisher, *redis_pub.py*:

```
import redis
import random

conn = redis.Redis()
cats = ['siamese', 'persian', 'maine coon', 'norwegian forest']
hats = ['stovepipe', 'bowler', 'tam-o-shanter', 'fedora']
for msg in range(10):
    cat = random.choice(cats)
    hat = random.choice(hats)
    print('Publish: %s wears a %s' % (cat, hat))
    conn.publish(cat, hat)
```

Each topic is a breed of cat, and the accompanying message is a type of hat.

Here's a single subscriber, *redis_sub.py*:

```
import redis
conn = redis.Redis()

topics = ['maine coon', 'persian']
sub = conn.pubsub()
sub.subscribe(topics)
for msg in sub.listen():
    if msg['type'] == 'message':
        cat = msg['channel']
        hat = msg['data']
        print('Subscribe: %s wears a %s' % (cat, hat))
```

The subscriber just shown wants all messages for cat types 'maine coon' and 'persian', and no others. The listen() method returns a dictionary. If its type is 'message', it was sent by the publisher and matches our criteria. The 'channel' key is the topic (cat), and the 'data' key contains the message (hat).

If you start the publisher first and no one is listening, it's like a mime falling in the forest (does he make a sound?), so start the subscriber first:

```
$ python redis_sub.py
```

Next, start the publisher. It will send 10 messages, and then quit:

```
$ python redis_pub.py
Publish: maine coon wears a stovepipe
Publish: norwegian forest wears a stovepipe
Publish: norwegian forest wears a tam-o-shanter
Publish: maine coon wears a bowler
Publish: siamese wears a stovepipe
Publish: norwegian forest wears a tam-o-shanter
```

```
Publish: maine coon wears a bowler
Publish: persian wears a bowler
Publish: norwegian forest wears a bowler
Publish: maine coon wears a stovepipe
```

The subscriber cares about only two types of cat:

```
$ python redis_sub.py
Subscribe: maine coon wears a stovepipe
Subscribe: maine coon wears a bowler
Subscribe: maine coon wears a bowler
Subscribe: persian wears a bowler
Subscribe: maine coon wears a stovepipe
```

We didn't tell the subscriber to quit, so it's still waiting for messages. If you restart the publisher, the subscriber will grab a few more messages and print them.

You can have as many subscribers (and publishers) as you want. If there's no subscriber for a message, it disappears from the Redis server. However, if there are subscribers, the messages stay in the server until all subscribers have retrieved them.

ZeroMQ

ZeroMQ is a library for writing networked applications. We'll go into more detail about it a little later in this chapter. Right now, we'll show how the cat-hat pub-sub example could be handled by ZeroMQ.

ZeroMQ has no central server, so each publisher writes to all subscribers. The publisher, *zmq_pub.py*, looks like this:

```python
import zmq
import random
import time
host = '*'
port = 6789
ctx = zmq.Context()
pub = ctx.socket(zmq.PUB)
pub.bind('tcp://%s:%s' % (host, port))
cats = ['siamese', 'persian', 'maine coon', 'norwegian forest']
hats = ['stovepipe', 'bowler', 'tam-o-shanter', 'fedora']
time.sleep(1)
for msg in range(10):
    cat = random.choice(cats)
    cat_bytes = cat.encode('utf-8')
    hat = random.choice(hats)
    hat_bytes = hat.encode('utf-8')
    print('Publish: %s wears a %s' % (cat, hat))
    pub.send_multipart([cat_bytes, hat_bytes])
```

Notice how this code uses UTF-8 encoding for the topic and value strings.

The file for the subscriber is *zmq_sub.py*:

```
import zmq
host = '127.0.0.1'
port = 6789
ctx = zmq.Context()
sub = ctx.socket(zmq.SUB)
sub.connect('tcp://%s:%s' % (host, port))
topics = ['maine coon', 'persian']
for topic in topics:
    sub.setsockopt(zmq.SUBSCRIBE, topic.encode('utf-8'))
while True:
    cat_bytes, hat_bytes = sub.recv_multipart()
    cat = cat_bytes.decode('utf-8')
    hat = hat_bytes.decode('utf-8')
    print('Subscribe: %s wears a %s' % (cat, hat))
```

In this code, we subscribe to two different byte values: the two strings in `topics`, encoded as UTF-8.

 It seems a little backward, but if you want *all* topics, you need to subscribe to the empty bytestring b''; if you don't, you'll get nothing.

Notice that we call `send_multipart()` in the publisher and `recv_multipart()` in the subscriber. This makes it possible for us to send multipart messages, and use the first part as the topic. We could also send the topic and message as a single string or bytestring, but it seems cleaner to keep cats and hats separate.

Start the subscriber:

```
$ python zmq_sub.py
```

Start the publisher. It immediately sends 10 messages, and then quits:

```
$ python zmq_pub.py
Publish: norwegian forest wears a stovepipe
Publish: siamese wears a bowler
Publish: persian wears a stovepipe
Publish: norwegian forest wears a fedora
Publish: maine coon wears a tam-o-shanter
Publish: maine coon wears a stovepipe
Publish: persian wears a stovepipe
Publish: norwegian forest wears a fedora
Publish: norwegian forest wears a bowler
Publish: maine coon wears a bowler
```

The subscriber prints what it requested and received:

```
Subscribe: persian wears a stovepipe
Subscribe: maine coon wears a tam-o-shanter
Subscribe: maine coon wears a stovepipe
```

```
Subscribe: persian wears a stovepipe
Subscribe: maine coon wears a bowler
```

Other Pub-sub Tools

You might like to explore some of these other Python pub-sub links:

RabbitMQ
> This is a well-known messaging broker, and `pika` is a Python API for it. See the `pika` documentation (*http://pika.readthedocs.org/*) and a pub-sub tutorial (*http://bit.ly/pub-sub-tut*).

`pypi.python.org`
> Go to the upper-right corner of the search window and type `pubsub` to find Python packages like `pypubsub` (*http://pubsub.sourceforge.net/*).

`pubsubhubbub`
> This mellifluous protocol (*https://code.google.com/p/pubsubhubbub/*) enables subscribers to register callbacks with publishers.

TCP/IP

We've been walking through the networking house, taking for granted that whatever's in the basement works correctly. Now, let's actually visit the basement and look at the wires and pipes that keep everything running above ground.

The Internet is based on rules about how to make connections, exchange data, terminate connections, handle timeouts, and so on. These are called *protocols*, and they are arranged in *layers*. The purpose of layers is to allow innovation and alternative ways of doing things; you can do anything you want on one layer as long as you follow the conventions in dealing with the layers above and below you.

The very lowest layer governs aspects such as electrical signals; each higher layer builds on those below. In the middle, more or less, is the IP (Internet Protocol) layer, which specifies how network locations are addressed and how *packets* (chunks) of data flow. In the layer above that, two protocols describe how to move bytes between locations:

UDP (User Datagram Protocol)
> This is used for short exchanges. A *datagram* is a tiny message sent in a single burst, like a note on a postcard.

TCP (Transmission Control Protocol)
> This protocol is used for longer-lived connections. It sends *streams* of bytes and ensures that they arrive in order without duplication.

UDP messages are not acknowledged, so you're never sure if they arrive at their destination. If you wanted to tell a joke over UDP:

```
Here's a UDP joke. Get it?
```

TCP sets up a secret handshake between sender and receiver to ensure a good connection. A TCP joke would start like this:

```
Do you want to hear a TCP joke?
Yes, I want to hear a TCP joke.
Okay, I'll tell you a TCP joke.
Okay, I'll hear a TCP joke.
Okay, I'll send you a TCP joke now.
Okay, I'll receive the TCP joke now.
... (and so on)
```

Your local machine always has the IP address 127.0.0.1 and the name localhost. You might see this called the *loopback interface*. If it's connected to the Internet, your machine will also have a *public* IP. If you're just using a home computer, it's behind equipment such as a cable modem or router. You can run Internet protocols even between processes on the same machine.

Most of the Internet with which we interact—the Web, database servers, and so on—is based on the TCP protocol running atop the IP protocol; for brevity, TCP/IP. Let's first look at some basic Internet services. After that, we'll explore general networking patterns.

Sockets

We've saved this topic until now because you don't need to know all the low-level details to use the higher levels of the Internet. But if you like to know how things work, this is for you.

The lowest level of network programming uses a *socket*, borrowed from the C language and the Unix operating system. Socket-level coding is tedious. You'll have more fun using something like ZeroMQ, but it's useful to see what lies beneath. For instance, messages about sockets often turn up when networking errors take place.

Let's write a very simple client-server exchange. The client sends a string in a UDP datagram to a server, and the server returns a packet of data containing a string. The server needs to listen at a particular address and port—like a post office and a post office box. The client needs to know these two values to deliver its message, and receive any reply.

In the following client and server code, address is a tuple of (*address*, *port*). The address is a string, which can be a name or an *IP address*. When your programs are just talking to one another on the same machine, you can use the name 'localhost' or the equivalent address '127.0.0.1'.

First, let's send a little data from one process to another and return a little data back to the originator. The first program is the client and the second is the server. In each program, we'll print the time and open a socket. The server will listen for connections to its socket, and the client will write to its socket, which transmits a message to the server.

Here's the first program, *udp_server.py*:

```
from datetime import datetime
import socket

server_address = ('localhost', 6789)
max_size = 4096

print('Starting the server at', datetime.now())
print('Waiting for a client to call.')
server = socket.socket(socket.AF_INET, socket.SOCK_DGRAM)
server.bind(server_address)

data, client = server.recvfrom(max_size)

print('At', datetime.now(), client, 'said', data)
server.sendto(b'Are you talking to me?', client)
server.close()
```

The server has to set up networking through two methods imported from the socket package. The first method, socket.socket, creates a socket, and the second, bind, *binds* to it (listens to any data arriving at that IP address and port). AF_INET means we'll create an Internet (IP) socket. (There's another type for *Unix domain sockets*, but those work only on the local machine.) SOCK_DGRAM means we'll send and receive datagrams—in other words, we'll use UDP.

At this point, the server sits and waits for a datagram to come in (recvfrom). When one arrives, the server wakes up and gets both the data and information about the client. The client variable contains the address and port combination needed to reach the client. The server ends by sending a reply and closing its connection.

Let's take a look at *udp_client.py*:

```
import socket
from datetime import datetime

server_address = ('localhost', 6789)
max_size = 4096

print('Starting the client at', datetime.now())
client = socket.socket(socket.AF_INET, socket.SOCK_DGRAM)
client.sendto(b'Hey!', server_address)
data, server = client.recvfrom(max_size)
```

```
print('At', datetime.now(), server, 'said', data)
client.close()
```

The client has most of the same methods as the server (with the exception of bind()). The client sends and then receives, whereas the server receives first.

Start the server first, in its own window. It will print its greeting and then wait with an eerie calm until a client sends it some data:

```
$ python udp_server.py
Starting the server at 2014-02-05 21:17:41.945649
Waiting for a client to call.
```

Next, start the client in another window. It will print its greeting, send data to the server, print the reply, and then exit:

```
$ python udp_client.py
Starting the client at 2014-02-05 21:24:56.509682
At 2014-02-05 21:24:56.518670 ('127.0.0.1', 6789) said b'Are you talking to me?'
```

Finally, the server will print something like this, and then exit:

```
At 2014-02-05 21:24:56.518473 ('127.0.0.1', 56267) said b'Hey!'
```

The client needed to know the server's address and port number but didn't need to specify a port number for itself. That was automatically assigned by the system—in this case, it was 56267.

UDP sends data in single chunks. It does not guarantee delivery. If you send multiple messages via UDP, they can arrive out of order, or not at all. It's fast, light, connectionless, and unreliable.

Which brings us to TCP (Transmission Control Protocol). TCP is used for longer-lived connections, such as the Web. TCP delivers data in the order in which you send it. If there were any problems, it tries to send it again. Let's shoot a few packets from client to server and back with TCP.

tcp_client.py acts like the previous UDP client, sending only one string to the server, but there are small differences in the socket calls, illustrated here:

```
import socket
from datetime import datetime

address = ('localhost', 6789)
max_size = 1000

print('Starting the client at', datetime.now())
client = socket.socket(socket.AF_INET, socket.SOCK_STREAM)
client.connect(address)
client.sendall(b'Hey!')
```

```
data = client.recv(max_size)
print('At', datetime.now(), 'someone replied', data)
client.close()
```

We've replaced SOCK_DGRAM with SOCK_STREAM to get the streaming protocol, TCP. We also added a connect() call to set up the stream. We didn't need that for UDP because each datagram was on its own in the wild, wooly Internet.

tcp_server.py also differs from its UDP cousin:

```
from datetime import datetime
import socket

address = ('localhost', 6789)
max_size = 1000

print('Starting the server at', datetime.now())
print('Waiting for a client to call.')
server = socket.socket(socket.AF_INET, socket.SOCK_STREAM)
server.bind(address)
server.listen(5)

client, addr = server.accept()
data = client.recv(max_size)

print('At', datetime.now(), client, 'said', data)
client.sendall(b'Are you talking to me?')
client.close()
server.close()
```

server.listen(5) is configured to queue up to five client connections before refusing new ones. server.accept() gets the first available message as it arrives. The cli ent.recv(1000) sets a maximum acceptable message length of 1,000 bytes.

As you did earlier, start the server and then the client, and watch the fun. First, the server:

```
$ python tcp_server.py
Starting the server at 2014-02-06 22:45:13.306971
Waiting for a client to call.
At 2014-02-06 22:45:16.048865 <socket.socket object, fd=6, family=2, type=1,
    proto=0> said b'Hey!'
```

Now, start the client. It will send its message to the server, receive a response, and then exit:

```
$ python tcp_client.py
Starting the client at 2014-02-06 22:45:16.038642
At 2014-02-06 22:45:16.049078 someone replied b'Are you talking to me?'
```

The server collects the message, prints it, responds, and then quits:

```
At 2014-02-06 22:45:16.048865 <socket.socket object, fd=6, family=2, type=1,
    proto=0> said b'Hey!'
```

Notice that the TCP server called `client.sendall()` to respond, and the earlier UDP server called `client.sendto()`. TCP maintains the client-server connection across multiple socket calls and remembers the client's IP address.

This didn't look so bad, but if you try to write anything more complex, you'll see how low-level sockets really are. Here are some of the complications with which you need to cope:

- UDP sends messages, but their size is limited, and they're not guaranteed to reach their destination.
- TCP sends streams of bytes, not messages. You don't know how many bytes the system will send or receive with each call.
- To exchange entire messages with TCP, you need some extra information to reassemble the full message from its segments: a fixed message size (bytes), or the size of the full message, or some delimiting character.
- Because messages are bytes, not Unicode text strings, you need to use the Python `bytes` type. For more information on that, see Chapter 7.

After all of this, if you find yourself fascinated by socket programming, check out the Python socket programming HOWTO (*http://bit.ly/socket-howto*) for more details.

ZeroMQ

We've already seen ZeroMQ sockets used for pub-sub. ZeroMQ is a library. Sometimes described as *sockets on steroids*, ZeroMQ sockets do the things that you sort of expected plain sockets to do:

- Exchange entire messages
- Retry connections
- Buffer data to preserve it when the timing between senders and receivers doesn't line up

The online guide (*http://zguide.zeromq.org/*) is well written and witty, and it presents the best description of networking patterns that I've seen. The printed version (*ZeroMQ: Messaging for Many Applications*, by Pieter Hintjens, from that animal house, O'Reilly) has that good code smell and a big fish on the cover, rather than the other way around. All the examples in the printed guide are in the C language, but the online version lets you pick from multiple languages for each code example. The Python examples are also viewable (*http://bit.ly/zeromq-py*). In this chapter, I'll show you some basic uses for ZeroMQ in Python.

ZeroMQ is like a Lego set, and we all know that you can build an amazing variety of things from a few Lego shapes. In this case, you construct networks from a few socket types and patterns. The basic "Lego pieces" presented in the following list are the ZeroMQ socket types, which by some twist of fate look like the network patterns we've already discussed:

- REQ (synchronous request)
- REP (synchronous reply)
- DEALER (asynchronous request)
- ROUTER (asynchronous reply)
- PUB (publish)
- SUB (subscribe)
- PUSH (fanout)
- PULL (fanin)

To try these yourself, you'll need to install the Python ZeroMQ library by typing this command:

```
$ pip install pyzmq
```

The simplest pattern is a single request-reply pair. This is synchronous: one socket makes a request and then the other replies. First, the code for the reply (server), *zmq_server.py*:

```
import zmq

host = '127.0.0.1'
port = 6789
context = zmq.Context()
server = context.socket(zmq.REP)
server.bind("tcp://%s:%s" % (host, port))
while True:
    # Wait for next request from client
    request_bytes = server.recv()
    request_str = request_bytes.decode('utf-8')
    print("That voice in my head says: %s" % request_str)
    reply_str = "Stop saying: %s" % request_str
    reply_bytes = bytes(reply_str, 'utf-8')
    server.send(reply_bytes)
```

We create a Context object: this is a ZeroMQ object that maintains state. Then, we make a ZeroMQ socket of type REP (for REPly). We call bind() to make it listen on a particular IP address and port. Notice that they're specified in a string such as 'tcp://localhost:6789' rather than a tuple, as in the plain socket examples.

This example keeps receiving requests from a sender and sending a response. The messages can be very long—ZeroMQ takes care of the details.

Following is the code for the corresponding request (client), *zmq_client.py*. Its type is REQ (for REQuest), and it calls connect() rather than bind().

```python
import zmq

host = '127.0.0.1'
port = 6789
context = zmq.Context()
client = context.socket(zmq.REQ)
client.connect("tcp://%s:%s" % (host, port))
for num in range(1, 6):
    request_str = "message #%s" % num
    request_bytes = request_str.encode('utf-8')
    client.send(request_bytes)
    reply_bytes = client.recv()
    reply_str = reply_bytes.decode('utf-8')
    print("Sent %s, received %s" % (request_str, reply_str))
```

Now it's time to start them. One interesting difference from the plain socket examples is that you can start the server and client in either order. Go ahead and start the server in one window in the background:

```
$ python zmq_server.py &
```

Start the client in the same window:

```
$ python zmq_client.py
```

You'll see these alternating output lines from the client and server:

```
That voice in my head says 'message #1'
Sent 'message #1', received 'Stop saying message #1'
That voice in my head says 'message #2'
Sent 'message #2', received 'Stop saying message #2'
That voice in my head says 'message #3'
Sent 'message #3', received 'Stop saying message #3'
That voice in my head says 'message #4'
Sent 'message #4', received 'Stop saying message #4'
That voice in my head says 'message #5'
Sent 'message #5', received 'Stop saying message #5'
```

Our client ends after sending its fifth message, but we didn't tell the server to quit, so it sits by the phone, waiting for another message. If you run the client again, it will print the same five lines, and the server will print its five also. If you don't kill the *zmq_server.py* process and try to run another one, Python will complain that the address is already is use:

```
$ python zmq_server.py
[2] 356
Traceback (most recent call last):
```

```
  File "zmq_server.py", line 7, in <module>
    server.bind("tcp://%s:%s" % (host, port))
  File "socket.pyx", line 444, in zmq.backend.cython.socket.Socket.bind
      (zmq/backend/cython/socket.c:4076)
  File "checkrc.pxd", line 21, in zmq.backend.cython.checkrc._check_rc
      (zmq/backend/cython/socket.c:6032)
zmq.error.ZMQError: Address already in use</pre>
```

The messages need to be sent as byte strings, so we encoded our example's text strings in UTF-8 format. You can send any kind of message you like, as long as you convert it to bytes. We used simple text strings as the source of our messages, so encode() and decode() were enough to convert to and from byte strings. If your messages have other data types, you can use a library such as MessagePack (*http://msgpack.org/*).

Even this basic REQ-REP pattern allows for some fancy communication patterns, because any number of REQ clients can connect() to a single REP server. The server handles requests one at a time, synchronously, but doesn't drop other requests that are arriving in the meantime. ZeroMQ buffers messages, up to some specified limit, until they can get through; that's where it earns the Q in its name. The Q stands for Queue, the M stands for Message, and the Zero means there doesn't need to be any broker.

Although ZeroMQ doesn't impose any central brokers (intermediaries), you can build them where needed. For example, use DEALER and ROUTER sockets to connect multiple sources and/or destinations asynchronously.

Multiple REQ sockets connect to a single ROUTER, which passes each request to a DEALER, which then contacts any REP sockets that have connected to it (Figure 11-1). This is similar to a bunch of browsers contacting a proxy server in front of a web server farm. It lets you add multiple clients and servers as needed.

The REQ sockets connect only to the ROUTER socket; the DEALER connects to the multiple REP sockets behind it. ZeroMQ takes care of the nasty details, ensuring that the requests are load balanced and that the replies go back to the right place.

Another networking pattern called the *ventilator* uses PUSH sockets to farm out asynchronous tasks, and PULL sockets to gather the results.

The last notable feature of ZeroMQ is that it scales up *and* down, just by changing the connection type of the socket when it's created:

- tcp between processes, on one or more machines
- ipc between processes on one machine
- inproc between threads in a single process

That last one, inproc, is a way to pass data between threads without locks, and an alternative to the threading example in "Threads" on page 271.

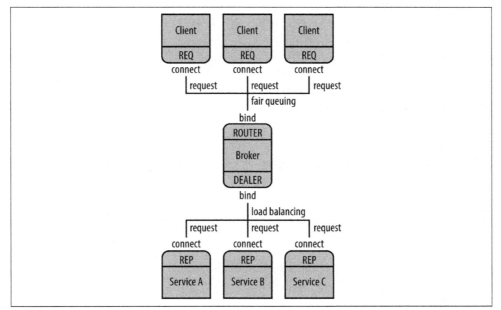

Figure 11-1. Using a broker to connect multiple clients and services

After using ZeroMQ, you might never want to write raw socket code again.

 ZeroMQ is certainly not the only message-passing library that Python supports. Message passing is one of the most popular ideas in networking, and Python keeps up with other languages. The Apache project, whose web server we saw in "Apache" on page 239, also maintains the ActiveMQ (*https://activemq.apache.org*) project, including several Python interfaces using the simple-text STOMP (*http://stomp.github.io/implementations.html*) protocol. RabbitMQ (*http://www.rabbitmq.com*) is also popular, and has useful online Python tutorials (*http://bit.ly/rabbitmq-tut*).

Scapy

Sometimes you need to dip into the networking stream and see the bytes swimming by. You might want to debug a web API, or track down some security issue. The scapy library is an excellent Python tool for packet investigation, and much easier than writing and debugging C programs. It's actually a little language for constructing and analyzing packets.

I planned to include some example code here but changed my mind for two reasons:

- scapy hasn't been ported to Python 3 yet. That hasn't stopped us before, when we've used pip2 and python2, but …
- The installation instructions (*http://bit.ly/scapy-install*) for scapy are, I think, too intimidating for an introductory book.

If you're so inclined, take a look at the examples in the main documentation site (*http://bit.ly/scapy-docs*). They might encourage you to brave an installation on your machine.

Finally, don't confuse scapy with scrapy, which is covered in "Crawl and Scrape" on page 244.

Internet Services

Python has an extensive networking toolset. In the following sections, we'll look at ways to automate some of the most popular Internet services. The official, comprehensive documentation (*http://bit.ly/py-internet*) is available online.

Domain Name System

Computers have numeric IP addresses such as 85.2.101.94, but we remember names better than numbers. The Domain Name System (DNS) is a critical Internet service that converts IP addresses to and from names via a distributed database. Whenever you're using a web browser and suddenly see a message like "looking up host," you've probably lost your Internet connection, and your first clue is a DNS failure.

Some DNS functions are found in the low-level socket module. gethostbyname() returns the IP address for a domain name, and the extended edition gethostby name_ex() returns the name, a list of alternative names, and a list of addresses:

```
>>> import socket
>>> socket.gethostbyname('www.crappytaxidermy.com')
'66.6.44.4'
>>> socket.gethostbyname_ex('www.crappytaxidermy.com')
('crappytaxidermy.com', ['www.crappytaxidermy.com'], ['66.6.44.4'])
```

The getaddrinfo() method looks up the IP address, but it also returns enough information to create a socket to connect to it:

```
>>> socket.getaddrinfo('www.crappytaxidermy.com', 80)
[(2, 2, 17, '', ('66.6.44.4', 80)), (2, 1, 6, '', ('66.6.44.4', 80))]
```

The preceding call returned two tuples, the first for UDP, and the second for TCP (the 6 in the 2, 1, 6 is the value for TCP).

You can ask for TCP or UDP information only:

```
>>> socket.getaddrinfo('www.crappytaxidermy.com', 80, socket.AF_INET,
socket.SOCK_STREAM)
[(2, 1, 6, '', ('66.6.44.4', 80))]
```

Some TCP and UDP port numbers (*http://bit.ly/tcp-udp-ports*) are reserved for certain services by IANA, and are associated with service names. For example, HTTP is named http and is assigned TCP port 80.

These functions convert between service names and port numbers:

```
>>> import socket
>>> socket.getservbyname('http')
80
>>> socket.getservbyport(80)
'http'
```

Python Email Modules

The standard library contains these email modules:

- smtplib for sending email messages via Simple Mail Transfer Protocol (SMTP)
- email for creating and parsing email messages
- poplib for reading email via Post Office Protocol 3 (POP3)
- imaplib for reading email via Internet Message Access Protocol (IMAP)

The official documentation contains sample code (*http://bit.ly/py-email*) for all of these libraries.

If you want to write your own Python SMTP server, try smtpd (*http://bit.ly/py-smtpd*).

A pure-python SMTP server called Lamson (*http://lamsonproject.org/*) allows you to store messages in databases, and you can even block spam.

Other protocols

Using the standard ftplib module (*http://bit.ly/py-ftplib*), you can push bytes around by using the File Transfer Protocol (FTP). Although it's an old protocol, FTP still performs very well.

You've seen many of these modules in various places in this book, but also try the documentation for standard library support of Internet protocols (*http://bit.ly/py-internet*).

Web Services and APIs

Information providers always have a website, but those are targeted for human eyes, not automation. If data is published only on a website, anyone who wants to access and structure the data needs to write scrapers (as shown in "Crawl and Scrape" on page 244), and rewrite them each time a page format changes. This is usually tedious. In contrast, if a website offers an API to its data, the data becomes directly available to client programs. APIs change less often than web page layouts, so client rewrites are less common. A fast, clean data pipeline also makes it easier to build *mashups*—combinations that might not have been foreseen but can be useful and even profitable.

In many ways, the easiest API is a web interface, but one that provides data in a structured format such as JSON or XML rather than plain text or HTML. The API might be minimal or a full-fledged RESTful API (defined in "Web APIs and Representational State Transfer" on page 243), but it provides another outlet for those restless bytes.

At the very beginning of this book, you can see a web API: it picks up the most popular videos from YouTube. This next example might make more sense now that you've read about web requests, JSON, dictionaries, lists, and slices:

```
import requests
url = "https://gdata.youtube.com/feeds/api/standardfeeds/top_rated?alt=json"
response = requests.get(url)
data = response.json()
for video in data['feed']['entry'][0:6]:
    print(video['title']['$t'])
```

APIs are especially useful for mining well-known social media sites such as Twitter, Facebook, and LinkedIn. All these sites provide APIs that are free to use, but they require you to register and get a key (a long-generated text string, sometimes also known as a *token*) to use when connecting. The key lets a site determine who's accessing its data. It can also serve as a way to limit request traffic to servers. The YouTube example you just looked at did not require an API key for searching, but it would if you made calls that updated data at YouTube.

Here are some interesting service APIs:

- New York Times (*http://developer.nytimes.com/*)
- YouTube (*http://gdata.youtube.com/demo/index.html*)
- Twitter (*https://dev.twitter.com/docs/twitter-libraries*)
- Facebook (*https://developers.facebook.com/tools/*)
- Weather Underground (*http://www.wunderground.com/weather/api/*)
- Marvel Comics (*http://developer.marvel.com/*)

You can see examples of APIs for maps in Appendix B, and others in Appendix C.

Remote Processing

Most of the examples in this book have demonstrated how to call Python code on the same machine, and usually in the same process. Thanks to Python's expressiveness, you can also call code on other machines as though they were local. In advanced settings, if you run out of space on your single machine, you can expand beyond it. A network of machines gives you access to more processes and/or threads.

Remote Procedure Calls

Remote Procedure Calls (RPCs) look like normal functions but execute on remote machines across a network. Instead of calling a RESTful API with arguments encoded in the URL or request body, you call an RPC function on your own machine. Here's what happens under the hood of the RPC client:

1. It converts your function arguments into bytes (sometimes this is called *marshalling*, or *serializing*, or just *encoding*).
2. It sends the encoded bytes to the remote machine.

And here's what happens on the remote machine:

1. It receives the encoded request bytes.
2. After receiving the bytes, the RPC client decodes the bytes back to the original data structures (or equivalent ones, if the hardware and software differ between the two machines).
3. The client then finds and calls the local function with the decoded data.
4. Next, it encodes the function results.
5. Last, the client sends the encoded bytes back to the caller.

And finally, the machine that started it all decodes the bytes to return values.

RPC is a popular technique, and people have implemented it in many ways. On the server side, you start a server program, connect it with some byte transport and encoding/decoding method, define some service functions, and light up your *RPC is open for business* sign. The client connects to the server and calls one of its functions via RPC.

The standard library includes one RPC implementation that uses XML as the exchange format: xmlrpc. You define and register functions on the server, and the client calls them as though they were imported. First, let's explore the file *xmlrpc_server.py*:

```
from xmlrpc.server import SimpleXMLRPCServer

def double(num):
```

```
    return num * 2

server = SimpleXMLRPCServer(("localhost", 6789))
server.register_function(double, "double")
server.serve_forever()
```

The function we're providing on the server is called double(). It expects a number as an argument and returns the value of that number times two. The server starts up on an address and port. We need to *register* the function to make it available to clients via RPC. Finally, start serving and carry on.

Now, you guessed it, *xmlrpc_client.py*:

```
import xmlrpc.client

proxy = xmlrpc.client.ServerProxy("http://localhost:6789/")
num = 7
result = proxy.double(num)
print("Double %s is %s" % (num, result))
```

The client connects to the server by using ServerProxy(). Then, it calls the function proxy.double(). Where did that come from? It was created dynamically by the server. The RPC machinery magically hooks this function name into a call to the remote server.

Give it a try—start the server and then run the client:

```
$ python xmlrpc_server.py
```

Next, run the client:

```
$ python xmlrpc_client.py
Double 7 is 14
```

The server then prints the following:

```
127.0.0.1 - - [13/Feb/2014 20:16:23] "POST / HTTP/1.1" 200 -
```

Popular transport methods are HTTP and ZeroMQ. Common encodings besides XML include JSON, Protocol Buffers, and MessagePack. There are many Python packages for JSON-based RPC, but many of them either don't support Python 3 or seem a bit tangled. Let's look at something different: MessagePack's own Python RPC implementation (*http://bit.ly/msgpack-rpc*). Here's how to install it:

```
$ pip install msgpack-rpc-python
```

This will also install tornado, a Python event-based web server that this library uses as a transport. As usual, the server comes first (*msgpack_server.py*):

```
from msgpackrpc import Server, Address

class Services():
    def double(self, num):
```

```
        return num * 2

server = Server(Services())
server.listen(Address("localhost", 6789))
server.start()
```

The `Services` class exposes its methods as RPC services. Go ahead and start the client, *msgpack_client.py*:

```
from msgpackrpc import Client, Address

client = Client(Address("localhost", 6789))
num = 8
result =  client.call('double', num)
print("Double %s is %s" % (num, result))
```

To run these, follow the usual drill: start the server, start the client, see the results:

```
$ python msgpack_server.py
```

```
$ python msgpack_client.py
Double 8 is 16
```

fabric

The `fabric` package lets you run remote or local commands, upload or download files, and run as a privileged user with `sudo`. The package uses Secure Shell (SSH; the encrypted text protocol that has largely replaced `telnet`) to run programs on remote machines. You write functions (in Python) in a so-called *fabric file* and indicate if they should be run locally or remotely. When you run these with the `fabric` program (called `fab`, but not as a tribute to the Beatles or detergent) you indicate which remote machines to use and which functions to call. It's simpler than the RPC examples we've seen.

 As this was written, the author of `fabric` was merging some fixes to work with Python 3. If those go through, the examples below will work. Until then, you'll need to run them using Python 2.

First, install `fabric` by typing the following:

```
$ pip2 install fabric
```

You can run Python code locally from a `fabric` file directly without SSH. Save this first file as *fab1.py*:

```
def iso():
    from datetime import date
    print(date.today().isoformat())
```

Now, type the following to run it:

```
$ fab -f fab1.py -H localhost iso
[localhost] Executing task 'iso'
2014-02-22

Done.
```

The `-f fab1.py` option specifies to use fabric file *fab1.py* instead of the default *fab-file.py*. The `-H localhost` option indicates to run the command on your local machine. Finally, `iso` is the name of the function in the fab file to run. It works like the RPCs that you saw earlier. You can find options on the site's documentation (*http://docs.fabfile.org/*).

To run external programs on your local or remote machines, they need to have an SSH server running. On Unix-like systems, this server is `sshd`; `service sshd status` will report if it's up, and `service sshd start` will start it, if needed. On a Mac, open System Preferences, click the Sharing tab, and then click the Remote Login checkbox. Windows doesn't have built-in SSH support; your best bet is to install putty (*http://bit.ly/putty-ssh*).

We'll reuse the function name `iso`, but this time have it run a command by using `local()`. Here's the command and its output:

```
from fabric.api import local

def iso():
    local('date -u')
```

```
$ fab -f fab2.py -H localhost iso
[localhost] Executing task 'iso'
[localhost] local: date -u
Sun Feb 23 05:22:33 UTC 2014

Done.
Disconnecting from localhost... done.
```

The remote counterpart of `local()` is `run()`. Here's *fab3.py*:

```
from fabric.api import run

def iso():
    run('date -u')
```

Using `run()` instructs `fabric` to use SSH to connect to whatever hosts were specified on the command line with `-H`. If you have a local network and can connect via SSH to a host, use that hostname in the command after the `-H` (shown in the example that follows). If not, use `localhost`, and it will act as though it were talking to another machine; this can be handy for testing. For this example, let's use `localhost` again:

```
$ fab -f fab3.py -H localhost iso
```
```
[localhost] Executing task 'iso'
[localhost] run: date -u
[localhost] Login password for 'yourname':
[localhost] out: Sun Feb 23 05:26:05 UTC 2014
[localhost] out:


Done.
Disconnecting from localhost... done.
```

Notice that it prompted for my login password. To avoid this, you can embed your password in the fabric file as follows:

```
from fabric.api import run
from fabric.context_managers import env

env.password = "your password goes here"

def iso():
    run('date -u')
```

Go ahead and run it:

```
$ fab -f fab4.py -H localhost iso
```
```
[localhost] Executing task 'iso'
[localhost] run: date -u
[localhost] out: Sun Feb 23 05:31:00 UTC 2014
[localhost] out:


Done.
Disconnecting from localhost... done.
```

 Putting your password in your code is both brittle and insecure. A better way to specify the necessary password is to configure SSH with public and private keys, by using ssh-keygen (*http://bit.ly/ genkeys*).

Salt

Salt (*http://www.saltstack.com/*) started as a way to implement remote execution, but it grew to a full-fledged systems management platform. Based on ZeroMQ rather than SSH, it can scale to thousands of servers.

Salt has not yet been ported to Python 3. In this case, I won't show Python 2 examples. If you're interested in this area, read the documents, and watch for announcements when they do complete the port.

Alternative products include puppet (*http://puppetlabs.com/*) and chef (*http://www.getchef.com/chef/*), which are closely tied to Ruby. The ansible (*http://www.ansible.com/home*) package, which like Salt is written in Python, is also comparable. It's free to download and use, but support and some add-on packages require a commercial license. It uses SSH by default and does not require any special software to be installed on the machines that it will manage.

salt and ansible are both functional supersets of fabric, handling initial configuration, deployment, and remote execution.

Big Fat Data and MapReduce

As Google and other Internet companies grew, they found that traditional computing solutions didn't scale. Software that worked for single machines, or even a few dozen, could not keep up with thousands.

Disk storage for databases and files involved too much *seeking*, which requires mechanical movement of disk heads. (Think of a vinyl record, and the time it takes to move the needle from one track to another manually. And think of the screeching sound it makes when you drop it too hard, not to mention the sounds made by the record's owner.) But you could *stream* consecutive segments of the disk more quickly.

Developers found that it was faster to distribute and analyze data on many networked machines than on individual ones. They could use algorithms that sounded simplistic, but actually worked better overall with massively distributed data. One of these is MapReduce, which spreads a calculation across many machines and then gathers the results. It's similar to working with queues.

After Google published its results in a paper, Yahoo followed with an open source Java-based package named *Hadoop* (named after the toy stuffed elephant of the lead programmer's son).

The phrase *big data* applies here. Often it just means "data too big to fit on my machine": data that exceeds the disk, memory, CPU time, or all of the above. To some organizations, if *big data* is mentioned somewhere in a question, the answer is always Hadoop. Hadoop copies data among machines, running them through map and reduce programs, and saving the results on disk at each step.

This batch process can be slow. A quicker method called *Hadoop streaming* works like Unix pipes, streaming the data through programs without requiring disk writes at each step. You can write Hadoop streaming programs in any language, including Python.

Many Python modules have been written for Hadoop, and some are discussed in the blog post "A Guide to Python Frameworks for Hadoop" (*http://bit.ly/py-hadoop*). The Spotify company, known for streaming music, open sourced its Python component for Hadoop streaming, Luigi (*https://github.com/spotify/luigi*). The Python 3 port is still incomplete.

A rival named Spark (*http://bit.ly/about-spark*) was designed to run ten to a hundred times faster than Hadoop. It can read and process any Hadoop data source and format. Spark includes APIs for Python and other languages. You can find the installation documents online (*http://bit.ly/dl-spark*).

Another alternative to Hadoop is Disco (*http://discoproject.org/*), which uses Python for MapReduce processing and Erlang for communication. Alas, you can't install it with `pip`; see the documentation (*http://bit.ly/get-disco*).

See Appendix C for related examples of *parallel programming*, in which a large structured calculation is distributed among many machines.

Working in the Clouds

Not so long ago, you would buy your own servers, bolt them into racks in data centers, and install layers of software on them: operating systems, device drivers, file systems, databases, web servers, email servers, name servers, load balancers, monitors, and more. Any initial novelty wore off as you tried to keep multiple systems alive and responsive. And you worried constantly about security.

Many hosting services offered to take care of your servers for a fee, but you still leased the physical devices and had to pay for your peak load configuration at all times.

With more individual machines, failures are no longer infrequent: they're very common. You need to scale services horizontally and store data redundantly. You can't assume that the network operates like a single machine. The eight fallacies of distributed computing, according to Peter Deutsch, are as follows:

- The network is reliable.
- Latency is zero.
- Bandwidth is infinite.
- The network is secure.
- Topology doesn't change.
- There is one administrator.
- Transport cost is zero.
- The network is homogeneous.

You can try to build these complex distributed systems, but it's a lot of work, and a different toolset is needed. To borrow an analogy, when you have a handful of servers, you treat them like pets—you give them names, know their personalities, and nurse them back to health when needed. But at scale, you treat servers more like livestock: they look alike, have numbers, and are just replaced if they have any problems.

Instead of building, you can rent servers in the *cloud*. By adopting this model, maintenance is someone else's problem, and you can concentrate on your service, or blog, or whatever you want to show the world. Using web dashboards and APIs, you can spin up servers with whatever configuration you need, quickly and easily—they're *elastic*. You can monitor their status, and be alerted if some metric exceeds a given threshold. Clouds are currently a pretty hot topic, and corporate spending on cloud components has spiked.

Let's see how Python interacts with some popular clouds.

Google

Google uses Python a lot internally, and it employs some prominent Python developers (even Guido van Rossum himself, for some time).

Go to the App Engine site (*https://developers.google.com/appengine/*) and then, under "Choose a Language," click in the Python box. You can type Python code into the Cloud Playground and see results just below. Just after that are links and directions to download the Python SDK to your machine. This allows you to develop against Google's cloud APIs on your own hardware. Following this are details on how to deploy your application to AppEngine itself.

From Google's main cloud page (*https://cloud.google.com/*), you can find details on its services, including these:

App Engine
   A high-level platform, including Python tools such as `flask` and `django`.

Compute Engine
   Create clusters of virtual machines for large distributed computing tasks.

Cloud Storage
   Object storage (objects are files, but there are no directory hierarchies).

Cloud Datastore
   A large NoSQL database.

Cloud SQL
   A large SQL database.

Cloud Endpoints
   Restful access to applications.

BigQuery
   Hadoop-like big data.

Google services compete with Amazon and OpenStack, a segue if there ever was one.

Amazon

As Amazon was growing from hundreds to thousands to millions of servers, developers ran into all the nasty problems of distributed systems. One day in 2002 or thereabouts, CEO Jeff Bezos declared to Amazon employees that, henceforth, all data and functionality needed to be exposed only via network service interfaces—not files, or databases, or local function calls. They had to design these interfaces as though they were being offered to the public. The memo ended with a motivational nugget: *"Anyone who doesn't do this will be fired."*

Not surprisingly, developers got to work, and over time built a very large service-oriented architecture. They borrowed or innovated many solutions, evolving into Amazon Web Services (AWS) (*http://aws.amazon.com/*), which now dominates the market. It now contains dozens of services, but the most relevant are the following:

Elastic Beanstalk
    High-level application platform

EC2 (Elastic Compute)
    Distributed computing

S3 (Simple Storage Service)
    Object storage

RDS
    Relational databases (MySQL, PostgreSQL, Oracle, MSSQL)

DynamoDB
    NoSQL database

Redshift
    Data warehouse

EMR
    Hadoop

For details on these and other AWS services, download the Amazon Python SDK (*http://bit.ly/aws-py-sdk*) and read the help section.

The official Python AWS library, boto (*http://docs.pythonboto.org/*), is another foot-dragger, not yet fully ported to Python 3. You'll need to use Python 2, or try an alternative, which you can do by searching the Python Package Index (*http://pypi.python.org*) for "aws" or "amazon."

OpenStack

The second most popular cloud service provider has been Rackspace. In 2010, it formed an unusual partnership with NASA to merge some of their cloud infrastructure into OpenStack (*http://www.openstack.org*). This is a freely available open source platform to build public, private, and hybrid clouds. A new release is made every six months, the most recent containing over 1.25 million lines of Python from many contributors. OpenStack is used in production by a growing number of organizations, including CERN and PayPal.

OpenStack's main APIs are RESTful, with Python modules providing programmatic interfaces, and command-line Python programs for shell automation. Here are some of the standard services in the current release:

Keystone
> *Identity* service, providing authentication (for example, user/password), authorization (capabilities), and service discovery.

Nova
> *Compute* service, distributing work across networked servers.

Swift
> *Object storage*, such as Amazon's S3. It's used by Rackspace's Cloud Files service.

Glance
> Mid-level *image storage* service.

Cinder
> Low-level *block storage* service.

Horizon
> Web-based *dashboard* for all the services.

Neutron
> *Network management* service.

Heat
> *Orchestration* (multicloud) service.

Ceilometer
> *Telemetry* (metrics, monitoring, and metering) service.

Other services are proposed from time to time, which then go through an incubation process and might become part of the standard OpenStack platform.

OpenStack runs on Linux or within a Linux virtual machine (VM). The installation of its core services is still somewhat involved. The fastest way to install OpenStack on Linux is to use Devstack (*http://devstack.org/*) and watch all the explanatory text fly-

---

ing by as it runs. You'll end up with a web dashboard that can view and control the other services.

If you want to install some or all of OpenStack manually, use your Linux distribution's package manager. All of the major Linux vendors support OpenStack and are providing official packages on their download servers. Browse the main OpenStack site for installation documents, news, and related information.

OpenStack development and corporate support are accelerating. It's been compared to Linux when it was disrupting the proprietary Unix versions.

Things to Do

11.1 Use a plain `socket` to implement a current-time-service. When a client sends the string *time* to the server, return the current date and time as an ISO string.

11.2 Use ZeroMQ REQ and REP sockets to do the same thing.

11.3 Try the same with XMLRPC.

11.4 You may have seen the old *I Love Lucy* television episode in which Lucy and Ethel worked in a chocolate factory (it's a classic). The duo fell behind as the conveyor belt that supplied the confections for them to process began operating at an ever-faster rate. Write a simulation that pushes different types of chocolates to a Redis list, and Lucy is a client doing blocking pops of this list. She needs 0.5 seconds to handle a piece of chocolate. Print the time and type of each chocolate as Lucy gets it, and how many remain to be handled.

11.5 Use ZeroMQ to publish the poem from exercise 7.7 (from "Things to Do" on page 173), one word at a time. Write a ZeroMQ consumer that prints every word that starts with a vowel, and another that prints every word that contains five letters. Ignore punctuation characters.

CHAPTER 12

Be a Pythonista

Always wanted to travel back in time to try fighting a younger version of yourself? Software development is the career for you!
—Elliot Loh (*http://bit.ly/loh-tweet*)

This chapter is devoted to the art and science of Python development, with "best practice" recommendations. Absorb them, and you too can be a card-carrying Pythonista.

About Programming

First, a few notes about programming, based on personal experience.

My original career path was science, and I taught myself programming to analyze and display experimental data. I expected computer programming to be like my impression of accounting—precise but dull. I was surprised to find that I enjoyed it. Part of the fun was its logical aspects—like solving puzzles—but part was creative. You had to write your program correctly to get the right results, but you had the freedom to write it any way you wanted. It was an unusual balance of right-brain and left-brain thinking.

After I wandered off into a career in programming, I also learned that the field had many niches, with very different tasks and types of people. You could delve into computer graphics, operating systems, business applications—even science.

If you're a programmer, you might have had a similar experience yourself. If you're not, you might try programming a bit to see if it fits your personality, or at least helps you to get something done. As I may have mentioned much earlier in this book, math skills are not so important. It seems that the ability to think logically is most important, and that an aptitude for languages seems to help. Finally, patience helps, especially when you're tracking down an elusive bug in your code.

Find Python Code

When you need to develop some code, the fastest solution is to steal it. Well…that is, from a source from which you're allowed to steal code.

The Python standard library (*http://docs.python.org/3/library/*) is wide, deep, and mostly clear. Dive in and look for those pearls.

Like the halls of fame for various sports, it takes time for a module to get into the standard library. New packages are appearing outside constantly, and throughout this book I've highlighted some that either do something new or do something old better. Python is advertised as *batteries included*, but you might need a new kind of battery.

So where, outside the standard library, should you look for good Python code?

The first place to look is the Python Package Index (PyPI) (*https://pypi.python.org/pypi*). Formerly named the *Cheese Shop* after a Monty Python skit, this site is constantly updated with Python packages—over 39,000 as I write this. When you use `pip` (see the next section), it searches PyPI. The main PyPI page shows the most recently added packages. You can also conduct a direct search. For instance, Table 12-1 lists the results of a search for `genealogy`.

Table 12-1. Packages on genealogy that you can find on PyPi

Package	Weight*	Description
Gramps 3.4.2	5	Research, organize, and share your family genealogy
python-fs-stack 0.2	2	Python wrapper for all FamilySearch APIs
human-names 0.1.1	1	Human names
nameparser 0.2.8	1	A simple Python module for parsing human names into their individual components

The best matches have higher weight values, so `Gramps` looks like your best bet here. Go to the Python website (*https://pypi.python.org/pypi/Gramps/3.4.2*) to see the documentation and download links.

Another popular repository is GitHub. See what Python packages are currently popular (*https://github.com/trending?l=python*).

Popular Python recipes (*http://bit.ly/popular-recipes*) has over four thousand short Python programs on every subject.

Install Packages

There are three ways to install Python packages:

- Use `pip` if you can. You can install most of the Python packages you're likely to encounter with `pip`.
- Sometimes, you can use a package manager for your operating system.
- Install from source.

If you're interested in several packages in the same area, you might find a Python distribution that already includes them. For instance, in Appendix C, you can try out a number of numeric and scientific programs that would be tedious to install individually but are included with distributions such as Anaconda.

Use pip

Python packaging has had some limitations. An earlier installation tool called `easy_install` has been replaced by one called `pip`, but neither had been in the standard Python installation. If you're supposed to install things by using `pip`, from where did you get `pip`? Starting with Python 3.4, `pip` will finally be included with the rest of Python to avoid such existential crises. If you're using an earlier version of Python 3 and don't have `pip`, you can get it from *http://www.pip-installer.org*.

The simplest use of `pip` is to install the latest version of a single package by using the following command:

```
$ pip install flask
```

You will see details on what it's doing, just so you don't think it's goofing off: downloading, running `setup.py`, installing files on your disk, and other details.

You can also ask `pip` to install a specific version:

```
$ pip install flask==0.9.0
```

Or, a minimum version (this is useful when some feature that you can't live without turns up in a particular version):

```
$ pip install flask≥0.9.0
```

In the preceding example, those single quotes prevent the > from being interpreted by the shell to redirect output to a file called `=0.9.0`.

If you want to install more than one Python package, you can use a requirements file (*http://bit.ly/pip-require*). Although it has many options, the simplest use is a list of packages, one per line, optionally with a specific or relative version:

```
$ pip -r requirements.txt
```

Your sample *requirements.txt* file might contain this:

```
flask==0.9.0
django
psycopg2
```

Use a Package Manager

Apple's OS X includes the third-party packagers homebrew (*http://brew.sh/*) (`brew`) and `ports` (*http://www.macports.org/*). They work a little like `pip`, but aren't restricted to Python packages.

Linux has a different manager for each distribution. The most popular are `apt-get`, `yum`, `dpkg`, and `zypper`.

Windows has the Windows Installer and package files with a `.msi` suffix. If you installed Python for Windows, it was probably in the MSI format.

Install from Source

Occasionally, a Python package is new, or the author hasn't managed to make it available with `pip`. To build the package, you generally do the following:

1. Download the code.
2. Extract the files by using `zip`, `tar`, or another appropriate tool if they're archived or compressed.
3. Run `python install setup.py` in the directory containing a *setup.py* file.

 As always, be careful what you download and install. It's a little harder to hide malware in Python programs, which are readable text, but it has happened.

Integrated Development Environments

I've used a plain-text interface for programs in this book, but that doesn't mean that you need to run everything in a console or text window. There are many free and commercial integrated development environments (IDEs), which are GUIs with support for such tools as text editors, debuggers, library searching, and so on.

IDLE

IDLE (*http://bit.ly/py-idle*) is the only Python IDE that's included with the standard distribution. It's based on tkinter, and its GUI is plain.

PyCharm

PyCharm (*http://www.jetbrains.com/pycharm/*) is a recent graphic IDE with many features. The community edition is free, and you can get a free license for the professional edition to use in a classroom or an open source project. Figure 12-1 shows its initial display.

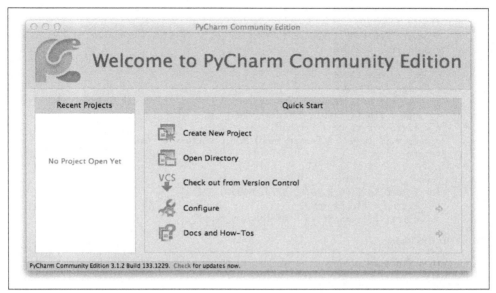

Figure 12-1. Startup screen for PyCharm

IPython

iPython (*http://ipython.org*), which you can see in Appendix C, is a publishing platform as well as an extensive IDE.

Name and Document

You won't remember what you wrote. There are times when I look at code I wrote even recently and wonder where on earth it came from. That's why it helps to document your code. Documentation can include comments and docstrings, but it can also incorporate informative naming of variables, functions, modules, and classes. Don't be obsessive, as in this example:

```
>>> # I'm going to assign 10 to the variable "num" here:
... num = 10
>>> # I hope that worked
... print(num)
```

```
10
>>> # Whew.
```

Instead, say *why* you assigned the value 10. Point out why you called the variable num. If you were writing the venerable Fahrenheit to Celsius converter, you might name variables to explain what they do, rather than a lump of magic code. And a little test code wouldn't hurt:

```python
def ftoc(f_temp):
    "Convert Fahrenheit temperature <f_temp> to Celsius and return it."
    f_boil_temp = 212.0
    f_freeze_temp = 32.0
    c_boil_temp = 100.0
    c_freeze_temp = 0.0
    f_range = f_boil_temp - f_freeze_temp
    c_range = c_boil_temp - c_freeze_temp
    f_c_ratio = c_range / f_range
    c_temp = (f_temp - f_freeze_temp) * f_c_ratio + c_freeze_temp
    return c_temp

if __name__ == '__main__':
    for f_temp in [-40.0, 0.0, 32.0, 100.0, 212.0]:
        c_temp = ftoc(f_temp)
        print('%f F => %f C' % (f_temp, c_temp))
```

Let's run the tests:

```
$ python ftoc1.py

-40.000000 F => -40.000000 C
0.000000 F => -17.777778 C
32.000000 F => 0.000000 C
100.000000 F => 37.777778 C
212.000000 F => 100.000000 C
```

We can make (at least) two improvements:

- Python doesn't have constants, but the PEP8 stylesheet recommends (*http://bit.ly/pep-constant*) using capital letters and underscores (e.g., ALL_CAPS) when naming variables that should be considered constants. Let's rename those constant-y variables in our example.

- Because we precompute values based on constant values, let's move them to the top level of the module. Then, they'll only be calculated once rather than in every call to the ftoc() function.

Here's the result of our rework:

```python
F_BOIL_TEMP = 212.0
F_FREEZE_TEMP = 32.0
C_BOIL_TEMP = 100.0
C_FREEZE_TEMP = 0.0
```

```
F_RANGE = F_BOIL_TEMP - F_FREEZE_TEMP
C_RANGE = C_BOIL_TEMP - C_FREEZE_TEMP
F_C_RATIO = C_RANGE / F_RANGE

def ftoc(f_temp):
    "Convert Fahrenheit temperature <f_temp> to Celsius and return it."
    c_temp = (f_temp - F_FREEZE_TEMP) * F_C_RATIO + C_FREEZE_TEMP
    return c_temp

if __name__ == '__main__':
    for f_temp in [-40.0, 0.0, 32.0, 100.0, 212.0]:
        c_temp = ftoc(f_temp)
        print('%f F => %f C' % (f_temp, c_temp))
```

Testing Your Code

Once in a while, I'll make some trivial code change and say to myself, "Looks good, ship it." And then it breaks. Oops. Every time I do this (thankfully, less and less over time) I feel like a doofus, and I swear to write even more tests next time.

The very simplest way to test Python programs is to add `print()` statements. The Python interactive interpreter's Read-Evaluate-Print Loop (REPL) lets you edit and test changes quickly. However, you probably don't want `print()` statements in production code, so you need to remember to take them all out. Furthermore, cut-and-paste errors are really easy to make.

Check with pylint, pyflakes, and pep8

The next step, before creating actual test programs, is to run a Python code checker. The most popular are `pylint` (*http://www.pylint.org/*) and `pyflakes` (*http://bit.ly/pyflakes*). You can install either or both by using `pip`:

```
$ pip install pylint
$ pip install pyflakes
```

These check for actual code errors (such as referring to a variable before assigning it a value) and style faux pas (the code equivalent of wearing plaids and stripes). Here's a fairly meaningless program with a bug and style issue:

```
a = 1
b = 2
print(a)
print(b)
print(c)
```

Here's the initial output of `pylint`:

```
$ pylint style1.py
No config file found, using default configuration
************* Module style1
```

```
C:  1,0: Missing docstring
C:  1,0: Invalid name "a" for type constant
   (should match (([A-Z_][A-Z0-9_]*)|(__.*__))$)
C:  2,0: Invalid name "b" for type constant
   (should match (([A-Z_][A-Z0-9_]*)|(__.*__))$)
E:  5,6: Undefined variable 'c'
```

Much further down, under `Global evaluation`, is our score (10.0 is perfect):

```
Your code has been rated at -3.33/10
```

Ouch. Let's fix the bug first. That `pylint` output line starting with an `E` indicates an `Error`, which occurred because we didn't assign a value to `c` before we printed it. Let's fix that:

```
a = 1
b = 2
c = 3
print(a)
print(b)
print(c)
```

$ **pylint style2.py**

```
No config file found, using default configuration
************* Module style2
C:  1,0: Missing docstring
C:  1,0: Invalid name "a" for type constant
   (should match (([A-Z_][A-Z0-9_]*)|(__.*__))$)
C:  2,0: Invalid name "b" for type constant
   (should match (([A-Z_][A-Z0-9_]*)|(__.*__))$)
C:  3,0: Invalid name "c" for type constant
   (should match (([A-Z_][A-Z0-9_]*)|(__.*__))$)
```

Good, no more `E` lines. And our score jumped from -3.33 to 4.29:

```
Your code has been rated at 4.29/10
```

`pylint` wants a docstring (a short text at the top of a module or function, describing the code), and it thinks short variable names such as `a`, `b`, and `c` are tacky. Let's make `pylint` happier and improve *style2.py* to *style3.py*:

```
"Module docstring goes here"

def func():
    "Function docstring goes here. Hi, Mom!"
    first = 1
    second = 2
    third = 3
    print(first)
    print(second)
    print(third)

func()
```

```
$ pylint style3.py
No config file found, using default configuration
```

Hey, no complaints. And our score?

```
Your code has been rated at 10.00/10
```

Not too shabby at all, right?

Another style checker is pep8 (*https://pypi.python.org/pypi/pep8*), which you can install in the usual way:

```
$ pip install pep8
```

What does it say about our style makeover?

```
$ pep8 style3.py
style3.py:3:1: E302 expected 2 blank lines, found 1
```

To be really stylish, it's recommending that I add a blank line after the initial module docstring.

Test with unittest

We've verified that we're no longer insulting the style senses of the code gods, so let's move on to actual tests of the logic in your program.

It's a good practice to write independent test programs first, to ensure that they all pass before you commit your code to any source control system. Writing tests can seem tedious at first, but they really do help you find problems faster—especially *regressions* (breaking something that used to work). Painful experience teaches all developers that even the teeniest change, which they swear could not possibly affect anything else, actually does. If you look at well-written Python packages, they always include a test suite.

The standard library contains not one, but two test packages. Let's start with uni ttest (*https://docs.python.org/3/library/unittest.html*). We'll write a module that capitalizes words. Our first version just uses the standard string function capitalize(), with some unexpected results as we'll see. Save this as *cap.py*:

```
def just_do_it(text):
    return text.capitalize()
```

The basis of testing is to decide what outcome you want from a certain input (here, you want the capitalized version of whatever text you input), submit the input to the function you're testing, and then check whether it returned the expected results. The expected result is called an *assertion*, so in unittest you check your results by using methods with names that begin with assert, like the assertEqual method shown in the following example.

Save this test script as *test_cap.py*:

```
import unittest
import cap

class TestCap(unittest.TestCase):

    def setUp(self):
        pass

    def tearDown(self):
        pass

    def test_one_word(self):
        text = 'duck'
        result = cap.just_do_it(text)
        self.assertEqual(result, 'Duck')

    def test_multiple_words(self):
        text = 'a veritable flock of ducks'
        result = cap.just_do_it(text)
        self.assertEqual(result, 'A Veritable Flock Of Ducks')


if __name__ == '__main__':
    unittest.main()
```

The setUp() method is called before each test method, and the tearDown() method is called after each. Their purpose is to allocate and free external resources needed by the tests, such as a database connection or some test data. In this case, our tests are self-contained, and we wouldn't even need to define setUp() and tearDown(), but it doesn't hurt to have empty versions there. The heart of our test is the two functions named test_one_word() and test_multiple_words(). Each runs the just_do_it() function we defined with different input and checks whether we got back what we expect.

Okay, let's run it. This will call our two test methods:

```
$ python test_cap.py
F.
======================================================================
FAIL: test_multiple_words (__main__.TestCap)
----------------------------------------------------------------------
Traceback (most recent call last):
  File "test_cap.py", line 20, in test_multiple_words
  self.assertEqual(result, 'A Veritable Flock Of Ducks')
AssertionError: 'A veritable flock of ducks' != 'A Veritable Flock Of Ducks'
- A veritable flock of ducks
?   ^         ^    ^  ^
+ A Veritable Flock Of Ducks
?   ^         ^    ^  ^
```

```
--------------------------------------------------------------------
Ran 2 tests in 0.001s

FAILED (failures=1)
```

It liked the first test (`test_one_word`) but not the second (`test_multiple_words`). The up arrows (^) shows where the strings actually differed.

What's special about multiple words? Reading the documentation for the `string capi talize` (*https://docs.python.org/3/library/stdtypes.html#str.capitalize*) function yields an important clue: it capitalizes only the first letter of the first word. Maybe we should have read that first.

Consequently, we need another function. Gazing down that page a bit, we find `title()` (*https://docs.python.org/3/library/stdtypes.html#str.title*). So, let's change *cap.py* to use `title()` instead of `capitalize()`:

```
def just_do_it(text):
    return text.title()
```

Rerun the tests, and let's see what happens:

```
$ python test_cap.py

..
--------------------------------------------------------------------
Ran 2 tests in 0.000s

OK
```

Everything is great. Well, actually, they're not. We need to add at least one more method to *test_cap.py*:

```
    def test_words_with_apostrophes(self):
        text = "I'm fresh out of ideas"
        result = cap.just_do_it(text)
        self.assertEqual(result, "I'm Fresh Out Of Ideas")
```

Go ahead and try it again:

```
$ python test_cap.py

..F
====================================================================
FAIL: test_words_with_apostrophes (__main__.TestCap)
--------------------------------------------------------------------
Traceback (most recent call last):
  File "test_cap.py", line 25, in test_words_with_apostrophes
    self.assertEqual(result, "I'm Fresh Out Of Ideas")
AssertionError: "I'M Fresh Out Of Ideas" != "I'm Fresh Out Of Ideas"
- I'M Fresh Out Of Ideas
?   ^
+ I'm Fresh Out Of Ideas
?   ^
```

```
----------------------------------------------------------------
Ran 3 tests in 0.001s
```

```
FAILED (failures=1)
```

Our function capitalized the m in I'm. A quick run back to the documentation for
title() shows that it doesn't handle apostrophes well. We *really* should have read the
entire text first.

At the bottom of the standard library's string documentation is another candidate: a
helper function called capwords(). Let's use it in *cap.py*:

```
def just_do_it(text):
    from string import capwords
    return capwords(text)
```

```
$ python test_cap.py
```

```
...
----------------------------------------------------------------
Ran 3 tests in 0.004s
```

```
OK
```

At last, we're finally done! Uh, no. One more test to add to *test_cap.py*:

```
def test_words_with_quotes(self):
    text = "\"You're despicable,\" said Daffy Duck"
    result = cap.just_do_it(text)
    self.assertEqual(result, "\"You're Despicable,\" Said Daffy Duck")
```

Did it work?

```
$ python test_cap.py
```

```
...F
================================================================
FAIL: test_words_with_quotes (__main__.TestCap)
----------------------------------------------------------------
Traceback (most recent call last):
  File "test_cap.py", line 30, in test_words_with_quotes
    self.assertEqual(result, "\"You're
    Despicable,\" Said Daffy Duck")
AssertionError: '"you\'re Despicable," Said Daffy Duck'
 != '"You\'re Despicable," Said Daffy Duck'
- "you're Despicable," Said Daffy Duck
?  ^
+ "You're Despicable," Said Daffy Duck
?  ^


----------------------------------------------------------------
Ran 4 tests in 0.004s
```

```
FAILED (failures=1)
```

It looks like that first double quote confused even `capwords`, our favorite capitalizer thus far. It tried to capitalize the ", and lowercased the rest (`You're`). We should have also tested that our capitalizer left the rest of the string untouched.

People who do testing for a living have a knack for spotting these edge cases, but developers often have blind spots when it comes to their own code.

`unittest` provides a small but powerful set of assertions, letting you check values, confirm whether you have the class you want, determine whether an error was raised, and so on.

Test with doctest

The second test package in the standard library is `doctest` (*http://bit.ly/py-doctest*). With this package, you can write tests within the docstring itself, also serving as documentation. It looks like the interactive interpreter: the characters >>>, followed by the call, and then the results on the following line. You can run some tests in the interactive interpreter and just paste the results into your test file. We'll modify *cap.py* (without that troublesome last test with quotes):

```python
def just_do_it(text):
    """
    >>> just_do_it('duck')
    'Duck'
    >>> just_do_it('a veritable flock of ducks')
    'A Veritable Flock Of Ducks'
    >>> just_do_it("I'm fresh out of ideas")
    "I'm Fresh Out Of Ideas"
    """
    from string import capwords
    return capwords(text)

if __name__ == '__main__':
    import doctest
    doctest.testmod()
```

When you run it, it doesn't print anything if all tests passed:

```
$ python cap.py
```

Give it the verbose (`-v`) option to see what actually happened:

```
$ python cap.py -v
Trying:
    just_do_it('duck')
Expecting:
    'Duck'
ok
```

```
Trying:
    just_do_it('a veritable flock of ducks')
Expecting:
    'A Veritable Flock Of Ducks'
ok
Trying:
    just_do_it("I'm fresh out of ideas")
Expecting:
    "I'm Fresh Out Of Ideas"
ok
1 items had no tests:
    __main__
1 items passed all tests:
    3 tests in __main__.just_do_it
3 tests in 2 items.
3 passed and 0 failed.
Test passed.
```

Test with nose

The third-party package called nose (*https://nose.readthedocs.org/en/latest/*) is
another alternative to unittest. Here's the command to install it:

```
$ pip install nose
```

You don't need to create a class that includes test methods, as we did with unittest.
Any function with a name matching test somewhere in its name will be run. Let's
modify our last version of our unittest tester and save it as *test_cap_nose.py*:

```python
import cap
from nose.tools import eq_

def test_one_word():
    text = 'duck'
    result = cap.just_do_it(text)
    eq_(result, 'Duck')

def test_multiple_words():
    text = 'a veritable flock of ducks'
    result = cap.just_do_it(text)
    eq_(result, 'A Veritable Flock Of Ducks')

def test_words_with_apostrophes():
    text = "I'm fresh out of ideas"
    result = cap.just_do_it(text)
    eq_(result, "I'm Fresh Out Of Ideas")

def test_words_with_quotes():
    text = "\"You're despicable,\" said Daffy Duck"
    result = cap.just_do_it(text)
    eq_(result, "\"You're Despicable,\" Said Daffy Duck")
```

Run the tests:

```
$ nosetests test_cap_nose.py
...F
======================================================================
FAIL: test_cap_nose.test_words_with_quotes
----------------------------------------------------------------------
Traceback (most recent call last):
  File "/Users/.../site-packages/nose/case.py", line 198, in runTest
    self.test(*self.arg)
  File "/Users/.../book/test_cap_nose.py", line 23, in test_words_with_quotes
    eq_(result, "\"You're Despicable,\" Said Daffy Duck")
AssertionError: '"you\'re Despicable," Said Daffy Duck'
    != '"You\'re Despicable," Said Daffy Duck'

----------------------------------------------------------------------
Ran 4 tests in 0.005s

FAILED (failures=1)
```

This is the same bug we found when we used `unittest` for testing; fortunately, there's an exercise to fix it at the end of this chapter.

Other Test Frameworks

For some reason, people like to write Python test frameworks. If you're curious, you can check out some other popular ones, including `tox` (*http://tox.readthedocs.org/*) and `py.test` (*http://pytest.org/latest/*).

Continuous Integration

When your group is cranking out a lot of code daily, it helps to automate tests as soon as changes arrive. You can automate source control systems to run tests on all code as it's checked in. This way, everyone knows if someone *broke the build* and just disappeared for an early lunch.

These are big systems, and I'm not going into installation and usage details here. In case you need them someday, you'll know where to find them:

`buildbot` *(http://buildbot.net/)*
    Written in Python, this source control system automates building, testing, and releasing.

`jenkins` *(http://jenkins-ci.org/)*
    This is written in Java and seems to be the preferred CI tool of the moment.

`travis-ci` *(http://travis-ci.com/)*
    This automates projects hosted at GitHub, and it's free for open source projects.

Debugging Python Code

> *Debugging is twice as hard as writing the code in the first place. Therefore, if you write the*
> *code as cleverly as possible, you are, by definition, not smart enough to debug it.*
>
> —Brian Kernighan

Test first. The better your tests are, the less you'll have to fix later. Yet, bugs happen and need to be fixed when they're found later. Again, the simplest way to debug in Python is to print out strings. Some useful things to print include vars(), which extracts the values of your local variables, including function arguments:

```
>>> def func(*args, **kwargs):
...     print(vars())
...
>>> func(1, 2, 3)
{'args': (1, 2, 3), 'kwargs': {}}
>>> func(['a', 'b', 'argh'])
{'args': (['a', 'b', 'argh'],), 'kwargs': {}}
```

As you read in "Decorators" on page 102, a decorator can call code before or after a function without modifying the code within the function itself. This means that you can use a decorator to do something before or after any Python function, not just ones that you wrote. Let's define the decorator dump to print the input arguments and output values of any function as it's called (designers know that a dump often needs decorating):

```
def dump(func):
    "Print input arguments and output value(s)"
    def wrapped(*args, **kwargs):
        print("Function name: %s" % func.__name__)
        print("Input arguments: %s" % ' '.join(map(str, args)))
        print("Input keyword arguments: %s" % kwargs.items())
        output = func(*args, **kwargs)
        print("Output:", output)
        return output
    return wrapped
```

Now the decoratee. This is a function called double() that expects numeric arguments, either named or unnamed, and returns them in a list with their values doubled:

```
from dump1 import dump

@dump
def double(*args, **kwargs):
    "Double every argument"
    output_list = [ 2 * arg for arg in args ]
    output_dict =  { k:2*v for k,v in kwargs.items() }
    return output_list, output_dict
```

```
if __name__ == '__main__':
    output = double(3, 5, first=100, next=98.6, last=-40)
```

Take a moment to run it:

```
$ python test_dump.py

Function name: double
Input arguments: 3 5
Input keyword arguments: dict_items([('last', -40), ('first', 100),
 ('next', 98.6)])
Output: ([6, 10], {'last': -80, 'first': 200, 'next': 197.2})
```

Debug with pdb

These techniques help, but sometimes there's no substitute for a real debugger. Most IDEs include a debugger, with varying features and user interfaces. Here, I'll describe use of the standard Python debugger, pdb (*https://docs.python.org/3/library/pdb.html*).

 If you run your program with the -i flag, Python will drop you into its interactive interpreter if the program fails.

Here's a program with a bug that depends on data—the kind of bug that can be particularly hard to find. This is a real bug from the early days of computing, and it baffled programmers for quite a while.

We're going to read a file of countries and their capital cities, separated by a comma, and write them out as *capital*, *country*. They might be capitalized incorrectly, so we should fix that also when we print. Oh, and there might be extra spaces here and there, and you'll want to get rid of those, too. Finally, although it would make sense for the program to just read to the end of the file, for some reason our manager told us to stop when we encounter the word quit (in any mixture of uppercase and lowercase characters). Here's a sample data file:

```
France, Paris
venuzuela,caracas
  LithuniA,vilnius
    quit
```

Let's design our *algorithm* (method for solving the problem). This is *pseudocode*—it looks like a program, but is just a way to explain the logic in normal language before converting it to an actual program. One reason programmers like Python is because it *looks a lot like pseudocode*, so there's less work involved to convert it to a working program:

```
for each line in the text file:
    read the line
    strip leading and trailing spaces
    if `quit` occurs in the lower-case copy of the line:
        stop
    else:
        split the country and capital by the comma character
        trim any leading and trailing spaces
        convert the country and capital to titlecase
        print the capital, a comma, and the country
```

We need to strip initial and trailing spaces from the names because that was a requirement. Likewise for the lowercase comparison with quit and converting the city and country names to title case. That being the case, let's whip out *capitals.py*, which is sure to work perfectly:

```python
def process_cities(filename):
    with open(filename, 'rt') as file:
        for line in file:
            line = line.strip()
            if 'quit' in line.lower():
                return
            country, city = line.split(',')
            city = city.strip()
            country = country.strip()
            print(city.title(), country.title(), sep=',')

if __name__ == '__main__':
    import sys
    process_cities(sys.argv[1])
```

Let's try it with that sample data file we made earlier. Ready, fire, aim:

```
$ python capitals.py cities.csv
Paris,France
Caracas,Venuzuela
Vilnius,Lithunia
```

Looks great! It passed one test, so let's put it in production, processing capitals and countries from around the world—until it fails, but only for this data file:

```
argentina,buenos aires
bolivia,la paz
brazil,brasilia
chile,santiago
colombia,Bogotá
ecuador,quito
falkland islands,stanley
french guiana,cayenne
guyana,georgetown
paraguay,Asunción
peru,lima
suriname,paramaribo
```

```
uruguay,montevideo
venezuela,caracas
quit
```

The program ends after printing only 5 lines of the 15 in the data file, as demonstrated here:

```
$ python capitals.py cities2.csv
Buenos Aires,Argentina
La Paz,Bolivia
Brazilia,Brazil
Santiago,Chile
Bogotá,Colombia
```

What happened? We can keep editing *capitals.py*, putting print() statements in likely places, but let's see if the debugger can help us.

To use the debugger, import the pdb module from the command line by typing **-m pdb**, like so:

```
$ python -m pdb capitals.py cities2.csv

> /Users/williamlubanovic/book/capitals.py(1)<module>()
-> def process_cities(filename):
(Pdb)
```

This starts the program and places you at the first line. If you type **c** (*continue*), the program will run until it ends, either normally or with an error:

```
(Pdb) c

Buenos Aires,Argentina
La Paz,Bolivia
Brazilia,Brazil
Santiago,Chile
Bogotá,Colombia
The program finished and will be restarted
> /Users/williamlubanovic/book/capitals.py(1)<module>()
-> def process_cities(filename):
```

It completed normally, just as it did when we ran it earlier outside of the debugger. Let's try again, using some commands to narrow down where the problem lies. It seems to be a *logic error* rather than a syntax problem or exception (which would have printed error messages).

Type **s** (*step*) to single-step through Python lines. This steps through *all* Python code lines: yours, the standard library's, and any other modules you might be using. When you use s, you also go into functions and single-step within them. Type **n** (*next*) to single-step but *not* to go inside functions; when you get to a function, a single n causes the entire function to execute and take you to the next line of your program. Thus, use s when you're not sure where the problem is; use n when you're sure that a particular function isn't the cause, especially if it's a long function. Often you'll single-step through your own code and step over library code, which is presumably well tested. We'll use s to step from the beginning of the program, into the function process_cities():

```
(Pdb) s
> /Users/williamlubanovic/book/capitals.py(12)<module>()
-> if __name__ == '__main__':

(Pdb) s
> /Users/williamlubanovic/book/capitals.py(13)<module>()
-> import sys

(Pdb) s
> /Users/williamlubanovic/book/capitals.py(14)<module>()
-> process_cities(sys.argv[1])

(Pdb) s
--Call--
> /Users/williamlubanovic/book/capitals.py(1)process_cities()
-> def process_cities(filename):

(Pdb) s
> /Users/williamlubanovic/book/capitals.py(2)process_cities()
-> with open(filename, 'rt') as file:
```

Type l (*list*) to see the next few lines of your program:

```
(Pdb) l
  1     def process_cities(filename):
  2  ->     with open(filename, 'rt') as file:
  3             for line in file:
  4                 line = line.strip()
  5                 if 'quit' in line.lower():
  6                     return
  7                 country, city = line.split(',')
  8                 city = city.strip()
  9                 country = country.strip()
 10                 print(city.title(), country.title(), sep=',')
 11
(Pdb)
```

The arrow (->) denotes the current line.

We could continue using s or n, hoping to spot something, but let's use one of the main features of a debugger: *breakpoints*. A breakpoint stops execution at the line you indicate. In our case, we want to know why process_cities() bails out before it's read all of the input lines. Line 3 (for line in file:) will read every line in the input file, so that seems innocent. The only other place where we could return from the function before reading all of the data is at line 6 (return). Let's set a breakpoint on line 6:

```
(Pdb) b 6
Breakpoint 1 at /Users/williamlubanovic/book/capitals.py:6
```

Next, let's continue the program until it either hits the breakpoint or reads all of the input lines and finishes normally:

```
(Pdb) c
Buenos Aires,Argentina
La Paz,Bolivia
Brasilia,Brazil
Santiago,Chile
Bogotá,Colombia
> /Users/williamlubanovic/book/capitals.py(6)process_cities()
-> return
```

Aha, it stopped at our line 6 breakpoint. This indicates that the program wants to return early after reading the country after Colombia. Let's print the value of line to see what we just read:

```
(Pdb) p line
'ecuador,quito'
```

What's so special about—oh, never mind.

Really? *quit*o? Our manager never expected the string quit to turn up inside normal data, so using it as a *sentinel* (end indicator) value like this was a boneheaded idea. You march right in there and tell him that, while I wait here.

If at this point you still have a job, you can see all your breakpoints by using a plain b command:

```
(Pdb) b
Num Type         Disp Enb  Where
1   breakpoint   keep yes   at /Users/williamlubanovic/book/capitals.py:6
        breakpoint already hit 1 time
```

An l will show your code lines, the current line (->), and any breakpoints (B). A plain l will start listing from the end of your previous call to l, so include the optional starting line (here, let's start from line 1):

```
(Pdb) l 1
  1     def process_cities(filename):
  2         with open(filename, 'rt') as file:
  3             for line in file:
  4                 line = line.strip()
  5                 if 'quit' in line.lower():
  6 B->                 return
```

```
 7              country, city = line.split(',')
 8              city = city.strip()
 9              country = country.strip()
10              print(city.title(), country.title(), sep=',')
11
```

Okay, let's fix that quit test to only match the full line, not within other characters:

```
def process_cities(filename):
    with open(filename, 'rt') as file:
        for line in file:
            line = line.strip()
            if 'quit' == line.lower():
                return
            country, city = line.split(',')
            city = city.strip()
            country = country.strip()
            print(city.title(), country.title(), sep=',')

if __name__ == '__main__':
    import sys
    process_cities(sys.argv[1])
```

Once more, with feeling:

```
$ python capitals2.py cities2.csv

Buenos Aires,Argentina
La Paz,Bolivia
Brasilia,Brazil
Santiago,Chile
Bogotá,Colombia
Quito,Ecuador
Stanley,Falkland Islands
Cayenne,French Guiana
Georgetown,Guyana
Asunción,Paraguay
Lima,Peru
Paramaribo,Suriname
Montevideo,Uruguay
Caracas,Venezuela
```

That was a skimpy overview of the debugger—just enough to show you what it can do and what commands you'd use most of the time.

Remember: more tests, less debugging.

Logging Error Messages

At some point you might need to graduate from using print() statements to logging messages. A log is usually a system file that accumulates messages, often inserting useful information such as a timestamp or the name of the user who's running the

---

program. Often logs are *rotated* (renamed) daily and compressed; by doing so, they don't fill up your disk and cause problems themselves. When something goes wrong with your program, you can look at the appropriate log file to see what happened. The contents of exceptions are especially useful in logs because they show you the actual line at which your program croaked, and why.

The standard Python library module is logging (*http://bit.ly/py-logging*). I've found most descriptions of it somewhat confusing. After a while it makes more sense, but it does seem overly complicated at first. The logging module includes these concepts:

- The *message* that you want to save to the log
- Ranked priority *levels* and matching functions: debug(), info(), warn(), error(), and critical()
- One or more *logger* objects as the main connection with the module
- *Handlers* that direct the message to your terminal, a file, a database, or somewhere else
- *Formatters* that create the output
- *Filters* that make decisions based on the input

For the simplest logging example, just import the module and use some of its functions:

```
>>> import logging
>>> logging.debug("Looks like rain")
>>> logging.info("And hail")
>>> logging.warn("Did I hear thunder?")
WARNING:root:Did I hear thunder?
>>> logging.error("Was that lightning?")
ERROR:root:Was that lightning?
>>> logging.critical("Stop fencing and get inside!")
CRITICAL:root:Stop fencing and get inside!
```

Did you notice that debug() and info() didn't do anything, and the other two printed *LEVEL*:root: before each message? So far, it's like a print() statement with multiple personalities, some of them hostile.

But it is useful. You can scan for a particular value of *LEVEL* in a log file to find particular messages, compare timestamps to see what happened before your server crashed, and so on.

A lot of digging through the documentation answers the first mystery (we'll get to the second one in a page or two): the default priority *level* is WARNING, and that got locked in as soon as we called the first function (logging.debug()). We can set the default level by using basicConfig(). DEBUG is the lowest level, so this enables it and all the higher levels to flow through:

```
>>> import logging
>>> logging.basicConfig(level=logging.DEBUG)
>>> logging.debug("It's raining again")
DEBUG:root:It's raining again
>>> logging.info("With hail the size of hailstones")
INFO:root:With hail the size of hailstones
```

We did all that with the default `logging` functions, without actually creating a *logger* object. Each logger has a name. Let's make one called bunyan:

```
>>> import logging
>>> logging.basicConfig(level='DEBUG')
>>> logger = logging.getLogger('bunyan')
>>> logger.debug('Timber!')
DEBUG:bunyan:Timber!
```

If the logger name contains any dot characters, they separate levels of a hierarchy of loggers, each with potentially different properties. This means that a logger named quark is higher than one named quark.charmed. The special *root logger* is at the top, and is called `''`.

So far, we've just printed messages, which is not a great improvement over `print()`. We use *handlers* to direct the messages to different places. The most common is a *log file*, and here's how you do it:

```
>>> import logging
>>> logging.basicConfig(level='DEBUG', filename='blue_ox.log')
>>> logger = logging.getLogger('bunyan')
>>> logger.debug("Where's my axe?")
>>> logger.warn("I need my axe")
>>>
```

Aha, the lines aren't on the screen anymore; instead, they're in the file named *blue_ox.log*:

```
DEBUG:bunyan:Where's my axe?
WARNING:bunyan:I need my axe
```

Calling `basicConfig()` with a `filename` argument created a `FileHandler` for you and made it available to your logger. The `logging` module includes at least 15 handlers to send messages to places such as email and web servers as well as the screen and files.

Finally, you can control the *format* of your logged messages. In our first example, our default gave us something similar to this:

```
WARNING:root:Message...
```

If you provide a `format` string to `basicConfig()`, you can change to the format of your preference:

```
>>> import logging
>>> fmt = '%(asctime)s %(levelname)s %(lineno)s %(message)s'
>>> logging.basicConfig(level='DEBUG', format=fmt)
```

```
>>> logger = logging.getLogger('bunyan')
>>> logger.error("Where's my other plaid shirt?")
2014-04-08 23:13:59,899 ERROR 1 Where's my other plaid shirt?
```

We let the logger send output to the screen again, but changed the format. The logging module recognizes a number of variable names in the fmt format string. We used asctime (date and time as an ISO 8601 string), levelname, lineno (line number), and the message itself. There are other built-ins, and you can provide your own variables, as well.

There's much more to logging than this little overview can provide. You can log to more than one place at the same time, with different priorities and formats. The package has a lot of flexibility, but sometimes at the cost of simplicity.

Optimize Your Code

Python is usually fast enough—until it isn't. In many cases, you can gain speed by using a better algorithm or data structure. The trick is knowing where to do this. Even experienced programmers guess wrong surprisingly often. You need to be like the careful quiltmaker, and measure before you cut. And this leads us to *timers*.

Measure Timing

You've seen that the time function in the time module returns the current epoch time as a floating-point number of seconds. A quick way of timing something is to get the current time, do something, get the new time, and then subtract the original time from the new time. Let's write this up and call it *time1.py*:

```
from time import time

t1 = time()
num = 5
num *= 2
print(time() - t1)
```

In this example, we're measuring the the time it takes to assign the value 5 to the name num and multiply it by 2. This is *not* a realistic benchmark, just an example of how to measure some arbitrary Python code. Try running it a few times, just to see how much it can vary:

```
$ python time1.py
2.1457672119140625e-06
$ python time1.py
2.1457672119140625e-06
$ python time1.py
2.1457672119140625e-06
$ python time1.py
1.9073486328125e-06
```

```
$ python time1.py
3.0994415283203125e-06
```

That was about two or three millionths of a second. Let's try something slower, such as sleep. If we sleep for a second, our timer should take a tiny bit more than a second. Save this as *time2.py*:

```
from time import time, sleep

t1 = time()
sleep(1.0)
print(time() - t1)
```

Let's be certain of our results, so run it a few times:

```
$ python time2.py
1.000797986984253
$ python time2.py
1.0010130405426025
$ python time2.py
1.0010390281677246
```

As expected, it takes about a second to run. If it didn't, either our timer or sleep() should be embarrassed.

There's a handier way to measure code snippets like this: the standard module timeit (*http://bit.ly/py-timeit*). It has a function called (you guessed it) timeit(), which will run your test *code count* times and print some results. The syntax is: timeit.timeit(*code*, number= *count*).

In the examples in this section, the code needs to be within quotes so that it is not executed after you press the Return key but is executed inside timeit(). (In the next section, you'll see how to time a function by passing its name to timeit().) Let's run our previous example just once and time it. Call this file *timeit1.py*:

```
from timeit import timeit
print(timeit('num = 5; num *= 2', number=1))
```

Run it a few times:

```
$ python timeit1.py
2.5600020308047533e-06
$ python timeit1.py
1.9020008039660752e-06
$ python timeit1.py
1.7380007193423808e-06
```

Again, these two code lines ran in about two millionths of a second. We can use the repeat argument of the timeit module's repeat() function to run more sets. Save this as *timeit2.py*:

```
from timeit import repeat
print(repeat('num = 5; num *= 2', number=1, repeat=3))
```

Try running it to see what transpires:

```
$ python timeit2.py
[1.691998477326706e-06, 4.070025170221925e-07, 2.4700057110749185e-07]
```

The first run took two millionths of a second, and the second and third runs were faster. Why? There could be many reasons. For one thing, we're testing a very small piece of code, and its speed could depend on what else the computer was doing in those instants, how the Python system optimizes calculations, and many other things.

Or, it could be just chance. Let's try something more realistic than variable assignment and `sleep`. We'll measure some code to help compare the efficiency of a few algorithms (program logic) and data structures (storage mechanisms).

Algorithms and Data Structures

The Zen of Python (*http://bit.ly/zen-py*) declares that *There should be one—and preferably only one—obvious way to do it*. Unfortunately, sometimes it isn't obvious, and you need to compare alternatives. For example, is it better to use a `for` loop or a list comprehension to build a list? And what do we mean by *better*? Is it faster, easier to understand, using less memory, or more "Pythonic"?

In this next exercise, we'll build a list in different ways, comparing speed, readability, and Python style. Here's *time_lists.py*:

```
from timeit import timeit

def make_list_1():
    result = []
    for value in range(1000):
        result.append(value)
    return result

def make_list_2():
    result = [value for value in range(1000)]
    return result

print('make_list_1 takes', timeit(make_list_1, number=1000), 'seconds')
print('make_list_2 takes', timeit(make_list_2, number=1000), 'seconds')
```

In each function, we add 1,000 items to a list, and we call each function 1,000 times. Notice that in this test we called `timeit()` with the function name as the first argument rather than code as a string. Let's run it:

```
$ python time_lists.py

make_list_1 takes 0.14117428699682932 seconds
make_list_2 takes 0.061741459000149597 seconds
```

The list comprehension is at least twice as fast as adding items to the list by using `append()`. In general, comprehensions are faster than manual construction.

Use these ideas to make your own code faster.

Cython, NumPy, and C Extensions

If you're pushing Python as hard as you can and still can't get the performance you want, you have yet more options.

Cython (*http://cython.org/*) is a hybrid of Python and C, designed to translate Python with some performance annotations to compiled C code. These annotations are fairly small, like declaring the types of some variables, function arguments, or function returns. For scientific-style loops of numeric calculations, adding these hints will make them much faster—as much as a thousand times faster. See the Cython wiki (*https://github.com/cython/cython/wiki*) for documentation and examples.

You can read much more about NumPy in Appendix C. It's a Python math library, written in C for speed.

Many parts of Python and its standard library are written in C for speed and wrapped in Python for convenience. These hooks are available to you for your applications. If you know C and Python and really want to make your code fly, writing a C extension is harder but the improvements can be worth the trouble.

PyPy

When Java first appeared about 20 years ago, it was as slow as an arthritic schnauzer. When it started to mean real money to Sun and other companies, though, they put millions into optimizing the Java interpreter and the underlying Java virtual machine (JVM), borrowing techniques from earlier languages like Smalltalk and LISP. Microsoft likewise put great effort into optimizing its rival C# language and .NET VM.

No one owns Python, so no one has pushed that hard to make it faster. You're probably using the standard Python implementation. It's written in C, and often called CPython (not the same as Cython).

Like PHP, Perl, and even Java, Python is not compiled to machine language, but translated to an intermediate language (with names such as *bytecode* or p-code) which is then interpreted in a *virtual machine.*

PyPy (*http://pypy.org/*) is a new Python interpreter that applies some of the tricks that sped up Java. Its benchmarks (*http://speed.pypy.org/*) show that PyPy is faster than CPython in every test—over 6 times faster on average, and up to 20 times faster in some cases. It works with Python 2 and 3. You can download it and use it instead of CPython. PyPy is constantly being improved, and it might even replace CPython some day. Read the latest release notes on the site to see if it could work for your purposes.

Source Control

When you're working on a small group of programs, you can usually keep track of your changes—until you make a boneheaded mistake and clobber a few days of work. Source control systems help protect your code from dangerous forces, like you. If you work with a group of developers, source control becomes a necessity. There are many commercial and open source packages in this area. The most popular in the open source world where Python lives are Mercurial and Git. Both are examples of *distributed* version control systems, which produce multiple copies of code repositories. Earlier systems such as Subversion run on a single server.

Mercurial

Mercurial (*http://mercurial.selenic.com/*) is written in Python. It's fairly easy to learn, with a handful of subcommands to download code from a Mercurial repository, add files, check in changes, and merge changes from different sources. bitbucket (*https://bitbucket.org/*) and other sites (*http://bit.ly/merc-host*) offer free or commercial hosting.

Git

Git (*http://git-scm.com/*) was originally written for Linux kernel development, but now dominates open source in general. It's similar to Mercurial, although some find it slightly trickier to master. GitHub (*http://github.com*) is the largest git host, with over a million repositories, but there are many other hosts (*http://bit.ly/githost-scm*).

The standalone program examples in this book are available in a public git repository at GitHub (*https://github.com/madscheme/introducing-python*). If you have the `git` program on your computer, you can download these programs by using this command:

```
$ git clone https://github.com/madscheme/introducing-python
```

You can also download the code by pressing the following buttons on the GitHub page:

- Click "Clone in Desktop" to open your computer's version of `git`, if it's been installed.
- Click "Download ZIP" to get a zipped archive of the programs.

If you don't have `git` but would like to try it, read the installation guide (*http://bit.ly/git-install*). I'll talk about the command-line version here, but you might be interested in sites such as GitHub that have extra services and might be easier to use in some cases; `git` has many features, but is not always intuitive.

Let's take git for a test drive. We won't go far, but the ride will show a few commands and their output.

Make a new directory and change to it:

```
$ mkdir newdir
$ cd newdir
```

Create a local git repository in your current directory *newdir*:

```
$ git init
```

```
Initialized empty Git repository in /Users/williamlubanovic/newdir/.git/
```

Create a Python file called *test.py* with these contents in *newdir*:

```
print('Oops')
```

Add the file to the git repository:

```
$ git add test.py
```

What do you think of that, Mr. Git?

```
$ git status
```

```
On branch master

Initial commit

Changes to be committed:
  (use "git rm --cached <file>..." to unstage)

    new file:    test.py
```

This means that *test.py* is part of the local repository but its changes have not yet been committed. Let's commit it:

```
$ git commit -m "simple print program"
```

```
[master (root-commit) 52d60d7] my first commit
 1 file changed, 1 insertion(+)
 create mode 100644 test.py
```

That -m "my first commit" was your *commit message*. If you omitted that, git would pop you into an editor and coax you to enter the message that way. This becomes a part of the git change history for that file.

Let's see what our current status is:

```
$ git status
```

```
On branch master
nothing to commit, working directory clean
```

Okay, all current changes have been committed. This means that we can change things and not worry about losing the original version. Make an adjustment now to *test.py*—change Oops to Ops! and save the file:

```
print('Ops!')
```

Let's check to see what git thinks now:

```
$ git status
On branch master
Changes not staged for commit:
  (use "git add <file>..." to update what will be committed)
  (use "git checkout -- <file>..." to discard changes in working directory)

    modified:   test.py

no changes added to commit (use "git add" and/or "git commit -a")
```

Use git diff to see what lines have changed since the last commit:

```
$ git diff
diff --git a/test.py b/test.py
index 76b8c39..62782b2 100644
--- a/test.py
+++ b/test.py
@@ -1 +1 @@
-print('Oops')
+print('Ops!')
```

If you try to commit this change now, git complains:

```
$ git commit -m "change the print string"
On branch master
Changes not staged for commit:
    modified:   test.py

no changes added to commit
```

That staged for commit phrase means you need to add the file, which roughly translated means *hey git, look over here*:

```
$ git add test.py
```

You could have also typed git add . to add *all* changed files in the current directory; that's handy when you actually have edited multiple files and want to ensure that you check in all their changes. Now we can commit the change:

```
$ git commit -m "my first change"
 [master e1e11ec] my first change
  1 file changed, 1 insertion(+), 1 deletion(-)
```

If you'd like to see all the terrible things that you've done to *test.py*, most recent first, use `git log`:

```
$ git log test.py
commit e1e11ecf802ae1a78debe6193c552dcd15ca160a
Author: William Lubanovic <bill@madscheme.com>
Date:   Tue May 13 23:34:59 2014 -0500

    change the print string

commit 52d60d76594a62299f6fd561b2446c8b1227cfe1
Author: William Lubanovic <bill@madscheme.com>
Date:   Tue May 13 23:26:14 2014 -0500

    simple print program
```

Clone This Book

You can get a copy of all the programs in this book. Visit the git repository (*https://github.com/madscheme/introducing-python*) and follow the directions to copy it to your local machine. If you have `git`, run the command `git clone https://github.com/madscheme/introducing-python` to make a git repository on your computer. You can also download the files in zip format.

How You Can Learn More

This is an introduction. It almost certainly says too much about some things that you don't care about and not enough about some things that you do. Let me recommend some Python resources that I've found helpful.

Books

I've found the books in the list that follows to be especially useful. These range from introductory to advanced, with mixtures of Python 2 and 3.

- Barry, Paul. *Head First Python*. O'Reilly, 2010.
- Beazley, David M. *Python Essential Reference (4th Edition)*. Addison-Wesley, 2009.
- Beazley, David M. and Brian K. Jones. *Python Cookbook (3rd Edition)*. O'Reilly, 2013.
- Chun, Wesley. *Core Python Applications Programming (3rd Edition)*. Prentice Hall, 2012.
- McKinney, Wes. *Python for Data Analysis: Data Wrangling with Pandas, NumPy, and IPython*. O'Reilly, 2012.

- Summerfield, Mark. *Python in Practice: Create Better Programs Using Concurrency, Libraries, and Patterns*. Addison-Wesley, 2013.

Of course, there are many more (*https://wiki.python.org/moin/PythonBooks*).

Websites

Here are some websites where you can find helpful tutorials:

- Learn Python the Hard Way (*http://learnpythonthehardway.org/book/*) by Zed Shaw.
- Dive Into Python 3 (*http://www.diveintopython3.net/*) by Mark Pilgrim.
- Mouse Vs. Python (*http://www.blog.pythonlibrary.org/*) by Michael Driscoll.

If you're interested in keeping up with what's going on in the Pythonic world, check out these news websites:

- comp.lang.python (*http://bit.ly/comp-lang-python*)
- comp.lang.python.announce (*http://bit.ly/comp-lang-py-announce*)
- python subreddit (*http://www.reddit.com/r/python*)
- Planet Python (*http://planet.python.org/*)

Finally, here are some good websites for downloading code:

- The Python Package Index (*https://pypi.python.org/pypi*)
- stackoverflow Python questions (*http://stackoverflow.com/questions/tagged/python*)
- ActiveState Python recipes (*http://code.activestate.com/recipes/langs/python/*)
- Python packages trending on GitHub (*https://github.com/trending?l=python*)

Groups

Computing communities have varied personalities: enthusiastic, argumentative, dull, hipster, button-down, and many others across a broad range. The Python community is friendly and civil. You can find Python groups based on location—meetups (*http://python.meetup.com/*) and local user groups around the world (*https://wiki.python.org/moin/LocalUserGroups*). Other groups are distributed and based on common interests. For instance, PyLadies (*http://www.pyladies.com/*) is a support network for women who are interested in Python and open source.

Conferences

Of the many conferences (*http://www.pycon.org/*) and workshops around the world (*https://www.python.org/community/workshops/*), the largest are held annually in North America (*https://us.pycon.org*) and Europe (*https://europython.eu/en/*).

Coming Attractions

But wait, there's more! Appendixes A, B, and C offer tours of Python in the arts, business, and science. You'll find at least one package that you'll want to explore.

Bright and shiny objects abound on the net. Only you can tell which are costume jewelry and which are silver bullets. And even if you're not currently pestered by werewolves, you might want some of those silver bullets in your pocket. Just in case.

Finally, we have answers to those annoying end-of-chapter exercises, details on installation of Python and friends, and a few cheat sheets for things that I always need to look up. Your brain is almost certainly better tuned, but they're there if you need them.

Py Art

Well, art is art, isn't it? Still, on the other hand, water is water! And east is east and west is west, and if you take cranberries and stew them like applesauce, they taste much more like prunes than rhubarb does.

—Groucho Marx

Maybe you're an artist, or a musician. Or maybe you just want to try something creative and different.

These first three appendices are explorations of some common human endeavors using Python. If your interest lies in any of these areas, you might get some ideas from the chapters, or the urge to try something new.

2-D Graphics

All computer languages have been applied to computer graphics to some degree. Many of the heavy-duty platforms in this chapter were written in C or C++ for speed, but added Python libraries for productivity. Let's begin by looking at some 2-D imaging libraries.

Standard Library

Only a few graphics-related modules are in the standard library. Here are two of them:

imghdr

This module detects the file type of some image files.

colorsys

This module converts colors between various systems: RGB, YIQ, HSV, and HLS.

If you downloaded the O'Reilly logo to a local file called *oreilly.png*, you could run this:

```
>>> import imghdr
>>> imghdr.what('oreilly.png')
'png'
```

To do anything serious with graphics in Python, we need to get some third-party packages. Let's see what's out there.

PIL and Pillow

For many years, the Python Image Library (*http://bit.ly/py-image*) (PIL), although not in the standard library, has been Python's best-known 2-D image processing library. It predated installers such as pip, so a "friendly fork" called Pillow (*http://pillow.readthe docs.org/*) was created. Pillow's imaging code is backward-compatible with PIL, and its documentation is good, so we'll use it here.

Installation is simple; just type the following command:

```
$ pip install Pillow
```

If you've already installed operating system packages such as libjpeg, libfreetype, and zlib, they'll be detected and used by Pillow. See the installation page (*http://bit.ly/pillow-install*) for details on this.

Open an image file:

```
>>> from PIL import Image
>>> img = Image.open('oreilly.png')
>>> img.format
'PNG'
>>> img.size
(154, 141)
>>> img.mode
'RGB'
```

Although the package is called Pillow, you import it as PIL to make it compatible with the older PIL.

To display the image on your screen using the Image object's show() method, you'll first need to install the ImageMagick package described in the next section, and then try this:

```
>>> img.show()
```

The image displayed in Figure A-1 opens in another window. (This screenshot was captured on a Mac, where the show() function used the Preview application. Your window's appearance might vary.)

Figure A-1. Image opened via the Python library

Let's crop the image in memory, save the result as a new object called img2, and display it. Images are always measured by horizontal (x) values and vertical (y) values, with one corner of the image known as the *origin* and arbitrarily assigned an x and y of 0. In this library, the origin (0, 0) is at the upper left of the image, x increases to the right, and y increases as you move down. We want to give the values of left x (55), top y (70), right x (85), and bottom y (100) to the crop() method, so we'll pass it a tuple with those values in that order.

```
>>> crop = (55, 70, 85, 100)
>>> img2 = img.crop(crop)
>>> img2.show()
```

The results are shown in Figure A-2.

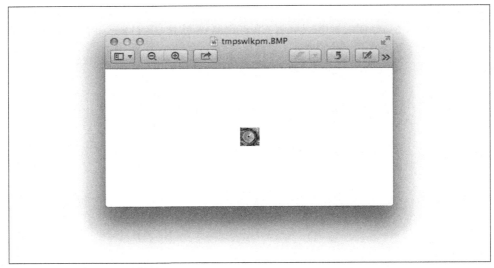

Figure A-2. The cropped image

Save an image file with the `save` method. It takes a filename and an optional type. If the filename has a suffix, the library uses that to determine the type. But, you can also specify the type explicitly. To save our cropped image as a GIF file, do the following:

```
>>> img2.save('cropped.gif', 'GIF')
>>> img3 = Image.open('cropped.gif')
>>> img3.format
'GIF'
>>> img3.size
(30, 30)
```

Let's "improve" our little mascot. First download an image of moustaches (*http://bit.ly/moustaches-png*) to *moustaches.png*. We'll load it, crop it suitably, and then overlay it on our spokescritter:

```
>>> mustache = Image.open('moustaches.png')
>>> handlebar = mustache.crop( (316, 282, 394, 310) )
>>> handlebar.size
(78, 28)
>>> img.paste(handlebar, (45, 90) )
>>> img.show()
```

Figure A-3 presents the highly satisfactory results.

Figure A-3. Our new, dapper mascot

It would be nice to make that moustache background transparent. Hey, there's an exercise for you! If you'd like to play with this, look up *transparency* and *alpha channel* in the Pillow tutorial (*http://bit.ly/pil-fork*).

ImageMagick

ImageMagick (*http://www.imagemagick.org/*) is a suite of programs to convert, modify, and display 2-D bitmap images. It's been around for more than 20 years. Various Python libraries have connected to the ImageMagick C library. A recent one that supports Python 3 is wand (*http://docs.wand-py.org/*). To install it, type the following command:

```
$ pip install Wand
```

You can do many of the same things with wand as you can with Pillow:

```
>>> from wand.image import Image
>>> from wand.display import display
>>>
>>> img = Image(filename='oreilly.png')
>>> img.size
(154, 141)
>>> img.format
'PNG'
```

As with Pillow, this displays the image on the screen:

```
>>> display(img)
```

wand includes rotation, resizing, text and line drawing, format conversion, and other features that you can also find in Pillow. Both have good APIs and documentation.

Graphical User Interfaces (GUIs)

The name includes the word graphic, but GUIs concentrate more on the user interface: widgets to present data, input methods, menus, buttons, and windows to frame everything.

The GUI programming (*http://bit.ly/gui-program*) wiki page and FAQ (*http://bit.ly/gui-faq*) list many Python-powered GUIs. Let's begin with the only one that's built into the standard library: Tkinter (*https://wiki.python.org/moin/TkInter*). It's plain, but it works on all platforms to produce native-looking windows and widgets.

Here's a teeny, tiny Tkinter program to display our favorite googly-eyed mascot in a window:

```
>>> import tkinter
>>> from PIL import Image, ImageTk
>>>
>>> main = tkinter.Tk()
>>> img = Image.open('oreilly.png')
>>> tkimg = ImageTk.PhotoImage(img)
>>> tkinter.Label(main, image=tkimg).pack()
>>> main.mainloop()
```

Notice that it used some modules from PIL/Pillow. You should see the O'Reilly logo again, as shown in Figure A-4.

Figure A-4. Image shown through Tkinter library

To make the window go away, click its close button, or leave your Python interpreter.

Read more about Tkinter at the tkinter wiki (*http://tkinter.unpythonic.net/wiki/*) and the Python wiki (*https://wiki.python.org/moin/TkInter*). Now for the GUIs that are not in the standard library.

Qt (http://qt-project.org/)
> This is a professional GUI and application toolkit, originated about 20 years ago by Trolltech in Norway. It's been used to help build applications such as Google Earth, Maya, and Skype. It was also used as the base for KDE, a Linux desktop. There are two main Python libraries for Qt: PySide (*http://qt-project.org/wiki/*

PySide) is free (LGPL license), and PyQt (*http://bit.ly/pyqt-info*) is licensed either with the GPL or commercially. The Qt folks see these differences (*http://bit.ly/qt-diff*). Download PySide from PyPI (*https://pypi.python.org/pypi/PySide*) or Qt (*http://qt-project.org/wiki/Get-PySide*) and read the tutorial (*http://qt-project.org/wiki/PySide_Tutorials*). You can download Qt for free online (*http://bit.ly/qt-dl*).

GTK+ (http://www.gtk.org/)

GTK+ is a competitor of Qt, and it, too, has been used to create many applications (*http://gtk-apps.org/*), including GIMP and the Gnome desktop for Linux. The Python binding is PyGTK (*http://www.pygtk.org/*). To download the code, go to the PyGTK site (*http://bit.ly/pygtk-dl*), where you can also read the documents (*http://bit.ly/py-gtk-docs*).

WxPython (http://www.wxpython.org/)

This is the Python binding for WxWidgets (*http://www.wxwidgets.org/*). It's another hefty package, free to download online (*http://wxpython.org/download.php*).

Kivy (http://kivy.org/)

Kivy is a free modern library for building multimedia user interfaces portably across platforms—desktop (Windows, OS X, Linux), and mobile (Android, iOS). It includes multitouch support. You can download for all the platforms on the Kivy website (*http://kivy.org/#download*). Kivy includes application development tutorials (*http://bit.ly/kivy-intro*).

The Web

Frameworks such as Qt use native components, but some others use the Web. After all, the Web is a universal GUI, and it has graphics (SVG), text (HTML), and even multimedia now (in HTML5). Some web-based GUI tools written in Python include RCTK (Remote Control Toolkit) (*https://code.google.com/p/rctk/*) and Muntjac (*http://www.muntiacus.org/*). You can build web applications with any combination of frontend (browser-based) and backend (web server) tools. A *thin client* lets the backend do most of the work. If the frontend dominates, it's a *thick*, or *fat*, or *rich* client; the last adjective sounds more flattering. It's common for the sides to communicate with RESTful APIs, AJAX, and JSON.

3-D Graphics and Animation

Watch the long end-credits for almost any contemporary movie, and you'll see mass quantities of people doing special effects and animation. Most of the big studios—Walt Disney Animation, ILM, Weta, Dreamworks, Pixar—hire people with Python experience. Do a web search for "python animation jobs" or visit vfxjobs (*http://vfxjobs.com/search/*) and search for "python" to see what's available now.

If you'd like to experiment with Python and 3-D, animation, multimedia, and games, try Panda3D (*http://www.panda3d.org/*). It's open source and free to use, even for commercial applications. You can download a version for your computer from the Panda3D website (*http://bit.ly/dl-panda*). To try some sample programs, change to the directory */Developer/Examples/Panda3D*. Each subdirectory contains one or more *.py* files. Run one of them by using the ppython command that came with Panda3D. For example:

```
$ cd /Developer/Examples/Panda3D
$ cd Ball-in-Maze/
$ ppython Tut-Ball-in-Maze.py

DirectStart: Starting the game.
Known pipe types:
  osxGraphicsPipe
(all display modules loaded.)
```

A window similar to Figure A-5 opens.

Figure A-5. An image shown through the Panda3D library

Use your mouse to tilt the box and move the ball in the maze.

If that all worked, and the base Panda3D installation looks good, then you can start playing with the Python library.

Here's a simple example application from the Panda3D documentation; save it as *panda1.py*:

```python
from direct.showbase.ShowBase import ShowBase

class MyApp(ShowBase):

    def __init__(self):
        ShowBase.__init__(self)

        # Load the environment model.
        self.environ = self.loader.loadModel("models/environment")
        # Reparent the model to render.
        self.environ.reparentTo(self.render)
        # Apply scale and position transforms on the model.
        self.environ.setScale(0.25, 0.25, 0.25)
        self.environ.setPos(-8, 42, 0)

app = MyApp()
app.run()
```

Run it by using this command:

```
$ ppython panda1.py

Known pipe types:
  osxGraphicsPipe
(all display modules loaded.)
```

A window opens displaying the scene in Figure A-6.

The rock and tree are floating above the ground. Click the Next buttons to continue the guided tour and fix these problems.

Following are some other 3-D packages with Python:

Blender (http://www.blender.org/)
Blender is a free 3-D animation and game creator. When you download and install it from *www.blender.org/download*, it comes bundled with its own copy of Python 3.

Maya (http://www.autodesk.com/products/autodesk-maya/overview)
This is a commercial 3-D animation and graphic system. It also comes bundled with a version of Python, currently 2.6. Chad Vernon has written a free downloadable book, *Python Scripting for Maya Artists* (*http://bit.ly/py-maya*). If you search for Python and Maya on the Web, you'll find many other resources, both free and commercial, including videos.

Houdini (https://www.sidefx.com/)

>   Houdini is commercial, although you can download a free version called Apprentice. Like the other animation packages, it comes with a Python binding (*http://bit.ly/py-bind*).

Figure A-6. Scaled image shown through Panda3D library

Plots, Graphs, and Visualization

Python has become a leading solution for plots, graphs, and data visualization. It's especially popular in science, which is covered in Appendix C. The official Python site has an overview (*https://wiki.python.org/moin/NumericAndScientific/Plotting*). Allow me to take a few moments to say a little more about some of these.

matplotlib

The free `matplotlib` (*http://matplotlib.org/*) 2-D plotting library can be installed by using the following command:

```
$ pip install matplotlib
```

The examples in the gallery (*http://matplotlib.org/gallery.html*) show the breadth of `matplotlib`. Let's try the same image display application (with results shown in Figure A-7), just to see how the code and presentation look:

```
import matplotlib.pyplot as plot
import matplotlib.image as image

img = image.imread('oreilly.png')
plot.imshow(img)
plot.show()
```

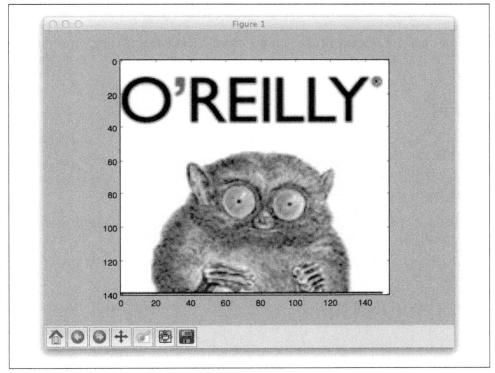

Figure A-7. Image shown through the matplotlib library

You can see more of `matplotlib` in Appendix C; it has strong ties to NumPy and other scientific applications.

bokeh

In the old web days, developers would generate graphics on the server and give the web browser some URL to access them. More recently, JavaScript has gained performance and client-side graphics generation tools like D3. A page or two ago, I mentioned the possibility of using Python as part of a frontend-backend architecture for graphics and GUIs. A new tool called bokeh (*http://bokeh.pydata.org/*) combines the strengths of Python (large data sets, ease of use) and JavaScript (interactivity, less graphics latency). Its emphasis is quick visualization of large data sets.

If you've already installed its prerequisites (NumPy, Pandas, and Redis) you can install bokeh by typing this command:

```
$ pip install bokeh
```

(You can see NumPy and Pandas in action in Appendix C.)

Or, install everything at once from the Bokeh website (*http://bit.ly/bokeh-dl*). Although matplotlib runs on the server, bokeh runs mainly in the browser and can take advantage of recent advances on the client side. Click any image in the gallery (*http://bokeh.pydata.org/docs/gallery.html*) for an interactive view of the display and its Python code.

Games

Python is good at data wrangling, and you've seen in this appendix that it's also good at multimedia. How about games?

It happens that Python is such a good game development platform that people have written books about it. Here are a couple of them:

- *Invent Your Own Computer Games with Python* (*http://inventwithpython.com/*) by Al Sweigart
- *The Python Game Book* (*http://thepythongamebook.com/*), by Horst Jens (a docu-wiki book)

There's a general discussion at the Python wiki (*https://wiki.python.org/moin/Python Games*) with even more links.

The best known Python game platform is probably pygame (*http://pygame.org/*). You can download an executable installer for your platform from the Pygame website (*http://pygame.org/download.shtml*), and read a line-by-line example of a "pummel the chimp" game (*http://bit.ly/line-chimp*).

Audio and Music

What about sound, and music, and cats singing Jingle Bells?

Well, maybe just the first two.

The standard library has some rudimentary audio modules under multimedia services (*http://docs.python.org/3/library/mm.html*). There's also a discussion of third-party modules (*https://wiki.python.org/moin/Audio*).

The following libraries can help you generate music:

- pyknon (*https://github.com/kroger/pyknon*) is used by the book *Music for Geeks and Nerds* (*http://musicforgeeksandnerds.com/*) by Pedro Kroger (CreateSpace).
- mingus (*https://code.google.com/p/mingus/*) is a music sequencer that can read and produce MIDI files.
- remix (*http://echonest.github.io/remix/python.html*), as the name implies, is an API to remix music. One example of its use is morecowbell.dj, which adds more cowbell to uploaded songs.
- sebastian (*https://github.com/jtauber/sebastian/*) is a library for music theory and analysis.
- Piano (*http://bit.ly/py-piano*) lets you play piano on your computer keyboard with the keys C, D, E, F, A, B, and C.

Finally, the libraries in the following list can help you organize your collection or give you access to music data:

- Beets (*http://beets.radbox.org/*) manages your music collection.
- Echonest (*http://developer.echonest.com/*) APIs access music metadata.
- Monstermash (*http://bit.ly/mm-karlgrz*) mashes song fragments together; it's built on Echonest, Flask, ZeroMQ, and Amazon EC2.
- Shiva (*http://bit.ly/shiva-api*) is a RESTful API and server (*https://github.com/tooxie/shiva-server*) to query your collection.
- Get album art (*http://jameh.github.io/mpd-album-art/*) to match your music.

Py at Work

"Business!" cried the Ghost, wringing its hands again. "Mankind was my business..."
—Charles Dickens, A Christmas Carol

The businessman's uniform is a suit and tie. But for some reason, when he decides to *get down to business*, he tosses his jacket over a chair, loosens his tie, rolls up his sleeves, and pours some coffee. Meanwhile the business woman, with little fanfare, is actually getting work done. Maybe with a latte.

In business, we use all of the technologies from the earlier chapters—databases, the Web, systems, and networks. Python's productivity is making it more popular in the enterprise (*http://bit.ly/py-enterprise*) and with startups (*http://bit.ly/py-startups*).

Businesses have long sought silver bullets to slay their legacy werewolves—incompatible file formats, arcane network protocols, language lock-in, and the universal lack of accurate documentation. However, today we see some technologies and techniques that can actually interoperate and scale. Businesses can create faster, cheaper, stretchier applications by employing the following:

- Dynamic languages like Python
- The Web as a universal graphical user interface
- RESTful APIs as language-independent service interfaces
- Relational and NoSQL databases
- "Big data" and analytics
- Clouds for deployment and capital savings

The Microsoft Office Suite

Business is heavily dependent on Microsoft Office applications and file formats. Although they are not well known, and in some cases poorly documented, there are some Python libraries that can help. Here are some that process Microsoft Office documents:

docx (https://pypi.python.org/pypi/docx)
>   This library creates, reads, and writes Microsoft Office Word 2007 .docx files.

python-excel (http://www.python-excel.org/)
>   This one discusses the xlrd, xlwt, and xlutils modules via a PDF tutorial (*http://bit.ly/py-excel*). Excel can also read and write Comma-Separated Value (CSV) files, which you know how to process by using the standard csv module.

oletools (http://bit.ly/oletools)
>   This library extracts data from Office formats.

These modules automate Windows applications:

pywin32 (http://sourceforge.net/projects/pywin32/)
>   This module automates many Windows applications. However, it's limited to Python 2, and has sparse documentation; see this blog post (*http://bit.ly/pywin32-lib*) and this one (*http://bit.ly/pywin-mo*).

pywinauto (https://code.google.com/p/pywinauto/)
>   This one also automates Windows applications and is limited to Python 2; see this blog post (*http://bit.ly/saju-pywinauto*).

swapy (https://code.google.com/p/swapy/)
>   swapy generates Python code for pywinauto from native controls.

OpenOffice (*http://openoffice.org*) is an open source alternative to Office. It runs on Linux, Unix, Windows, and OS X, and reads and writes Office file formats, It also installs a version of Python 3 for its own use. You can program OpenOffice in Python (*https://wiki.openoffice.org/wiki/Python*) with the PyUNO (*http://www.openoffice.org/udk/python/python-bridge.html*) library.

OpenOffice was owned by Sun Microsystems, and when Oracle acquired Sun, some people feared for its future availability. LibreOffice (*https://www.libreoffice.org/*) was spun off as a result. DocumentHacker (*http://bit.ly/docu-hacker*) describes using the Python UNO library with LibreOffice.

OpenOffice and LibreOffice had to reverse engineer the Microsoft file formats, which is not easy. The Universal Office Converter (*http://dag.wiee.rs/home-made/unoconv/*) module depends on the UNO library in OpenOffice or LibreOffice. It can convert many file formats: documents, spreadsheets, graphics, and presentations.

If you have a mystery file, python-magic (*https://github.com/ahupp/python-magic*) can guess its format by analyzing specific byte sequences.

The python open document (*http://appyframework.org/pod.html*) library lets you provide Python code within templates to create dynamic documents.

Although not a Microsoft format, Adobe's PDF is very common in business. ReportLab (*http://www.reportlab.com/opensource/*) has open source and commercial versions of its Python-based PDF generator. If you need to edit a PDF, you might find some help at StackOverflow (*http://bit.ly/add-text-pdf*).

Carrying Out Business Tasks

You can find a Python module for almost anything. Visit PyPI (*https://pypi.python.org/pypi*) and type something into the search box. Many modules are interfaces to the public APIs of various services. You might be interested in some examples related to business tasks:

- Ship via Fedex (*https://github.com/gtaylor/python-fedex*) or UPS (*https://github.com/openlabs/PyUPS*).

- Mail with the stamps.com (*https://github.com/jzempel/stamps*) API.

- Read a discussion of *Python for business intelligence* (*http://bit.ly/py-biz*).

- If Aeropresses are flying off the shelves in Anoka, was it customer activity or poltergeists? Cubes (*http://cubes.databrewery.org/*) is an Online Analytical Processing (OLAP) web server and data browser.

- OpenERP (*https://www.openerp.com/*) is a large commercial Enterprise Resource Planning (ERP) system written in Python and JavaScript, with thousands of add-on modules.

Processing Business Data

Businesses have a particular fondness for data. Sadly, many of them conjure up perverse ways of making data harder to use.

Spreadsheets were a good invention, and over time businesses became addicted to them. Many non-programmers were tricked into programming because they were called *macros* instead of programs. But the universe is expanding and data is trying to keep up. Older versions of Excel were limited to 65,536 rows, and even newer versions choke at a million or so. When an organization's data outgrow the limits of a single computer, it's like headcount growing past a hundred people or so—suddenly you need new layers, intermediaries, and communication.

Excessive data programs aren't caused by the size of data on single desktops; rather, they're the result of the aggregate of data pouring into the business. Relational databases handle millions of rows without exploding, but only so many writes or updates at a time. A plain old text or binary file can grow gigabytes in size, but if you need to process it all at once, you need enough memory. Traditional desktop software isn't designed for all this. Companies such as Google and Amazon had to invent solutions to handle so much data at scale. Netflix (*http://bit.ly/py-netflix*) is an example built on Amazon's AWS cloud, using Python to glue together RESTful APIs, security, deployment, and databases.

Extracting, Transforming, and Loading

The underwater portions of the data icebergs include all the work to get the data in the first place. If you speak enterprise, the common term is extract, transform, load, or *ETL*. Synonyms such as *data munging* or *data wrangling* give the impression of taming an unruly beast, which might be apt metaphors. This would seem to be a solved engineering matter by now, but it remains largely an art. We'll address *data science* more broadly in Appendix C, because this is where most developers spend a large part of their time.

If you've seen *The Wizard of Oz*, you probably remember (besides the flying monkeys) the part at the end—when the good witch told Dorothy that she could always go home to Kansas just by clicking her ruby slippers. Even when I was young I thought, "Now she tells her!" Although, in retrospect, I realize the movie would have been much shorter if she'd shared that tip earlier.

But this isn't a movie; we're talking about the world of business here, where making tasks shorter is a good thing. So, let me share some tips with you now. Most of the tools that you need for day-to-day data work in business are those that you've already read about here. Those include high-level data structures such as dictionaries and objects, thousands of standard and third-party libraries, and an expert community that's just a google away.

If you're a computer programmer working for some business, your workflow almost always includes:

1. Extracting data from weird file formats or databases
2. "Cleaning up" the data, which covers a lot of ground, all strewn with pointy objects
3. Converting things like dates, times, and character sets
4. Actually doing something with the data
5. Storing resulting data in a file or database

6. Rolling back to step 1 again; lather, rinse, repeat

Here's an example: you want to move data from a spreadsheet to a database. You can save the spreadsheet in CSV format and use the Python libraries from Chapter 8. Or, you can look for a module that reads the binary spreadsheet format directly. Your fingers know how to type python excel into Google, and find sites such as Working with Excel files in Python (*http://www.python-excel.org/*). You can install one of the packages by using pip, and locate a Python database driver for the last part of the task. I mentioned SQLAlchemy and the direct low-level database drivers in that same chapter. Now you need some code in the middle, and that's where Python's data structures and libraries can save you time.

Let's try an example here, and then we'll try again with a library that saves a few steps. We'll read a CSV file, aggregate the counts in one column by unique values in another, and print the results. If we did this in SQL, we would use SELECT, JOIN, and GROUP BY.

First, the file, *zoo.csv*, which has columns for the type of animal, how many times it has bitten a visitor, the number of stitches required, and how much we've paid the visitor not to tell local television stations:

```
animal,bites,stitches,hush
bear,1,35,300
marmoset,1,2,250
bear,2,42,500
elk,1,30,100
weasel,4,7,50
duck,2,0,10
```

We want to see which animal is costing us the most, so we'll aggregate the total hush money by the type of animal. (We'll leave bites and stitches to an intern.) We'll use the csv module from "CSV" on page 185 and Counter from "Count Items with Counter()" on page 118. Save this code as *zoo_counts.py*:

```
import csv
from collections import Counter

counts = Counter()
with open('zoo.csv', 'rt') as fin:
    cin = csv.reader(fin)
    for num, row in enumerate(cin):
        if num > 0:
            counts[row[0]] += int(row[-1])
for animal, hush in counts.items():
    print("%10s %10s" % (animal, hush))
```

We skipped the first row because it contained only the column names. counts is a Counter object, and takes care of initializing the sum for each animal to zero. We also applied a little formatting to right-align the output. Let's try it:

```
$ python zoo_counts.py
    duck         10
     elk        100
    bear        800
  weasel         50
marmoset        250
```

Ha! It was the bear. He was our prime suspect all along, but now we have the numbers.

Next, let's replicate this with a data processing toolkit called Bubbles (*http://bubbles.databrewery.org/*). You can install it by typing this command:

```
$ pip install bubbles
```

It requires SQLAlchemy; if you don't have that, `pip install sqlalchemy` will do the trick. Here's the test program (call it *bubbles1.py*), adapted from the documentation (*http://bit.ly/py-bubbles*):

```
import bubbles

p = bubbles.Pipeline()
p.source(bubbles.data_object('csv_source', 'zoo.csv', infer_fields=True))
p.aggregate('animal', 'hush')
p.pretty_print()
```

And now, the moment of truth:

```
$ python bubbles1.py
2014-03-11 19:46:36,806 DEBUG calling aggregate(rows)
2014-03-11 19:46:36,807 INFO called aggregate(rows)
2014-03-11 19:46:36,807 DEBUG calling pretty_print(records)
+--------+--------+------------+
|animal  |hush_sum|record_count|
+--------+--------+------------+
|duck    |      10|           1|
|weasel  |      50|           1|
|bear    |     800|           2|
|elk     |     100|           1|
|marmoset|     250|           1|
+--------+--------+------------+
2014-03-11 19:46:36,807 INFO called pretty_print(records)
```

If you read the documentation, you can avoid those debug print lines, and maybe change the format of the table.

Looking at the two examples, we see that the `bubbles` example used a single function call (`aggregate`) to replace our manual reading and counting of the CSV format. Depending on your needs, data toolkits can save a lot of work.

In a more realistic example, our zoo file might have thousands of rows (it's a dangerous place), with misspellings such as `bare`, commas in numbers, and so on. For good examples of practical data problems with Python and Java code, I'd also recommend Greg Wilson's book *Data Crunching: Solve Everyday Problems Using Java, Python, and More* (*http://bit.ly/data_crunching*) (Pragmatic Bookshelf).

Data cleanup tools can save a lot of time, and Python has many of them. For another example, PETL (*http://petl.readthedocs.org/*) does row and column extraction and renaming. Its related work (*http://bit.ly/petl-related*) page lists many useful modules and products. Appendix C has detailed discussions of some especially useful data tools: Pandas, NumPy, and IPython. Although they're currently best known among scientists, they're becoming popular among financial and data developers. At the 2012 Pydata conference, AppData (*http://bit.ly/py-big-data*) discussed how these three and other Python tools help process 15 terabytes of data daily. Make no mistake: Python can handle very large real-world data loads.

Additional Sources of Information

Sometimes, you need data that originates somewhere else. Some business and government data sources include:

data.gov (https://www.data.gov/)
A gateway to thousands of data sets and tools. Its APIs (*https://www.data.gov/developers/apis*) are built on CKAN (*http://ckan.org/*), a Python data management system.

Opening government with Python (http://sunlightfoundation.com)
See the video (*http://bit.ly/opengov-py*) and slides (*http://goo.gl/8Yh3s*).

python-sunlight (http://bit.ly/py-sun)
Libraries to access the Sunlight APIs (*http://sunlightfoundation.com/api/*).

froide (http://stefanw.github.io/froide/)
A Django-based platform for managing freedom of information requests.

30 places to find open data on the Web (http://blog.visual.ly/data-sources/)
Some handy links.

Python in Finance

Recently, the financial industry has developed a great interest in Python. Adapting software from Appendix C as well as some of their own, *quants* are building a new generation of financial tools:

Quantitative economics (http://quant-econ.net/)
This is a tool for economic modeling, with lots of math and Python code.

Python for finance (http://www.python-for-finance.com/)
    This features the book *Derivatives Analytics with Python: Data Analytics, Models, Simulation, Calibration, and Hedging* by Yves Hilpisch (Wiley).

Quantopian (https://www.quantopian.com/)
    Quantopian is an interactive website on which you can write your own Python code and run it against historic stock data to see how it would have done.

PyAlgoTrade (http://gbeced.github.io/pyalgotrade/)
    This is another that you can use for stock backtesting, but on your own computer.

Quandl (http://www.quandl.com/)
    Use this to search millions of financial datasets.

Ultra-finance (https://code.google.com/p/ultra-finance/)
    A real-time stock collection library.

Python for Finance (http://bit.ly/python-finance) (O'Reilly)
    A book by Yves Hilpisch with Python examples for financial modeling.

Business Data Security

Security is a special concern for business. Entire books are devoted to this topic, so we'll just mention a few Python-related tips here.

- "Scapy" on page 295 discusses `scapy`, a Python-powered language for packet forensics. It has been used to explain some major network attacks.

- The Python Security (*http://www.pythonsecurity.org/*) site has discussions of security topics, details on some Python modules, and cheat sheets.

- The book *Violent Python* (*http://bit.ly/violent-python*) (subtitled *A Cookbook for Hackers, Forensic Analysts, Penetration Testers and Security Engineers*) by TJ O'Connor (Syngress) is an extensive review of Python and computer security.

Maps

Maps have become valuable to many businesses. Python is very good at making maps, so we're going to spend a little more time in this area. Managers love graphics, and if you can quickly whip up a nice map for your organization's website it wouldn't hurt.

In the early days of the Web, I used to visit an experimental mapmaking website at Xerox. When big sites such as Google Maps came along, they were a revelation (along the lines of "why didn't I think of that and make millions?"). Now mapping and *location-based services* are everywhere, and are particularly useful in mobile devices.

Many terms overlap here: mapping, cartography, GIS (geographic information system), GPS (Global Positioning System), geospatial analysis, and many more. The blog at Geospatial Python (*http://bit.ly/geospatial-py*) has an image of the "800-pound gorilla" systems—GDAL/OGR, GEOS, and PROJ.4 (projections)--and surrounding systems, represented as monkeys. Many of these have Python interfaces. Let's talk about some of these, beginning with the simplest formats.

Formats

The mapping world has lots of formats: vector (lines), raster (images), metadata (words), and various combinations.

Esri, a pioneer of geographic systems, invented the *shapefile* format over 20 years ago. A shapefile actually consists of multiple files, including at the very least the following:

`.shp`
   The "shape" (vector) information

`.shx`
   The shape index

`.dbf`
   An attribute database

Some useful Python shapefile modules include the following:

- pyshp (*https://code.google.com/p/pyshp/*) is a pure-Python shapefile library.
- shapely (*http://toblerity.org/shapely/*) addresses geometric questions such as, "What buildings in this town are within the 50-year flood contour?"
- fiona (*https://github.com/Toblerity/Fiona*) wraps the OGR library, which handles shapefiles and other vector formats.
- kartograph (*http://kartograph.org/*) renders shapefiles into SVG maps on the server or client.
- basemap (*http://matplotlib.org/basemap/*) plots 2-D data on maps, and uses `mat plotlib`.
- cartopy (*http://scitools.org.uk/cartopy/docs/latest/*) uses `matplotlib` and `shapely` to draw maps.

Let's grab a shapefile for our next example- visit the Natural Earth 1:110m Cultural Vectors page (*http://bit.ly/cultural-vectors*). Under "Admin 1 - States and Provinces," click the green download states and provinces (*http://bit.ly/dl-states*) box to download a zip file. After it downloads to your computer, unzip it; you should see these result-ing files:

```
ne_110m_admin_1_states_provinces_shp.README.html
ne_110m_admin_1_states_provinces_shp.sbn
ne_110m_admin_1_states_provinces_shp.VERSION.txt
ne_110m_admin_1_states_provinces_shp.sbx
ne_110m_admin_1_states_provinces_shp.dbf
ne_110m_admin_1_states_provinces_shp.shp
ne_110m_admin_1_states_provinces_shp.prj
ne_110m_admin_1_states_provinces_shp.shx
```

We'll use these for our examples.

Draw a Map

You'll need this library to read a shapefile:

```
$ pip install pyshp
```

Now for the program, *map1.py*, which I've modified from a Geospatial Python blog post (*http://bit.ly/raster-shape*):

```python
def display_shapefile(name, iwidth=500, iheight=500):
    import shapefile
    from PIL import Image, ImageDraw
    r = shapefile.Reader(name)
    mleft, mbottom, mright, mtop = r.bbox
    # map units
    mwidth = mright - mleft
    mheight = mtop - mbottom
    # scale map units to image units
    hscale = iwidth/mwidth
    vscale = iheight/mheight
    img = Image.new("RGB", (iwidth, iheight), "white")
    draw = ImageDraw.Draw(img)
    for shape in r.shapes():
        pixels = [
            (int(iwidth - ((mright - x) * hscale)), int((mtop - y) * vscale))
            for x, y in shape.points]
        if shape.shapeType == shapefile.POLYGON:
            draw.polygon(pixels, outline='black')
        elif shape.shapeType == shapefile.POLYLINE:
            draw.line(pixels, fill='black')
    img.show()

if __name__ == '__main__':
    import sys
    display_shapefile(sys.argv[1], 700, 700)
```

This reads the shapefile and iterates through its individual shapes. I'm checking for only two shape types: a polygon, which connects the last point to the first, and a polyline, which doesn't. I've based my logic on the original post and a quick look at the documentation for pyshp, so I'm not really sure how it will work. Sometimes, we just need to make a start and deal with any problems as we find them.

So, let's run it. The argument is the base name of the shapefile files, without any extension:

```
$ python map1.py ne_110m_admin_1_states_provinces_shp
```

You should see something like Figure B-1.

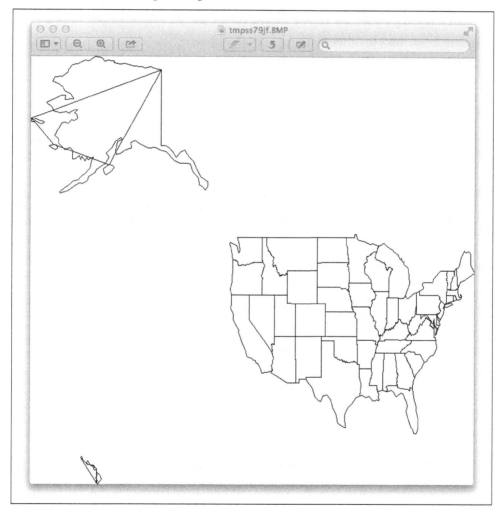

Figure B-1. Preliminary map

Well, it drew a map that resembles the United States, but:

- It looks like a cat dragged yarn across Alaska and Hawaii; this is a *bug*.
- The country is squished; I need a *projection*.
- The picture isn't pretty; I need better *style* control.

To address the first point: I have a problem somewhere in my logic, but what should I do? Chapter 12 discusses development tips, including debugging, but we can consider other options here. I could write some tests and bear down until I fix this, or I could just try some other mapping library. Maybe something at a higher level would solve all three of my problems (the stray lines, squished appearance, and primitive style).

Here are some links to other Python mapping software:

basemap (http://matplotlib.org/basemap/)
    Based on `matplotlib`, draws maps and data overlays

mapnik (http://mapnik.org/)
    A C++ library with Python bindings, for vector (line) and raster (image) maps

tilemill (https://www.mapbox.com/tilemill/)
    A map design studio based on `mapnik`

Vincent (http://vincent.readthedocs.org/)
    Translates to Vega, a JavaScript visualization tool; see the tutorial Mapping data in Python with pandas and vincent (*http://wrobstory.github.io/2013/10/mapping-data-python.html*)

Python for ArcGIS (http://bit.ly/py-arcgis)
    Links to Python resources for Esri's commercial ArcGIS product

Spatial analysis with python (http://bit.ly/spacial-analysis)
    Links to tutorials, packages, and videos

Using geospatial data with python (http://bit.ly/geos-py)
    Video presentations

So you'd like to make a map using Python (http://bit.ly/pythonmap)
    Uses `pandas`, `matplotlib`, `shapely`, and other Python modules to create maps of historic plaque locations

Python Geospatial Development (http://bit.ly/py-geo-dev) (Packt)
    A book by Eric Westra with examples using `mapnik` and other tools

Learning Geospatial Analysis with Python (http://bit.ly/learn-geo-py) (Packt)
    Another book by Joel Lawhead reviewing formats and libraries, with geospatial algorithms

These modules all make beautiful maps, but are harder to install and learn. Some depend on other software you haven't seen yet, such as numpy or pandas. Will the benefits outweigh the costs? As developers, we often need to make these trade-offs based on incomplete information. If you're interested in maps, try downloading and installing one of these packages and see what you can do. Or, you can avoid installing software and try connecting to a remote web service API yourself; Chapter 9 shows you how to connect to web servers and decode JSON responses.

Applications and Data

We've been talking about drawing maps, but you can do a lot more with map data. *Geocoding* converts between addresses and geographic coordinates. There are many geocoding APIs (*http://www.programmableweb.com/apitag/geocoding*) (see ProgrammableWeb's comparison (*http://bit.ly/free-geo-api*)) and Python libraries: geopy (*https://code.google.com/p/geopy/*), pygeocoder (*https://pypi.python.org/pypi/pygeo coder*), and googlemaps (*http://py-googlemaps.sourceforge.net/*). If you sign up with Google or another source to get an API key, you can access other services such as step-by-step travel directions or local search.

Here are a few sources of mapping data:

http://www.census.gov/geo/maps-data/
Overview of the U.S. Census Bureau's map files

http://www.census.gov/geo/maps-data/data/tiger.html
Heaps of geographic and demographic map data

http://wiki.openstreetmap.org/wiki/Potential_Datasources
Worldwide sources

http://www.naturalearthdata.com/
Vector and raster map data at three scales

We should mention the Data Science Toolkit (*http://www.datasciencetoolkit.org/*) here. It includes free bidirectional geocoding, coordinates to political boundaries and statistics, and more. You can also download all the data and software as a virtual machine (VM) and run it self-contained on your own computer.

Py Sci

In her reign the power of steam
On land and sea became supreme,
And all now have strong reliance
In fresh victories of science.
—James McIntyre, Queen's Jubilee Ode
1887

In the past few years, largely because of the software you'll see in this appendix, Python has become extremely popular with scientists. If you're a scientist or student yourself, you might have used tools like MATLAB and R, or traditional languages such as Java, C, or C++. In this appendix, you'll see how Python makes an excellent platform for scientific analysis and publishing.

Math and Statistics in the Standard Library

First, let's take a little trip back to the standard library and visit some features and modules that we've ignored.

Math Functions

Python has a menagerie of math functions in the standard math (*https://docs.python.org/3/library/math.html*) library. Just type **import math** to access them from your programs.

It has a few constants such as pi and e:

```
>>> import math
>>> math.pi
>>> 3.141592653589793
>>> math.e
2.718281828459045
```

Most of it consists of functions, so let's look at the most useful ones.

`fabs()` returns the absolute value of its argument:

```
>>> math.fabs(98.6)
98.6
>>> math.fabs(-271.1)
271.1
```

Get the integer below (`floor()`) and above (`ceil()`) some number:

```
>>> math.floor(98.6)
98
>>> math.floor(-271.1)
-272
>>> math.ceil(98.6)
99
>>> math.ceil(-271.1)
-271
```

Calculate the factorial (in math, n !) by using `factorial()`:

```
>>> math.factorial(0)
1
>>> math.factorial(1)
1
>>> math.factorial(2)
2
>>> math.factorial(3)
6
>>> math.factorial(10)
3628800
```

Get the logarithm of the argument in base e with `log()`:

```
>>> math.log(1.0)
0.0
>>> math.log(math.e)
1.0
```

If you want a different base for the log, provide it as a second argument:

```
>>> math.log(8, 2)
3.0
```

The function `pow()` does the opposite, raising a number to a power:

```
>>> math.pow(2, 3)
8.0
```

Python also has the built-in exponentiation operator `**` to do the same, but it doesn't automatically convert the result to a float if the base and power are both integers:

```
>>> 2**3
8
```

```
>>> 2.0**3
8.0
```

Get a square root with `sqrt()`:

```
>>> math.sqrt(100.0)
10.0
```

Don't try to trick this function; it's seen it all before:

```
>>> math.sqrt(-100.0)
Traceback (most recent call last):
  File "<stdin>", line 1, in <module>
ValueError: math domain error
```

The usual trigonometric functions are all there, and I'll just list their names here: `sin()`, `cos()`, `tan()`, `asin()`, `acos()`, `atan()`, and `atan2()`. If you remember the Pythagorean theorem (or can say it fast three times without spitting), the math library also has a `hypot()` function to calculate the hypotenuse from two sides:

```
>>> x = 3.0
>>> y = 4.0
>>> math.hypot(x, y)
5.0
```

If you don't trust all these fancy functions, you can work it out yourself:

```
>>> math.sqrt(x*x + y*y)
5.0
>>> math.sqrt(x**2 + y**2)
5.0
```

A last set of functions converts angular coordinates:

```
>>> math.radians(180.0)
3.141592653589793
>>> math.degrees(math.pi)
180.0
```

Working with Complex Numbers

Complex numbers are fully supported in the base Python language, with their familiar notation of *real* and *imaginary* parts:

```
>>> # a real number
... 5
5
>>> # an imaginary number
... 8j
8j
>>> # an imaginary number
... 3 + 2j
(3+2j)
```

Because the imaginary number i (1j in Python) is defined as the square root of –1, we can execute the following:

```
>>> 1j * 1j
(-1+0j)
>>> (7 + 1j) * 1j
(-1+7j)
```

Some complex math functions are in the standard cmath (*http://docs.python.org/3/library/cmath.html*) module.

Calculate Accurate Floating Point with decimal

Floating-point numbers in computers are not quite like the real numbers we learned in school. Because computer CPUs are designed for binary math, numbers that aren't exact powers of two often can't be represented exactly:

```
>>> x = 10.0 / 3.0
>>> x
3.3333333333333335
```

Whoa, what's that 5 at the end? It should be 3 all the way down. With Python's decimal (*http://docs.python.org/3/library/decimal.html*) module, you can represent numbers to your desired level of significance. This is especially important for calculations involving money. US currency doesn't go lower than a cent (a hundredth of a dollar), so if we're calculating money amounts as dollars and cents, we want to be accurate to the penny. If we try to represent dollars and cents through floating-point values such as 19.99 and 0.06, we'll lose some significance way down in the end bits before we even begin calculating with them. How do we handle this? Easy. We use the decimal module, instead:

```
>>> from decimal import Decimal
>>> price = Decimal('19.99')
>>> tax = Decimal('0.06')
>>> total = price + (price * tax)
>>> total
Decimal('21.1894')
```

We created the price and tax with string values to preserve their significance. The total calculation maintained all the significant fractions of a cent, but we want to get the nearest cent:

```
>>> penny = Decimal('0.01')
>>> total.quantize(penny)
Decimal('21.19')
```

You might get the same results with plain old floats and rounding, but not always. You could also multiply everything by 100 and use integer cents in your calculations, but that will bite you eventually, too. There's a nice discussion of these issues at *www.itmaybeahack.com* (*http://bit.ly/fixed-point-num*).

Perform Rational Arithmetic with fractions

You can represent numbers as a numerator divided by a denominator through the standard Python fractions (*http://docs.python.org/3/library/fractions.html*) module. Here is a simple operation multiplying one-third by two-thirds:

```
>>> from fractions import Fraction
>>> Fraction(1,  3) * Fraction(2, 3)
Fraction(2, 9)
```

Floating-point arguments can be inexact, so you can use Decimal within Fraction:

```
>>> Fraction(1.0/3.0)
Fraction(6004799503160661, 18014398509481984)
>>> Fraction(Decimal('1.0')/Decimal('3.0'))
Fraction(3333333333333333333333333333, 10000000000000000000000000000)
```

Get the greatest common divisor of two numbers with the gcd function:

```
>>> import fractions
>>> fractions.gcd(24, 16)
8
```

Use Packed Sequences with array

A Python list is more like a linked list than an array. If you want a one-dimensional sequence of the same type, use the array (*http://docs.python.org/3/library/array.html*) type. It uses less space than a list and supports many list methods. Create one with array(*typecode* , *initializer*). The *typecode* specifies the data type (like int or float) and the optional *initializer* contains initial values, which you can specify as a list, string, or iterable.

I've never used this package for real work. It's a low-level data structure, useful for things such as image data. If you actually need an array—especially with more then one dimension—to do numeric calculations, you're much better off with NumPy, which we'll discuss momentarily.

Handling Simple Stats by Using statistics

Beginning with Python 3.4, statistics (*http://docs.python.org/3.4/library/statistics.html*) is a standard module. It has the usual functions: mean, media, mode, standard deviation, variance, and so on. Input arguments are sequences (lists or tuples) or iterators of various numeric data types: int, float, decimal, and fraction. One function, mode, also accepts strings. Many more statistical functions are available in packages such as SciPy and Pandas, featured later in this appendix.

Matrix Multiplication

Starting with Python 3.5, you'll see the @ character doing something out of character. It will still be used for decorators, but it will also have a new use for *matrix multiplication* (*http://legacy.python.org/dev/peps/pep-0465/*). However, until it arrives, NumPy (coming right up) is your best bet.

Scientific Python

The rest of this appendix covers third-party Python packages for science and math. Although you can install them individually, you should consider downloading all of them at once as part of a scientific Python distribution. Here are your main choices:

Anaconda (https://store.continuum.io/cshop/anaconda/)
> This package is free, extensive, up-to-the-minute, supports Python 2 and 3, and won't clobber your existing system Python.

Enthought Canopy (https://www.enthought.com/products/canopy/)
> This package is available in both free and commercial versions.

Python(x,y) (https://code.google.com/p/pythonxy/)
> This is a Windows-only release.

Pyzo (http://www.pyzo.org/)
> This package is based on some tools from Anaconda, plus a few others.

ALGORETE Loopy (http://algorete.org/)
> This is also based on Anaconda, with extras.

I recommend installing Anaconda. It's big, but everything in this appendix is in there. See Appendix D for details on using Python 3 with Anaconda. The examples in the rest of this appendix will assume that you've installed the required packages, either individually or as part of Anaconda.

NumPy

NumPy (*http://www.numpy.org/*) is one of the main reasons for Python's popularity among scientists. You've heard that dynamic languages such as Python are often slower than compiled languages like C, or even other interpreted languages such as Java. NumPy was written to provide fast multidimensional numeric arrays, similar to scientific languages like FORTRAN. You get the speed of C with the developer-friendliness of Python.

If you've downloaded one of the scientific distributions, you already have NumPy. If not, follow the instructions on the NumPy download page (*http://www.scipy.org/scipy lib/download.html*).

To begin with NumPy, you should understand a core data structure, a multidimensional array called an ndarray (for *N-dimensional array*) or just an array. Unlike Python's lists and tuples, each element needs to be of the same type. NumPy refers to an array's number of dimensions as its *rank*. A one-dimensional array is like a row of values, a two-dimensional array is like a table of rows and columns, and a three-dimensional array is like a Rubik's Cube. The lengths of the dimensions need not be the same.

 The NumPy array and the standard Python array are not the same thing. For the rest of this appendix, when I say *array*, I'm referring to a NumPy array.

But why do you need an array?

- Scientific data often consists of large sequences of data.
- Scientific calculations on this data often use matrix math, regression, simulation, and other techniques that process many data points at a time.
- NumPy handles arrays *much* faster than standard Python lists or tuples.

There are many ways to make a NumPy array.

Make an Array with array()

You can make an array from a normal list or tuple:

```
>>> b = np.array( [2, 4, 6, 8] )
>>> b
array([2, 4, 6, 8])
```

The attribute ndim returns the rank:

```
>>> b.ndim
1
```

The total number of values in the array are given by size:

```
>>> b.size
4
```

The number of values in each rank are returned by shape:

```
>>> b.shape
(4,)
```

Make an Array with arange()

NumPy's `arange()` method is similar to Python's standard `range()`. If you call `arange()` with a single integer argument num, it returns an `ndarray` from 0 to num-1:

```
>>> import numpy as np
>>> a = np.arange(10)
>>> a
array([0, 1, 2, 3, 4, 5, 6, 7, 8, 9])
>>> a.ndim
1
>>> a.shape
(10,)
>>> a.size
10
```

With two values, it creates an array from the first to the last minus one:

```
>>> a = np.arange(7, 11)
>>> a
array([ 7,  8,  9, 10])
```

And you can provide a step size to use instead of one as a third argument:

```
>>> a = np.arange(7, 11, 2)
>>> a
array([7, 9])
```

So far, our examples have used integers, but floats work just fine:

```
>>> f = np.arange(2.0, 9.8, 0.3)
>>> f
array([ 2. ,  2.3,  2.6,  2.9,  3.2,  3.5,  3.8,  4.1,  4.4,  4.7,  5. ,
        5.3,  5.6,  5.9,  6.2,  6.5,  6.8,  7.1,  7.4,  7.7,  8. ,  8.3,
        8.6,  8.9,  9.2,  9.5,  9.8])
```

And one last trick: the `dtype` argument tells `arange` what type of values to produce:

```
>>> g = np.arange(10, 4, -1.5, dtype=np.float)
>>> g
array([ 10. ,   8.5,   7. ,   5.5])
```

Make an Array with zeros(), ones(), or random()

The `zeros()` method returns an array in which all the values are zero. The argument you provide is a tuple with the shape that you want. Here's a one-dimensional array:

```
>>> a = np.zeros((3,))
>>> a
array([ 0.,  0.,  0.])
>>> a.ndim
1
>>> a.shape
(3,)
```

```
>>> a.size
3
```

This one is of rank two:

```
>>> b = np.zeros((2, 4))
>>> b
array([[ 0.,   0.,   0.,   0.],
       [ 0.,   0.,   0.,   0.]])
>>> b.ndim
2
>>> b.shape
(2, 4)
>>> b.size
8
```

The other special function that fills an array with the same value is ones():

```
>>> import numpy as np
>>> k = np.ones((3, 5))
>>> k
array([[ 1.,   1.,   1.,   1.,   1.],
       [ 1.,   1.,   1.,   1.,   1.],
       [ 1.,   1.,   1.,   1.,   1.]])
```

One last initializer creates an array with random values between 0.0 and 1.0:

```
>>> m = np.random.random((3, 5))
>>> m
array([[  1.92415699e-01,   4.43131404e-01,   7.99226773e-01,
          1.14301942e-01,   2.85383430e-04],
       [  6.53705749e-01,   7.48034559e-01,   4.49463241e-01,
          4.87906915e-01,   9.34341118e-01],
       [  9.47575562e-01,   2.21152583e-01,   2.49031209e-01,
          3.46190961e-01,   8.94842676e-01]])
```

Change an Array's Shape with reshape()

So far, an array doesn't seem that different from a list or tuple. One difference is that you can get it to do tricks, such as change its shape by using reshape():

```
>>> a = np.arange(10)
>>> a
array([0, 1, 2, 3, 4, 5, 6, 7, 8, 9])
>>> a = a.reshape(2, 5)
>>> a
array([[0, 1, 2, 3, 4],
       [5, 6, 7, 8, 9]])
>>> a.ndim
2
>>> a.shape
(2, 5)
>>> a.size
10
```

You can reshape the same array in different ways:

```
>>> a = a.reshape(5, 2)
>>> a
array([[0, 1],
       [2, 3],
       [4, 5],
       [6, 7],
       [8, 9]])
>>> a.ndim
2
>>> a.shape
(5, 2)
>>> a.size
10
```

Assigning a shapely tuple to shape does the same thing:

```
>>> a.shape = (2, 5)
>>> a
array([[0, 1, 2, 3, 4],
       [5, 6, 7, 8, 9]])
```

The only restriction on a shape is that the product of the rank sizes needs to equal the total number of values (in this case, 10):

```
>>> a = a.reshape(3, 4)
Traceback (most recent call last):
  File "<stdin>", line 1, in <module>
ValueError: total size of new array must be unchanged
```

Get an Element with []

A one-dimensional array works like a list:

```
>>> a = np.arange(10)
>>> a[7]
7
>>> a[-1]
9
```

However, if the array has a different shape, use comma-separated indices:

```
>>> a.shape = (2, 5)
>>> a
array([[0, 1, 2, 3, 4],
       [5, 6, 7, 8, 9]])
>>> a[1,2]
7
```

That's different from a two-dimensional Python list:

```
>>> l = [ [0, 1, 2, 3, 4], [5, 6, 7, 8, 9] ]
>>> l
[[0, 1, 2, 3, 4], [5, 6, 7, 8, 9]]
```

```
>>> l[1,2]
Traceback (most recent call last):
  File "<stdin>", line 1, in <module>
TypeError: list indices must be integers, not tuple
>>> l[1][2]
7
```

One last thing: slices work, but again, only within one set of square brackets. Let's make our familiar test array again:

```
>>> a = np.arange(10)
>>> a = a.reshape(2, 5)
>>> a
array([[0, 1, 2, 3, 4],
       [5, 6, 7, 8, 9]])
```

Use a slice to get the first row, elements from offset 2 to the end:

```
>>> a[0, 2:]
array([2, 3, 4])
```

Now, get the last row, elements up to the third from the end:

```
>>> a[-1, :3]
array([5, 6, 7])
```

You can also assign a value to more than one element with a slice. The following statement assigns the value 1000 to columns (offsets) 2 and 3 of all rows:

```
>>> a[:, 2:4] = 1000
>>> a
array([[   0,    1, 1000, 1000,    4],
       [   5,    6, 1000, 1000,    9]])
```

Array Math

Making and reshaping arrays was so much fun that we almost forgot to actually *do* something with them. For our first trick, we'll use NumPy's redefined multiplication (*) operator to multiply all the values in a NumPy array at once:

```
>>> from numpy import *
>>> a = arange(4)
>>> a
array([0, 1, 2, 3])
>>> a *= 3
>>> a
array([0, 3, 6, 9])
```

If you tried to multiply each element in a normal Python list by a number, you'd need a loop or a list comprehension:

```
>>> plain_list = list(range(4))
>>> plain_list
[0, 1, 2, 3]
```

```
>>> plain_list = [num * 3 for num in plain_list]
>>> plain_list
[0, 3, 6, 9]
```

This all-at-once behavior also applies to addition, subtraction, division, and other functions in the NumPy library. For example, you can initialize all members of an array to any value by using `zeros()` and `+`:

```
>>> from numpy import *
>>> a = zeros((2, 5)) + 17.0
>>> a
array([[ 17.,   17.,   17.,   17.,   17.],
       [ 17.,   17.,   17.,   17.,   17.]])
```

Linear Algebra

NumPy includes many functions for linear algebra. For example, let's define this system of linear equations:

```
4x + 5y = 20
 x + 2y = 13
```

How do we solve for x and y? We'll build two arrays:

- The *coefficients* (multipliers for x and y)
- The *dependent* variables (right side of the equation)

```
>>> import numpy as np
>>> coefficients = np.array([ [4, 5], [1, 2] ])
>>> dependents = np.array( [20, 13] )
```

Now, use the `solve()` function in the `linalg` module:

```
>>> answers = np.linalg.solve(coefficients, dependents)
>>> answers
array([ -8.33333333,  10.66666667])
```

The result says that x is about –8.3 and y is about 10.6. Did these numbers solve the equation?

```
>>> 4 * answers[0] + 5 * answers[1]
20.0
>>> 1 * answers[0] + 2 * answers[1]
13.0
```

How about that. To avoid all that typing, you can also ask NumPy to get the *dot product* of the arrays for you:

```
>>> product = np.dot(coefficients, answers)
>>> product
array([ 20.,   13.])
```

The values in the `product` array should be close to the values in `dependents` if this solution is correct. You can use the `allclose()` function to check whether the arrays are approximately equal (they might not be exactly equal because of floating-point rounding):

```
>>> np.allclose(product, dependents)
True
```

NumPy also has modules for polynomials, Fourier transforms, statistics, and some probability distributions.

The SciPy Library

There's even more in a library of mathematical and statistical functions built on top of NumPy: SciPy (*http://www.scipy.org/*). The SciPy release (*http://www.scipy.org/scipy lib/download.html*) includes NumPy, SciPy, Pandas (coming later in this appendix), and other libraries.

SciPy includes many modules, including some for the following tasks:

- Optimization
- Statistics
- Interpolation
- Linear regression
- Integration
- Image processing
- Signal processing

If you've worked with other scientific computing tools, you'll find that Python, NumPy, and SciPy cover some of the same ground as the commercial MATLAB (*http://www.mathworks.com/products/matlab/*) or open source R (*http://www.r-project.org/*).

The SciKit Library

In the same pattern of building on earlier software, SciKit (*https://scikits.appspot.com/scikits*) is a group of scientific packages built on SciPy. SciKit's specialty is *machine learning*: it supports modeling, classification, clustering, and various algorithms.

The IPython Library

IPython (*http://ipython.org/*) is worth your time for many reasons. Here are some of them:

- An improved interactive interpreter (an alternative to the >>> examples that we've used throughout this book)
- Publishing code, plots, text, and other media in web-based *notebooks*
- Support for *parallel computing* (*http://bit.ly/parallel-comp*)

Let's look at the interpreter and notebooks.

A Better Interpreter

IPython has different versions for Python 2 and 3, and both are installed by Anaconda or other modern scientific Python releases. Use ipython3 for the Python 3 version.

```
$ ipython3
Python 3.3.3 (v3.3.3:c3896275c0f6, Nov 16 2013, 23:39:35)
Type "copyright", "credits" or "license" for more information.

IPython 0.13.1 -- An enhanced Interactive Python.
?         -> Introduction and overview of IPython's features.
%quickref -> Quick reference.
help      -> Python's own help system.
object?   -> Details about 'object', use 'object??' for extra details.

In [1]:
```

The standard Python interpreter uses the input prompts >>> and ... to indicate where and when you should type code. IPython tracks everything you type in a list called In, and all your output in Out. Each input can be more than one line, so you submit it by holding the Shift key while pressing Enter. Here's a one-line example:

```
In [1]: print("Hello? World?")
Hello? World?

In [2]:
```

In and Out are automatically numbered lists, letting you access any of the inputs you typed or outputs you received.

If you type ? after a variable, IPython tells you its type, value, ways of making a variable of that type, and some explanation:

```
In [4]: answer = 42

In [5]: answer?
Type:        int
String Form:42
Docstring:
int(x=0) -> integer
int(x, base=10) -> integer

Convert a number or string to an integer, or return 0 if no arguments
are given.  If x is a number, return x.__int__().  For floating point
numbers, this truncates towards zero.

If x is not a number or if base is given, then x must be a string,
bytes, or bytearray instance representing an integer literal in the
given base.  The literal can be preceded by '+' or '-' and be surrounded
by whitespace.  The base defaults to 10.  Valid bases are 0 and 2-36.
Base 0 means to interpret the base from the string as an integer literal.
>>> int('0b100', base=0)
4
```

Name lookup is a popular feature of IDEs such as IPython. If you press the Tab key right after some characters, IPython shows all variables, keywords, and functions that begin with those characters. Let's define some variables and then find everything that begins with the letter f:

```
In [6]: fee = 1

In [7]: fie = 2

In [8]: fo = 3

In [9]: fum = 4

In [10]: ftab
%%file     fie        finally    fo         format     frozenset
fee        filter     float      for        from       fum
```

If you type fe followed by the Tab key, it expands to the variable fee, which, in this program, is the only thing that starts with fe:

```
In [11]: fee
Out[11]: 1
```

IPython Notebook

If you prefer graphical interfaces, you might enjoy IPython's web-based implementation. You start from the Anaconda launcher window (Figure C-1).

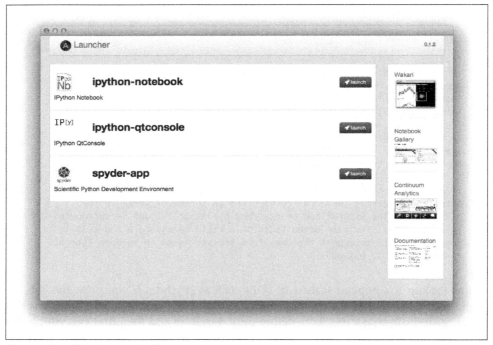

Figure C-1. The Anaconda home page

To launch the notebook in a web browser, click the "launch" icon to the right of "ipython-notebook." Figure C-2 shows the initial display.

Figure C-2. The iPython home page

Now, click the New Notebook button. A window similar to Figure C-3 opens.

Figure C-3. The iPython Notebook page

For a graphical version of our previous text-based example, type the same command that we used in the previous section, as shown in Figure C-4.

Figure C-4. Entering code in iPython

Click the solid black triangle icon to run it. The result is depicted in Figure C-5.

Figure C-5. Running code in iPython

The notebook is more than just a graphical version of an improved interpreter. Besides code, it can contain text, images, and formatted mathematical expressions.

In the row of icons at the top of the notebook, there's a pull-down menu (Figure C-6) that specifies how you can enter content. Here are the choices:

Code
  The default, for Python code

Markdown
  An alternative to HTML that serves as readable text and a preprocessor format

Raw Text

Unformatted text Heading 1 through Heading 6: HTML <H1> through <H6> heading tags

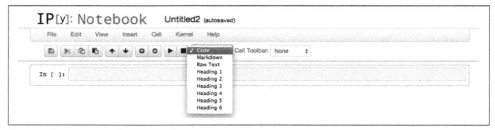

Figure C-6. Menu of content choices

Let's intersperse some text with our code, making it sort of a wiki. Select Heading 1 from the pull-down menu, type "Humble Brag Example," and then hold the Shift key while pressing the Enter key. You should see those three words in a large bold font. Then, select Code from the pull-down menu and type some code like this:

```
print("Some people say this code is ingenious")
```

Again, press Shift + Enter to complete this entry. You should now see your formatted title and code, as shown in Figure C-7.

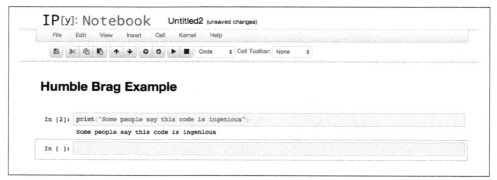

Figure C-7. Formatted text and code

By interspersing code input, output results, text, and even images, you can create an interactive notebook. Because it's served over the Web, you can access it from any browser.

You can see some notebooks converted to static HTML (*http://nbviewer.ipython.org*) or in a gallery (*http://bit.ly/ipy-notebooks*). For a specific example, try the notebook about the passengers on the Titanic (*http://bit.ly/titanic-noteb*). It includes charts showing how gender, wealth, and position on the ship affected survival. As a bonus, you can read how to apply different machine learning techniques.

Scientists are starting to use IPython notebooks to publish their research, including all the code and data used to reach their conclusions.

Pandas

Recently, the phrase *data science* has become common. Some definitions that I've seen include "statistics done on a Mac," or "statistics done in San Francisco." However you define it, the tools we've talked about in this chapter—NumPy, SciPy, and the subject of this section, Pandas—are components of a growing popular data-science toolkit. (Mac and San Francisco are optional.)

Pandas (*http://pandas.pydata.org/*) is a new package for interactive data analysis. It's especially useful for real world data manipulation, combining the matrix math of NumPy with the processing ability of spreadsheets and relational databases. The book *Python for Data Analysis: Data Wrangling with Pandas, NumPy, and IPython* (*http://bit.ly/python_for_data_analysis*) by Wes McKinney (O'Reilly) covers data wrangling with NumPy, IPython, and Pandas.

NumPy is oriented toward traditional scientific computing, which tends to manipulate multidimensional data sets of a single type, usually floating point. Pandas is more like a database editor, handling multiple data types in groups. In some languages, such groups are called *records* or *structures*. Pandas defines a base data structure called a `DataFrame`. This is an ordered collection of columns with names and types. It has some resemblance to a database table, a Python named tuple, and a Python nested dictionary. Its purpose is to simplify the handling of the kind of data you're likely to encounter not just in science, but also in business. In fact, Pandas was originally designed to manipulate financial data, for which the most common alternative is a spreadsheet.

Pandas is an ETL tool for real world, messy data—missing values, oddball formats, scattered measurements—of all data types. You can split, join, extend, fill in, convert, reshape, slice, and load and save files. It integrates with the tools we've just discussed —NumPy, SciPy, iPython—to calculate statistics, fit data to models, draw plots, publish, and so on.

Most scientists just want to get their work done, without spending months to become experts in esoteric computer languages or applications. With Python, they can become productive more quickly.

Python and Scientific Areas

We've been looking at Python tools that could be used in almost any area of science. What about software and documentation targeted to specific scientific domains?

Here's a small sample of Python's use for specific problems, and some special-purpose libraries:

General
- Python computations in science and engineering (*http://bit.ly/py-comp-sci*)
- A crash course in Python for scientists (*http://bit.ly/pyforsci*)

Physics
- Computational physics (*http://bit.ly/comp-phys-py*)

Biology and medicine
- Python for biologists (*http://pythonforbiologists.com/*)
- Neuroimaging in Python (*http://nipy.org/*)

International conferences on Python and scientific data include the following:

- PyData (*http://pydata.org*)
- SciPy (*http://conference.scipy.org/*)
- EuroSciPy (*https://www.euroscipy.org/*)

Install Python 3

By the time Python 3 is preinstalled on every machine, toasters will be replaced by 3-D printers that crank out daily doughnuts with sprinkles. Windows doesn't have Python at all, and OS X, Linux, and Unix tend to have old versions. Until they catch up, you'll probably need to install Python 3 yourself.

The following sections describe how to carry out these tasks:

- Find out what version of Python you have on your computer, if any
- Install the standard distribution of Python 3, if you don't have it
- Install the Anaconda distribution of scientific Python modules
- Install `pip` and `virtualenv`, if you can't modify your system
- Install `conda` as an alternative to `pip`

Most of the examples in this book were written and tested with Python 3.3, the most recent stable version at the time of writing. Some used 3.4, which was released during the editing process. The What's New in Python page (*https://docs.python.org/3/what snew/*) presents what was added in each version. There are many sources of Python and many ways to install a new version. In this appendix, I'll describe two of these ways:

- If you just want the standard interpreter and libraries, I recommend going to the official language site (*http://www.python.org*).
- If you would like Python together with the standard library, and the great scientific libraries described in Appendix C, use Anaconda.

Install Standard Python

Go to the Python download page (*http://www.python.org/download/*) with your web browser. It tries to guess your operating system and present the appropriate choices, but if it guesses wrong, you can use these:

- Python Releases for Windows (*https://www.python.org/downloads/windows/*)
- Python Releases for Mac OS X (*https://www.python.org/downloads/mac-osx/*)
- Python Source Releases (Linux and Unix) (*https://www.python.org/downloads/source/*)

You'll see a page similar to that shown in Figure D-1.

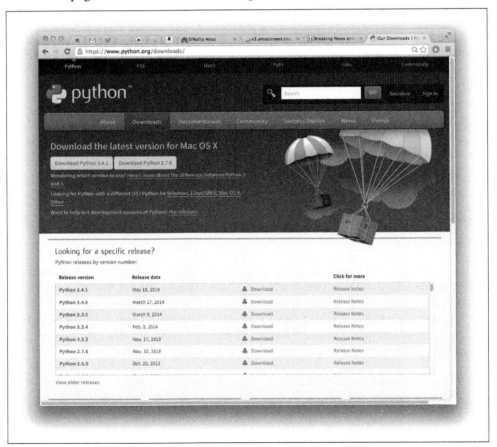

Figure D-1. Sample download page

Click the Download link for the most recent version. In our case, that's 3.4.1. This takes you to an information page like the one shown in Figure D-2.

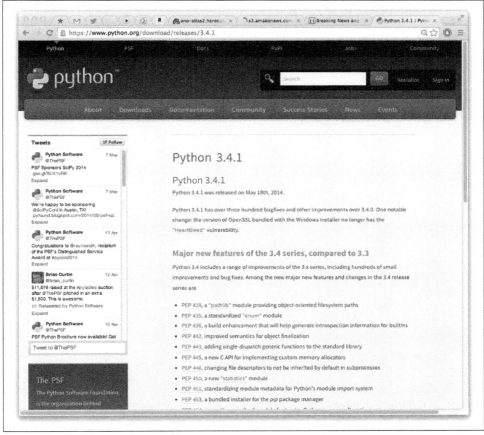

Figure D-2. Detail page for download

You need to scroll down the page to see the actual download link (Figure D-3).

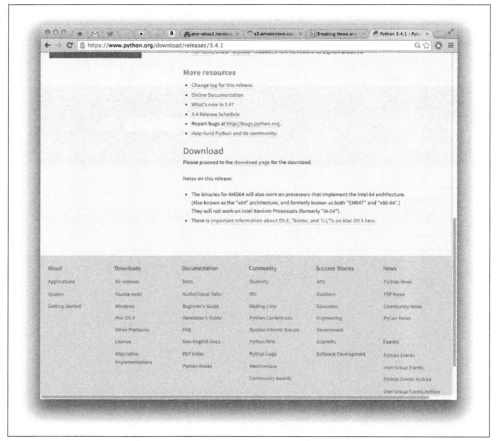

Figure D-3. Bottom of page offering download

Click the download link to get to the actual release-specific page (Figure D-4).

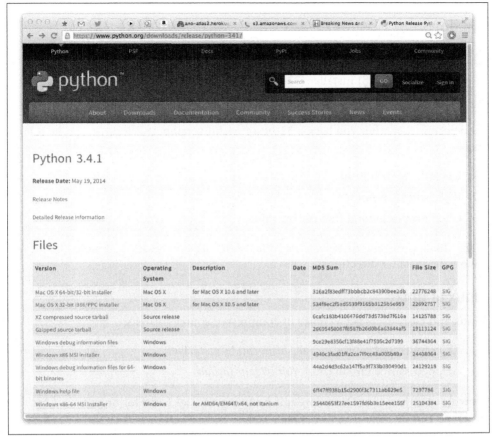

Figure D-4. Files to download

Now, click the correct version for your computer.

Mac OS X

Click the Mac OS X 64-bit/32-bit installer (*http://bit.ly/macosx-64*) link to download a
Mac *.dmg* file. Double-click it after the download completes. A window with four
icons opens. Right-click *Python.mpkg* and then, in the dialog box that opens, click
Open. Click the Continue button three times or so to step through the legalese, and
then, when the appropriate dialog box opens, click Install. Python 3 will be installed
as */usr/local/bin/python3*, leaving any existing Python 2 on your computer
unchanged.

Windows

For Windows, download one of these:

- Windows x86 MSI installer (32-bit) (*http://bit.ly/win-x86*)
- Windows x86-64 MSI installer (64-bit) (*http://bit.ly/win-x86-64*)

To determine whether you have a 32-bit or 64-bit version of Windows, do the following:

1. Click the Start button.
2. Right-click Computer.
3. Click Properties and find the bit value.

Click the appropriate installer (`.msi` file). After it's downloaded, double-click it and follow the installer directions.

Linux or Unix

Linux and Unix users get a choice of compressed source formats:

- XZ compressed source tarball (*http://bit.ly/xz-tarball*)
- Gzipped source tarball (*http://bit.ly/gzip-tarball*)

Download either one. Decompress it by using `tar xJ` (*.xz* file) or `tar xz` (*.tgz* file) and then run the resulting shell script.

Install Anaconda

Anaconda is an all-in-one installer with an emphasis on science: it includes Python, the standard library, and many useful third-party libraries. Until recently, it included Python 2 as its standard interpreter, although there was a workaround to install Python 3.

The new upgrade, Anaconda 2.0, installs the latest version of Python and its standard library (3.4 when this was written). Other goodies include libraries that we've talked about in this book: `beautifulsoup4`, `flask`, `ipython`, `matplotlib`, `nose`, `numpy`, `pandas`, `pillow`, `pip`, `scipy`, `tables`, `zmq`, and many others. It includes a cross-platform installation program called `conda` that improves on `pip`; we'll talk about that shortly.

To install Anaconda 2, go to the download page (*https://www.continuum.io/down loads*) for the Python 3 versions. Click the appropriate link for your platform (version numbers might have changed since this was written, but you can figure it out):

- To download for the Mac, click Anaconda3-2.0.0-MacOSX-x86_64.pkg (*http:// bit.ly/ana-3-2*). Double-click the file when it's done downloading, and then follow the usual steps for installing Mac software. It will install everything to the *anaconda* directory under your home directory.

- For Windows, click the 32-bit version (*http://bit.ly/win-32b*) or 64-bit version (*http://bit.ly/win-64b*). Double-click the *.exe* file after it downloads.

- For Linux, click the 32-bit version (*http://bit.ly/linux-32*) or 64-bit version (*http:// bit.ly/linux-64*). When it has downloaded, execute it (it's a big shell script).

 Ensure that the name of the file you download starts with *Anaconda3*. If it starts with just *Anaconda*, that's the Python 2 version.

Anaconda installs everything to its own directory (*anaconda* under your home directory). This means that it won't interfere with any versions of Python that might already be on your computer. It also means that you don't need any special permission (names like `admin` or `root`) to install it either.

To see what packages are included, visit the Anaconda docs page (*http://docs.contin uum.io/anaconda/pkg-docs.html*) and then, in the box at the top of the page, click "Python version: 3.4." It listed 141 packages when I last looked.

After installing Anaconda 2, you can see what Santa put on your computer by typing this command:

```
$ ./conda list
# packages in environment at /Users/williamlubanovic/anaconda:
#
anaconda                   2.0.0                np18py34_0
argcomplete                0.6.7                   py34_0
astropy                    0.3.2                np18py34_0
backports.ssl-match-hostname 3.4.0.2                 <pip>
beautiful-soup             4.3.1                   py34_0
beautifulsoup4             4.3.1                    <pip>
binstar                    0.5.3                   py34_0
bitarray                   0.8.1                   py34_0
blaze                      0.5.0                np18py34_0
blz                        0.6.2                np18py34_0
bokeh                      0.4.4                np18py34_1
cdecimal                   2.3                     py34_0
```

colorama	0.2.7	py34_0
conda	3.5.2	py34_0
conda-build	1.3.3	py34_0
configobj	5.0.5	py34_0
curl	7.30.0	2
cython	0.20.1	py34_0
datashape	0.2.0	np18py34_1
dateutil	2.1	py34_2
docutils	0.11	py34_0
dynd-python	0.6.2	np18py34_0
flask	0.10.1	py34_1
freetype	2.4.10	1
future	0.12.1	py34_0
greenlet	0.4.2	py34_0
h5py	2.3.0	np18py34_0
hdf5	1.8.9	2
ipython	2.1.0	py34_0
ipython-notebook	2.1.0	py34_0
ipython-qtconsole	2.1.0	py34_0
itsdangerous	0.24	py34_0
jdcal	1.0	py34_0
jinja2	2.7.2	py34_0
jpeg	8d	1
libdynd	0.6.2	0
libpng	1.5.13	1
libsodium	0.4.5	0
libtiff	4.0.2	0
libxml2	2.9.0	1
libxslt	1.1.28	2
llvm	3.3	0
llvmpy	0.12.4	py34_0
lxml	3.3.5	py34_0
markupsafe	0.18	py34_0
matplotlib	1.3.1	np18py34_1
mock	1.0.1	py34_0
multipledispatch	0.4.3	py34_0
networkx	1.8.1	py34_0
nose	1.3.3	py34_0
numba	0.13.1	np18py34_0
numexpr	2.3.1	np18py34_0
numpy	1.8.1	py34_0
openpyxl	2.0.2	py34_0
openssl	1.0.1g	0
pandas	0.13.1	np18py34_0
patsy	0.2.1	np18py34_0
pillow	2.4.0	py34_0
pip	1.5.6	py34_0
ply	3.4	py34_0
psutil	2.1.1	py34_0
py	1.4.20	py34_0
pycosat	0.6.1	py34_0
pycparser	2.10	py34_0

pycrypto	2.6.1	py34_0
pyflakes	0.8.1	py34_0
pygments	1.6	py34_0
pyparsing	2.0.1	py34_0
pyqt	4.10.4	py34_0
pytables	3.1.1	np18py34_0
pytest	2.5.2	py34_0
python	3.4.1	0
python-dateutil	2.1	<pip>
python.app	1.2	py34_2
pytz	2014.3	py34_0
pyyaml	3.11	py34_0
pyzmq	14.3.0	py34_0
qt	4.8.5	3
readline	6.2	2
redis	2.6.9	0
redis-py	2.9.1	py34_0
requests	2.3.0	py34_0
rope	0.9.4	py34_1
rope-py3k	0.9.4	<pip>
runipy	0.1.0	py34_0
scikit-image	0.9.3	np18py34_0
scipy	0.14.0	np18py34_0
setuptools	3.6	py34_0
sip	4.15.5	py34_0
six	1.6.1	py34_0
sphinx	1.2.2	py34_0
spyder	2.3.0rc1	py34_0
spyder-app	2.3.0rc1	py34_0
sqlalchemy	0.9.4	py34_0
sqlite	3.8.4.1	0
ssl_match_hostname	3.4.0.2	py34_0
sympy	0.7.5	py34_0
tables	3.1.1	<pip>
tk	8.5.15	0
tornado	3.2.1	py34_0
ujson	1.33	py34_0
werkzeug	0.9.4	py34_0
xlrd	0.9.3	py34_0
xlsxwriter	0.5.5	py34_0
yaml	0.1.4	1
zeromq	4.0.4	0
zlib	1.2.7	1

Install and Use pip and virtualenv

The pip package is the most popular way to install third-party (nonstandard) Python packages. It has been annoying that such a useful tool isn't part of standard Python, and that you've needed to download and install it yourself. As a friend of mine used to say, it's a cruel hazing ritual. The good news is that `pip` is a standard part of Python, starting with the 3.4 release.

Often used with `pip`, the `virtualenv` program is a way to install Python packages in a specified directory (folder) to avoid interactions with any preexisting system Python packages. This lets you use whatever Python goodies you want, even if you don't have permission to change the existing installation.

If you have Python 3 but only the Python 2 version of `pip`, here's how to get the Python 3 version on Linux or OS X:

```
$ curl -O http://python-distribute.org/distribute_setup.py
$ sudo python3 distribute_setup.py
$ curl -O https://raw.github.com/pypa/pip/master/contrib/get-pip.py
$ sudo python3 get-pip.py
```

This installs `pip-3.3` in the `bin` directory of your Python 3 installation. Then, use `pip-3.3` to install third-party Python packages rather than Python 2's `pip`.

Some good guides to `pip` and `virtualenv` are:

- A non-magical introduction to Pip and Virtualenv for Python beginners (*http://bit.ly/jm-pip-vlenv*)
- The hitchhiker's guide to packaging: pip (*http://bit.ly/hhgp-pip*)

Install and Use conda

Until recently, `pip` always downloaded source files rather than binaries. This can be a problem with Python modules that are built on C libraries. Recently, the Anaconda developers built conda (*http://www.continuum.io/blog/conda*) to address the problems they've seen with `pip` and other tools. `pip` is a Python package manager, but `conda` works with any software and language. `conda` also avoids the need for something like `virtualenv` to keep installations from stepping on one another.

If you installed the Anaconda distribution, you already have the `conda` program. If not, you can get Python 3 and `conda` from the miniconda page (*http://conda.pydata.org/miniconda.html*). As with Anaconda, make sure the file you download starts with `Miniconda3`; if it starts with `Miniconda` alone, it's the Python 2 version.

conda works with pip. Although it has its own public package repository (*http://binstar.org*), commands like `conda search` will also search the PyPi repository (*http://pypi.python.org*). If you have problems with `pip`, `conda` might be a good alternative.

Answers to Exercises

Chapter 1, *A Taste of Py*

1.1 If you don't already have Python 3 installed on your computer, do it now. Read Appendix D for the details for your computer system.

1.2 Start the Python 3 interactive interpreter. Again, details are in Appendix D. It should print a few lines about itself and then a single line starting with >>>. That's your prompt to type Python commands.

Here's what it looks like on my MacBook Pro:

```
$ python
Python 3.3.0 (v3.3.0:bd8afb90ebf2, Sep 29 2012, 01:25:11)
[GCC 4.2.1 (Apple Inc. build 5666) (dot 3)] on darwin
Type "help", "copyright", "credits" or "license" for more information.
>>>
```

1.3 Play with the interpreter a little. Use it like a calculator and type this: **8 * 9**. *Press the Enter key to see the result. Python should print 72.*

```
>>> 8 * 9
72
```

1.4 Type the number **47** *and press the Enter key. Did it print 47 for you on the next line?*

```
>>> 47
47
```

1.5 Now type **print(47)** *and press Enter. Did that also print 47 for you on the next line?*

```
>>> print(47)
47
```

Chapter 2, *Py Ingredients: Numbers, Strings, and Variables*

2.1 *How many seconds are in an hour? Use the interactive interpreter as a calculator and multiply the number of seconds in a minute (60) by the number of minutes in an hour (also 60).*

```
>>> 60 * 60
3600
```

2.2 *Assign the result from the previous task (seconds in an hour) to a variable called* seconds_per_hour.

```
>>> seconds_per_hour = 60 * 60
>>> seconds_per_hour
3600
```

2.3 *How many seconds are in a day? Use your* seconds_per_hour *variable.*

```
>>> seconds_per_hour * 24
86400
```

2.4 *Calculate seconds per day again, but this time save the result in a variable called* seconds_per_day.

```
>>> seconds_per_day = seconds_per_hour * 24
>>> seconds_per_day
86400
```

2.5 *Divide* seconds_per_day *by* seconds_per_hour. *Use floating-point (/) division.*

```
>>> seconds_per_day / seconds_per_hour
24.0
```

2.6 *Divide* seconds_per_day *by* seconds_per_hour, *using integer (//) division. Did this number agree with the floating-point value from the previous question, aside from the final `.0`?*

```
>>> seconds_per_day // seconds_per_hour
24
```

Chapter 3, *Py Filling: Lists, Tuples, Dictionaries, and Sets*

3.1 *Create a list called* years_list, *starting with the year of your birth, and each year thereafter until the year of your fifth birthday. For example, if you were born in 1980, the list would be* years_list = [1980, 1981, 1982, 1983, 1984, 1985].

If you were born in 1980, you would type:

```
>>> years_list = [1980, 1981, 1982, 1983, 1984, 1985]
```

3.2 In which of these years was your third birthday? Remember, you were 0 years of age for your first year.

You want offset 3. Thus, if you were born in 1980:

```
>>> years_list[3]
1983
```

3.3 In which year in `years_list` *were you the oldest?*

You want the last year, so use offset -1. You could also say 5 because you know this list has six items, but -1 gets the last item from a list of any size. For a 1980-vintage person:

```
>>> years_list[-1]
1985
```

3.4. Make and print a list called `things` *with these three strings as elements:* `"mozzarella"`, `"cinderella"`, `"salmonella"`.

```
>>> things = ["mozzarella", "cinderella", "salmonella"]
>>> things
['mozzarella', 'cinderella', 'salmonella']
```

3.5. Capitalize the element in `things` *that refers to a person and then print the list. Did it change the element in the list?*

This capitalizes the word, but doesn't change it in the list:

```
>>> things[1].capitalize()
'Cinderella'
>>> things
['mozzarella', 'cinderella', 'salmonella']
```

If you want to change it in the list, you need to assign it back:

```
>>> things[1] = things[1].capitalize()
>>> things
['mozzarella', 'Cinderella', 'salmonella']
```

3.6. Make the cheesy element of `things` *all uppercase and then print the list.*

```
>>> things[0] = things[0].upper()
>>> things
['MOZZARELLA', 'Cinderella', 'salmonella']
```

3.7. Delete the disease element, collect your Nobel Prize, and then print the list.

This would remove it by value:

```
>>> things.remove("salmonella")
>>> things
['MOZZARELLA', 'Cinderella']
```

Because it was last in the list, the following would have worked also:

```
>>> del things[-1]
```

And you could have deleted by offset from the beginning:

```
>>> del things[2]
```

3.8. *Create a list called* surprise *with the elements* "Groucho", "Chico", *and* "Harpo".

```
>>> surprise = ['Groucho', 'Chico', 'Harpo']
>>> surprise
['Groucho', 'Chico', 'Harpo']
```

3.9. *Lowercase the last element of the* surprise *list, reverse it, and then capitalize it.*

```
>>> surprise[-1] = surprise[-1].lower()
>>> surprise[-1] = surprise[-1][::-1]
>>> surprise[-1].capitalize()
'Oprah'
```

3.10. *Make an English-to-French dictionary called* e2f *and print it. Here are your starter words:* dog *is* chien, cat *is* chat, *and* walrus *is* morse.

```
>>> e2f = {'dog': 'chien', 'cat': 'chat', 'walrus': 'morse'}
>>> e2f
{'cat': 'chat', 'walrus': 'morse', 'dog': 'chien'}
```

3.11. *Using your three-word dictionary* e2f, *print the French word for* walrus.

```
>>> e2f['walrus']
'morse'
```

3.12. *Make a French-to-English dictionary called* f2e *from* e2f. *Use the* items *method.*

```
>>> f2e = {}
>>> for english, french in e2f.items():
        f2e[french] = english
>>> f2e
{'morse': 'walrus', 'chien': 'dog', 'chat': 'cat'}
```

3.13. *Print the English equivalent of the French word* chien.

```
>>> f2e['chien']
'dog'
```

3.14. *Print the set of English words from* e2f.

```
>>> set(e2f.keys())
{'cat', 'walrus', 'dog'}
```

3.15. *Make a multilevel dictionary called* life. *Use these strings for the topmost keys:* 'animals', 'plants', *and* 'other'. *Make the* 'animals' *key refer to another dictionary with the keys* 'cats', 'octopi', *and* 'emus'. *Make the* 'cats' *key refer to a list of strings with the values* 'Henri', 'Grumpy', *and* 'Lucy'. *Make all the other keys refer to empty dictionaries.*

This is a hard one, so don't feel bad if you peeked here first.

```
>>> life = {
...     'animals': {
...         'cats': [
...             'Henri', 'Grumpy', 'Lucy'
...             ],
...         'octopi': {},
...         'emus': {}
...         },
...     'plants': {},
...     'other': {}
...     }
>>>
```

3.16. *Print the top-level keys of* life.

```
>>> print(life.keys())
dict_keys(['animals', 'other', 'plants'])
```

Python 3 includes that dict_keys stuff. To print them as a plain list, use this:

```
>>> print(list(life.keys()))
['animals', 'other', 'plants']
```

By the way, you can use spaces to make your code easier to read:

```
>>> print ( list ( life.keys() ) )
['animals', 'other', 'plants']
```

3.17. *Print the keys for* life['animals'].

```
>>> print(life['animals'].keys())
dict_keys(['cats', 'octopi', 'emus'])
```

3.18. *Print the values for* life['animals']['cats'].

```
>>> print(life['animals']['cats'])
['Henri', 'Grumpy', 'Lucy']
```

Chapter 4, *Py Crust: Code Structures*

4.1. *Assign the value 7 to the variable* guess_me. *Then, write the conditional tests (*if*,* else*, and* elif*) to print the string* 'too low' *if* guess_me *is less than 7,* 'too high' *if greater than 7, and* 'just right' *if equal to 7.*

```
guess_me = 7
if guess_me < 7:
    print('too low')
elif guess_me > 7:
    print('too high')
else:
    print('just right')
```

Run this program and you should see the following:

```
just right
```

4.2. *Assign the value* 7 *to the variable* guess_me *and the value* 1 *to the variable* start. *Write a* while *loop that compares* start *with* guess_me. *Print* 'too low' *if* start *is less than* guess me. *If* start *equals* guess_me, *print* 'found it!' *and exit the loop. If* start *is greater than* guess_me, *print* 'oops' *and exit the loop. Increment* start *at the end of the loop.*

```
guess_me = 7
start = 1
while True:
    if start < guess_me:
        print('too low')
    elif start == guess_me:
        print('found it!')
        break
    elif start > guess_me:
        print('oops')
        break
    start += 1
```

If you did this right, you should see this:

```
too low
too low
too low
too low
too low
too low
found it!
```

Notice that the elif start > guess_me: line could have been a simple else:, because if start is not less than or equal to guess_me, it must be greater. At least in this universe.

4.3. *Use a* for *loop to print the values of the list* [3, 2, 1, 0].

```
>>> for value in [3, 2, 1, 0]:
...     print(value)
...
3
2
1
0
```

4.4. *Use a list comprehension to make a list called* even *of the even numbers in* range(10).

```
>>> even = [number for number in range(10) if number % 2 == 0]
>>> even
[0, 2, 4, 6, 8]
```

4.5. Use a dictionary comprehension to create the dictionary squares. *Use* range(10) *to return the keys, and use the square of each key as its value.*

```
>>> squares = {key: key*key for key in range(10)}
>>> squares
{0: 0, 1: 1, 2: 4, 3: 9, 4: 16, 5: 25, 6: 36, 7: 49, 8: 64, 9: 81}
```

4.6. Use a set comprehension to create the set odd *from the odd numbers in* range(10).

```
>>> odd = {number for number in range(10) if number % 2 == 1}
>>> odd
{1, 3, 9, 5, 7}
```

4.7. Use a generator comprehension to return the string 'Got ' *and a number for the numbers in* range(10). *Iterate through this by using a* for *loop.*

```
>>> for thing in ('Got %s' % number for number in range(10)):
...       print(thing)
...
Got 0
Got 1
Got 2
Got 3
Got 4
Got 5
Got 6
Got 7
Got 8
Got 9
```

4.8. Define a function called good() *that returns the list* ['Harry', 'Ron', 'Her mione'].

```
>>> def good():
...       return ['Harry', 'Ron', 'Hermione']
...
>>> good()
['Harry', 'Ron', 'Hermione']
```

4.9. Define a generator function called get_odds() *that returns the odd numbers from* range(10). *Use a* for *loop to find and print the third value returned.*

```
>>> def get_odds():
...       for number in range(1, 10, 2):
...           yield number
...
>>> count = 1
>>> for number in get_odds():
...       if count == 3:
...           print("The third odd number is", number)
...           break
...       count += 1
```

```
...
The third odd number is 5
```

4.10. Define a decorator called `test` *that prints* `'start'` *when a function is called and* `'end'` *when it finishes.*

```
>>> def test(func):
...     def new_func(*args, **kwargs):
...         print('start')
...         result = func(*args, **kwargs)
...         print('end')
...         return result
...     return new_func
...
>>>
>>> @test
... def greeting():
...     print("Greetings, Earthling")
...
>>> greeting()
start
Greetings, Earthling
end
```

4.11. Define an exception called `OopsException`. *Raise this exception to see what happens. Then, write the code to catch this exception and print* `'Caught an oops'`.

```
>>> class OopsException(Exception):
...     pass
...
>>> raise OopsException()
Traceback (most recent call last):
  File "<stdin>", line 1, in <module>
__main__.OopsException
>>>
>>> try:
...     raise OopsException
... except OopsException:
...     print('Caught an oops')
...
Caught an oops
```

4.12. Use `zip()` *to make a dictionary called* `movies` *that pairs these lists:* `titles = ['Creature of Habit', 'Crewel Fate']` *and* `plots = ['A nun turns into a monster', 'A haunted yarn shop']`.

```
>>> titles = ['Creature of Habit', 'Crewel Fate']
>>> plots = ['A nun turns into a monster', 'A haunted yarn shop']
>>> movies = dict(zip(titles, plots))
>>> movies
{'Crewel Fate': 'A haunted yarn shop', 'Creature of Habit': 'A nun turns
into a monster'}
```

Chapter 5, *Py Boxes: Modules, Packages, and Programs*

5.1. *Make a file called* zoo.py. *In it, define a function called* hours *that prints the string* 'Open 9-5 daily'. *Then, use the interactive interpreter to import the* zoo *module and call its* hours *function. Here's* zoo.py:

```
def hours():
    print('Open 9-5 daily')
```

And now, let's import it interactively:

```
>>> import zoo
>>> zoo.hours()
Open 9-5 daily
```

5.2. *In the interactive interpreter, import the* zoo *module as* menagerie *and call its* hours() *function.*

```
>>> import zoo as menagerie
>>> menagerie.hours()
Open 9-5 daily
```

5.3. *Staying in the interpreter, import the* hours() *function from* zoo *directly and call it.*

```
>>> from zoo import hours
>>> hours()
Open 9-5 daily
```

5.4. *Import the* hours() *function as* info *and call it.*

```
>>> from zoo import hours as info
>>> info()
Open 9-5 daily
```

5.5 *Make a dictionary called* plain *with the key-value pairs* 'a': 1, 'b': 2, *and* 'c': 3, *and then print it.*

```
>>> plain = {'a': 1, 'b': 2, 'c': 3}
>>> plain
{'a': 1, 'c': 3, 'b': 2}
```

5.6. *Make an* OrderedDict *called* fancy *from the same pairs and print it. Did it print in the same order as* plain?

```
>>> from collections import OrderedDict
>>> fancy = OrderedDict([('a', 1), ('b', 2), ('c', 3)])
>>> fancy
OrderedDict([('a', 1), ('b', 2), ('c', 3)])
```

5.7. *Make a* defaultdict *called* dict_of_lists *and pass it the argument* list. *Make the list* dict_of_lists['a'] *and append the value* 'something for a' *to it in one assignment. Print* dict_of_lists['a'].

```
>>> from collections import defaultdict
>>> dict_of_lists = defaultdict(list)
>>> dict_of_lists['a'].append('something for a')
>>> dict_of_lists['a']
['something for a']
```

Chapter 6, *Oh Oh: Objects and Classes*

6.1. *Make a class called* Thing *with no contents and print it. Then, create an object called* example *from this class and also print it. Are the printed values the same or different?*

```
>>> class Thing:
...     pass
...
>>> print(Thing)
<class '__main__.Thing'>
>>> example = Thing()
>>> print(example)
<__main__.Thing object at 0x1006f3fd0>
```

6.2. *Make a new class called* Thing2 *and assign the value* 'abc' *to a class variable called* letters. *Print* letters.

```
>>> class Thing2:
...     letters = 'abc'
...
>>> print(Thing2.letters)
abc
```

6.3. *Make yet another class called (of course)* Thing3. *This time, assign the value* 'xyz' *to an instance (object) variable called* letters. *Print* letters. *Do you need to make an object from the class to do this?*

```
>>> class Thing3:
...     def __init__(self):
...         self.letters = 'xyz'
...
```

The variable letters belongs to any objects made from Thing3, not the Thing3 class itself:

```
>>> print(Thing3.letters)
Traceback (most recent call last):
  File "<stdin>", line 1, in <module>
AttributeError: type object 'Thing3' has no attribute 'letters'
>>> something = Thing3()
>>> print(something.letters)
xyz
```

6.4. *Make a class called* Element, *with instance attributes* name, symbol, *and* number. *Create an object called* hydrogen *of this class with the values* 'Hydrogen', 'H', *and 1.*

```
>>> class Element:
...     def __init__(self, name, symbol, number):
...         self.name = name
...         self.symbol = symbol
...         self.number = number
...
>>> hydrogen = Element('Hydrogen', 'H', 1)
```

6.5. *Make a dictionary with these keys and values:* 'name': 'Hydrogen', 'symbol': 'H', 'number': 1. *Then, create an object called* hydrogen *from class* Element *using this dictionary.*

Start with the dictionary:

```
>>> el_dict = {'name': 'Hydrogen', 'symbol': 'H', 'number': 1}
```

This works, although it takes a bit of typing:

```
>>> hydrogen = Element(el_dict['name'], el_dict['symbol'], el_dict['number'])
```

Let's check that it worked:

```
>>> hydrogen.name
'Hydrogen'
```

However, you can also initialize the object directly from the dictionary, because its key names match the arguments to __init__ (refer to Chapter 3 for a discussion of keyword arguments):

```
>>> hydrogen = Element(**el_dict)
>>> hydrogen.name
'Hydrogen'
```

6.6. *For the* Element *class, define a method called* dump() *that prints the values of the object's attributes* (name, symbol, *and* number). *Create the* hydrogen *object from this new definition and use* dump() *to print its attributes.*

```
>>> class Element:
...     def __init__(self, name, symbol, number):
...         self.name = name
...         self.symbol = symbol
...         self.number = number
...     def dump(self):
...         print('name=%s, symbol=%s, number=%s' %
...             (self.name, self.symbol, self.number))
...
>>> hydrogen = Element(**el_dict)
>>> hydrogen.dump()
name=Hydrogen, symbol=H, number=1
```

6.7. *Call* print(hydrogen). *In the definition of* Element, *change the name of method* dump *to* __str__, *create a new* hydrogen *object, and call* print(hydrogen) *again.*

```
>>> print(hydrogen)
<__main__.Element object at 0x1006f5310>
>>> class Element:
...     def __init__(self, name, symbol, number):
...         self.name = name
...         self.symbol = symbol
...         self.number = number
...     def __str__(self):
...         return ('name=%s, symbol=%s, number=%s' %
...             (self.name, self.symbol, self.number))
...
>>> hydrogen = Element(**el_dict)
>>> print(hydrogen)
name=Hydrogen, symbol=H, number=1
```

__str__() is one of Python's *magic methods*. The print function calls an object's __str__() method to get its string representation. If it doesn't have a __str__() method, it gets the default method from its parent Object class, which returns a string like <__main__.Element object at 0x1006f5310>.

6.8. *Modify* Element *to make the attributes* name, symbol, *and* number *private. Define a getter property for each to return its value.*

```
>>> class Element:
...     def __init__(self, name, symbol, number):
...         self.__name = name
...         self.__symbol = symbol
...         self.__number = number
...     @property
...     def name(self):
...         return self.__name
...     @property
...     def symbol(self):
...         return self.__symbol
...     @property
...     def number(self):
...         return self.__number
...
>>> hydrogen = Element('Hydrogen', 'H', 1)
>>> hydrogen.name
'Hydrogen'
>>> hydrogen.symbol
'H'
>>> hydrogen.number
1
```

6.9 *Define three classes:* Bear, Rabbit, *and* Octothorpe. *For each, define only one method:* eats(). *This should return* 'berries' (Bear), 'clover' (Rabbit), *and* 'camp ers' (Octothorpe). *Create one object from each and print what it eats.*

```
>> class Bear:
...     def eats(self):
```

```
...             return 'berries'
...
>>> class Rabbit:
...       def eats(self):
...             return 'clover'
...
>>> class Octothorpe:
...       def eats(self):
...             return 'campers'
...
>>> b = Bear()
>>> r = Rabbit()
>>> o = Octothorpe()
>>> print(b.eats())
berries
>>> print(r.eats())
clover
>>> print(o.eats())
campers
```

6.10. *Define these classes:* Laser, Claw, *and* SmartPhone. *Each has only one method:* does(). *This returns* 'disintegrate' (Laser), 'crush' (Claw), *or* 'ring' (Smart Phone). *Then, define the class* Robot *that has one instance (object) of each of these. Define a* does() *method for the* Robot *that prints what its component objects do.*

```
>>> class Laser:
...       def does(self):
...             return 'disintegrate'
...
>>> class Claw:
...       def does(self):
...             return 'crush'
...
>>> class SmartPhone:
...       def does(self):
...             return 'ring'
...
>>> class Robot:
...       def __init__(self):
...             self.laser = Laser()
...             self.claw = Claw()
...             self.smartphone = SmartPhone()
...       def does(self):
...             return '''I have many attachments:
... My laser, to %s.
... My claw, to %s.
... My smartphone, to %s.''' % (
...         self.laser.does(),
...         self.claw.does(),
...         self.smartphone.does() )
...
>>> robbie = Robot()
```

```
>>> print( robbie.does() )
I have many attachments:
My laser, to disintegrate.
My claw, to crush.
My smartphone, to ring.
```

Chapter 7, *Mangle Data Like a Pro*

7.1. *Create a Unicode string called* mystery *and assign it the value* '\U0001f4a9'. *Print* mystery. *Look up the Unicode name for* mystery.

```
>>> import unicodedata
>>> mystery = '\U0001f4a9'
>>> mystery
'💩'
>>> unicodedata.name(mystery)
'PILE OF POO'
```

Oh my. What else have they got in there?

7.2. *Encode* mystery, *this time using UTF-8, into the* bytes *variable* pop_bytes. *Print* pop_bytes.

```
>>> pop_bytes = mystery.encode('utf-8')
>>> pop_bytes
b'\xf0\x9f\x92\xa9'
```

7.3. *Using UTF-8, decode* pop_bytes *into the string variable* pop_string. *Print* pop_string. *Is* pop_string *equal to* mystery?

```
>>> pop_string = pop_bytes.decode('utf-8')
>>> pop_string
'💩'
>>> pop_string == mystery
True
```

7.4. *Write the following poem by using old-style formatting. Substitute the strings* 'roast beef', 'ham', 'head', *and* 'clam' *into this string:*

```
My kitty cat likes %s,
My kitty cat likes %s,
My kitty cat fell on his %s
And now thinks he's a %s.

>>> poem = '''
... My kitty cat likes %s,
... My kitty cat likes %s,
... My kitty cat fell on his %s
... And now thinks he's a %s.
... '''
>>> args = ('roast beef', 'ham', 'head', 'clam')
>>> print(poem % args)
```

```
My kitty cat likes roast beef,
My kitty cat likes ham,
My kitty cat fell on his head
And now thinks he's a clam.
```

7.5. Write a form letter by using new-style formatting. Save the following string as let
ter *(you'll use it in the next exercise):*

```
Dear {salutation} {name},

Thank you for your letter. We are sorry that our {product} {verbed} in your
{room}. Please note that it should never be used in a {room}, especially
near any {animals}.

Send us your receipt and {amount} for shipping and handling. We will send
you another {product} that, in our tests, is {percent}% less likely to
have {verbed}.

Thank you for your support.

Sincerely,
{spokesman}
{job_title}
>>> letter = '''
... Dear {salutation} {name},
...
... Thank you for your letter. We are sorry that our {product} {verb} in your
... {room}. Please note that it should never be used in a {room}, especially
... near any {animals}.
...
... Send us your receipt and {amount} for shipping and handling. We will send
... you another {product} that, in our tests, is {percent}% less likely to
... have {verbed}.
...
... Thank you for your support.
...
... Sincerely,
... {spokesman}
... {job_title}
... '''
```

7.6. Make a dictionary called response *with values for the string keys* 'salutation',
'name', 'product', 'verbed' *(past tense verb),* 'room', 'animals', 'percent',
'spokesman', *and* 'job_title'. *Print* letter *with the values from* response.

```
>>> response = {
...     'salutation': 'Colonel',
...     'name': 'Hackenbush',
...     'product': 'duck blind',
...     'verbed': 'imploded',
...     'room': 'conservatory',
...     'animals': 'emus',
...     'amount': '$1.38',
...     'percent': '1',
```

```
...         'spokesman': 'Edgar Schmeltz',
...         'job_title': 'Licensed Podiatrist'
...     }
...
>>> print( letter.format(**response) )

Dear Colonel Hackenbush,

Thank you for your letter. We are sorry that our duck blind imploded in your
conservatory. Please note that it should never be used in a conservatory,
especially near any emus.

Send us your receipt and $1.38 for shipping and handling. We will send
you another duck blind that, in our tests, is 1% less likely to have imploded.

Thank you for your support.

Sincerely,
Edgar Schmeltz
Licensed Podiatrist
```

7.7. *When you're working with text, regular expressions come in very handy. We'll apply them in a number of ways to our featured text sample. It's a poem titled "Ode on the Mammoth Cheese," written by James McIntyre in 1866 in homage to a seven-thousand-pound cheese that was crafted in Ontario and sent on an international tour. If you'd rather not type all of it, use your favorite search engine and cut and paste the words into your Python program. Or, just grab it from Project Gutenberg (http://bit.ly/mcintyre-poetry). Call the text string* mammoth.

```
>>> mammoth = '''
... We have seen thee, queen of cheese,
... Lying quietly at your ease,
... Gently fanned by evening breeze,
... Thy fair form no flies dare seize.
...
... All gaily dressed soon you'll go
... To the great Provincial show,
... To be admired by many a beau
... In the city of Toronto.
...
... Cows numerous as a swarm of bees,
... Or as the leaves upon the trees,
... It did require to make thee please,
... And stand unrivalled, queen of cheese.
...
... May you not receive a scar as
... We have heard that Mr. Harris
... Intends to send you off as far as
... The great world's show at Paris.
...
... Of the youth beware of these,
```

```
... For some of them might rudely squeeze
... And bite your cheek, then songs or glees
... We could not sing, oh! queen of cheese.
...
... We'rt thou suspended from balloon,
... You'd cast a shade even at noon,
... Folks would think it was the moon
... About to fall and crush them soon.
... '''
```

7.8 Import the re *module to use Python's regular expression functions. Use* re.fin dall() *to print all the words that begin with* 'c'.

We'll define the variable pat for the pattern and then search for it in mammoth:

```
>>> import re
>>> pat = r'\bc\w*'
>>> re.findall(pat, mammoth)
['cheese', 'city', 'cheese', 'cheek', 'could', 'cheese', 'cast', 'crush']
```

The \b means to begin at a boundary between a word and a nonword. Use this to specify either the beginning or end of a word. The literal c is the first letter of the words we're looking for. The \w means any *word character*, which includes letters, digits, and underscores (_). The * means *zero or more* of these word characters. Together, this finds words that begin with c, including 'c' itself. If you didn't use a raw string (with an r right before the starting quote), Python would interpret \b as a backspace and the search would mysteriously fail:

```
>>> pat = '\bc\w*'
>>> re.findall(pat, mammoth)
[]
```

7.9 Find all four-letter words that begin with c.

```
>>> pat = r'\bc\w{3}\b'
>>> re.findall(pat, mammoth)
['city', 'cast']
```

You need that final \b to indicate the end of the word. Otherwise, you'll get the first four letters of all words that begin with c and have at least four letters:

```
>>> pat = r'\bc\w{3}'
>>> re.findall(pat, mammoth)
['chee', 'city', 'chee', 'chee', 'coul', 'chee', 'cast', 'crus']
```

7.10. Find all the words that end with r.

This is a little tricky. We get the right result for words that end with r:

```
>>> pat = r'\b\w*r\b'
>>> re.findall(pat,mammoth)
['your', 'fair', 'Or', 'scar', 'Mr', 'far', 'For', 'your', 'or']
```

However, the results aren't so good for words that end with l:

```
>>> pat = r'\b\w*l\b'
>>> re.findall(pat,mammoth)
['All', 'll', 'Provincial', 'fall']
```

But what's that ll doing there? The \w pattern only matches letters, numbers, and underscores—not ASCII apostrophes. As a result, it grabs the final ll from you'll. We can handle this by adding an apostrophe to the set of characters to match. Our first try fails:

```
>>> >>> pat = r'\b[\w']*l\b'
  File "<stdin>", line 1
    pat = r'\b[\w']*l\b'
```

Python points to the vicinity of the error, but it might take a while to see that the mistake was that the pattern string is surrounded by the same apostrophe/quote character. One way to solve this is to escape it with a backslash:

```
>>> pat = r'\b[\w\']*l\b'
>>> re.findall(pat, mammoth)
['All', "you'll", 'Provincial', 'fall']
```

Another way is to surround the pattern string with double quotes:

```
>>> pat = r"\b[\w']*l\b"
>>> re.findall(pat, mammoth)
['All', "you'll", 'Provincial', 'fall']
```

7.11. *Find all the words that contain exactly three vowels in a row.*

Begin with a word boundary, any number of *word* characters, three vowels, and then any non-vowel characters to the end of the word:

```
>>> pat = r'\b[^aeiou]*[aeiou]{3}[^aeiou]*\b'
>>> re.findall(pat, mammoth)
['queen', 'quietly', 'beau\nIn', 'queen', 'squeeze', 'queen']
```

This looks right, except for that 'beau\nIn' string. We searched mammoth as a single multiline string. Our [^aeiou] matches any non-vowels, including \n (line feed, which marks the end of a text line). We need to add one more thing to the ignore set: \s matches any space characters, including \n:

```
>>> pat = r'\b\w*[aeiou]{3}[^aeiou\s]\w*\b'
>>> re.findall(pat, mammoth)
['queen', 'quietly', 'queen', 'squeeze', 'queen']
```

We didn't find beau this time, so we need one more tweak to the pattern: match any number (even zero) of non-vowels after the three vowels. Our previous pattern always matched one non-vowel.

```
>>> pat = r'\b\w*[aeiou]{3}[^aeiou\s]*\w*\b'
>>> re.findall(pat, mammoth)
['queen', 'quietly', 'beau', 'queen', 'squeeze', 'queen']
```

What does all of this show? Among other things, that regular expressions can do a lot, but they can be very tricky to get right.

7.12. *Use* `unhexlify()` *to convert this hex string (combined from two strings to fit on a page) to a* `bytes` *variable called* `gif`:

```
'474946383961010001008000000000000ffffff21f9' +
'0401000000002c000000000100010000020144003b'
```

```
>>> import binascii
>>> hex_str = '474946383961010001008000000000000ffffff21f9' + \
...           '0401000000002c000000000100010000020144003b'
>>> gif = binascii.unhexlify(hex_str)
>>> len(gif)
42
```

7.13. *The bytes in* `gif` *define a one-pixel transparent GIF file, one of the most common graphics file formats. A legal GIF starts with the string GIF89a. Does* `gif` *match this?*

```
>>> gif[:6] == b'GIF89a'
True
```

Notice that we needed to use a b to define a byte string rather than a Unicode character string. You can compare bytes with bytes, but you cannot compare bytes with strings:

```
>>> gif[:6] == 'GIF89a'
False
>>> type(gif)
<class 'bytes'>
>>> type('GIF89a')
<class 'str'>
>>> type(b'GIF89a')
<class 'bytes'>
```

7.14. *The pixel width of a GIF is a 16-bit little-endian integer starting at byte offset 6, and the height is the same size, starting at offset 8. Extract and print these values for* `gif`. *Are they both* 1?

```
>>> import struct
>>> width, height = struct.unpack('<HH', gif[6:10])
>>> width, height
(1, 1)
```

Chapter 8, *Data Has to Go Somewhere*

8.1. *Assign the string* `'This is a test of the emergency text system'` *to the variable* `test1`, *and write* `test1` *to a file called* test.txt.

```
>>> test1 = 'This is a test of the emergency text system'
>>> len(test1)
43
```

Here's how to do it by using open, write, and close:

```
>>> outfile = open('test.txt', 'wt')
>>> outfile.write(test1)
43
>>> outfile.close()
```

Or, you can use with and avoid calling close (Python does it for you):

```
>>> with open('test.txt', 'wt') as outfile:
...     outfile.write(test1)
...
43
```

8.2. *Open the file* test.txt *and read its contents into the string* test2. *Are* test1 *and* test2 *the same?*

```
>>> with open('test.txt', 'rt') as infile:
...     test2 = infile.read()
...
>>> len(test2)
43
>>> test1 == test2
True
```

8.3. *Save these text lines to a file called* test.csv. *Notice that if the fields are separated by commas, you need to surround a field with quotes if it contains a comma.*

```
author,book
J R R Tolkien,The Hobbit
Lynne Truss,"Eats, Shoots & Leaves"
>>> text = '''author,book
... J R R Tolkien,The Hobbit
... Lynne Truss,"Eats, Shoots & Leaves"
... '''
>>> with open('test.csv', 'wt') as outfile:
...     outfile.write(text)
...
73
```

8.4. *Use the* csv *module and its* DictReader() *method to read* test.csv *to the variable* books. *Print the values in* books. *Did* DictReader() *handle the quotes and commas in the second book's title?*

```
>>> with open('test.csv', 'rt') as infile:
...     books = csv.DictReader(infile)
...     for book in books:
...         print(book)
...
```

```
{'book': 'The Hobbit', 'author': 'J R R Tolkien'}
{'book': 'Eats, Shoots & Leaves', 'author': 'Lynne Truss'}
```

8.5. Create a CSV file called books.csv *by using these lines:*

```
title,author,year
The Weirdstone of Brisingamen,Alan Garner,1960
Perdido Street Station,China Miéville,2000
Thud!,Terry Pratchett,2005
The Spellman Files,Lisa Lutz,2007
Small Gods,Terry Pratchett,1992

>>> text = '''title,author,year
... The Weirdstone of Brisingamen,Alan Garner,1960
... Perdido Street Station,China Miéville,2000
... Thud!,Terry Pratchett,2005
... The Spellman Files,Lisa Lutz,2007
... Small Gods,Terry Pratchett,1992
... '''
>>> with open('books.csv', 'wt') as outfile:
...     outfile.write(text)
...
201
```

8.6. Use the sqlite3 *module to create a SQLite database called* books.db *and a table called* books *with these fields:* title *(text),* author *(text), and* year *(integer).*

```
>>> import sqlite3
>>> db = sqlite3.connect('books.db')
>>> curs = db.cursor()
>>> curs.execute('''create table book (title text, author text, year int)''')
<sqlite3.Cursor object at 0x1006e3b90>
>>> db.commit()
```

8.7. Read the data from books.csv *and insert them into the* book *table.*

```
>>> import csv
>>> import sqlite3
>>> ins_str = 'insert into book values(?, ?, ?)'
>>> with open('books.csv', 'rt') as infile:
...     books = csv.DictReader(infile)
...     for book in books:
...         curs.execute(ins_str, (book['title'], book['author'], book['year']))
...
<sqlite3.Cursor object at 0x1007b21f0>
<sqlite3.Cursor object at 0x1007b21f0>
<sqlite3.Cursor object at 0x1007b21f0>
<sqlite3.Cursor object at 0x1007b21f0>
<sqlite3.Cursor object at 0x1007b21f0>
>>> db.commit()
```

8.8. Select and print the title *column from the* book *table in alphabetical order.*

```
>>> sql = 'select title from book order by title asc'
>>> for row in db.execute(sql):
```

```
...       print(row)
...
('Perdido Street Station',)
('Small Gods',)
('The Spellman Files',)
('The Weirdstone of Brisingamen',)
('Thud!',)
```

If you just wanted to print the title value without that tuple stuff (parentheses and comma), try this:

```
>>> for row in db.execute(sql):
...       print(row[0])
...
Perdido Street Station
Small Gods
The Spellman Files
The Weirdstone of Brisingamen
Thud!
```

If you want to ignore the initial 'The' in titles, you need a little extra SQL fairy dust:

```
>>> sql = '''select title from book order by
... case when (title like "The %") then substr(title, 5) else title end'''
>>> for row in db.execute(sql):
...       print(row[0])
...
Perdido Street Station
Small Gods
The Spellman Files
Thud!
The Weirdstone of Brisingamen
```

8.9. *Select and print all columns from the* book *table in order of publication.*

```
>>> for row in db.execute('select * from book order by year'):
...       print(row)
...
('The Weirdstone of Brisingamen', 'Alan Garner', 1960)
('Small Gods', 'Terry Pratchett', 1992)
('Perdido Street Station', 'China Miéville', 2000)
('Thud!', 'Terry Pratchett', 2005)
('The Spellman Files', 'Lisa Lutz', 2007)
```

To print all the fields in each row, just separate with a comma and space:

```
>>> for row in db.execute('select * from book order by year'):
...       print(*row, sep=', ')
...
The Weirdstone of Brisingamen, Alan Garner, 1960
Small Gods, Terry Pratchett, 1992
Perdido Street Station, China Miéville, 2000
Thud!, Terry Pratchett, 2005
The Spellman Files, Lisa Lutz, 2007
```

8.10. *Use the* `sqlalchemy` *module to connect to the sqlite3 database* books.db *that you just made in exercise 8.6. As in 8.8, select and print the* `title` *column from the* book *table in alphabetical order.*

```
>>> import sqlalchemy
>>> conn = sqlalchemy.create_engine('sqlite:///books.db')
>>> sql = 'select title from book order by title asc'
>>> rows = conn.execute(sql)
>>> for row in rows:
...     print(row)
...
('Perdido Street Station',)
('Small Gods',)
('The Spellman Files',)
('The Weirdstone of Brisingamen',)
('Thud!',)
```

8.11. *Install the Redis server (see Appendix D) and the Python* `redis` *library (pip install redis) on your machine. Create a Redis hash called* test *with the fields* count *(1) and* name *('Fester Bestertester'). Print all the fields for* test.

```
>>> import redis
>>> conn = redis.Redis()
>>> conn.delete('test')
1
>>> conn.hmset('test', {'count': 1, 'name': 'Fester Bestertester'})
True
>>> conn.hgetall('test')
{b'name': b'Fester Bestertester', b'count': b'1'}
```

8.12. *Increment the* count *field of* test *and print it.*

```
>>> conn.hincrby('test', 'count', 3)
4
>>> conn.hget('test', 'count')
b'4'
```

Chapter 9, *The Web, Untangled*

9.1. *If you haven't installed* `flask` *yet, do so now. This will also install* `werkzeug`, `jinja2`, *and possibly other packages.*

9.2. *Make a skeleton website, using Flask's debug/reload development web server. Ensure that the server starts up for hostname* `localhost` *on default port* 5000. *If your machine is already using port* 5000 *for something else, use another port number.*

Here's *flask1.py*:

```
from flask import Flask

app = Flask(__name__)
```

```
    app.run(port=5000, debug=True)
```

Gentlemen, start your engines:

```
$ python flask1.py
 * Running on http://127.0.0.1:5000/
 * Restarting with reloader
```

9.3. Add a `home()` *function to handle requests for the home page. Set it up to return the string* `It's alive!`.

What should we call this one, *flask2.py*?

```
from flask import Flask

app = Flask(__name__)

@app.route('/')
def home():
    return "It's alive!"

app.run(debug=True)
```

Start the server:

```
$ python flask2.py
 * Running on http://127.0.0.1:5000/
 * Restarting with reloader
```

Finally, access the home page via a browser, command-line HTTP program such as `curl` or `wget`, or even `telnet`:

```
$ curl http://localhost:5000/
It's alive!
```

9.4. Create a Jinja2 template file called home.html *with the following contents:*

```
I'm of course referring to {{thing}}, which is {{height}} feet tall and {{color}}.
```

Make a directory called *templates* and create the file *home.html* with the contents just shown. If your Flask server is still running from the previous examples, it will detect the new content and restart itself.

9.5. Modify your server's `home()` *function to use the* home.html *template. Provide it with three* GET *parameters:* `thing`, `height`, *and* `color`.

Here comes *flask3.py*:

```
from flask import Flask, request, render_template

app = Flask(__name__)

@app.route('/')
def home():
```

```
    thing = request.values.get('thing')
    height = request.values.get('height')
    color = request.values.get('color')
    return render_template('home.html',
        thing=thing, height=height, color=color)

app.run(debug=True)
```

Go to this address in your web client:

```
http://localhost:5000/?thing=Octothorpe&height=7&color=green
```

You should see the following:

```
I'm of course referring to Octothorpe, which is 7 feet tall and green.
```

Chapter 10, *Systems*

10.1. *Write the current date as a string to the text file* today.txt.

```
>>> from datetime import date
>>> now = date.today()
>>> now_str = now.isoformat()
>>> with open('today', 'wt') as output:
...     print(now_str, file=output)
>>>
```

Instead of print, you could have also said something like output.write(now_str). Using print adds the final newline.

10.2. *Read the text file* today.txt *into the string* today_string.

```
>>> with open('today', 'rt') as input:
...     today_string = input.read()
...
>>> today_string
'2014-02-04\n'
```

10.3. *Parse the date from* today_string.

```
>>> fmt = '%Y-%m-%d\n'
>>> datetime.strptime(today_string, fmt)
datetime.datetime(2014, 2, 4, 0, 0)
```

If you wrote that final newline to the file, you need to match it in the format string.

10.4. *List the files in your current directory.*

If your current directory is *ohmy* and contains three files named after animals, it might look like this:

```
>>> import os
>>> os.listdir('.')
['bears', 'lions', 'tigers']
```

10.5. *List the files in your parent directory.*

If your parent directory contained two files plus the current *ohmy* directory, it might look like this:

```
>>> import os
>>> os.listdir('..')
['ohmy', 'paws', 'whiskers']
```

10.6. *Use* `multiprocessing` *to create three separate processes. Make each one wait a random number of seconds between zero and one, print the current time, and then exit.*

Save this as *multi_times.py*:

```
import multiprocessing

def now(seconds):
    from datetime import datetime
    from time import sleep
    sleep(seconds)
    print('wait', seconds, 'seconds, time is', datetime.utcnow())

if __name__ == '__main__':
    import random
    for n in range(3):
        seconds = random.random()
        proc = multiprocessing.Process(target=now, args=(seconds,))
        proc.start()
```

```
$ python multi_times.py
wait 0.4670532005508353 seconds, time is 2014-06-03 05:14:22.930541
wait 0.5908421960431798 seconds, time is 2014-06-03 05:14:23.054925
wait 0.8127669040699719 seconds, time is 2014-06-03 05:14:23.275767
```

10.7. *Create a date object of your day of birth.*

Let's say that you were born on August 14, 1982:

```
>>> my_day = date(1982, 8, 14)
>>> my_day
datetime.date(1982, 8, 14)
```

10.8. *What day of the week was your day of birth?*

```
>>> my_day.weekday()
5
>>> my_day.isoweekday()
6
```

With `weekday()`, Monday is 0 and Sunday is 6. With `isoweekday()`, Monday is 1 and Sunday is 7. Therefore, this date was a Saturday.

10.9. *When will you be (or when were you) 10,000 days old?*

```
>>> from datetime import timedelta
>>> party_day = my_day + timedelta(days=10000)
>>> party_day
datetime.date(2009, 12, 30)
```

If that was your birthday, you probably missed an excuse for a party.

Chapter 11, *Concurrency and Networks*

11.1. *Use a plain* socket *to implement a current-time service. When a client sends the string* 'time' *to the server, return the current date and time as an ISO string.*

Here's one way to write the server, *udp_time_server.py*:

```
from datetime import datetime
import socket

address = ('localhost', 6789)
max_size = 4096

print('Starting the server at', datetime.now())
print('Waiting for a client to call.')
server = socket.socket(socket.AF_INET, socket.SOCK_DGRAM)
server.bind(address)
while True:
    data, client_addr = server.recvfrom(max_size)
    if data == b'time':
        now = str(datetime.utcnow())
        data = now.encode('utf-8')
        server.sendto(data, client_addr)
        print('Server sent', data)
server.close()
```

And the client, *udp_time_client.py*:

```
import socket
from datetime import datetime
from time import sleep

address     = ('localhost', 6789)
max_size    = 4096

print('Starting the client at', datetime.now())
client = socket.socket(socket.AF_INET, socket.SOCK_DGRAM)
while True:
    sleep(5)
    client.sendto(b'time', address)
    data, server_addr = client.recvfrom(max_size)
    print('Client read', data)
client.close()
```

I put in a `sleep(5)` call at the top of the client loop to make the data exchange less supersonic. Start the server in one window:

```
$ python udp_time_server.py
Starting the server at 2014-06-02 20:28:47.415176
Waiting for a client to call.
```

Start the client in another window:

```
$ python udp_time_client.py
Starting the client at 2014-06-02 20:28:51.454805
```

After five seconds, you'll start getting output in both windows. Here are the first three lines from the server:

```
Server sent b'2014-06-03 01:28:56.462565'
Server sent b'2014-06-03 01:29:01.463906'
Server sent b'2014-06-03 01:29:06.465802'
```

And here are the first three from the client:

```
Client read b'2014-06-03 01:28:56.462565'
Client read b'2014-06-03 01:29:01.463906'
Client read b'2014-06-03 01:29:06.465802'
```

Both of these programs run forever, so you'll need to cancel them manually.

11.2. *Use ZeroMQ REQ and REP sockets to do the same thing.*

Here's *zmq_time_server.py*:

```
import zmq
from datetime import datetime

host = '127.0.0.1'
port = 6789
context = zmq.Context()
server = context.socket(zmq.REP)
server.bind("tcp://%s:%s" % (host, port))
print('Server started at', datetime.utcnow())
while True:
    # Wait for next request from client
    message = server.recv()
    if message == b'time':
        now = datetime.utcnow()
        reply = str(now)
        server.send(bytes(reply, 'utf-8'))
        print('Server sent', reply)
```

And here's *zmq_time_client.py*:

```
import zmq
from datetime import datetime
from time import sleep
```

```
host = '127.0.0.1'
port = 6789
context = zmq.Context()
client = context.socket(zmq.REQ)
client.connect("tcp://%s:%s" % (host, port))
print('Client started at', datetime.utcnow())
while True:
    sleep(5)
    request = b'time'
    client.send(request)
    reply = client.recv()
    print("Client received %s" % reply)
```

With plain sockets, you need to start the server first. With ZeroMQ, you can start either the server or client first.

```
$ python zmq_time_server.py
Server started at 2014-06-03 01:39:36.933532

$ python zmq_time_client.py
Client started at 2014-06-03 01:39:42.538245
```

After 15 seconds or so, you should have some lines from the server:

```
Server sent 2014-06-03 01:39:47.539878
Server sent 2014-06-03 01:39:52.540659
Server sent 2014-06-03 01:39:57.541403
```

Here's what you should see from the client:

```
Client received b'2014-06-03 01:39:47.539878'
Client received b'2014-06-03 01:39:52.540659'
Client received b'2014-06-03 01:39:57.541403'
```

11.3. *Try the same with XMLRPC.*

The server, *xmlrpc_time_server.py*:

```
from xmlrpc.server import SimpleXMLRPCServer

def now():
    from datetime import datetime
    data = str(datetime.utcnow())
    print('Server sent', data)
    return data

server = SimpleXMLRPCServer(("localhost", 6789))
server.register_function(now, "now")
server.serve_forever()
```

And the client, *xmlrpc_time_client.py*:

```
import xmlrpc.client
from time import sleep

proxy = xmlrpc.client.ServerProxy("http://localhost:6789/")
```

```
while True:
    sleep(5)
    data = proxy.now()
    print('Client received', data)
```

Start the server:

```
$ python xmlrpc_time_server.py
```

Start the client:

```
$ python xmlrpc_time_client.py
```

Wait 15 seconds or so. Here are the first three lines of server output:

```
Server sent 2014-06-03 02:14:52.299122
127.0.0.1 - - [02/Jun/2014 21:14:52] "POST / HTTP/1.1" 200 -
Server sent 2014-06-03 02:14:57.304741
127.0.0.1 - - [02/Jun/2014 21:14:57] "POST / HTTP/1.1" 200 -
Server sent 2014-06-03 02:15:02.310377
127.0.0.1 - - [02/Jun/2014 21:15:02] "POST / HTTP/1.1" 200 -
```

And here are the first three lines from the client:

```
Client received 2014-06-03 02:14:52.299122
Client received 2014-06-03 02:14:57.304741
Client received 2014-06-03 02:15:02.310377
```

11.4. You may have seen the old I Love Lucy *television episode in which Lucy and Ethel worked in a chocolate factory (it's a classic). The duo fell behind as the conveyor belt that supplied the confections for them to process began operating at an ever-faster rate. Write a simulation that pushes different types of chocolates to a Redis list, and Lucy is a client doing blocking pops of this list. She needs 0.5 seconds to handle a piece of chocolate. Print the time and type of each chocolate as Lucy gets it, and how many remain to be handled.*

redis_choc_supply.py supplies the infinite treats:

```
import redis
import random
from time import sleep

conn = redis.Redis()
varieties = ['truffle', 'cherry', 'caramel', 'nougat']
conveyor = 'chocolates'
while True:
    seconds = random.random()
    sleep(seconds)
    piece = random.choice(varieties)
    conn.rpush(conveyor, piece)
```

redis_lucy.py might look like this:

```
import redis
from datetime import datetime
```

```
from time import sleep

conn = redis.Redis()
timeout = 10
conveyor = 'chocolates'
while True:
    sleep(0.5)
    msg = conn.blpop(conveyor, timeout)
    remaining = conn.llen(conveyor)
    if msg:
        piece = msg[1]
        print('Lucy got a', piece, 'at', datetime.utcnow(),
          ', only', remaining, 'left')
```

Start them in either order. Because Lucy takes a half second to handle each, and they're being produced every half second on average, it's a race to keep up. The more of a head start that you give to the conveyor belt, the harder you make Lucy's life.

```
$ python redis_choc_supply.py&
```

```
$ python redis_lucy.py
Lucy got a b'nougat' at 2014-06-03 03:15:08.721169 , only 4 left
Lucy got a b'cherry' at 2014-06-03 03:15:09.222816 , only 3 left
Lucy got a b'truffle' at 2014-06-03 03:15:09.723691 , only 5 left
Lucy got a b'truffle' at 2014-06-03 03:15:10.225008 , only 4 left
Lucy got a b'cherry' at 2014-06-03 03:15:10.727107 , only 4 left
Lucy got a b'cherry' at 2014-06-03 03:15:11.228226 , only 5 left
Lucy got a b'cherry' at 2014-06-03 03:15:11.729735 , only 4 left
Lucy got a b'truffle' at 2014-06-03 03:15:12.230894 , only 6 left
Lucy got a b'caramel' at 2014-06-03 03:15:12.732777 , only 7 left
Lucy got a b'cherry' at 2014-06-03 03:15:13.234785 , only 6 left
Lucy got a b'cherry' at 2014-06-03 03:15:13.736103 , only 7 left
Lucy got a b'caramel' at 2014-06-03 03:15:14.238152 , only 9 left
Lucy got a b'cherry' at 2014-06-03 03:15:14.739561 , only 8 left
```

Poor Lucy.

11.5. *Using the poem from exercise 7.7, use ZeroMQ to publish it, one word at a time. Write a ZeroMQ consumer that prints every word that starts with a vowel, and another that prints every word that contains five letters. Ignore punctuation characters.*

Here's the server, *poem_pub.py*, which plucks each word from the poem and publishes it to the topic vowels if it starts with a vowel, and the topic five if it has five letters. Some words might be in both topics, some in neither.

```
import string
import zmq

host = '127.0.0.1'
port = 6789
ctx = zmq.Context()
pub = ctx.socket(zmq.PUB)
pub.bind('tcp://%s:%s' % (host, port))
```

```
with open('mammoth.txt', 'rt') as poem:
    words = poem.read()
for word in words.split():
    word = word.strip(string.punctuation)
    data = word.encode('utf-8')
    if word.startswith(('a','e','i','o','u','A','e','i','o','u')):
        pub.send_multipart([b'vowels', data])
    if len(word) == 5:
        pub.send_multipart([b'five', data])
```

The client, *poem_sub.py*, subscribes to the topics vowels and five and prints the topic and word:

```
import string
import zmq

host = '127.0.0.1'
port = 6789
ctx = zmq.Context()
sub = ctx.socket(zmq.SUB)
sub.connect('tcp://%s:%s' % (host, port))
sub.setsockopt(zmq.SUBSCRIBE, b'vowels')
sub.setsockopt(zmq.SUBSCRIBE, b'five')
while True:
    topic, word = sub.recv_multipart()
    print(topic, word)
```

If you start these and run them, they *almost* work. Your code looks fine but nothing happens. You need to read the ZeroMQ guide (*http://zguide.zeromq.org/page:all*) to learn about the *slow joiner* problem: even if you start the client before the server, the server begins pushing data immediately after starting, and the client takes a little time to connect to the server. If you're publishing a constant stream of something and don't really care when the subscribers jump in, it's no problem. But in this case, the data stream is so short that it's flown past before the subscriber blinks, like a fastball past a batter.

The easiest way to fix this is to make the publisher sleep a second after it calls bind() and before it starts sending messages. Call this version *poem_pub_sleep.py*:

```
import string
import zmq
from time import sleep

host = '127.0.0.1'
port = 6789
ctx = zmq.Context()
pub = ctx.socket(zmq.PUB)
pub.bind('tcp://%s:%s' % (host, port))

sleep(1)
```

```
with open('mammoth.txt', 'rt') as poem:
    words = poem.read()
for word in words.split():
    word = word.strip(string.punctuation)
    data = word.encode('utf-8')
    if word.startswith(('a','e','i','o','u','A','e','i','o','u')):
        print('vowels', data)
        pub.send_multipart([b'vowels', data])
    if len(word) == 5:
        print('five', data)
        pub.send_multipart([b'five', data])
```

Start the subscriber and then the sleepy publisher:

```
$ python poem_sub.py
```

```
$ python poem_pub_sleep.py
```

Now, the subscriber has time to grab its two topics. Here are the first few lines of its output:

```
b'five' b'queen'
b'vowels' b'of'
b'five' b'Lying'
b'vowels' b'at'
b'vowels' b'ease'
b'vowels' b'evening'
b'five' b'flies'
b'five' b'seize'
b'vowels' b'All'
b'five' b'gaily'
b'five' b'great'
b'vowels' b'admired'
```

If you can't add a sleep() to your publisher, you can synchronize publisher and subscriber programs by using REQ and REP sockets. See the *publisher.py* and *subscriber.py* examples on GitHub (*http://bit.ly/pyzmq-gh*).

Cheat Sheets

I find myself looking up certain things a little too often. Here are some tables that I hope you'll find useful.

Operator Precedence

This table is a remix of the official documentation on precedence in Python 3, with the *highest* precedence operators at the top.

Operator	Description and examples
[*v1*, ...], { *v1*, ...}, { *k1*: *v1*, ...}, (...)	List/set/dict/generator creation or comprehension, parenthesized expression
seq [*n*], *seq* [*n* : *m*], *func* (*args*...), *obj* .*attr*	Index, slice, function call, attribute reference
**	Exponentiation
`+`x, `-`x, `~`x	Positive, negative, bitwise not
*, /, //, %	Multiplication, float division, int division, remainder
+, -	Addition, subtraction
<<, >>	Bitwise left, right shifts
&	Bitwise and
|	Bitwise or

Operator	Description and examples
in, not in, is, is not, <, <=, >, >=, !=, ==	Membership and equality tests
not *x*	Boolean (logical) not
and	Boolean and
or	Boolean or
if ... else	Conditional expression
lambda ...	lambda expression

String Methods

Python offers both string *methods* (can be used with any `str` object) and a `string` module with some useful definitions. Let's use these test variables:

```
>>> s = "OH, my paws and whiskers!"
>>> t = "I'm late!"
```

Change Case

```
>>> s.capitalize()
'Oh, my paws and whiskers!'
>>> s.lower()
'oh, my paws and whiskers!'
>>> s.swapcase()
'oh, MY PAWS AND WHISKERS!'
>>> s.title()
'Oh, My Paws And Whiskers!'
>>> s.upper()
'OH, MY PAWS AND WHISKERS!'
```

Search

```
>>> s.count('w')
2
>>> s.find('w')
9
>>> s.index('w')
9
>>> s.rfind('w')
16
>>> s.rindex('w')
16
>>> s.startswith('OH')
True
```

Modify

```
>>> ''.join(s)
'OH, my paws and whiskers!'
>>> ' '.join(s)
'O H ,   m y   p a w s   a n d   w h i s k e r s !'
>>> ' '.join((s, t))
"OH, my paws and whiskers! I'm late!"
>>> s.lstrip('HO')
', my paws and whiskers!'
>>> s.replace('H', 'MG')
'OMG, my paws and whiskers!'
>>> s.rsplit()
['OH,', 'my', 'paws', 'and', 'whiskers!']
>>> s.rsplit(' ', 1)
['OH, my paws and', 'whiskers!']
>>> s.split()
['OH,', 'my', 'paws', 'and', 'whiskers!']
>>> s.split(' ')
['OH,', 'my', 'paws', 'and', 'whiskers!']
>>> s.splitlines()
['OH, my paws and whiskers!']
>>> s.strip()
'OH, my paws and whiskers!'
>>> s.strip('s!')
'OH, my paws and whisker'
```

Format

```
>>> s.center(30)
'  OH, my paws and whiskers!   '
>>> s.expandtabs()
'OH, my paws and whiskers!'
>>> s.ljust(30)
'OH, my paws and whiskers!     '
>>> s.rjust(30)
'     OH, my paws and whiskers!'
```

String Type

```
>>> s.isalnum()
False
>>> s.isalpha()
False
>>> s.isprintable()
True
>>> s.istitle()
False
>>> s.isupper()
False
>>> s.isdecimal()
False
```

```
>>> s.isnumeric()
False
```

String Module Attributes

These are class attributes that are used as constant definitions.

Attribute	Example
ascii_letters	`'abcdefghijklmnopqrstuvwxyzABCDEFGHIJKLMNOPQRSTUVWXYZ'`
ascii_lowercase	`'abcdefghijklmnopqrstuvwxyz'`
ascii_uppercase	`'ABCDEFGHIJKLMNOPQRSTUVWXYZ'`
digits	`'0123456789'`
hexdigits	`'0123456789abcdefABCDEF'`
octdigits	`'01234567'`
punctuation	`'!"#$%&\'()*+,-./:;<=>?@[\\]^_\{|}~`'`
printable	`'0123456789abcdefghijklmnopqrstuvwxyz'` + `'ABCDEFGHIJKLMNOPQRSTUVWXYZ'` + `'!"#$%&\'()*+,-./:;<=>?@[\\]^_`{|}~'` + `'\t\n\r\x0b\x0c`'`
whitespace	`' \t\n\r\x0b\x0c'`

Fin

This page intentionally left blank.

No, wait...it isn't.

Index

benefits of, 80
canceling, 82
check break, 82
continuing, 82
generating number sequences, 83
iterating over multiple sequences, 83
itertools and, 121
foreground programs, 279
foreign keys, 198
formatting
curly brackets/format, 157
old and new styles, 154
string % data, 155
frameworks, 230, 232
full-text search, 220
functions
anonymous, 100
arguments and, 90
as first-class citizens, 96
callback functions, 101
closures, 99
default parameter values, 93
defining, 89
definition of term, 2, 37, 89
docstrings, 96
inner functions, 98
keyword arguments and, 93, 95
math, 373
monkey-patching functions, 274
positional arguments and, 92, 94
running as separate process, 255

G

games, 356
generator comprehensions, 88
generators, 101
GET command, 225
get() function, 61
gethostbyname() function, 296
getoutput() function, 253
getstatusoutput() function, 254
getter methods, 133
get_description() function, 113
gevent library, 242, 273
Git, 339
github, 123
glob() function, 252
Global Interpreter Lock (GIL), 273
global namespace, 104

global variables, 104
glue code, 10
Google, 306
graphical user interfaces (GUIs), 350
graphics
2D, 345
3D, 351
graphs, 354
green threads, 273
group ids, 253
GTK+ user interface, 351

H

h5py module, 197
hachoir, 171
Hadoop streaming, 304
hard links, 249
hash character (#), 71
hashes (see dictionaries)
hashmaps (see dictionaries)
HDF5 format, 197
HEAD command, 225
hex (base 16), 26
Houdini, 354
HTML (Hypertext Markup Language), 189, 223
HTTP (Hypertext Transfer Protocol)
client-server communication via, 223, 224
GET command, 225
HEAD command, 225
POST command, 226
response headers, 226
statelessness of, 224
status codes, 227
text-based protocol of, 225
verbs in, 225
http package, 226
human-readable code, 71, 96

I

I/O bound, 268
IDLE, 314
if statement, 73
ImageMagick, 349
images, 346
(see also graphics)
immutable, definition of, 18
import alias, 205
import statement, 112
in statement, 50, 60, 64, 74

About the Author

Bill Lubanovic has developed software with Unix since 1977, GUIs since 1981, databases since 1990, and the Web since 1993.

In 1982, at a startup named Intran, he developed MetaForm, one of the first commercial GUIs (before the Mac or Windows), on one of the first graphic workstations. In the early 1990s, while at Northwest Airlines, he wrote a graphic yield management system that generated millions of dollars in revenue; established a presence for the company on the Internet; and wrote its first Internet marketing test. Later, he cofounded an ISP (Tela) in 1994, and a web development company (Mad Scheme) in 1999.

Recently, he developed core services and distributed systems with a remote team for a Manhattan startup. Currently, he's integrating OpenStack services for a supercomputer company.

Bill enjoys life in Minnesota with his wonderful wife Mary, children Tom and Karin, and cats Inga, Chester, and Lucy.

Colophon

The animal on the cover of *Introducing Python* is an Asiatic Python (*Python reticulatus*). This snake is not quite as scary as it looks: it is nonvenomous and only occasionally attacks humans. Approaching lengths of seven meters (and sometimes over nine), this can be the longest snake or reptile in the world, but most individuals are closer to three or four meters long. The Latin terminology in its name refers to the netlike appearance of its patterns and coloring. The size and color of the shapes varies widely, particularly according to location, but diamonds are common on the python's back. Their appearance often allows them to blend in well with their surroundings in the wild.

The Asiatic python lives throughout Southeast Asia. There may be three subspecies with distinct geographical boundaries, but the scientific community does not formally recognize this idea. Pythons are most commonly found in rainforests, woodlands, grasslands, and bodies of water, since their swimming skills are superb. They have even been known to swim out to remote islands. Their diet consists mainly of mammals and birds.

This is an increasingly popular species to have in captivity, due to their striking appearance and good behavior, but this species can be unpredictable. There are documented instances of Asiatic pythons eating or otherwise killing people. Exact length measurements are very hard to take on a fairly aggressive snake, so only figures on dead or anesthetized Asiatic pythons are really considered accurate. While many captive pythons are obese, ones in the wild tend to be lighter, and they may be more fairly described as erratic rather than genuinely dangerous.

Many of the animals on O'Reilly covers are endangered; all of them are important to the world. To learn more about how you can help, go to *http://animals.oreilly.com*.

The cover image is from Johnson's *Natural History*. The cover font is Adobe ITC Garamond. The text font is Adobe Minion Pro; the heading font is Adobe Myriad Condensed; and the code font is Dalton Maag's Ubuntu Mono.

Have it your way.

Get even more for your money.

Join the O'Reilly Community, and register the O'Reilly books you own. It's free, and you'll get:

- $4.99 ebook upgrade offer
- 40% upgrade offer on O'Reilly print books
- Membership discounts on books and events
- Free lifetime updates to ebooks and videos
- Multiple ebook formats, DRM FREE
- Participation in the O'Reilly community
- Newsletters
- Account management
- 100% Satisfaction Guarantee

Signing up is easy:

1. Go to: oreilly.com/go/register
2. Create an O'Reilly login.
3. Provide your address.
4. Register your books.

Note: English-language books only

To order books online:
oreilly.com/store

For questions about products or an order:
orders@oreilly.com

To sign up to get topic-specific email announcements and/or news about upcoming books, conferences, special offers, and new technologies:
elists@oreilly.com

For technical questions about book content:
booktech@oreilly.com

To submit new book proposals to our editors:
proposals@oreilly.com

O'Reilly books are available in multiple DRM-free ebook formats. For more information:
oreilly.com/ebooks

O'REILLY®

CPSIA information can be obtained
at www.ICGtesting.com
Printed in the USA
BVOW07s1143260816
460268BV00014B/51/P

9 781449 359362